dialogic
moments

Raphael Patai Series in Jewish Folklore and Anthropology

For a complete listing of the books in this series please visit our Web site at
http://wsupress.wayne.edu

General Editor:
Dan Ben-Amos
University of Pennsylvania

Advisory Editors:
Jane S. Gerber
City University of New York

Barbara Kirshenblatt-Gimblett
New York University

Aliza Shenhar
University of Haifa

Amnon Shiloah
Hebrew University

Harvey E. Goldberg
Hebrew University

Samuel G. Armistead
University of California, Davis

Guy H. Haskell

dialogic
moments

From

Soul Talks

to

Talk Radio

in

Israeli Culture

Tamar Katriel

 WAYNE STATE UNIVERSITY PRESS
DETROIT

Library of Congress Cataloging-in-Publication Data

Katriel, Tamar.
   Dialogic moments : from soul talks to talk radio in Israeli culture / Tamar Katriel.
      p.   cm. — (Raphael Patai series in Jewish folklore and anthropology)
   Includes bibliographical references and index.
   ISBN 0-8143-2774-5 (unjacketed cloth : alk. paper) — ISBN 0-8143-2775-3 (pbk. :
alk. paper)
   1. Oral communication—Israel—History.   I. Title.   II. Series.
P95.43.I75K38 2004
302.2'242'095694—dc22   2004011623

⊗The paper used in this publication meets the minimum requirements of the American National Standard for Information Sciences—Permanence of Paper for Printed Library Materials, ANSI Z39.48–1984.

Contents

Acknowledgments

Like all books, this book owes a great deal to a great many people. It is not only a book about dialogue but also the product of my own dialogue with persons and texts. I am grateful to all those who gracefully accepted my rather slippery role as auto-ethnographer and joined me in probing implicit dimensions of meaning that are part of our shared cultural world. They invariably helped me to note unsuspected nuances and subtle changes in Israeli cultural style. Of the numerous people I have talked to over the years, I'd like to single out for special thanks the author Netiva Ben-Yehuda, whose book I discuss in the second section of this book, and the two radio hosts, Yovav Katz and Yosi Saias, whose programs I discuss in the third section, for their generous hospitality and willingness to share their craft and thoughts with me.

I acknowledge with gratitude the help I received in several archives, including the ones at Giv'at Haviva, at kibbutz Yif'at, and at kibbutz Beit-Alfa. I am also grateful to the many friends and colleagues, in Israel and elsewhere, who discussed aspects of this work with me in the context of scholarly collaboration, conferences, formal presentations, and personal conversations. Several people have read and commented on earlier versions of the work included in these pages, in whole or in part. Their comments have been invaluable in helping me shape the final version of the book. They include Dan Ben-Amos, Donal Carbaugh, Debbie Golden, Amy Horowitz, Haggai Katriel, Jacob Katriel, Yovav Katz, Barbara Kirshenblatt-Gimblett, Andre Levy, Yael Maschler, Darya Maoz, David McKie, Rivki Ribak, Miri Talmon, Michelle Rosenthal, and Anna Wierbicka.

Revisiting my earlier work on Israeli ways of speaking, I have come to appreciate the extent to which the research program initially formulated by Dell Hymes under the heading of the "ethnography of speaking" has shaped my own research agenda. Apart from this intellectual debt, I am indebted to Professor Hymes for his warm support of my scholarly work in its early stages. I also owe a debt of gratitude to Gerry Philipsen for introducing me to this research paradigm and for supporting my own way of engaging it ever since my graduate years.

I feel fortunate to have been able to work with Dan Ben-Amos as series editor for the press. His patience, genuine interest, and faith in this project helped me feel that writing about Israeli culture in the face of the devastating political reality that has engulfed us in the past two years may not be as futile as it often feels.

I am grateful to Cambridge University Press for giving me back the copyright of my 1986 *Talking Straight: "Dugri" Speech in Israeli Sabra Culture,* thereby making it possible for me to rework that study as part of the present volume. Part of the work on this book was carried out during an extended sabbatical leave, which I spent as a visiting scholar at the Center for the Study of Jewish Life at Rutgers University and at the Graduate School of Education at Harvard University. I am grateful to Yael Zerubavel of the former and to Catherine Snow of the latter for their warm hospitality during my stay with them. My thanks also to Adela Garcia and the staff at Wayne State University Press for their professional and courteous assistance.

Finally, I would like to gratefully acknowledge a research grant I received from the Israel Science Foundation Founded by the Israel Academy of Sciences and Humanities (ISF 824/95).

These pages are dedicated with love and gratitude to my life-partner, Jacob, who was the first to introduce me to Martin Buber's writings. He has accompanied me every step of the way, and has read more versions of this book than either of us would care to admit.

Introduction
The Social Life of Dialogue

DIALOGUE AS A LOCUS OF AUTHENTICITY

The vision of communication as authentic dialogue, as the mutual communion of souls, has animated many twentieth-century discussions of language and communication. In its diverse manifestations, both in scholarly writings and in various forms of vernacular culture, this communicative utopia has identified dialogue, or conversation, as a locus of authenticity of both individuals and groups. This study traces the ways utopian visions of communication have played themselves out in particular contexts of Israeli society through the past century, encapsulating central trends in the evolving Israeli cultural conversation over the years.

Spanning the twentieth century, the following exploration is composed of three separate yet intertwined case studies that relate to different periods in Israeli history: the study of the communal conversations known as "soul talks" among early Zionist settler groups in the 1920s; the study of the cultural style of straight talk (or *dugri* speech) that is traceable to the emerging Sabra culture of native-born Israeli Jews in the 1930s and 1940s; and the study of personally oriented broadcasting styles that became a distinctive feature of radio programming in the 1980s and 1990s. In one sense, this book is a historically situated study of the cultural fluctuations of a given society in all its particularity. In another sense, however, it seeks to offer a more general statement about the culturally constructed nature of the quest for authenticity as a project of modernity by focusing on conceptions of communication and language as its quintessential loci.

The quest for genuine dialogue is one facet of the more encompassing search for authenticity that has been a central theme in discussions of modernity, especially as they appeared in the writings of continental philosophers, such as Kierkegaard, Nietzsche, Sartre, and

Camus, in the past two centuries.[1] While the notion of authenticity has been given different interpretations by these various existentialist philosophers, it is generally conceptualized as involving a commitment to the project of forming one's own self, often in rebellion against the prevailing social ethic. Thus, the search for authenticity is frequently viewed as involving an essential tension between the individual and society in "what seems to be a paradoxical situation: it [authenticity] cannot be materialized without society, nor can it be lived within its framework."[2]

As Charles Taylor has argued, the search for authenticity involves creation and originality, often expressed as opposition to the rules of society while simultaneously requiring openness to socially constituted horizons of significance and a "self-definition in dialogue."[3] The quest for authenticity thus becomes a quest for "authentic dialogue," a dialogue that is marked by an absence of pretense and intertwines self-discovery and self-creation for both individuals and groups. This quest has been a recurrent theme in writings about language and communication, both descriptive and contemplative, and has been addressed in a range of scholarly fields: philosophy, communication, anthropology, literary criticism, folklore, and sociolinguistics. A wide range of scholars have discussed the language practices and ideological discourses associated with the notion of authentic dialogue in relation to the predicament of modernity.[4] At the same time, the search for authentic experience has permeated artistic and vernacular discourses of different kinds, and has colored a variety of increasingly popular cultural practices, such as museum-making and tourism. These involve appeals to nature, to territorially marked national or ethnic roots, or to an exotic "other," as loci of authenticity.

In the forthcoming analysis, I bring to bear insights from several fields of inquiry in exploring the forms and meanings of historically situated quests for dialogue, taking Israeli speech culture as my ethnographic site. Part of a self-conscious and popular cultural project of identity production, the Israeli quest for authentic dialogue has its roots in ideological and philosophical trends that flourished in Europe in the first part of the twentieth century and became part of mainstream scholarly writings in its second part. This ongoing scholarly discussion has, in turn, colored a larger cultural conversation in which the notion of dialogue has assumed localized inflections and has carried various degrees of social and ideational weight.

As the following studies will show, mainstream Israeli culture has been haunted by visions of dialogue as an authenticating resource in communal and interpersonal life. Thus, crossing the lines between philosophical, social-scientific, and vernacular discourses, I will argue for a cultural approach to the study of language ideologies and dialogic practices by illuminating some of the different ways in which the notion of genuine dialogue has been conceptualized and enacted in Israeli culture over the years. The three "dialogic moments" I have identified as significant to the evolution of Israeli speech culture will allow me to bring out the ethnographic richness of the quest for authentic dialogue and its historical fluctuations.[5]

As I reflect on my ongoing interest in authentic dialogue as both a human possibility and a philosophical concern, I am taken back to my high school years when I first encountered Martin Buber's philosophy of dialogue, a time when he was still a living presence in Israeli intellectual life. I found his affirmative approach both exhilarating and comforting: "There is genuine dialogue—no matter whether spoken or silent—where each of the participants really has in mind the other or others in their present and particular being and turns to them with the intention of establishing a living mutual relation between himself and them."[6] This early encounter with Buber's thought has stayed with me through the years; it has become blended with my reading of the body of literature I review below. In his philosophical writing and teaching, Buber elaborated a view of conversation as a transcendent moment, as a communion of souls. In this perspective, the dialogic quality of human encounters relates to the promise of interpersonal relationships and to the possibility of personal authenticity. Thus, a focus on dialogue (or its absence) becomes a way of reflecting on the resources of interpersonal life and the sources of the self.[7]

In Buber's account, "I-and-Thou" relations of direct human contact and interpersonal immediacy are the social products of moments of sharing in dialogue, whether in speech or in the silent interlocking of gazes. Such moments have a powerful transformative impact—they turn an alienated world suffused with instrumental, objectifying "I-It" relations, as Buber called them, into a world in which individuals' humanity is affirmed and new communicative possibilities emerge. The extensive scholarly work dealing with the dialogic dimensions of communication and with the sociological analysis of dialogue confirms the ongoing relevance of a Buberian perspective.[8] Indeed, Buber's work has been drawn upon in a range of communication studies in recent years. In a 1998 article that revisits the 1957 Buber-Rogers public exchange on the nature of therapy as a form of dialogue and discusses their perspectives on dialogue in relation to postmodernist themes, philosophers of communication Kenneth Cissna and Rob Anderson recapture the major tenets of Buber's philosophy of dialogue in the following way: "(a) an awareness that others are unique and whole persons, encouraging genuineness or authenticity that does not mandate full disclosure, but (b) suggests that dialogic partners are not pretending and are not holding back what needs to be said; and (c) a respect for the other that inclines one not to impose but to help the reality and possibility of the other unfold."[9] The same authors highlight the shared conception Buber and Rogers held of the fleeting, emergent nature of dialogic encounters as follows: "The basic character of such a dialogic moment, therefore, is the experience of inventive surprise shared by the dialogic partners as each 'turns towards' the other and both mutually perceive the impact of each other's turning. It is a brief interlude of focused awareness or acceptance of otherness and difference that somehow simultaneously transcends the perception of difference itself."[10]

Buber and Rogers, philosopher and therapist, debated whether authentic dialogic moments can emerge in contexts of unequal, role-regulated encounters such as those involving therapeutic relations. They differed in their assessment of the distinctive temporality of dialogue. For Rogers, it was precisely the ephemeral nature of dialogue that was responsible for its reenergizing potential in therapeutic encounters. Buber, on the other hand, viewed the ephemeral existence of dialogue as a human limitation grounded in the particular sociocultural conditions of modernity, when people's lives are no longer anchored in a sustained and life-sustaining sense of communal affiliation. Both of them, however, fully agreed that dialogue "lives in moments," and that at this point in history it is through the emergence of such moments that human affirmation and growth can be attained.

Both the notion of dialogue as communion, as celebrated in Buber's writings, and the analytic perspectives I later encountered in the scholarly literature on expressive culture and language use, some of which will be reviewed below, have significantly shaped my scholarly path. The choice to study the quest for authentic dialogue within an ethnographic framework, taking the shifting Israeli cultural scene as my empirical site, has been my way of acknowledging the deep existential roots of my concern with language and an attempt to elucidate what seems to me a hallmark of contemporary discursive life in Westernized cultures.

The scholarly discussion of "dialogic moments" by philosophers and social theorists has informed the study of face-to-face communication and expressive culture in a variety of ways.[11] I will therefore turn to a consideration of a number of studies that I have found most pertinent to my understanding of the quest for "authentic dialogue" as applied to the Israeli case. I do not claim that these studies delineate a coherently organized line of inquiry. On the contrary, in presenting the following intellectual collage I wish to draw attention to a shared intellectual concern with the quest for authentic dialogue in disparate fields of inquiry as well as to the ways in which the insights offered in these various fields can enrich our understanding of forms of dialogue and their symbolic import. In thus remapping the scholarly domain in which my analysis has taken shape, I also hope to further illuminate continuities between everyday enactments of ideologically charged ways of speaking and intellectual explorations of the social life of language.

A recent book titled *In Search of Authenticity,* by Regina Bendix, deconstructs the cultural discourses of authenticity that shaped the formation of the field of folklore studies in the German and North American scholarly contexts between the eighteenth and twentieth centuries. It usefully addresses the cultural sensibilities associated with the quest for authenticity in academic and other institutional contexts, describing the search for an authentic expressive culture as part of the predicament of modernity:

> The quest for authenticity is a peculiar longing, at once modern and anti-modern. It is oriented towards the recovery of an essence whose loss has been realized only through modernity, and whose recovery is feasible only through methods and sentiments created in modernity. . . . The continued craving for experiences of unmediated genuineness seeks to cut through what Rousseau called "the wounds of reflection," a reaction to modernization's demythologization, detraditionalization, and disenchantment.[12]

The quest for authenticity is thus an expression of a utopian and anti-modern spirit. Its elevation of emotions over reason is rooted in Romanticism and in the anti-Enlightenment movement. This originally implied a "critical stance against urban manners, artifice in language, behavior, and art, and against aristocratic excesses."[13] In individual terms, it promised to restore a pure and unaffected state of being, and contributed to the emergence of the idea of the "authentic self." In its communal interpretation, this quest promoted the project of nationalism as a modern political movement and its essentializing dimensions. Bendix points to the problematic standing of this essentializing tendency at a time when "the idea of homogeneous national culture confronts the reality of multicultural demographics."[14]

A related, though very different, treatment of these issues appears in the field of communication studies. Thus, John Durham Peters, too, historicizes the notion of authentic dialogue in a recent book concerned with the history of the idea of communication:

> "Communication" is a registry of modern longings. The term evokes a utopia where nothing is misunderstood, hearts are open, and expression is uninhibited. Desire being most intense when the object is absent, longings for communication also index a deep sense of dereliction in social relationships. How do we get to the pass where such a pathos attaches to the act of speaking with another person?[15]

Peters's interesting analysis counterposes the dream of communication-as-dialogue as a specifically addressed and reciprocal form of communication to a conception of communication-as-dissemination, which involves the indiscriminate broadcasting of messages to "all who would listen." The latter is, of course, the hallmark of mass communication media. Peters goes on to critique the privileged position that visions of dialogue have assumed in modern communication ideologies and theories. His reservations have to do with the exclusionary potential of direct communication within close-knit social groups, a point made by Bendix in her discussion of the essentializing role of the traditionalist view of expressive culture.

Peters contrasts the role played by face-to-face dialogue—as specifically addressed communication characterized by reciprocity—in demarcating group boundaries, with the inclusiveness implied by a dissemination view of communication. The latter involves the broadcasting of a controlled message from a central source to a wide audience. He points out that both dialogue and dissemination are essential modes of human communication and that different social occasions call for an emphasis on one conception of communication or the other:

> The horrors of broken dialogue can also be the blessings of just treatment. In some settings we would like to be treated as unique individuals (with family or friends); in others we want to be treated exactly the same as any other human (in court or the market). One's personal uniqueness can be a hindrance to justice and the basis of love. A life without individuated interaction (dialogue) would lack love; one without generalized access (dissemination) would lack justice.[16]

Notably, however, communicative events involving dissemination, such as the Sermon on the Mount discussed by Peters, even when appearing to be universally addressed, nevertheless imply the existence of interpretive communities for whom the address is meaningful in similar ways. The same can be said for the process of disseminating media messages. The characterization of this process as unidirectional and nonreciprocal depends on downplaying the role of the audience as an interpretive community, as Peters has done in proposing a dichotomous view of communication as either dialogue or dissemination. The recent development of interactive mass-mediated forms and genres, greatly facilitated by the advent of electronic communication, has most clearly brought this dichotomy into question.

Indeed, it seems that contemporary forms of mass-mediated communication often involve a combination of dialogue and dissemination. If we consider them as dimensions rather than modes of communication, we can explore the ways in which these dimensions become intertwined in particular cases. Viewed in dialectical terms, then, these two dimensions of communicative conduct provide a language with which to discuss cultural-communicative processes, such as inclusion and exclusion, that are central to the construction of group life.

The conditions of social fragmentation and alienation that characterize modern Western societies provide the backdrop against which the quest for dialogue as "a registry of modern longings" can be read. This quest is articulated in a variety of expressive genres that have made their way into popular culture, such as romantic literature, communal ideologies, self-help books, talk shows, and soap operas. Indeed, it is precisely in response to this rather overwhelming surfeit in yearnings for authentic dialogue that Peters seeks to swing the pendulum the other way. He defines today's task as that of finding a less romantic and more pragmatic account of communication, one "that erases neither the curious fact of otherness at its core nor the possibility of doing things with words."[17]

Indeed, the exploration of the search for authenticity in face-to-face dialogic encounters in the past should be accompanied by a consideration of how dialogue is continually shaped and reshaped by new media formats and communication environments. While the yearning for dialogue must be acknowledged as part of our modern heritage, the ways in which it plays itself out in our contemporary media-saturated cultural landscapes deserve to be explored in empirical detail. Indeed, my study of the quest for dialogue in the context of Israeli society is an attempt at a historically and culturally situated analysis of this kind. It traces the varied possibilities and manifestations of visions of communication-as-dialogue in the Israeli cultural ethos as they have emerged and unfolded over much of the twentieth century.

In invoking the notion of cultural ethos, I draw on an early anthropological line of work by such scholars as Ruth Benedict and Gregory Bateson. Their ideas have been revived and incorporated within a linguistic-anthropological framework in Penelope Brown and Stephen Levinson's influential study of "politeness phenomena" in language use.[18] In Brown and Levinson's wording, an "ethos" refers to "the affective quality of interaction characteristic of members of a society," and it is "a label for the quality of interaction characterizing groups, or social categories of persons, in a particular society."[19] The model of politeness strategies they develop provides a framework for a discussion of the interactional ethos of particular groups in particular times and places. They also provide a language for discussing cultural differences in the "overall stable flavor of interaction in a society"[20] through consideration of particular, culturally situated acts of speaking. While only part of the analysis offered in this book draws directly on the Brown and Levinson model, and while I seek to go beyond it in some ways, their ambitious and illuminating investigation of politeness phenomena as articulations of cultural ethos has been an important influence on my own thinking.

Another recent study that is similarly pertinent to my concerns, and which addresses contemporary yearnings for dialogue from a sociolinguistic and critical angle, is found in a recent book by Deborah Cameron, *Good to Talk? Living and Working in a Communication Culture*. The analysis in this book highlights a concern with the regulation, commodification, and regimentation of talk in everyday and institutional settings in contemporary societies.[21] Cameron's analysis in this book, as well as in her previous work, questions commonly accepted professional ideologies among linguists about the "naturalness" of talk as a feature of unimpeded natural conversation in everyday settings. Arguing that the evaluation of talk (for example, as good or bad, as more or less appropriate or effective) is intrinsic to language use, she asks about the nature and purpose of attempts to control speech behavior as forms of institutional authority.

Commenting on the communication scene around her, Cameron expresses misgivings reminiscent of those voiced by Peters regarding the "communication inflation" that characterizes modern life, whose ideological dimensions often remain hidden. She identifies changing attitudes toward communication practices in late modernity that have arisen in response to social and economic developments. One such change relates to the notion of "reflexive modernity," adopted from the work of sociologist Anthony Giddens.[22] It is linked to the view that the construction of individual identity has become a self-reflexive project of biographical construction. The requirement to construct oneself through the weaving of a coherent story line is a source of deep anxiety. Cameron claims that "at least some current anxieties about 'communication' are anxieties about the ability to tell that 'ongoing story about self,' either to oneself or to others."[23] People are aided in this task by what are considered to be "expert systems" of knowledge that are general and impersonal, and that involve codified procedures of expression and validation.

Therapy and the self-help industry are variously institutionalized examples of systems geared to providing such aid. As Cameron points out, the quasi-therapeutic discourses that are such a pervasive aspect of contemporary public culture have the important moral function "of disseminating ideas about what it means to be a 'good person,' and, more concretely, of providing models for the behavior of such a person towards other people."[24] Such beliefs are often encapsulated in norms regulating communicative conduct.

In discussing the notion of "enterprise culture," Cameron notes that the values and behaviors associated with organizational cultures that promote "enterprising" employees are very often articulated in communicative terms as well. The requirements made of these individuals, who are expected to display self-motivation, self-discipline, and self-directedness in pursuing their tasks, are formulated as expectations regarding interactional behavior and ways of speaking. She points to the fundamental paradox that accompanies contemporary expressive regimes that enshrine "open communication" yet at the same time regiment it in a variety of ways. Contemporary communicative ideologies promoting greater expressive license and creativity are counteracted by more and more invasive standardizing and disciplinary measures that curtail the authenticity of natural talk.

Thus, by combining the notions of "reflexive modernity" and "enterprise culture," Cameron offers an account of why the quest for dialogue—or "communication" in more contemporary parlance—is both thematized and subverted in the culture of late modernity. The reflexive project of constructing self-identities makes communication crucial. The discursive regimes that have emerged in order to socially regulate this process in the workplace, in public media, and in the home have resulted in widespread linguistic regimentation.

Like Peters, but for other reasons, Cameron finds the dominance of a relational focus and a consensus orientation highly problematic. This is not only because such a focus opens up the relational domain to the kind of linguistic regimentation described earlier, but also because it devalues the pragmatic and instrumental role of language. She concludes by arguing for a more complex view of communication, one that would incorporate agonistic exchanges on the one hand and playfulness on the other, and particularly a view of communication that would release it of its overburdened social agenda: "I would like to see the subject of communication 'liberated' from the rationalizing apparatus of scripts and checklists, and from the inflationary discourse that represents it as the cause and the remedy for all the world's problems."[25] Both Peters and Cameron recognize the lure of authentic dialogue as intimately addressed communication and its attendant "horror of broken dialogue," in Peters's words, as culturally compelling forces. They both locate the problematic of communication in the burdens of individuation—for Peters it has to do with interpersonal distance and the gap between self and other, while for Cameron it lies in both social and inner fragmentation, and the consequent difficulty of maintaining an ongoing, coherent story line about the self. Both object to what they see as the exaggerated emphasis placed on the relational dimension of communication rather than on "doing things with words."

This objection could be profitably linked to Vincent Carpanzano's critique of the "ideology of dialogue" current in existential-phenomenological approaches and its anthropological applications. He claims that this ideology overstresses the view of dialogue as contributing to "the constitution of a shared world, a shared understanding, a coming together."[26] According to Carpanzano, the lack of attention to the differentiating function of dialogue and the emphasis on integration "mystifies, [and] certainly simplifies, the dynamics of dialogue. Agonism gives way to an often saccharine communion."[27] He claims, in a way reminiscent of Cameron and Peters, that what is missing from the communion-oriented views of dialogue are the dimensions of power and desire that "can contradict the amity that dialogue connotes."[28]

I came upon the ideas presented in the work of Bendix, Peters, Cameron, and Carpanzano at a very late point in the formulation of my three intertwined case studies. Nevertheless, their different accounts of the idea of expressive culture or communication as ideology, and as embodied practice, provide me with a congruent framework against which to set the theoretical underpinnings for my own work. My analysis of Israeli ways of speaking will show that many of the general theoretical concerns raised by these authors have their counterparts in the cultural ideologies, controversies, and ritual practices that have shaped and continue to shape the specific Israeli quests for authentic dialogue.

My inquiry has been situated within the general framework of the research program known as the ethnography of speaking.[29] This scholarly approach draws on folklore's interest in expressive culture, anthropology's concern with cultural meanings, and the modern rhetorical tradition, particularly as elaborated in Kenneth Burke's writings on language as symbolic action.[30] Ethnographies of speaking explore both vernacular speech cultures in their everyday use and high-profile ritualized and artistic expressions.

Studies within this framework have made many distinctive contributions to the understanding of the interplay of language use and social life since the early 1960s. This was long after Bakhtin originally made his contribution to the study of language as dialogue, but before his work was translated into English and became influential in the West.[31] Scholars working within this framework have contributed to the development of a discourse-focused and anthropologically oriented approach to the study of culturally shared "ways of speaking," "speech events," and "speech communities"—concepts that have been proposed by Dell Hymes as key analytic terms.[32]

A way of speaking, or speech style, is an amalgamation of the Whorfian notion of "fashions of speaking," which refers to the lingual means and their organization, and the commonsense notion of "ways of life," which relates to the cultural world in which speaking takes place. Speech events are spatio-temporally bounded social occasions in which speaking is a focal activity and whose internal organization is socioculturally shaped. Speech communities are groups—which may be as small as a family or as large as a nation—that share rules and norms for the production and the interpretation of speech. Culturally focal ways of speaking and named speech events that are widely recognized within particular speech communities testify to sociolinguistic processes of structuration that relate to the dialectical tension between individual expression and the social regulation of human conduct. They involve the stylization of communicative conduct and the patterning of speech occasions within a shared framework of cultural assumptions about speaking.

A speech community's cultural ways of speaking and its named speech events are often widely recognized by cultural members as intertwined categories. Speech events are partly constituted in terms of the distinctive ways of speaking they give rise to, whereas the meaning of speech styles arises out of the speech occasions in which they are appropriately employed. Thus, for example, a court hearing as a culturally situated speech event is discursively constituted through the use of legal language and a formal style of address. Similarly, a particular style, like the measured, emotionally detached cadence of news reporting, becomes associated with such culturally valued notions as objectivity and impartiality. Ethnographic studies of speech may take a particular way of speaking or particular speech events, or both, as their point of departure. Often this choice is in response to the kind of structuration processes that are most visible and available for documentation and analysis in particular cultural contexts. Speech events that are highly visible and dramatized and speech styles whose features are clearly "hearable" form prime candidates for such studies.

The naming of ways of speaking and speech events is a cultural-linguistic strategy that points to the sociolinguistic consolidation of vernacular verbal forms. Terms for talk, as Donal Carbaugh has called them,[33] can often serve as important tools for analysis as well. Hymes himself pointed out that a good ethnographic technique for identifying culturally focal speech events is through words that name them.[34] The metapragmatic terms used in everyday discourse have an important indexical dimension, linking form and meaning by pointing to identity and relational claims made by speakers. Such terms also delineate a metacommunicative repertoire that cultural members can employ in discussing and evaluating verbal performances.[35]

Attending to metacommunicative "naming" practices is a major and well-recognized strategy of exploration in ethnographic studies of speaking. Kenneth Burke has suggested an additional strategy for exploring the interrelationship between form and meaning in the study of speech, proposing to complement the study of everyday speech with the study of artistic expressive forms, such as the novels and plays I draw on in the forthcoming chapters. As we shall see, the critical points in works of fiction relate to moments of action and choice, moments of self-making, emplotting the possibility of either attaining authenticity or of sliding into "bad faith." Burke has identified such "critical points" in a work of art as having the potential to "give us a 'way in' to the discovery of the motivation, or situation, of a poetic strategy,"[36] and thus shed light on the work as a whole. In other words, these critical moments have a metonymic function and can clarify the interrelationship between the underlying thematics of a work of art and the expressive form in which it is cast. Burke further said:

> When you begin to consider the situations behind the tactics of expression, you will find tactics that organize a work technically because they organize it emotionally. The two aspects . . . are but two modes of the same substance. Hence, if you look for a man's burden you will find the principle that reveals the structure of his unburdening; or, in attenuated form, if you look for his problem, you will find the lead that explains the structure of his solution.[37]

Thus, viewing verbal-artistic productions as culturally focal utterances that in some ways resonate with everyday speech patterns and speech events, I have been guided by Kenneth Burke's critical insights in drawing on literary works and media texts as a cultural resource. This move reflects the recognition that the range of cultural texts used by ethnographers of speaking is continually expanding. In the field of communication studies, Gerry Philipsen and his students have explored a variety of cultural texts as sites for the understanding of the role of speaking in sociocultural life.[38] A central focus of these studies is the role of speech in articulating the dialectical tension between individual and community. In Philipsen's terms, these studies explored the ways in which culturally focal speech styles and speech events fulfill the "cultural communication" function. Negotiating the dialectical tension between the individual self and a community of others is clearly subject to cultural coloration, yet it is posited as a central concern of communication systems in all cultural groups:

> Every people manages somehow to deal with the inevitable tension between the impulse of individuals to be free and the constraints of communal life. . . . Locating a culture on this axis reveals a partial truth about it, a kind of cultural snapshot, but in order to perceive the culture fully, one must also know the culture's direction of movement along the axis and the relative strengths of the competing forces pushing it one way or another.[39]

The analytic focus on the personal/communal dialectic draws our attention to issues that are central to both the perspective and the materials of the present study. It enables us to attend to discursive processes associated with the construction of personhood and communal affiliation, the maintenance of autonomy, and the accomplishment of connectedness.[40] This theme has played a central role in the changing communication ideologies and practices of the Israeli cultural scene, and became intertwined in its highly explicit nation-building agenda.

One important way in which the personal/communal dialectical tension finds its expression is in moments of publicly enacted social strife in which central cultural norms and values are contested, violated, and renegotiated. In an attempt to avoid an unwarranted focus on issues of shared meaning and consensus-building, Philipsen has drawn attention to the research potential of the study of social dramas in which speech-related cultural norms and meanings "hearably" clash. To this end, he has incorporated Victor Turner's framework for the analysis of "social dramas," making it an integral part of the analytic tool kit employed in the exploration of ways of speaking.

Turner discusses the notion of a "social drama" as a processual unit identifiable in terms of its dynamic, four-phase structure. This includes the initial phase of the *breach*, "a symbolic trigger of confrontation or encounter," which takes the form of "the deliberate non-fulfillment of some crucial norm regulating the intercourse of the parties."[41] The symbolic breach is a social statement by an individual who "always acts, or believes he acts, on behalf of other parties, whether they are aware of it or not. He sees himself as a representative, not as a lone hand."[42] The second phase of social drama, the *crisis* phase, is characterized as a turning point that may invite the response of representatives of the established social order. It has liminal characteristics and occurs at those moments "when it is least easy to don masks or pretend that there is nothing rotten in the village."[43] The third phase of the social drama involves *redressive action* and is designed to limit the spread of the confrontation through the use of corrective mechanisms that are brought into play. The fourth and last phase of a social drama consists either of the *reintegration* of the disturbed social group or of the recognition and legitimization of an irreparable *schism* between the contesting parties.

Turner furthermore makes an intriguing suggestion that articulates a link between his analysis of social dramas and a sociolinguistic concern with ways of speaking. He says:

> At the linguistic level of "parole," each phase has its own speech forms and styles, its own rhetoric, its own kinds of nonverbal languages and symbolisms. These vary greatly, of course, cross-culturally and cross-temporally, but I postulate that there will be certain important generic affinities between the speeches and languages of the crisis phase everywhere, or the

redressive phase everywhere, or the restoration of peace phase everywhere. Cross-cultural comparison has never applied itself to such a task.[44]

With the following studies of Israeli ways of speaking I hope to contribute to the cross-cultural enterprise ultimately envisioned by Turner. As this book attempts to show, the quest for authentic dialogue, articulated as a preference for open and direct speech, is associated with both the ritualization of social intimacy in special times and places and the confrontational style typical of the breach and crisis phases of social dramas. These are versions of what Van Gennep has identified as liminal, transitional contexts of betwixt-and-between associated with rites of passage, which are characterized by the counterstructural relations that hold in them.[45] In Turner's terms, this is the social modality of *communitas*—in other words, a state of existence located outside or at the margins of social time and place, which involves the creation of egalitarian, undifferentiated, individuating relationships and the suspension of the roles and rules that hold in the realm of social structure, or *societas*.

The modality of *spontaneous communitas* cannot be sustained for long if society is to proceed with its workaday, instrumental functions. It marks a ritual space where a qualitatively different type of social bonding is generated and new expressive possibilities are allowed to flourish in a moment of authentic interpersonal contact, experienced as a "flash of lucid mutual understanding on the existential level."[46] Turner describes this social state as follows:

> When the mood, style or "fit" of spontaneous *communitas* is upon us, we place a high value on personal honesty, openness and lack of pretensions or pretentiousness. We feel that it is important to relate directly to another person as he presents himself in the here-and-now, to understand him in his sympathetic . . . way, free from the culturally defined encumbrances of his role, status, reputation, class, caste, sex, or other structural niche.[47]

Inevitably, spontaneous *communitas* becomes routinized into the normative structure of social life, and social groups guided by its spirit attempt to cultivate and regulate relationships of *communitas* in a more sustained framework. The idioms of normative *communitas* are thus part of the larger social life of language, as suggested by Gerry Philipsen in his proposal to incorporate Turner's anthropological insights within an ethnography of speaking framework, rendering the sociocultural units of narrative, ritual, and social drama as basic to the study of spoken life.[48] Indeed, the dialogic quests described in the forthcoming chapters are designed to institute moments of "true dialogue" associated with the authentic and egalitarian spirit of *communitas* as part of the expressive repertoires of social groups.

Studying such moments involves an attempt to articulate the vibrant yet elusive quality of mutual presence and mutual recognition, touching on what Martin Buber referred to as "the spokenness of speech."[49] This could be part of what we might term a "sociolinguistics of human recognition." Studies falling under this rubric have often focused on the role of linguistic communication as a social regulator associated with hierarchical arrangements and power displays. Prime examples of such studies are Goffman's discussion of "face-work" as the considerateness we demand from and extend to each other in everyday interaction, and Brown and Levinson's work on politeness strategies mentioned earlier.[50] This latter study, and the many studies of politeness phenomena that came in its wake, are concerned with the affirmation or the violation of interactional partners' social "selves" as they are enacted and displayed in everyday exchanges.

This, however, does not extend to the uses of speech in the service of unique address, or in the creation of liminal, performative spaces in which the spirit of *communitas* can emerge. Such dialogic moments are intrinsically spontaneous and fleeting. They defy social expectations and, at least in Buber's version of them, often emerge in the absence of language, in lieu of speech. Cameron herself, while so eloquently arguing against the regimentation of talk, does not specify the nature and form of the authentic communication she would like to see. She tells us about authentic communication indirectly, by exploring examples of inauthentic cases, communication that has undergone "styling" in the sense of being regulated, regimented, commodified, overly self-reflexive. She is not alone in trying to capture the distinctive quality of the dialogic dimension of "communication" by putting it in quotation marks, but this is at best a suggestive, not a clarifying, move.

Indeed, the attempt to incorporate the study of dialogic moments into our exploration of the social life of language seems almost like a contradiction in terms. It takes us away from the study of communication rules and social norms and into the unchartered realm of emergence, surprise, and the essential fluidity and uncertainty of human interaction. At the same time, leaving such dialogic moments out of the sphere of our study of linguistic practices prevents us from attending to a highly ideologized and possibly defining element of modern social life, one that is central to the understanding of the quest for dialogue as a contemporary locus of authenticity and as a potentially humanizing force.

In exploring the search for authentic dialogue as involving a distinctive quality of human communication, I have approached the study of the life of dialogue as a cultural rather than as an interpersonal or even group phenomenon. This line of inquiry thus differs from the philosophical and communicational perspectives often applied to the study of dialogue.[51] I do not ask what dialogue is; I explore the discourses constructing and surrounding what I have identified as "dialogic moments" in the cultural life of one particular group—one to which I claim some degree of affiliation. I look at how members of given subgroups, in particular times and places, have articulated and enacted their longings for dialogic communication as they themselves conceptualized it in their own search for meaning and identity. The centrality of such moments in Israeli cultural life is evidenced by the fact that I could identify cultural junctures in which visions of dialogue and dialogic practices became explicitly thematized, negotiated, contested, and cultivated in a variety of ways. Interestingly, while dialogic moments themselves are both emergent and fleeting, the ideologies that promote their humanizing potential have been an ongoing though multifarious presence in Israeli cultural life.

Another intriguing extension of the ethnography of speaking scholarship has emerged in recent years in a field of interdisciplinary research that has brought linguistic anthropologists and historians into dialogue. The work of these scholars, who are interested in the social and historical life of language from their different scholarly perspectives, has also informed my overall approach. Thus, Richard Bauman's study of the symbolism of speaking and silence among seventeenth-century Quakers is an early and seminal example of a language-oriented anthropologist working within a historical framework.[52] Peter Burke's work on the art of conversation in early modern Italy is an example of historical studies that take the social life of language as their focus. Burke, indeed, has cogently argued for a systematic application of concepts and methods drawn from the ethnography of speaking to the study of historical materials, characterizing such a scholarly enterprise as "the attempt to add a social dimension to the history of language and a historical dimension to the work of sociolinguists and ethnographers of speaking."[53]

By attending to vernacular discourses about communication—specifically, about the possibilities, promises, and dangers of authentic dialogue—I will explore how these issues have played into the formation and transformation of modern Israeli culture. Thus, I explore the debates about the nature and value of spontaneity and emotional expressivity in dialogue; the dialectical tension between dialogue and dissemination; the mutual pull of the relational and the instrumental dimensions of language use; the role and nature of regulation, regimentation, and ritualization of discursive patterns. Underwriting all of this is my interest in the processes whereby selves and communities are constituted in and through everyday forms of talk, set in the particular context of Israel as an arena of cultural production and reproduction over time.

IN SEARCH OF AUTHENTICITY IN ISRAELI SPEECH CULTURE

The quest for authentic dialogue has been central to the making of Israeli culture since the first decades of the twentieth century, when early Zionist groups began to settle in Palestine. Over the years, this quest has remained central to the shaping of the Israeli expressive ethos despite significant changes in the specific cultural contents associated with it at different points in time. An exploration of these changes thus provides an opportunity to study the dynamics of Israeli speechways as a culturally focal arena. The quest for authenticity in Israeli speech culture is, of course, part of a larger cultural focus on the creation of an authentic new Hebrew culture and new Jewish person, which has been central to the Israeli nation-building ethos.[54] The authentic image of the New Jew is anchored in the reclamation of Jewish roots in the Land of Israel, which was conceptualized within the Zionist ethos as a place of authentic origins. The Zionists' "return" to the land of Israel was designed to reclaim and revitalize their ancient national roots. Much of the Zionist agenda involved the attempt to reestablish direct contact with the land of national origin through agricultural activities, hiking, archaeological excavations, and the study of the country's native flora and fauna.[55]

The vision of the New Jew was also centrally anchored in a vision of authentic dialogue and the new forms of sociality it was hoped to engender. As Rina Peled has pointed out, the image of the "New Man" of the Zionist revolution was not a monolithic one. Indeed, there were two major versions of it: one was the neo-Romantic version inspired by the German youth culture of the turn of the twentieth century and its individualist-humanist ethos, which sought to attain personal redemption through the re-creation of an organic-national community. A central vehicle in this quest for personal-communal redemption were the rituals of spontaneous confession, or "soul talks," addressed in chapter 1. The other version of the New Jew was influenced by Russian pre-revolutionary movements that preached the return to nature and to the simple life via menial, productive work. Leo Tolstoy, whose teachings permeated the early Zionist movement, was a primary motivating and influential figure in the shaping of the latter version. Within this ideological orientation, the image of the early Jewish settler in Palestine, natively known in Zionist discourse as *halutz* (pioneer), was elevated. The personal authenticity of the *halutz* was grounded in the ability and willingness to pursue national goals through communally oriented action. Thus, in the neo-Romantic version of the New Jew, talk became the locus of authenticity and a major vehicle of self-formation. In the activist-pioneering version, the pursuit of effective social action became the test of an authentic, shared will. In this latter scheme of things, the prevailing language ideology conceptualized the value of talk in terms of speaking efficiency rather than expressive license.

Both of these alternative images of the New Jew as an authentic emblem of a new society and culture were grounded in the modernist, European-based image of the New Man who "tries to disengage from the external dictates of the 'anachronistic' bourgeois-liberal ethos, which no longer fit the context of modernity, and shape his world in terms of internal-authentic codes."[56] As we shall see, these different versions of the authentic New Jew gave rise to different culturally focal ways of speaking at different points in Israeli history, and both served as cultural resources for the discursive construction of alternative versions of Israeli identity at different points in time.

This book thus explores the cultural roots as well as the cultural consequences of various articulations of the quest for authentic dialogue in Israeli culture by tracing the construction and deconstruction of historically situated "dialogic moments" and the ethos they embody. Despite its diachronic orientation, this study is not a historical one, however. It does not purport to draw a straight line between the case studies explored, but nevertheless emplots a historical narrative and lays out a historical argument about Israeli modes of communication and the ways in which they have been interwoven within Israeli life. Exploring the ways in which the three "case studies" considered here resonate with each other and combine to offer a larger picture of Israel's shifting speech culture is a major goal of this book.

Reflecting on the process of inquiry that has given rise to this book, it is worth noting that I have not pursued these studies in the chronological order in which they are presented here and that my exploration of Israeli speechways has been intertwined with studies addressing American ways of speaking. In fact, the discursive traces of what I have come to think of as a dialogic vision of communication attracted my attention from my very first steps in the ethnographic study of speech more than twenty years ago, but not in the Israeli context. My first venture in ethnographic analysis, conducted in the late 1970s and coauthored with Gerry Philipsen, was an attempt to elucidate popular American conceptions of the notion of "communication" as encountered in everyday discourse and in instances of popular culture (such as television talk shows).[57]

Upon coming to the United States, I was struck by the ongoing American talk about the virtues of communicating, as well as the expressed sensitivity toward the quality of interpersonal communication. The exhortations to communicate more and better struck my foreigner's sensibilities as peculiar to the American setting in which I was a sojourner. In the language I am currently employing, I would say that "communication" serves as a locus of authenticity in American culture, a discursive site in and through which "selves" and "relationships" are constructed and affirmed. At that time I wondered what Americans meant when they said "we talked but we didn't communicate," or when they testified that "we really communicated."

The term "communication" rang to my outsider's ears as simultaneously foreign and familiar. At the time, there was no ready-to-hand Hebrew equivalent for "communication" that would comfortably allow me to check how it would have played out in my own cultural-linguistic world. Attending to American everyday and media discourses, I often heard the term "communication" and its derivatives used in ways and with an emotional intensity that I found surprising. I began to hear it in the context of related terms such as "relationship" and "self" for which I could find no easy-sounding translations to Hebrew either. Notably, at the time of this writing, the noun *tikshoret* (communication) and the verb *letaksher* (to communicate) have become much more prevalent in Hebrew vernacular usage in a sense similar to the American one. Talk about the need for "communication" and the value of "communicating" as relational "work" have also become commonplace.

Initial seeds of this change could already be gleaned in the mid-seventies, when Israeli popular discourse had already begun to incorporate American-imported therapeutic parlance through the proliferation of various forms of group therapy as well as therapy-oriented radio programs. The therapeutic ethos has become increasingly widespread since the late 1960s, especially following the 1973 war between Israel and its neighboring Arab states and the widespread political disillusionment that marked its aftermath. This traumatic war undercut the sense of national euphoria that had engulfed the country after its victory over the same Arab states in the 1967 Six Day War. It was followed by a growing rejection of collective ideologies and national narratives as a source of shared meanings and sense of purpose and a foregrounding of personal concerns.

In the late seventies and early eighties, I found myself once again listening for echoes of a vision of communication as authentic dialogue—this time in my own culture, the mainstream culture of middle-class native-Israeli Jews, which by then had clearly begun to lose some of its privileged standing. Just as my hearing of American "communication" as a cultural idiom was colored by my non-American cultural baggage, my sensitivity to the Israeli idiom of *dugri* speech, translatable as "straight talk," was colored by my exposure to the American idiom of "communication" and its growing impact on Israeli culture. The *dugri* way of speaking is associated with the Israeli Sabra ethos of the 1940s and 1950s and its idiom of straight talk realism.[58] *Dugri* speech involves a confrontational dialogic idiom. Its locus of authenticity is to be found in participants' cultural persona—the image of the Sabras, the native-born Israeli Jews who will assume a confrontational stance and speak their mind. It is an idiom of responsibility, not of emotionality, and its employment signals communal affiliation through the forceful assertion of a culturally shaped and valorized personal identity.

In this case, too, the authenticity of dialogue is the underlying issue, though it finds its expression in an essentially agonistic mode. By focusing on the ritual dimension of *dugri* speech and the explicit use of the term *dugri* as an indexical sign,[59] I have highlighted its role in the affirmation of the image of the Sabra as the New Jew within the Israeli nation-building context. My early treatment of *dugri* speech as a particular enactment of authentic dialogue, probably colored by my study of American "communication," included a passing reference to the soul talk ethos, which preceded it in historical terms. Yet it was only later that I realized the profound sense in which the soul talk ethos can be seen as a cultural alternative to the *dugri* ethos, but one that was discarded as the Sabra generation took the place of the early generation of diaspora born-and-bred early settlers.

With the soul talk ethos identified as one cultural possibility and the *dugri* idiom as another, both are cast into a comparative and dynamic perspective. A further dynamic and comparative dimension is added by attending to the ways in which the production of an Israeli cultural style has rubbed against the cultural styles of other groups with which it came into contact. Thus, this more fully historicized and updated version of my earlier *dugri* study locates it within a broader cultural field. The *dugri* idiom is discussed here in conjunction with the Arabic ethos of respectful indirectness, encapsulated in the notion of doing *musayara* (roughly, going along with), and its decline as a dominant cultural idiom is considered within the broader landscape of Israeli ethnic relations and contemporary multiculturalism.

Indeed, as already mentioned, the intense nocturnal encounters held among early Zionist settlement groups in the Palestine of the 1920s and 1930s, which have been referred to as soul talks, prefigured the rise of *dugri* speech. In this early context, the locus of authenticity lay in transcendent experiences of communal conversations. These encounters represented an attempt to generate a spirit of group solidarity, or *communitas*, through the medium of face-to-face personal disclosure in small groups of like-minded youngsters, ensconced in the often isolated social enclaves of settlers' work camps.[60]

The early settlement mythology woven around the soul talk ethos involves an exploration of a central dynamic associated with Israeli speech culture—the quest for authentic dialogue in a communal setting. While the soul talk ethos dates back to the 1920s and must be understood with reference to its particular historical time and place, my study takes the reader through a historical trajectory of reenactments and retextualizations in which the soul talk format has figured up until the mid-1990s.

Concerns that were focal in the 1920s are revisited in the 1960s through a study of the encounters of soldiers who participated in the 1967 war, which were publicized in the publication *Si'ah Lohamim* (Fighters' Talk),[61] and again in the 1990s through a consideration of three Israeli plays that have addressed the soul talk ethos as both a site of nostalgia and an occasion for cultural critique.[62] These various treatments have shown how the soul talks continued to serve as a template for authentic dialogue, how they changed, and how the views of them shifted in later years. These changes were associated with shifts in notions of community and the introduction of new media and communicative contexts—specifically, the shift away from the intimate group format toward more diffuse notions of mass-mediated ones.

The last in the series of studies that make up my larger exploration of the quest for dialogue on the Israeli cultural scene relates to late-night call-in radio programs that focus on the personal domain. It addresses the mass-mediated refiguring of the quest for dialogue and the generation of "public intimacy" in this particular genre of audience-animated call-in programs on Israeli radio. The establishment of such programs in the 1970s and their growing popularity is part of the foregrounding of the personal domain and the emergence of a psychotherapeutic subculture in Israel of the 1970s.

Beit-Hallahmi has discussed the growing acceptance and popularity of psychotherapy at that time as part of the "private salvation" movement that swept the country following the aforementioned 1973 war—a collective experience that was accompanied by a profound sense of existential threat and both personal and communal trauma.[63] This trauma gave rise to a variety of spiritual revival movements, including cult-oriented communities and folk-religious, return-to-Judaism ones. The national disorientation following the 1973 war, when Israel's sense of confidence and superiority were critically undermined, led many Israelis to respond to this historical crisis through various forms of private salvation.

The psychotherapeutic subculture is a secular form of this quest for private salvation. This private salvation both signals and fosters a focus on individuals and their inner worlds, on emotional expression, and on meaning-making as personal projects. According to Beit-Hallahmi, psychotherapy shares with religious traditions an ideology that favors positive thinking and willpower whereas "the quest for meaning and quest for intimacy are the two cornerstones of secular psychotherapy."[64] Until the early 1970s, the therapeutic subculture in Israel remained culturally marginal. Indeed, for most Israelis the need for therapy amounted to "a confession of deviance from the conventional norm of toughness and independence."[65] In the 1970s, psychotherapy had become part of the fabric of Israeli society, marking a path to private salvation open to its secular members, on a par with the various religious paths toward salvation open to its more traditionally inclined members.

The media had a central role in the quick adoption of the therapeutic subculture in Israel. As Beit-Hallahmi points out, the "growing legitimacy of psychotherapy in Israel is demonstrated by the success of radio and television programs offering it to the masses, which have reached a remarkable level of popularity."[66] The late-night radio programs I will focus on are thus a product of a particular juncture in Israeli recent history. Like other roads to private salvation, they are anchored in the idea of the personal and "represent attempts to turn away from collective distress, to ignore the political crisis, and to become apolitical."[67]

Indeed, the verbal exchanges on the nocturnal radio programs I discuss in this book are centrally concerned with participants' private worlds and emotional experiences.[68] They testify to a search for authentic dialogue that is focused on the domain of personal life. This private domain is culturally constructed in and through particular forms of talk and expressive regimes. Refiguring the private/public relationship, these mass-mediated dialogues are held by participants to have a "humanizing" effect on the Israeli public sphere. They reaffirm the viability of interpersonal relationships and the possibility of human contact through attention to relationship trouble and personal alienation. In a sense, call-in radio invokes the public/communal intimacy associated with the pioneers' soul talks and can be seen in new light when considered with reference to the confrontational yet solidaristic dimensions of *dugri* speech as an alternative cultural possibility.

I have chosen to focus on two programs that allow me to explore two distinctive idioms of personal talk that I believe are marked by ethnicity and social class. One of them employs a more "traditional," Mizrahi (Middle Eastern) code of social support while the other speaks in the voice of the middle-class Western-oriented therapeutic code of "communication" discussed by Cameron, and which harks back to my earlier work on American speech. Both represent quests for the spirit of dialogue in late modernity, and their juxtaposition in Israeli mediascape seems to testify to the emergence of a multivocal public sphere.

While the first two case studies addressed here—the study of soul talks and the study of *dugri* speech—are devoted to explorations of particular kinds of culturally situated face-to-face dialogues, the third one explores the call-in radio format as an early and powerful example of a changing media context, in which communication as dialogue and as dissemination go hand in hand. The nature of dialogue is different in face-to-face and mass-mediated encounters. The early settlers' soul talk format was deployed within a context of highly accentuated in-group intimacy among familiar and rather homogenous participants. They shared much of their life with each other, far beyond the "dialogic moments" of transcendence that marked the soul talks themselves. Set apart from the flow of everyday life, these encounters nevertheless colored their relationships with each other in everyday contexts as well. There were times when they proved to be a relationally energizing resource; at other times they became a relational burden, coloring and impeding daily contacts among group members.

By contrast, the late-night call-in radio programs involve speaking anonymously to unseen others in a public arena about intimate matters of personal import. The anonymity of audience participants in these mass-mediated encounters means that even though they are largely devoted to a discussion of poignantly felt relational matters, they carry no direct relational consequences for callers' everyday lives, unless callers are urged into direct dialogue with significant others through the mediation services of the host (a strategy frequently used by one of the hosts).

These encounters are asymmetrical and nonreciprocal in the sense that the callers' anonymity is counteracted by the performative cultivation of the hosts' personal charisma. Thus, they clearly exemplify a new kind of dialogue and locus of interpersonal authenticity, and they speak to a new kind of "public intimacy." Radio intimacy is bred of expressive freedom; its emergence is facilitated by the program's decontextualized format that is divorced from specific relational histories. It is grounded in the objectification and reification of the relational domain and charts a world of human pain and suffering that is potentially shared by all who care to listen. Callers' stories are about everyday matters that are simultaneously reportable and mundane, of concern to everyone and to no one in particular (except, of course, to the person whose personal problem is being discussed).

My study thus combines a synchronic concern with contemporary ways of speaking with a diachronic concern with the evolution of speechways. In dealing with aspects of Israeli communicative ethos that have been by now largely relegated to the mists of the past, I have also chosen to trace their continued impact on the wider cultural landscape and assess their changing role over the years. While not strictly historical, my work is diachronically oriented in its own way. By assembling the three case studies within the same overarching framework, I aim to offer a more complex analytic argument than any of them taken separately would have allowed. This point seems worth emphasizing given the overwhelmingly synchronic orientation of so much of the research conducted within the ethnography of speaking perspective.

In what follows I therefore try to make a wide-ranging case for the centrality of the quest for authentic dialogue in Israeli speech culture. It is not a claim about the prevalence of "dialogic moments" in my field of inquiry but about an ongoing ideological concern with authentic encounters, direct address, and interpersonal openness as loci of cultural authenticity. Such a concern has been amply articulated in metatalk about authentic dialogue, attempts to orchestrate cultural conditions that would enhance it, and laments about its impossibility or demise.

In approaching the quest for dialogue through an exploration of the shifting contours of Israeli speech culture, I will address the changing meanings and values associated with different forms of dialogue, with different conceptions of community, with different notions of authenticity, and with different articulations of the personal/communal dialectic. Each of these themes involves localized tensions such as that between the persistent longing for the experience of spontaneous engagements in "authentic dialogue" and processes of ritualization accompanying it,[69] or the tension between the inward-looking gesture of communal self-making and its attendant social and cultural exclusions.

While this book is essentially about the quest for authentic dialogue and the discursive occasions in which it has taken shape in Israeli culture at various points in time, it also makes an attempt to use a dialogic perspective in its method of inquiry. In this sense, "dialogue" is employed as a vehicle of understanding and relating various research foci, as represented in the three case studies that make up the book's larger argument. It refers to relations of intertextuality, or mutual responsiveness, between cultural-expressive forms such as ways of speaking or speech events. This view of dialogism is grounded in a Bakhtinian conception of communicative forms through the notion of "dialogized heteroglossia."[70] Proposing a radically contextual version of the meaning of utterances, Bakhtin viewed linguistic communication as a historically grounded, multilayered, and multivocal social enterprise. He stressed the intrinsic openness of utterances as responses inviting further responses, pointed backward and forward, and interlocked in actuality as well as in anticipation. He described the essentially dialogic process of meaning-making as follows:

The living utterance, having taken meaning and shape at a particular historical moment in a socially specific environment, cannot fail to brush up
against thousands of living dialogic threads, woven by socio-ideological
consciousness around the given object of an utterance; it cannot fail to
become an active participant in social dialogue. After all, the utterance
arises out of this dialogue as a continuation of it and as a rejoinder to
it—it does not approach the object from the sideline.[71]

Thus, I construct the overall argument of this book by applying a dialogic perspective to the study of the historically situated and culturally
focal ways of speaking under investigation here. The three chapters of
the book take up ways of speaking and speech events that highlight the
role of dialogue as a locus of authenticity at different points in the making of Israeli culture, more or less spanning the twentieth century. Each
of them gains its full meaning when considered in conjunction with
the other two, each "dialogic moment" responding to and anticipating
those that came before and those that come after.

This attention to the intertextual relations between cultural ways
of speaking allows me to treat them as components in a multivocal and
constantly evolving cultural repertoire. The three case studies demonstrate the potential usefulness of the analytic perspective developed
within the ethnography of speaking program. Yet each of them also
attempts to push this perspective a step further in theoretical, methodological, and substantive terms. I have come to visualize the book as
a three-part mobile whose music-making emerges from the combined
movement of its interconnected parts. Any modification in one of the
parts inevitably affects the motion of the others and the music the three
make together. While each of the book's three chapters can be said to
play its own separate tune, I hope the reader who approaches this text
in the spirit of dialogue will find that its real meaning lies in the playful
intermingling of all three.[72]

Chapter 1

Community of Dialogue
Soul Talks in Israeli Pioneering Ethos

VISIONS OF DIALOGUE

The desolate, gloomy-looking, tent-shaped monument perched on top of a mountain overlooking the Lake of Galilee a little south of Tiberias can no more than suggest the depths of the human drama it was designed to commemorate. Today most Israelis are unfamiliar with the story of the group of twenty-six young pioneers who inhabited the work camp on that spot of mountainous terrain for six months in 1920–21. Indeed, only very few of those who drive by this monument daily ever take the trouble to stop and read the modest but decorative wooden plaque that welcomes visitors to the site, called Bitaniya Ilit (Upper Bitaniya) in pioneering days. The wording on the plaque reads as follows:

> In the year 1921 in the month of Tishrei [the first month of the Jewish year], a group of young men and women of Hashomer Hatza'ir [The young guard] established a tent camp on this site as their first encounter with the landscape of the homeland, with manual labor, with the wilderness and the hardships. Here they wove courageous dreams, which gradually came true all across the land. On the fiftieth anniversary of Hashomer Hatza'ir youth movement in 1964 the Kibbutz Artzi movement erected a tent-shaped monument on this site, commemorating a dream that has become a reality, as a note of hope for the dreamers of tomorrow.
> From a tent camp in 1921
> To 73 kibbutzim [collective settlements] in 1964
> To 85 kibbutzim in 1985.

The deserted, unkempt surroundings of the monument stand in stark contrast to the high-soaring language of the plaque, or the historical weight claimed by the dozens of *kibbutzim* established by Hashomer Hatza'ir movement over the years, whose names are etched in gray concrete on the inner side of the tent-shaped monument. The brief description on the plaque only hints at the legendary tale of Bitaniya

29

Ilit as it has been inscribed in Israeli collective memory. Yet the sorry state of the monument site makes a statement that is no less eloquent than the triumphant note sounded by the plaque itself.

Since the monument was built in 1964, the kibbutz movement has lost much of its ideological fervor and original sense of purpose. It is no longer considered to be a vehicle for the cultivation of the utopian dream it once nourished. The widespread processes of privatization and social fragmentation that now dominate the Israeli social scene as a whole have resulted in the practical abandonment of the socialist visions of the early pioneering groups that founded the first *kibbutzim*.[1] The pioneering ethos inscribed on the plaque commemorating the site of Bitaniya Ilit can therefore no longer be thought of as "a dream that has become a reality."

The saga of Bitaniya Ilit marks an extraordinary though little-known chapter in Israeli foundation mythology. The master-narrative of Socialist Zionism is replete with tales and symbols of heroic deeds and sacrificial acts of settlement. In fact, one of the most famous of these heroic tales, the story of Yosef Trumpeldor's death in the battle of Tel Hai, dates back to events that took place in the very same year as the saga of Bitaniya Ilit, 1920.[2] The heroic settlement activities enshrined in mainstream versions of Israeli pioneering are usually associated with the physical hardiness and material accomplishments encompassed within the notions of the "conquest of the land" and "the conquest of labor." These phrases referred to symbolically charged activities such as draining the swamps or plowing "virginal" fields. They were also interlaced with tales of combat heroism associated with the need to defend the settlements against attacks by local Arabs.[3] The settlement project as represented within mainstream Zionist mythology thus involved action-filled ventures of personal and communal sacrifice in which ecstatic visions of place-making and the exhausting routines of hard labor came together in an often uneasy, yet livable, tension. A paradigmatic example of such heroic representations of Zionist settlement is found in the well-known "Tower and Stockade" narrative, which became an emblem of Jewish settlement activism in the late 1930s.[4]

The saga of Bitaniya Ilit is both part of the Israeli hegemonic pioneering ethos and a counterpart to it. The group of twenty-six young pioneers (four of them women) who made their temporary home in Bitaniya Ilit supported and promoted the Zionist pioneering agenda as a national goal, yet gave it their own very particular inflection. They were centrally concerned with Zionist fulfillment as both a cultural and a personal project of self-transformation to be accomplished by the reinvention of social relations within a revitalized communal setting. They belonged to the Hashomer Hatza'ir Zionist socialist youth movement, many of whose members flowed into Palestine from Poland, Galicia, and Central Europe after World War I, making up the bulk of what is known as the Third Immigration Wave (Aliyah) of Jewish newcomers to the land of Israel between 1919 and 1923.

Some of them came from poverty-stricken, traditional Jewish homes while others were from well-to-do middle-class, urban Jewish families. They were mainly in their late teens and early twenties. The older among them carried traumatic memories of war-torn Europe and the pogroms perpetrated on the Jews in Eastern Europe at the end of the war. The Hashomer Hatza'ir pioneers formed small groups of laborers scattered in different parts of the country, where they found work in road construction, land development, and agricultural labor. Through these various labor engagements, they took an active part in the larger project of the "productivization" of Jewish society and the settlement of the land of Israel. In that respect, they had much in common with other worker groups that did not share their particular brand of youth movement background.

A succinct collective portrait of this group of pioneers is given by Aviva Ufaz, a leading researcher of the literary productions of this Jewish immigration wave:

> The founders of Hashomer Hatza'ir arrived in Vienna as refugees toward the end of the First World War. They lived in a reality in which communal frameworks were falling apart and families were increasingly breaking up. But in Vienna, which was a center of European culture in those days, they were exposed to a rich spiritual climate with which they became utterly infatuated. In Vienna they encountered the ideas and theories that captivated the cultural life of the West in those days. They became acquainted with the writings of Marx, Freud, Nietzsche, Weininger, Landauer, Bernfeld and Buber, and even personally met some of them. They were exposed to the influences of the "youth culture" and the German youth movement. Hand in hand with those influences, they also cultivated their links to Jewish history and tradition.[5]

In developing their version of a community of dialogue, these Hashomer Hatza'ir youths were influenced by the ethos of early twentieth-century Russian revolutionary groups, the *narodniks,* who preached a return to the land, the love of nature, and the moral superiority of the simple and authentic life. They were also influenced by the spirit of the German youth movement, the Wandervogel. This youth culture ethos was rooted in a romantic rejection of the regime of rationality and in a revolt against the social atomization and alienation of modern urban societies. Its goal was to create a new society and a new Jewish person.[6]

In the spirit of social experimentation that was part of the youth culture ethos, these young pioneers regarded themselves as constituting a "social laboratory" for the radical reconstruction of self and community in the context of the close-knit "intimate group." The social model of the "intimate group" took after the German youth culture notion of the Bund. It referred to a small group of highly committed and spiritually inclined individuals who chose to share their lives and souls with each other in close touch with nature and through highly introspective rituals of confession. The proponents of the "intimate group" model envisioned the establishment of a confederation of such groups that would be spread all over the land.

This communal project resonated with the teachings of social thinkers of the time. Notably, the young Hashomer Hatza'ir pioneers were influenced by Martin Buber, whose teachings had greatly affected some of them during their formative years in Vienna before their arrival in Palestine. Buber highlighted the pressing need for social renewal in a society that had become fragmented and alienated by processes of industrialization, urbanization, and secularization. His call for the cultivation of a spirit of dialogue that could reach beyond the functional and interest-related dimensions of social exchange spoke directly to their spiritual and social concerns.

Buber drew on Ferdinand Tonnies's well-known distinction between the notion of a Gemeinschaft (community), which is based in the shared orientation and sense of affiliation generated by ongoing face-to-face contact, and the notion of Gesellschaft (society), which is based on contractual relations and negotiated differences.[7] He argued for the need to deliberately reinvent social life so as to combat the isolation and social fragmentation experienced by so many citizens of modernity. Such a consciously designed process of cultural construction would respond to what he identified as "the enormous desire for communal living that has gripped all people with a soul in Western culture."[8] He felt this desire had to be attended to even though there was obviously no going back to preindustrial forms of social organization: "Indeed, we cannot avoid mechanical society, but we can transcend it and attain a new form of organicism. It is true that we cannot renew ancient origins of growth, but we can sketch the way toward a new social vision that will grow out of deliberately designed social action."[9] This social vision involved first and foremost reconfiguring social relations in a way that would transform both individuals and communities. Buber described this process in organismic terms, stressing again and again that the desired social renewal could not be externally imposed but must come from within the relevant groups themselves—be they local communities, labor unions, friendship circles, or religious groups:

> Only from within, by reviving the tissue of the cells, can there be healing and renewal. The community in all its forms needs to be infused with the new reality, a reality of more direct, more pure, more just social relations between one person and another, so that a true larger community can emerge of the unification of smaller communities, watching with gratification how the system's rusty wheels turn one by one into a pile of debris.[10]

This relational view of communal life involved a special emphasis on the group's internal dialogue, charting a central domain of social experience that was held to be distinct from the realm of politics. In this view, communal participation was a matter of genuine human contact that was oriented toward group "we-ness" rather than involving mere cooperation between individuals who shared personal interests or even group goals. The young pioneers enacted Buber's philosophical search for new and authentic forms of social relationships both in their day-to-day living but especially in the ritualized context of their nocturnal encounters.

These enactments involved an attempt to create a new expressive regime, privileging particular speech events as loci of authenticity. They took the form of confessional group dialogues that characterized the ritualized speech events natively known as soul talks *(sihot nefesh)*, or simply "the talk" *(hasiha)*. These soul talks were designed to facilitate direct contact and enhance interpersonal openness among group members by providing a site for self-disclosure and communal sharing. They followed a model of group conversations led by a charismatic group leader that had been cultivated by Hashomer Hatza'ir groups in Europe. In the context of Bitaniya Ilit, these communal conversations were intended to color the social climate of group life as a whole. Indeed, as focal speech events, the soul talks became an emblem for the possibility of a new and authentic form of communal life. Providing a discursive site for the mediation of self and others, the early pioneers' soul talks can be seen as unique, historically situated forms of cultural communication. They are thus a promising point of departure for my analysis of the life of dialogue as a distinctive cultural project.

The pioneers' encampment in Bitaniya was made up of a workers' camp located along the shore of the Lake of Galilee and of an upper encampment called Bitaniya Ilit, which was perched close to the top of the mountain overlooking the lake. It was one of several concentrations of Hashomer Hatza'ir members, where the special spirit of that youth movement, with its special blend of youth culture and Jewish-Hasidic roots, was nurtured within a close-knit communal setting.[11]

Members of the Bitaniya Ilit group were engaged in clearing the terrain and preparing it for tree planting. They worked hard from early morning to the middle of the day. The women sometimes joined the men's work in the fields, but were often assigned to cooking and other menial service tasks within the encampment, often against their wishes. During the extremely hot hours of midday and early afternoon they took a rest, gathering strength for their evening social pursuits. In the late afternoons they gathered for a shared meal, followed by nightly discussions, singing, and folk dancing. While all pioneering groups of the day shared the experience of engaging in exhausting manual labor, this particular group of well-educated pioneers, who were highly conversant with the intellectual currents of the time, became known for its dense emotional soul talks and the spiritualism attending their distinctive utopian vision of a community of dialogue.

The very process of forming this "intimate group" of Hashomer Hatza'ir pioneers was colored by the communal vision they cultivated. Thus, the Bitaniya Ilit group was formed through a gradual and painful process of social selection, whereby every new group member was chosen by those who already belonged, beginning with a core group of central figures. This selection process was designed to ensure a maximum degree of affinity and compatibility in members' ideological orientations and spiritual inclinations so that they could join hands in conducting their social experiment. Many members of the group later joined the budding kibbutz movement, and some became leading figures in Israeli public life, notably Meir Ya'ari, who was the leader of the left-wing socialist movement and party Mapam for many years, and David Horowitz, who became a leading figure in Israel's economic establishment in the early years of statehood.

This mechanism of group formation encouraged the exploration of individual feelings and motivations as well as the nurturing of shared sensibilities. It involved an attempt to merge individual worlds within a compelling sense of group camaraderie (often referred to as "group eros").[12] Committed to the ideal camaraderie and group feeling, members came to experience interpersonal differences and cultural incompatibilities as an ever-present source of anxiety. Therefore, even while they capitalized on self-disclosure, personal expression, and introspection, individuals' public confessions were felt to be a matter of personal sacrifice to the communal spirit and not of self-fulfillment. The unique spirit of Bitaniya Ilit as a site of social experimentation and innovation is captured in an account by Muky Tsur, a foremost student of the early pioneering days, who contributed greatly to the inscription of the Bitaniya Ilit pioneers in Israeli collective memory:

> They abhorred the old social order. The place of institutions was taken by the [soul] talks, which were a quasi ritual of confession and prayer that gave expression to their anxiety-ridden inner world. These talks revealed an enormous thirst for a life of togetherness, an exhilaration with the new way of life, and unarticulated longings for the idyllic world of the youth movement, which became both unsettled and more mature as a result of the encounter with the realities of life in Palestine. Indeed, the depths of these talks, and the tension that filled them, had consequences for the group's social organization. In the spirit of Buber's and Landauer's teachings, they wanted to prove that their group did not require an organizational structure but sought a deepening of human connection through group encounters. One needs no institutions, only dialogue, and the rules of society can be replaced by the desire for mutual recognition. But along with the dream, there was also a great deal of disorientation, inexperience, longings for the parental home, and a sense of embarrassment that facilitated the rise of a strong leadership. Thus, the person who could articulate their feelings, who had the power to chart a clear direction, gained authority.[13]

The pioneers' soul talks were emotionally intense group encounters in which participants experienced moments of authentic human contact through confessional exchanges and evocative silence. These encounters took place in the communal dining hall, a centrally located public space that often doubled as a library and recreational room. They were convened by either the group's leader or a group member who felt a pressing need to unburden the pain in his or her heart to sympathetic ears. Members of the group were summoned by the sound of a bell that hung outside the communal dining hall and became a symbol of group solidarity and mutual care.

The talks always took place in the evenings after a long day's work, followed by a short rest and a communal supper. They often extended late into the night. Encircled in the intimacy of semidarkness, partaking of the liminality of this "time out of time,"[14] participants shared their most personal thoughts and feelings with each other. The meetings were usually presided over by the group's charismatic leader. They sometimes began with a prolonged, tense silence and were characterized by highly expressive forms of discourse, combining confessional and philosophical monologues on the one hand and pragmatic deliberations concerning the minutae of pioneering life on the other.

As indicated, these gatherings were designed to enact a distinctive communicative ethos of openness and spiritual sharing, concretizing the pioneers' vision of authentic dialogue. This utopian vision of a community of dialogue galvanized considerable emotion, admiration, anticipation, and speculation within socialist Zionist circles, but it also gave rise to a good deal of skepticism and censure among other groups, both at the time and in later days. In serving as a symbol of a spiritual quest enacted through dialogic moments, the saga of Bitaniya Ilit carved for itself a unique, if marginal, place in Israeli collective memory. Indeed, over the years, the story of Bitaniya Ilit has come to constitute a singular version of dialogic yearnings and of spiritual fulfillment within the Israeli settlement mythology.

By foregrounding the spiritual and dialogic dimensions of the Zionist pioneering ethos rather than its pragmatic and political ones, the soul talk ethos challenged the mainstream Zionist view that action and fact-creating deeds were the main loci of authentic Jewish revival, whether expressed in productive manual labor or in activities geared toward self-defense. Since talk became such a central element of their communal experience, these early pioneers engaged in a good deal of reflexive commentary about ways of speaking and speech occasions. This commentary is interspersed in their retrospective accounts of pioneering days, both the accounts that were formulated shortly after the six months they had spent in the isolated encampment in Bitaniya Ilit and those they compiled many years later. Throughout this chapter, I will draw on the early pioneers' own participant accounts, which testify to the ways in which they perceived and assessed the culturally focal discursive sites they named "soul talks" and the communicative activities occasioned by them.

I begin with two excerpts that exemplify the kinds of ecstatic accounts that circulated about the group's soul talks. The first excerpt is taken from a fragment contributed by Shulamit, one of the four young women in the group, to the communal diary *Kehiliyatenu*

(Our commune), the story of whose compilation will be addressed below.[15] Shulamit's account brings forth the liberating potential of self-disclosure and emotional sharing in a setting that combined an ascetic attitude and a puritanical sexual climate with a belief in psychoanalysis as "a revolutionary doctrine essential for the building of a utopian enterprise."[16]

As the following excerpt indicates, Shulamit experienced the group's nocturnal encounters as highly charged dialogic and erotic moments. Her account illustrates the blend of spiritualism and eroticism in terms of which some of the participants in these encounters presented their thoughts and feelings about the soul talks:

> And the nights we spent in the reading room—(Oh, how beautiful it was!), when we all participated in long talks, nights of seeking out the path from one person to the other—this is how I call these nights of holiness [*leilot kodesh*]. Hours, long hours of confessions and listening. Some of us were blessed with the power of expression; others stuttered; many kept silent . . . and in moments of silence—utter silence [*dmama daka*]—it seemed to me that a ray of light [*zik*] springs out of every heart and the rays merge [*mizdavgim*, copulate] into one big flame that reaches into the heart of the sky; and it seemed to me that one large spirit is walking silently around the hall and leaving the stamp of a kiss [*hotam neshika*] on our foreheads. And the stamp left on us by our talks will forever light our foreheads: It will be the sign that will allow us to know each other to the end of our days. And I loved these nights more than any other night, our nights of sharing.[17]

A similarly enthusiastic account of the group's soul talks is found in a letter that was written in Polish by Meir Ya'ari, the group's charismatic leader, and sent to Hashomer Hatza'ir members who were still in Europe at the time. It was later translated and printed in the 1988 edition of *Kehiliyatenu*. In this letter, Ya'ari attributed the uniqueness of the Bitaniya Ilit group to the spiritual sharing they attained in the dialogic moments that punctuated their nocturnal talks. Ya'ari, as a major participant in these talks, fully subscribed to this elevated ideal of authentic dialogue, and his leadership position was intimately implicated with his capacity to orchestrate the group's encounters. Proposing another version of the meaning of the soul talks as ecstatic moments of dialogic sharing, the letter says:

> People around us view us as some kind of Free Masons, or "Free Love Association," or hallucinating youngsters. Some regard us as a danger, others— as an exotic phenomenon. Interpretations pile up, while we are still so far from realizing our main ideas.

And to my point, where do people celebrate such a spiritual feast after a day's hard work as they do here? We are completely addicted to the infatuating flavor of the confession and to the ritual of the talk. The boys may represent polar stances in this spiritual feast, but they are nevertheless so close to each other. Therefore one's breast fills up with pride. You feel that *we are really different.* Not you or that other person, but that small group that is neither formally regulated nor cohesive, yet shines with spirituality.

Sometimes our song flies up high and there are no hills that can send back its echo, as Bitaniya is higher than the surrounding mountains. Our song is not strong and artificial—it is not a forced cry. *It is different.* Sometimes a few concrete words are thrown in, and again there is silence, mountainous and profound. *Our silence—is different.*

Sometimes a cloud throws its shadow on the Sea of Galilee. Our eyes unintentionally interlock and lose themselves in the shadow of the lake in a moment of evening grace. The wild, drunken mountain air invites people to denude themselves. . . . They cannot find their way. *Our communal spirit is different.*[18]

Through individual and collective acts of inscription and narration, members of the pioneering generation itself, as well as some of their descendants and occasional followers, made concerted efforts to keep alive the memory of the spiritual fervor that attended this early Zionist quest for a community of dialogue. Others have invoked the legacy of Bitaniya Ilit in direct or indirect ways to make poignant statements about the Zionist dream and the realities it has fostered. It is mainly through these repeated allusions and invocations that the saga of Bitaniya Ilit has made its repeated, phoenix-like reappearances on the Israeli cultural scene.

The story of Bitaniya Ilit has been inscribed in Israeli cultural imagination as an unfulfilled—yet unforgettable—spiritual possibility. Never quite part of mainstream Israeli myths of place-making, heroism, and sacrifice, it was nevertheless kept alive in kibbutz local histories and has been resurrected now and again in Israeli literature and drama. The marginality of this saga attests to the fact that the spiritualized version of the Zionist project was overwhelmingly superseded both by its more insistent, pragmatic strands and by the embattled reality that has shaped it. However, the fact that the Bitaniya Ilit story has lurked at the edges of the Israeli cultural imagination for so many years, providing a point of reference for both nostalgic and critical reflections on the Zionist project, testifies to its ongoing symbolic resonance.

Therefore, a more sustained look at the cultural conversation surrounding the early pioneers' soul talk format and its attendant vision of a community of dialogue may be rewarding despite (or, indeed, because of) their secondary position in Israeli nation-building mythology. As utopian models for a life of dialogue, these soul talks have emerged as nostalgic cultural sites in and through which the ongoing search for a spiritually meaningful yet secular Jewish existence could be contemplated. The cultural conversation that has surrounded them gives voice to the ideational tension between a life-world dominated by "words," which encapsulates spiritual leanings, and one dominated by deeds, which reflects a down-to-earth, pragmatic attitude. In mainstream Zionist conceptions, "deeds" designate materially and instrumentally oriented endeavors whereas "words" designate "up in the air" talk that is basically purposeless and ineffectual. The devaluing of words and the celebration of deeds goes hand in hand with the rejection of traditional Jewish word-centered spiritual traditions. This attitude was part and parcel of the Zionist cultural revolution.

The saga of Bitaniya Ilit reintroduced the possibility of a spiritualized, word-centered ethos, albeit one that was very different from that of the traditional Jewish world the young pioneers had left behind. In the controversy that surrounded this saga, action-oriented settlement endeavors associated with the mainstream Zionist ethos and the logocentric practices of the pioneers' quest for authentic dialogue were formulated in polar terms. In the hegemonic version of pioneering, "deeds" were recognized as foundational to the settlement project of nation-building and to the attainment of group solidarity, a culturally prized state of cohesion natively known as *gibush* (crystallization).[19] Clearly, the logocentric dialogic quest of Bitaniya Ilit could not be easily accommodated within mainstream Zionist ethos.

The secularized spirituality of these pioneering groups was a largely unsuccessful attempt to break down the words versus deeds dichotomy, to infuse the world of deeds with the spiritual resonances of the authentically addressed spoken word. Though the pioneers rejected traditional Jewish religiosity, they reconfigured some of its basic sentiments, sacralizing productive physical labor as the material and ideological base for the establishment of a new Jewish pioneering society. They thus invented their own distinctive version of a "secular religion," which assumed its own localized version of youthful ecstasy overlaid with Hasidic overtones. The Bitaniya Ilit group turned the search for authentic dialogue into a cornerstone of their secular spiritualism.

The story of the soul talks, as told within the context of the Zionist nation-building ethos, is thus a localized tale of culturally sanctioned soul searchings and utopian strivings. It is a story as full of pain and disillusionment as of ecstatic hopes and spiritual endeavors. It is as much about the search for interpersonal connection and personal transcendence as about the struggle for social position and ideological control. Tracing the contours of this story thus provides an opportunity to rearticulate the early pioneers' utopian quest for authentic dialogue as it became refracted through their nocturnal encounters. It also provides an opportunity to explore the role played by speech symbolism in sustaining communal life over time.

The saga of Bitaniya Ilit is a story of a "road not taken" within the Israeli settlement project. It offers intimations of a spiritualized form of pioneering that presents an alternative to the better-known, action-filled dramas of Israeli nation-building.[20] It offers a bottom-up vision of nation-building that starts from the close-knit, face-to-face community. These small "intimate groups"—in the language of the time—are then envisioned as the building blocks of larger social frameworks. These groups' quest for authentic dialogue can thus be seen as an emergent form of cultural communication through which the individual-community dialectic plays itself out in a particular way—by merging the personal and the communal in the "public intimacy" of group confession.

Yet turning such fleeting moments of authentic dialogue into the cornerstones of communal life is a risky move. It is a move that foregrounds the inevitable tensions between individual expressivity and the social-cultural regulation of talk. As we shall see, this underlying tension is an essential dimension of the ongoing, if highly ambivalent, cultural project of the search for authenticity in Israeli cultural life. In fact, the ways in which the saga of Bitaniya Ilit has been inscribed in Israeli collective memory underscores this ambivalence. This saga has turned into both a site of nostalgia and an arena of bitter ideological critique. For some, it is a symbol of sadly unattainable noble aspirations, while for others it has become a symbol of what they believed were the profoundly delusional dimensions of the pioneering spirit.

This double vision has played itself out by different cultural agents and in vastly different ways over the years. The myth of Bitaniya Ilit has thus been central to the negotiation of the Israeli pioneering ethos, challenging its univocal, mainstream version. In this counterpoint to the heroic pioneering saga, the quest for authentic dialogue has been reinstated as part of early pioneering efforts. Notably, the ephemeral moment of dialogic quest became the object of dissemination efforts, which were designed to share the soul talk ethos with Zionist circles in Palestine and around the Jewish diaspora in the early 1920s. The vision of a community of dialogue was then further disseminated to later generations and became inscribed in Israeli collective memory as part of the nation's utopian agenda.

Indeed, the soul talks of Bitaniya Ilit embodied an alternative form of sociability, a politics of counterpolitics that became the hallmark of some fringe groups within the pioneering movement. This alternative ethos involved an attempt to ground communal life in ongoing dialogic encounters that would replace social institutions and political parties and make them redundant. The rejection of institutionalized politics was an important underlying theme in the life of the spiritually oriented young pioneers of the Third Aliyah. Given their ideological stance against a centralized party apparatus that would stifle attempts to create new social forms, they did not become members of existing political factions of the Labor movement. Rather, they were intent on creating their own social groups with their own model of sociality. David Horowitz, one of the most down-to-earth members of the group, addressed the issue of institutionalized politics and social creativity. In his contribution to the communal diary compiled by the group, *Kehiliyatenu,* he said:

> Once we do away with the fiction of the [political] party—then new groups can be established: social formations, free kibbutzim will make up our movement, a movement of revival, construction and creativity—a movement of life. . . .
>
> It is not incidental that many members of the Third Aliyah have refrained from joining any parties. The reason for this was not apathy, I believe, but a negation of the party as a form of association within the Labor movement in Eretz Israel.[21]

The soul talk format later became a common feature of the life of other Hashomer Hatza'ir groups as well, among them the group called Shomriya, whose members were engaged in road construction. The Shomriya group was joined by many of the Bitaniya Ilit pioneers after they completed their six months of labor and social experimentation on their isolated mountaintop. They continued to hold their nocturnal soul talks within this new context while waiting for the land allocation that would later allow them to establish the first Hashomer Hatza'ir kibbutz in Palestine. In this time of betwixt-and-between, following the ecstatic communal experience in Bitaniya Ilit and just before the group embarked on the long-awaited settlement venture that would give them a home of their own, they decided to inscribe their experiences at Bitaniya Ilit in the form of a communal diary. As already mentioned, it was this diary, *Kehiliyatenu*, that made them famous within pioneering circles as a highly distinctive group with a communal spirit of its own.

Through the writing and dissemination of the diary to various parts of the Jewish world, the young pioneers sought to broadcast their quest for a distinctive communal soul, and to make sure their specific brand of spiritual pioneering was incorporated into the larger nation-building ethos. Indeed, *Kehiliyatenu* soon became a cult book among youth groups in Palestine, Europe, and even North America. It served to broadcast the rather feverish and mystical spirit of the social-spiritual experiment conducted in Bitaniya Ilit to other pioneering groups in Palestine and elsewhere, and eventually became the major resource for transmitting the saga of Bitaniya Ilit to later generations. During the 1920s and 1930s, other pioneering groups, not just those belonging to Hashomer Hatza'ir movement, adopted the soul talk format, and some also appropriated the practice of inscribing personal thoughts and feelings in a communal diary. A number of such diaries are still preserved in various kibbutz archives.

Following the initial interest in the saga of Bitaniya Ilit in the 1920s, the memory of the early pioneering experiment of Bitaniya Ilit, and the text of *Kehiliyatenu* itself, were kept out of public view for many years. The very people who had participated in this drama and in the compilation of *Kehiliyatenu* were reluctant to address it. Most of them preferred to think of the Bitaniya Ilit experience as a misguided youthful venture. They felt that it had better be left behind as they embarked on their communal project of building a home for the group and its members. It was only about half a century later that *Kehiliyatenu* was salvaged from oblivion and reprinted in celebration of the fiftieth anniversary of the Hashomer Hatza'ir movement. At that time, in the mid-1960s, Bitaniya Ilit became crowned as the "cradle" of that pioneering movement in Palestine. This coincided with the emergence of a new wave of spiritual explorations among second-generation kibbutz members, which engendered a new quest for dialogic sharing. As we shall see, this search became intensified following the Six Day War in 1967, when groups of kibbutz members who had participated in the war used a latter-day version of the soul talk format to share thoughts and feelings about the war and its aftermath.

   Kehiliyatenu was again republished in a festive, album-like format by the Yad Ben-Tzvi Institute for the study of Eretz Israel in 1988, reedited by Muky Tsur, a scholar and prominent leader and ideologue of the kibbutz movement, who took up the cultural project begun by Nathan Bistritsky, the original editor of *Kehiliyatenu*, in the 1920s. This edition included an introduction and extensive commentary and visual illustrations, and made this foundational text accessible to the public at large, taking it far beyond the boundaries of the kibbutz movement itself. The re-publication of the communal diary marked a renewed, nostalgic interest in this text as a form of early Israeli protoliterature. Several important scholarly publications exploring it in relation to other early expressive genres of the pioneering era soon followed.[22] In 1995, a second communal diary, written by members of Kvutzat Hasharon between the years 1923 and 1931, was published in a similar format by Yad Ben-Tzvi, this time under the editorship of Aviva Ufaz. A third appeared in 2001.[23]

   Interwoven in the publication history of *Kehiliyatenu* there is the story of the publication of memoirs and literary works that have thematized the saga of Bitaniya Ilit. The various inscriptions and textualizations of this pioneering saga probably account for the fact that it became part of Israeli collective memory in spite of the rather obscure position it has occupied in Israeli pioneering mythology. In what follows, I will draw on the main retextualizations of the Bitaniya Ilit experience, such as the novel *Days and Nights,* by Nathan Bistritsky (originally published in 1926 and later in shortened versions in 1940 and 1978)[24]; the memoir published by David Horowitz in 1970, *My Yesterday;*[25] and plays that thematize or allude to the saga of Bitaniya Ilit, chief among them Yehoshua Sobol's *The Night of the Twentieth.*[26]

   These writings offer layers of individual and collective commentary, artistic appropriations, and reformulations of this saga and its meanings. They provide different glimpses of the soul talk ethos by attending to the ways in which it was remembered, mythologized, and contested at various junctures in Israeli cultural history. The intertextual threads linking these texts to one another, as well as their public reception as gleaned from critical responses in the popular press, offer a promising perspective from which to consider the symbolic career of the "intimate group" ideal and of the soul talk ethos in Israeli culture.

Thus, the vision of authentic dialogue charted by the saga of Bitaniya Ilit offers an intriguing vantage point for the exploration of the symbolism of speaking and action in Israeli cultural imagination. The young pioneers inhabiting the isolated mountain spot overlooking the Lake of Galilee both proclaimed and explored the possibility of what Buber called "true/authentic dialogue" *(hasiha kehavayata)*.[27] Even though the saga of Bitaniya Ilit has been overshadowed by national myths centered on heroic endeavors and patriotic deeds, its memory has continued to hover at the edges of Israeli cultural imagination as a symbol of an alternative communal order grounded in spirituality. Over the years, the quest for authentic dialogue has been pursued in other communicative contexts and forms on the Israeli scene, signaling significant cultural changes in it. Some of them will be addressed in the other chapters of this book.

TEXTUALIZATIONS: *KEHILIYATENU* AND AFTER

The publication of *Kehiliyatenu* was the first step toward inscribing the ethos of Bitaniya Ilit and the pioneers' soul talks in Israeli collective memory. In fact, accounts of the process whereby the diary was compiled have themselves become part of the mythic construction of the saga of Bitaniya Ilit. The writing of the diary was viewed as a communal rite of passage, marking an important juncture in the group's life. It was, indeed, a transitional moment of mythic proportions, marking the end of the group's self-focused, rather delirious immersion in a utopian quest, and the beginning of the workaday, pragmatic, and adult venture of establishing a permanent home. The communal diary was designed to help the pioneers remember the Bitaniya Ilit experience and remind others of it. It was, however, also designed to help them put a sense of closure on this youthful experience and leave it behind them.

The special lure of the confessional genre of the soul talks as inscribed in *Kehiliyatenu* is largely responsible for the communal diary's great popularity at the time of its initial publication in 1922. *Kehiliyatenu*, in turn, further served to popularize the soul talk format, which had been a central element of the ethos of Hashomer Hatza'ir in both Europe and Palestine. Consequently, *Kehiliyatenu* has become wedded in Israeli cultural imagination with the saga of Bitaniya Ilit. This communal diary is indeed an extraordinary text. It is considered to be the most authentic expression of Hashomer Hatza'ir spirit in its early days, before the movement's turn to Marxism. It is the main, though not only, text in which the saga of Bitaniya Ilit has been elaborated. Through it we get a glimpse of the nature of the soul talks with which the young pioneers experimented during and after their stay on their secluded mountaintop. In both content and tenor, the diary was a direct extension of the pioneers' dialogic, face-to-face encounters. However, it was clearly designed to be disseminated to a wider audience, inscribing the intense communal experience of the Bitaniya Ilit group in a gesture of self-celebration.

As mentioned, the group entrusted the task of compiling and editing the diary to Nathan Bistritsky. Bistritsky served as a traveling lecturer, moving among pioneering groups around the country and sharing with them his knowledge of the newly emerging Hebrew culture. He had visited the group in their encampment after they left Bitaniya Ilit and they were very impressed with the literary talk he gave them. He, on his part, was touched by their unique group spirit, and seemed to be just the right person to undertake the delicate task of putting together the bits and pieces of writing they brought to the "editorial tent." This tent became a center of activity, where individuals dispatched their written contributions or orally dictated them to the editor, who was also the translator of segments written in Polish and Yiddish. At times the youngsters read their fragments to each other before handing them over to the editor. He patched them all together into the compilation he titled *Kehiliyatenu*, after the title of a Hasidic text.

The contributions to *Kehiliyatenu* varied greatly in both content and tenor. They were very personal statements reflecting the concerns of particular individuals at the time of writing—their unfulfilled dreams and passions, their disappointments and longings, their beliefs and doubts. These highly emotional outpourings followed the tradition of confessional group talks the young pioneers had brought with them from their experience in Hashomer Hatza'ir. They gave voice to their extreme mood swings, to their struggles to endure the daily difficulties they encountered—their harsh living conditions, the disease and hunger, as well as the gnawing sense of inadequacy they wrestled with, given their lofty ideas on the possibilities of group life.

Thus, these youngsters questioned and rejected the bourgeois social norms and cultural beliefs they associated with the decadent Europe they had left behind. In different ways, they expressed a desire to find new, elusive forms of love that would transcend the bourgeois arrangements of their parental homes. They raised questions about their projected utopian community, whose members would be bound together by their "group eros" rather than being grounded in possessive and exclusive conjugal bonds. They asked about the place of the family in the life of such a community and about the place of women in their male-oriented group setting. They discussed the emerging Zionist cult of agricultural productivity and the potential impact of the ongoing engagement in arduous manual labor on their personal and cultural life. They elaborated their stance toward the communal rituals and expressive forms developed within the group and in the pioneering movement more generally—the communal meal, the dancing, the rituals of confession. Some shared their sense of isolation and their longing for family and friends left behind, others shared humiliating memories they carried with them in relation to their Jewish experience in the *shtetl,* or their tension-filled relationships with either overbearing or painfully helpless parental figures. They invoked biblical stories, Jewish and Christian images, and classical myths as well as modern literary figures in discussing their life and concerns, thus indicating their complex, unresolved relationship toward both Jewish and European cultural traditions. A central theme that is of particular interest from the standpoint of this study and will be further elaborated on below is the youngsters' tormented discussion of their expressive difficulties, their yearning for human contact, and their keen awareness of the many barriers to true dialogue.

The textual form of *Kehiliyatenu* was particularly suited to incorporate this wide range of topics and expressionistic outpourings. It exemplifies a distinctive protoliterary genre that had emerged within early pioneering groups in Palestine in the first decades of the twentieth century. It was unique in that it consisted of intimate, self-reflective utterances by disparate individuals, which were then made part of a collective group project. Composed of a loosely coherent compilation of individual entries, it covered a broad range of topics associated with pioneering life. The pioneers' written fragments followed the flexible genre of the "short article" *(reshima)*, in which the textual organization of the diary brings together a wide range of writing styles. The genre of the short article, as described by literary scholar Shula Keshet, accounts for some of the special flavor of this communal text:

> A short and flexible text, with no constraining formal and thematic features, a simple and elementary textual form that sought to approximate reality as given, without any partitions. The short article gave expression to impressionistic moods, philosophical reflections; it described scenes from working life and tried to paint verbal pictures of the Israeli landscape.

The genre of the short article grew "naturally" out of the interpersonal writing habits that were common among the early pioneers (as a distinctive genre, the short article was preceded by such forms as the letter to a loved one, to the family or to a circle of friends who remained in the Diaspora, or by the personal diary). It also grew out of the custom of holding "written conversations," which was found among some of the early pioneering groups, whereby members used to "talk" to each other via collective notebooks or diaries. This channel enabled members, particularly the women, to express their positions in an unmediated fashion and not in the often stressful context of public discussion—in the general assembly or "the [soul] talk"—as this was called in the kibbutzim of Hashomer Hatza'ir.[28]

Indeed, the stylistic range of *Kehiliyatenu* spanned highly explosive, emotional outbursts and intimate confessions as well as carefully structured philosophical treatises about nature, love, and physical labor. The confessional entries were formulated in a first-person idiom of emotional authenticity, while the diary as a whole was organized around shared themes, constructing the community-at-large as its intended addressee. The philosophical and confessional segments in the diary dealt extensively with such highly charged themes as the place of eroticism and love in the life of the "intimate group." Some of the writings revealed a religious-pantheistic orientation centered on the notions of Love and Eros. Others gave voice to the basic tensions that pervaded the pioneers' everyday life and intellectual deliberations—the tensions between personal and communal expression, between social regulation and individual articulation, between structure and spontaneity. In the analysis proposed by Ufaz, *Kehiliyatenu* is first and foremost a multifaceted statement of such ideals and concerns:

> From what they said about the experience of Bitaniya, we can learn about the nature of the utopian community they envisioned under the name of *eda* (communal group). The distinctive features of the *eda*, as presented in *Kehiliyatenu*, lie in the texture of human relationships among its members, and in their terms—in the creation of a "new culture." The discussion of the texture of community is interwoven with concepts whose combination and repetition create a distinctive-esoteric linguistic universe. Terms such as "love," "eros," "family" lose their denotative meanings in this language and gain a variety of additional meanings.[29]

The group members' youthful struggle with their budding sexuality and with fundamental questions about the relationship between the individual and the group infuse many of the philosophical musings found in the diary. They wrestled with what they considered to be the decline of modern European culture and the social inadequacy of the Jewish communal frameworks they had been raised in; they nurtured their ties to European philosophical and literary thought and also found it difficult to relinquish their emotional ties with their families of origin in Europe.

In one way or another, many of the segments in the diary put forth the ideals of a new social order and a new Jewish person as the center of the group's discussion. Their fundamental philosophical concerns informed the diary as a whole but were specifically focused on in a section titled "From Our Reflections," which included six long essays that dealt with the ideological assumptions underlying such group concerns as the accommodation of family life within the group structure, education, work, settlement, and politics. While I cannot recapture all the idiosyncratic richness of the various philosophical contributions to the diary, the following examples give a sense of their overall flavor and the high degree of reflexivity that characterized their discourse. The first two excerpts are articulations of the ways in which two different members of the Bitaniya Ilit group viewed their communal enterprise. The first one, by David Kahana, stressed the importance of concrete social ties of love and commitment among the members of the "intimate group":

> Our social-cultural enterprise is inextricably linked to a whole set of beloved people and faces, and should one of them be missing, our enterprise would miss the special tune that person could have incorporated into it.
>
> A social enterprise, which involves the recreation of a familiar social or economic formation, is not a cultural enterprise. A social enterprise results bonds of friendship between a person who leads in the name of love and longing for particular individuals whose absence cannot be imagined, not in the name of an abstract idea. . . . Because the enterprise of cultural renewal is not a high-floating idea that was thrown into real life; it is concretized first and foremost through the individual who reaches out to his fellows, driven by the most elementary of desires: Eros.[30]

Another participant, Bistritsky himself, emphasized the unique value of the reflective and creative dimensions of the group's culture-making enterprise:

> The cultural enterprise: there's no other name for our goal and source of happiness. I couldn't call it a way of life because it still seems so remote, so remote. . . . We are experimenters, whose brows are marked by reflection; we are a generation that imposes on itself and its surroundings the tyranny of a spiritual ideal—willingly and out of a great affection. This power of

ours is the power of culture. Culture—as against nature—means that the person sees, envisions, faces several choices and selects among them. . . . The idea of culture for us is not an abstraction, and certainly not a matter of intellect, or of mystery. It is all of our complex being, in its struggle toward the highest, most generous quality. In our struggle for personal integrity, we feel we are among those few today who are cultivating in themselves a new, vital concept of culture.[31]

Several contributors to the diary spoke in familial rather than abstract terms of the cultural-personal renewal project described in the above excerpts. In their vision, the "intimate group" was to become an alternative family, one that would be able to supersede the stifling patriarchal family that was the cornerstone of both Jewish *shtetl* and bourgeois European life. Such proposals are found in another part of the above segment by Bistritsky and in the contribution by Eliyahu Rapaport, the philosophy student turned pioneer, who had been influenced by both the dialogic teachings of Buber and the pantheistic ideas of Spinoza. The diary segment he wrote is an intense treatment of the notion of the group as a family of the future, to be grounded in the lived experience of mutual love and daily care. He, too, spoke of love, or "group eros," in terms of concrete social relations, writing:

There exists no more difficult test than the demand to actualize the feelings of love in the small details of the moment. . . . It is easy to die for great things; it is hard to live for mundane ones. It is easy to carve flowers out of stone for your loved one; it is hard to present one's distant friend with the space between one moment and another. . . . But what is culture? To actualize the love of God from one object to another, from one moment to the other. Our culture is not imprisoned in a library, nor is it contained in grand ideals. It is—the way we attend to each other at table. Did everybody get what he needs? Does everyone have a spoon? . . . Every manifestation of love is an overcoming, an overcoming of the boundaries of the "self."[32]

A similarly spiritualized attitude was expressed with reference to the cult of work, which was an important element of the pioneering spirit in other groups as well. David Kahana expressed it thus: "From all that has been said so far it is clear that our profound attitude toward work is not related to our desire to solve social-pragmatic problems. Moreover, our attitude toward work must flow out of our need to solve cosmic questions, which have to be solved and overcome through sharing. Our solution lies in rooting the individual in the life of the community."[33]

This strong belief in the unique value and transformative potential of the "group eros" was, however, accompanied by ever-present doubts concerning the resilience of the individuals through whose efforts this group spirit would be crafted. One of the group members, Shimon, expressed it as follows:

> We have a group of people, who aspire together, who are tied to each other through a shared past and shared educational experiences, a shared fate and a desire to fulfill their mission—they are tied to each other inescapably. Sometimes one cannot help but note the weakness and lack of resilience vis-à-vis difficult life-conditions—the erosion of bodily strength, hysterical cries into the night, grief, feebleness and erasure. There's no faith in the power of the individual to stick by his "nevertheless" and pave his path, find a way out. And we stand there frightened and anxious, waiting to see how things will turn out. But there's always a ray of hope and there's faith in the depths of our hearts.[34]

In addition to the physical hardships they endured, the young pioneers also felt deprived of the cultural richness of their past life in Europe. While denigrating the decadent spirit of the European bourgeoisie and elevating the "true culture" of group bonding and dialogue, they also attempted to go on cultivating their intellectual life, mainly through reading and discussion. Nevertheless, they were keenly aware of the renunciations they had made when joining the pioneering project. Some of them, particularly those with strong artistic inclinations, experienced the renunciation of an artistically rich environment as a painful personal sacrifice. A touching example of such a moment of realization is narrated in a segment written by one of the girls in the group. It tells the story of a trip she took to the city. Walking along one of the city streets, she was suddenly taken aback by the sound of piano music coming out of one of the windows. This half-forgotten sound stirred buried longings, reminding her of the many years she had devoted to the piano in her parental home in Europe, and of the great personal sacrifice she had made by opting for a pioneering life over a musical career.

What the "intimate group" could offer these young, sensitive intellectuals in compensation for the things they had left behind was an intense climate of spiritual sharing and a life of meaning in a close-knit communal group. The soul talks provided group members with an arena in which they could actualize their innermost individuality within a communal setting. In these ritualized soul talks, speech had a redemptive force. Ecstatic language and total self-disclosure were intended to help overcome the ever-present threat of social alienation and isolation and to reinject a sense of spiritual sharing into a world

Weber has described as the "disenchanted" universe of modernity with its associated modes of fast-moving, urban living and bureaucratic engagements. The pioneers' soul-baring, confessional encounters were major vehicles through which this magical fusion of souls was to be accomplished.[35]

The sections of the communal diary "From Our General Talk," "From the Kibbutz Diary," and "In Our Tents" are confessional, intimate, and at times even lyrical in tone. The continuity between these confessional fragments and the confessional flavor of the ritualized soul talks as thematized both in *Kehiliyatenu* and in other writings describing the events in Bitaniya Ilit is quite evident. The written segments were extensions of the oral exchanges. As Aviva Ufaz put it: "The confessional fragments are an attempt to provide authentic documentation of the [soul] talk and the [oral] confession as they were institutionalized in Bitaniya Ilit and in the Shomriya camp, and as those who compiled the diary wanted to institute them in the utopian society they envisioned."[36] Given the central role played by these confessional rituals in the group's life, members' desire and ability to participate in them became crucial issues. While for some participants these dialogic occasions bore the mark of enchantment, others experienced them as highly charged moments of group tyranny. The sense of empowerment some group members derived from their active participation in these encounters was replaced by deep frustration for those who found it difficult to partake of these public confessions. Much of the metacommunicative discussion of the soul talk experience that appears on the pages of *Kehiliyatenu* relates to dilemmas of participation. A closer look at the rather effusive discussion about both talk and silence can give us a better sense of the soul talk format and the tensions associated with participation in it.

Dilemmas of Participation

The pioneers' contributions to the soul talks expressed their deep-seated dreams and yearnings for a life of meaning and value. Yet not all members of the group felt they could participate as wholeheartedly as Shulamit's and Meir Ya'ari's foregoing testimonies suggest. Other contributors to *Kehiliyatenu* gave voice to their personal sense of inadequacy vis-à-vis the demand to participate in the articulation of feelings, fantasies, and ideological positions in the public context of the group's soul talks. Among the many inadequacies the young pioneers confessed to, the communicative difficulties they described with reference to their participation in the soul talk format are of particular relevance to our concerns. These testimonies were, in fact, meditations on the dialogic process they were striving to enact. Their gnawing feelings of inadequacy created an ever-present sense of existential guilt, which found its outlet in the mode of confession. In this context, verbal acts of self-disclosure were felt to be self-sacrificial gestures of atonement. Since participation in the soul talks became an important measure of communal affirmation, the forms and degrees of participation in them became both a source of gratification and a matter of deep concern for group members.

The pioneers' soul talks and the communal diary in which they were inscribed were a hybrid form, combining elements of voluntary, spontaneous confession with features of institutionalization that are more typical of religious confessional occasions.[37] Aviva Ufaz explained the pioneers' strong emotional urge to engage in voluntary group confession, whether oral or written, as an outgrowth of their existential predicament. In particular, it responded to their keen sense of the enormous gap that existed between their lofty communal ideals and the day-to-day, grinding existence that group members were leading. Her explanation of this process runs as follows:

> The disappointment, the despair and the self-accusations are a result of the attempt to realize the utopian values and norms which were the basis for the *Kehiliyatenu* group. These feelings gave rise to the confessions and made up the bulk of their contents. The confession, from the point of view of its content, was highly personal, but it was enacted within the moral-spiritual world of the group.[38]

Given the youngsters' position of essential isolation and vulnerability, the act of confession was intended to lead group members into renewed contact with one another. For those for whom oral participation was too overwhelming, the outlet and channel provided by the possibility to write their thoughts in the communal diary provided a new opportunity for reconnection with their own feelings and with their peers. Ufaz speaks to these issues when she says: "The confession in *Kehiliyatenu* is involved, mostly, with a feeling of loneliness and an attempt to reconnect with the group. In self-disclosing, the persons confessing express their devotion, perhaps even sacrifice, to society and they feel therefore worthy and entitled, after the confession, to renewed appreciation and to social acceptance."[39]

The diary entries, like the soul talks on which they were modeled, were thus important arenas for the elaboration of social relations within the group. Combining philosophical reflections on social matters and confessional outpourings of personal thoughts and feelings, they served to wed the most abstract universal concerns with the most concrete of personal problems. The conversations and sharing of written fragments became occasions in which personal grievances and vulnerabilities were probed, objectionable behavior was brought up for public consideration, and communal ideals were examined in relation to their implementation in everyday life. The discussions were always grounded in a deeply felt personal reality and were cast in intense emotional tones, whether they touched upon the dynamics of interpersonal relations in the group, or whether they related to the more public dimensions of the group's relations with other Zionist groups.

Individual expression and personal sentiment were articulated against the background of the idealized images constructed in and through the group's dialogic encounters. As noted, a good deal of this talk involved explicit reference to talk and to impediments to self-expression, thematizing the nature of the group's ways of speaking and individuals' concerns about properly participating in them. The communal diary *Kehiliyatenu* was thus not only an inscription of the group's face-to-face soul talks, but also a reflection on the process of dialogic communication itself.

Whereas all members of the intimate group were ratified participants in the soul talks, individuals obviously differed in the form and degree of their participation. The most dominant participant was the group's self-appointed, charismatic leader, who usually presided over the talk and was often the one who summoned it. Both the summons and the soul talk that followed it were grounded in a culturally compelling ethics of dialogue, involving the demands for *presence* and mutual recognition between participants in an encounter. This dialogic vision resounded with the spirit of Buber's I-Thou relationships.[40] Or, in the formulation proposed by sociologist Zali Gurevitch, it was a vision of dialogue that was anchored in a regard for the Other, which was "structured in dialogue as obligated gestures and attitudes, the principle of which is *recognition*."[41] These gestures translated into a set of three obligations: 1. the obligation to *speak;* 2. the obligation to *listen;* and 3. the obligation to *respond.* These obligations formed the normative backbone of the soul talks as communal rituals, regulating participants' expectations as to the kind of mutual engagement these talks should produce.

The issue of participation as a form of affiliation and dialogic recognition looms large in many of the segments of *Kehiliyatenu* that point to the young pioneers' communicative competencies, whether participation is discussed in celebratory or skeptical tones. Examples of both these attitudes, and of a range of self-reflexive comments about the soul talks as discursive engagements, are given in what follows. Attending to the ways in which the pioneers expressed the inner difficulties they experienced with the implicit demand to share openly within the context of the soul talks can teach us a good deal about the nature of these speech occasions.

The diary entry written by Moshe F. expressed his intense belief in the power of words to create the kind of social relationship he was seeking. It begins as follows:

> It is hard for me to talk, because I struggle over the gift of words I want to bring you. I feel I have to say something definitive, and I weigh all my emotions, what you can receive from me and all that ties us together. . . . I didn't want to become captive of my own feelings. I wanted to build a Gothic Church with every word—towering up. The word has to pave the road to the individual. I want to build up our togetherness.[42]

Another diary entry, written by David Horowitz, indicated his recognition of the power of these dialogic encounters, and the sense of isolation he felt due to his inability to fully partake of the group's communal ritual of talk:

> I have always kept the shadowy parts of my life to myself; and whenever I spoke of the deepest and most tragic problems of my life I was afraid that the sanctity of these high matters would be violated by the ruthlessness of daylight, by the word and the dead concept. That's why I kept silent.
>
> But today I feel I must not keep silent; today we are all bound together in the web of shared life, and you are my brothers in sorrow and in great love. You have a right to demand all my truth, to demand and ask me: "Who are you, the silent, the lonely one amongst us?"[43]

In another entry, a pioneer by the name of Dov similarly gave voice to his expressive difficulties in the context of the group's gatherings. He attributed his reticence to his incapacity for love, finding some solace in the possibilities opened up by the communal diary as an alternative expressive outlet:

Yes, my brothers, I want to express myself this one time. I want to share my burden with you. The collection *[Kehiliyatenu]* is my only shelter. In the oral talk I cannot tell you anything. I can't, I haven't yet been able to relax. I would like this [the writing] to improve my situation in the kibbutz. Because I am scared: my [reticent] behavior may be due to the education I received, but I tend to retreat the moment I burst forth, right after giving of myself completely.

I would like you to teach me true love. I would like to struggle against the erosion of love. I succeed in loving most of you only in moments, moments of endless happiness.[44]

In a similar vein, the entry written by Yehoshua expressed the problematic associated with individuals' participation in the soul talks. It further pointed out the danger of routinization. The fear was that these encounters would turn into inauthentic, organizationally oriented gatherings concerned with pragmatic issues rather than occasions for spiritual sharing:

A while ago I approached you for the first time in my life and told you many things, if not everything, about myself. . . . But the things I told you I now want to inscribe for all my brothers, who are allowed to touch this Torah—this unwritten book of souls.

Listen! Our [soul] talk has turned into an assembly. We discuss all kinds of arrangements, we say a lot to each other, our lips move, our tongues move about, our brow wrinkles up, our brains work, the scream silences the restlessness within us—but there is no sharing of souls. . . .

My lips have addressed you many times, I—never did. I did not have the courage to break out of my hard shell, because I was afraid of your hard shell.[45]

And, finally, the entry written by Yehuda, who was a central figure among a group of young pioneers with Hasidic leanings and was active in the group's ecstatic dancing and singing rituals. In his reflections about participating in the soul talks, he linked individual reticence to the degree of supportiveness individuals could expect to find within the group:

I have had many doubts whether I should take part in this dialogue today. My doubts were due to the fact that to this day I have not seen two things that are, in my view, the basis for any society: understanding and pardon. We do not yet know how to understand the individual with all his weaknesses and love him for what he is. We see only external appearances, not the person himself, not the soul. And therefore we lack the ability to pardon. Because if we could see the soul that always contains a spark of holiness, and not only the outward appearance, which is sometimes homely, we would forgive each other.

Therefore, I decided not to participate in any [soul] talk until these two qualities become part of us. Because I recognize a great many shortcomings in myself, and I cannot open myself up in front of you unless I am assured that you can love me with all my faults.[46]

The highly troubled enactments of the vision of a community of dialogue alluded to in these segments came to symbolize both the vitality and the problematics of the pioneers' communal vision. Localized rules and ideals of group participation thus gained a normative force. As some of the foregoing confessional entries testify, they also fueled personal feelings of inadequacy and guilt, adding another layer of difficulty to the young pioneers' difficulties with their new life of physical hardship and, for many of them, the pains of separation from their parental homes. To talk or not to talk, how much to disclose when choosing to talk, how to respond to claims on one's listenership, how to overcome one's expressive limitations—all these were metacommunicative questions the young pioneers wrestled with in their oral and written exchanges.

In a sense, this metacommunicative commentary concerning the soul talk ethos is a meditation on the very possibility of forming a community of dialogue. It is also a reflection on the limitations of language as an instrument of social life, which brings together some of the multiple voices attending the ambitious cultural project of self-fashioning and community-building undertaken by the young pioneers. While they were adamant about maintaining a small-scale group framework, which would be anchored in face-to-face spontaneous encounters, they also sought to provide a social model for other Jewish groups around the country. The soul talks epitomized the dialogic possibilities of well-bounded groups, but they also brought out their rigid boundaries.

An issue that has emerged as particularly poignant with regards to the definition of group boundaries and the patterns of participation in the communal soul talks relates to women's inherently problematic position within the group.[47] The attitudes toward women, as expressed by the primarily male voices of the contributors to *Kehiliyatenu*, were extremely complex and conflicted. In particular, they moved between an exclusionary stance toward women on the one hand and an egalitarian rhetoric that sought to grant women an equal place in the group's life on the other. The "woman question" was intensely discussed within the pioneering group in relation to the possibility of egalitarian relations between men and women who fully share their work and social life. Yet the notion of a "group eros" encompassing men and women alike was interpreted within a basically patriarchal idiom that blended sexual and spiritual claims. In this patriarchal idiom the constitution of a desired group framework required the full participation of women, but they were mainly spoken of as elevated objects of male desire and as beneficiaries of male attentions.

Thus, in some instances, the men in the group gave expression to an ethos of male fraternization marked by homoerotic overtones in which women had no place.[48] This ethos had complex roots in the aforementioned cultural movements that informed the early pioneers' world—the German youth movement ethos, the East European Hasidic cult of male bonding, and the patterns of male comradeship associated with the Jewish enlightenment movement.[49] In a variety of ways, the young male pioneers expressed their reservations concerning women's participation in the utopian community they envisioned. Thus, Ya'ari wrote that "the women are not ripe for the commune . . . eroticism for them is just a high-sounding term."[50] He constructed his argument in historical terms, asking: "Did the woman ever take a real part in community life? Why has woman never taken part in a significant social movement? Isn't the commune a purely male entity, largely spiritual, rarely mundane and concrete?"[51] Binyamin Dror, too, invoked the historical precedents of the ancient Jews and Greeks to discuss the exclusion of women from the pioneering commune, saying: "The group of men, blended through an erotic relationship, tuned into a cultural circle, a spiritual center for the nation, a fountain from which the people drew strength through the generations . . . but they excluded women from their circle."[52]

The young women in the pioneering group were similarly excluded, according to Dror, because they "did not, in fact, live their spiritual lives with the same intensity and intellectual richness as did the men, but since they served as a center of attraction for the men's erotic needs they were cultivated by them without deliberate design and without a pedagogical plan."[53] Indeed, women's distinctive voices and points of view were not part of the empathetic yet ultimately paternalistic vision of gender equality and mutual concern expounded by Dror:

> Our community can be beautiful, but it cannot be complete as long as our young woman does not stand shoulder to shoulder with us. The group of

men can create a culture for itself and for the future generations; but we will be flawed as long as the woman, with whom the man shares the more important aspects of his life—the erotic and the sexual—will remain in a remote corner and will have no value in the life of the community. Making this the center for our communal aspirations is a goal we hardly dare to formulate. But I will not rest until we establish a community that will serve as an appropriate ground for this basic desire. I believe it is at the center of all our life's work.[54]

An even more pronounced patriarchal attitude is found in statements that extol women's matriarchal role as creators of life, but not as equal participants in a social dialogue. In a piece later included in the 1988 edition of *Kehiliyatenu,* Ya'ari called to women, "Come, enter our circle, subordinated girl. Come, give life, new life. A Baby and life. The spirit conquers wild, hungry hearts. You have to find the woman."[55] And Eliyahu Rapaport painted Woman as a birth-giving tool of mythical proportions, seeing her at the same time as requiring the insemination of Man so as to bring her production powers to fruition: "The world and the earth are created in the woman's womb, in the image of God. . . . But the world that emerges from the woman's womb is shapeless, lacks direction, strength and daring . . . the man will come and give it shape."[56]

Thus, even while not directly calling for the exclusion and marginalization of women, and while elevating Woman as an ideal, and even calling for gender equality of sorts, the early pioneers basically replicated the patriarchal worldview in which they had been brought up. Women's own voices were marginalized in *Kehiliyatenu*—only five of its dozens of contributions were written by women. So that even though the communal diary's intimate, confessional tones may have been conducive to the participation of women, the cultural conversation encompassed within it is mainly structured around a male speaker and a passive woman—listener and facilitator of men's talk. In the words of Ufaz, "The passivity and acceptance which characterize female presence are what enable the male discourse to emerge."[57]

The few women who wrote for *Kehiliyatenu* refrained from dwelling on socially expected "feminine" topics such as family, childbirth, and motherhood. They also downplayed the common pioneering women's complaint concerning their relegation to domestic service work, such as kitchen and laundry duty, rather than to "productive" labor in the field, which was a common feature in the diaries of women at the time. As is evident in Shulamit's glowing account of the nocturnal soul talks (segments of which were cited earlier), some of the women embraced the "group eros," finding in it the kind of spiritual fulfillment they sought.

However, in other instances, women's contributions to *Kehiliy-atenu* carried subversive overtones in both style and content, which gave them special resonance and unusual weight. Some of their writings were highly expressionistic and sharply formulated. Giving free reign to outbursts of emotion, they engaged in expressions of unbridled power and freedom that were stereotypically marked as male domains. They violated social rules of propriety and crossed gender boundaries, immersing themselves in ecstatic sensual displays. As Shenka put it: "Why don't you let me go crazy, act wild, run forward in an insane manner, follow the secret call of life?"[58] Yet this desire for free expression, while openly articulated, was nevertheless accompanied by self-doubts and social disappointments. Like Shenka, others, too, asked themselves such questions as: "Can you ever say to yourself—I am free? Can you find in yourself the ability to share and create? And there's no answer. Exhaustion. I spread my arms—and they fall down, tired . . . I look in your faces, seeking an answer, and instead—indifference, misunderstanding, ridicule, lack of respect."[59]

Alongside their expressed desire to participate fully in the group's communal life, the women expressed their rejection of the demands made on them by the pioneering reality of toil and hardship. They refused to lose themselves in ideological musings and repeatedly exposed the gap between the group's pioneering ideals of fraternity and equality and their own experiences of isolation and powerlessness within the group. By highlighting their experience of renunciation and self-effacement, they subverted the pioneering group ethos that was so centrally anchored in an ethic of expressiveness and sharing. This stance may partially account for the paucity of women's contributions to the communal diary. Both in the few statements they made and in holding themselves back, the women signaled their refusal to fully embrace the group's participatory ethos. As Ufaz points out, the women's guarded participation gave expression to their feeling that "the life of togetherness in the Hashomer group did not prevent despair, loneliness, alienation and exploitation—the symptoms of gender trouble in the old world."[60]

Even as they cast doubt on the human possibilities opened up by the group's discursive regime, participants in the soul talks turned the self-probings and intimate sharing of the men and the few women who made up the pioneering group into a tool of ideological dissemination. This was done through the publication of the communal diary *Kehiliy-atenu*, which was so avidly read and discussed by pioneering groups in Palestine, Europe, and North America. That the diary attained cult book status indicates that the dissemination effort paid off. The vision of a community of dialogue was attractive to Jewish youth at the time. And even though the dialogic option presented by the pioneering saga of Bitaniya Ilit did not in fact take root, its phantom presence in Israeli cultural conversation over the years has been both meaningful and instructive.

The retrospective participant accounts of the pioneers' nocturnal gatherings are obviously subjective recollections. They are drawn upon here so as to highlight the experiential dimensions and existential meanings of the soul talks from the point of view of the various participants in them. As we have already seen, these participant accounts provide important insights into the pioneers' utopian vision of dialogic sharing and its human ramifications. They help to further clarify the difficulties individual members experienced in trying to implement the group's vision of a communal dialogue. They also point to the ways in which participants as well as outsiders to the group have contested the saga of Bitaniya Ilit over the years, leaving us with a complexly textured narrative that interweaves nostalgia with ideological subversion.

CONTESTING THE SOUL TALK ETHOS

From the very first, the ecstatic voices promoting the saga of Bitaniya Ilit became entangled with voices contesting its spirit. These voices of contestation went far beyond the kind of questioning that attended the dilemmas of participation I have described earlier. Indeed, the most powerful subversion of the soul talk spirit was generated by the people who had been direct participants in the saga of Bitaniya Ilit and in the making of the communal diary. The saga of Bitaniya Ilit was interrogated in different ways by different critics, each illuminating a different point of contention related to it. In what follows, I will attend to three major ways in which the cultural aura of Bitaniya Ilit has been challenged over the years: first, through an attack on the group's lofty symbolism (Ya'ari); second, by reinterpreting the soul talks as expressions of the tyranny of group spirit (Horowitz); and third, by offering an implicit moral critique of the group's intense self-absorption in its confessional practices (Bistritsky). I will attend to these critiques one by one.

Rootless Symbols

In 1923, just a year following the publication of *Kehiliyatenu*, the group's leader, Meir Ya'ari, published an article titled "Rootless Symbols" *(Smalim Tlushim)*, which caused quite a bit of a stir among pioneering groups.[61] In this article, which was published in the literary journal *Hedim* after Ya'ari left the group in great anger, he was one of the first to publicly renounce as well as denounce the soul talk ethos and what he now described as its inauthentic, mystical orientation. This landmark article was republished in 1980 in the literary-cultural journal published by the kibbutz movement, *Shdemot*, followed by the text of two interviews with Meir Ya'ari, which were devoted to reflections on this early piece.

In this article, Ya'ari joined those who feared that the spiritualism and heightened expressive displays promoted in Bitaniya Ilit would undermine the pioneering movement's pragmatic and worldly orientation. The down-to-earth ethos of mainstream Socialist Zionism privileged masculinist images of "doing," distancing itself from the effeminacy associated with the logocentric image of diaspora Jews. Ya'ari echoed the concern voiced by others before him that the young pioneers' immersion in their spiritualized world might suggest an alternative to the path of productive endeavors, fact-creating deeds, and political alignments. In this early retrospective look, he was the first to publicly refer to the young pioneers' infatuation with the soul talk ethos as "a youthful sin." He described it as an expression of the "eccentric spiritualism" fostered by the German youth culture, which he now claimed to be foreign both to Jewish tradition and to the pioneers' actual life experience. At the same time, he confirmed the pioneers' need to elaborate their own symbols of cultural renewal, believing in the possibility of "vital symbols" such as the cult of work and the idea of peoplehood promulgated by laborer-philosopher A. D. Gordon and by Martin Buber's philosophy of dialogue.[62] Ya'ari now sought a middle ground between two polar positions that presented themselves as cultural alternatives—the rootless, mystical spirit of the European cult of youth on the one hand, and the new interest-oriented, calculating, and "heartless" political alliances of the local pioneering scene on the other.

In this surprisingly early reassessment of the myth of Bitaniya Ilit, Ya'ari questioned the authenticity of the symbolic world that was spun on the pages of *Kehiliyatenu*. His objection was twofold. First, invoking the pragmatic values he had earlier discarded, he now maintained that the group's vision of a spiritualized, communal life was an untenable, distracting utopia. It was not rooted in the real-life predicaments and possibilities of ordinary people who needed to wrestle with actual and concrete social situations, but in the decadent, bourgeois world of European intellectual circles. Second, harking back to deeply felt roots in Jewish culture, he also maintained that the seductive symbols adapted from the German youth culture, such as the glorification of youth and the vision of perfect bonding were inauthentic. They were alien to the Jewish tradition in which the young pioneers had their cultural roots.

Furthermore, pointing to the gap between the pioneering group's rhetoric of community and the grinding routine of its everyday life, Ya'ari questioned if there was any substance to the group's bookish symbols of social solidarity. He suggested that they may have been utterly vacuous, invoking a polarity between mere words and real-life experience:

> We live today in a world of rootless symbols, of modern Don Quixotes. . . . This century's intellectuals have no living symbols left. The symbols found in the literature peeking at us from the pages [of books] are pale and worn out, a danger to touch. . . . And indeed the working masses do not touch them. I often think that they will soon become unmarketable products. The workers consider the host of poems, images and symbols that appear in books and journals as a form of luxury. Only the bourgeoisie in the large cities of Europe enjoys them. . . .
>
> Our Youth movement in the large cities of Vienna and Lvov has attributed some of that leaning toward an eccentric spiritualism and uprooted symbols to the pioneering spirit and Socialist ideologies. . . . Here in Eretz-Israel we established places of refuge for this delirious spirituality and disproportional religiosity. The collection *Kehiliyatenu* shows clearly how we exchanged a straightforward religion with the unique religiosity of Western youth.[63]

In fact, Ya'ari did not reject the pioneers' concern with cultural symbolism, but argued that their task was to seek out "vital symbols" grounded in Jewish culture rather than the "rootless symbols" they borrowed from foreign cultural repertoires. In the interview he gave to a kibbutz ideologue of the younger generation, Yariv Ben-Aharon, following the republication of the article in 1980, he further commented: "We all entered a state of ecstasy, to the point of losing our sense of reality.

I criticized this sense of spiritual infatuation in my article 'Rootless Symbols.' It wasn't a criticism waged against others but self-criticism."[64]

Ya'ari stressed that his criticism was a call for spiritual caution rather than an outright repudiation of the spirit of Bitaniya Ilit, and he expressed his desire to reconnect the Jewish pioneering project to the historical reality in which it was embedded and to its "vital" Jewish roots.

The Tyranny of Group Spirit

Another line of opposition to the Bitaniya Ilit ethos was voiced by another central group member, David Horowitz, who left the group shortly after they left the work camp, and later became a leading figure in Israel's financial establishment. He strongly rejected both the soul talk spirit and Ya'ari's charismatic leadership style. During one of the group's nocturnal gatherings, before the compilation of the communal diary was completed, he confronted Ya'ari headlong, accusing him of exerting intolerable pressure on participants in the soul talks, and charging him with a tyrannical approach. Since none of the other group members rose to his defense, Ya'ari was deeply offended and left the group with his spouse and a few belongings the next morning. Before he left the group, he retrieved the written piece he had contributed to Kehiliyatenu and the diary was published without it.[65] Ya'ari's departure from the group, and the challenge that went with it, turned out to be a highly traumatic event for everybody involved. The scene of confrontation was later inscribed by Horowitz in his memoir and became a memorable moment of cultural contestation, underwritten as it was by personal rivalry.

David Horowitz's memoir was published some fifty years later, in 1970, and was titled My Yesterday. In this autobiographical document he reiterated his version of the story of the group, highlighting the "dark" side of its delirious experience. His account of the soul talk format was, of course, very different from the glowing descriptions given by Shulamit and Ya'ari in the excerpts cited at the beginning of this chapter. What became a flame of spiritual contact in Shulamit's account, and a touch of spiritual grace in Ya'ari's description, became a form of spiritual torment in Horowitz's personal reconstruction. In a rendition that has often been invoked as a countermemory to the enshrinement of the saga of Bitaniya Ilit, he described the group's soul talks in the following terms:

Bitaniya resembled a secluded monastery of a religious sect, a sect with its own charismatic leader and set of symbols, with its ritual of public confession, the kind of confession that calls to mind the attempts of religious mystics to wrestle with God and the devil at one and the same time. . . . It was also the peak of disconnection from real life and its material difficulties, a kind of escapism into spiritual suffering that involves the test of an ongoing confrontation with *memento mori*, in the dense atmosphere of a godless monasterial order, immersed in directionless search and longings. . . .

Work began at sunrise. . . . After a short break for a poor meal at noon, labor continued till sunset. . . . But all this was considered only secondary to the real life. Everyone knew that in Bitaniya life begins in the evening, with the "[soul]talk" *(hasiha)*, that public confession and lengthy and pain-filled dialogue about life, the individual, society, and anything that goes beyond real, concrete, daily reality. It was a rather rich spiritual feast, but full of useless self-recriminations. . . . The talks were conducted in semidarkness, in a dense and spiritually tense atmosphere, which bordered on lunacy. This mysticism, this state of mind, penetrated every spot of the group's life, leaving the individual not even one hidden corner for himself. Every person had to face constant social criticism and judgment by the group, to the point of spiritual cruelty.[66]

The publication of Horowitz's memoir, with its unfavorable portrayal of the soul talk ethos, seems to have struck Ya'ari in his very core. He responded with a long, three-part sequence of articles, which appeared in the left-wing daily *Al Hamishmar*.[67] In this extended reply, Ya'ari countered with an autobiographical statement of his own, rejecting the charges against his leadership style and vehemently denying the claim that the dense social climate induced by the soul talks in Bitaniya Ilit encouraged hysterical displays. Ya'ari's highly emotional rejection of Horowitz's allegations seemed to have more to do with his feeling that his image had been tarnished than with any nostalgic adherence to the spirit of Bitaniya Ilit. In explaining the group's spirit, which he himself had repudiated decades earlier in his well-known 1923 article, he rejected Horowitz's claims about its inauthenticity. This time he grounded its claims to authenticity in its ecstatic Hasidic roots, as well as in members' commitment to a vision of genuine dialogue. He claimed that Horowitz's account was inaccurate and overstated, and that his memoir reflected his personal agenda and sense of rivalry over leadership within the group.

This charge and countercharge turned into an acrimonious exchange, whose animated tones blurred the fact that it concerned events that went fifty years back in time. This was a testimony to the impact of the memory of Bitaniya Ilit on the lives of those who had participated in this unusual venture. The publication of the memoir brought forth old animosities, heated allegations, and self-justifications. For the younger generation for whom the soul talk spirit was a remote aspect of early Zionist mythology, the discussion of the memoir became an occasion for a reinterpretation of the saga of Bitaniya Ilit in more contemporary terms; for example, in terms that echoed the more recent Western countercultural movements of the 1960s. In his response to Horowitz's memoir, Ya'ari angrily mentioned a review of Horowitz's book by journalist and author Amos Elon, which was published in the daily paper *Ha'aretz*, as one that added offense to injury. In this review, titled "The Hippies of the Twenties," Elon likened the spirit of Bitaniya Ilit to that of the New Left in Europe and North America in the 1970s. Drawing on Horowitz's depiction, he described Ya'ari as the

> "guru" of a psychologically suspect set of fools. Ya'ari, something between a sincere spell-binder and a charismatic charlatan, threw the commune into a mystery-filled collective neurosis. Ya'ari was responsible for the hysterical manifestations that became more and more frequent in the group. Horowitz describes the cult of personal confessions that Ya'ari instated in the Bitaniya [Ilit] group. He reports on the violation of individuals' most intimate life, on ecstatic faintings, and on hysterical, tearful outbursts during the leader's ritual performances.[68]

The critique raised by Horowitz and picked up by those who responded to his account had to do with the social implications of the soul talk spirit. The depiction of soul talks as invasive, tyrannical dramas of group coercion served as a means of interrogating the viability of the intimate group model. Obliterating interpersonal distance and incorporating private realities into a common life-world were not perceived as contributing to a viable ideal of group cohesion. Rather, they were presented as an attempt to immerse individuals within the collective by forceful fiat.

There was another problematic dimension to the self-enclosed, inward-looking orientation of these early pioneering groups. Their goal was to enact the social revolution described by Buber as a renewal "from within." Indeed, the inner group focus and intense self-absorption that characterized the pioneers' communal rituals—of which the nocturnal soul talks were a prime example—drew a circle of belonging around group members. At the same time, however, the vexing problematic of the group's contacts with outsiders to it became foregrounded. These exclusionary implications of the Israeli ethos of group cohesion were addressed in both testimonial and fictional treatments of the soul talk spirit, as illustrated in the following discussion of what I refer to as the early pioneers' art of self-absorption.

The Art of Self-Absorption

Even before the publication of *Kehiliyatenu,* the word about the unique spirit of Bitaniya Ilit was disseminated by occasional visitors, such as Nathan Bistritsky, and through encounters with other pioneering groups. Outsiders to the group were both impressed and baffled by the intensity of the group's expressive displays. While Bistritsky obviously found them enchanting, others testified to the discomfort they felt upon encountering the pioneers' communicative style. A witness account published in the wake of a nationwide convention of members of Hashomer Hatza'ir that was held in Haifa in 1920 indicates the bewilderment of those who were not acquainted with the soul talk idiom and were struck by the ecstatic style that characterized the talk of the Bitaniya Ilit group. In the following excerpt, the soul talk idiom, as it appeared in its out-of-the-ordinary context of group intimacy, was put to ridicule by an external observer:

> "Discussed"—this is not the right word, young people don't discuss; youth does not weigh positions; the lyrical temperament of age 18–20 does not concern itself with issues. It ferments, it's like an Aeolian lute that produces music of its own accord when moved by the wind. They talked in the way one talks in a small, intimate kibbutz during winter nights, or in the attic of a dreamy friend—that's how they talked before the audience, in public.[69]

Despite his overall positive response to the group, Bistritsky's fictional account of its life in Bitaniya Ilit which appears in his 1926 novel, *Days and Nights,* clearly is a multivocal text. It includes a detailed, pathos-filled account of the production of *Kehiliyatenu* as a self-made, sacralized communal text. The novel further publicized and aggrandized the saga of Bitaniya Ilit, as did Bistritsky's later autobiography, published in 1980 under the title *The Hidden Myth.*[70] Yet *Days and Nights* also offered a more complex cultural commentary on this unique pioneering saga.

For some of the characters that populate the novel, the soul talks are ecstatic moments of communal soul-searching. For others they are social occasions filled with oppressive silences and overblown emotional outpourings orchestrated by the group's leader. Other voices appear in the novel as well, offering outsiders' perspectives that paint the scene in a parodical light. Thus, Nahum, one of the young pioneers in the book, invites a newcomer to the group to join him in subverting the somber spirit of the group's soul talk with the merry music of his balalaika, offering an irreverent account of the group's nocturnal encounters:

> Tonight we're having an encounter. . . . What's an encounter, Mishkale, do you know? You, son of a bull that you are, you don't know what that is. An encounter is when one person is silent and the other shuts up and the third is mute, and then, with God's help, all the others shut up, keep silent and are mute, too. Now you know what an encounter is. And then someone gets up and mutters three words into his royal nose, or into the ground—let the earth swallow him up as it did Korah and his people. This is how they make public speeches in Giv'at Aryeh [the fictional name of Bitaniya Ilit].[71]

Toward the end of the novel, this mocking portrayal is replaced by another, more complex version of an outsider's point of view. I would like to dwell on this scene, which I believe is critical to the novel's overall message. In a masterful stroke, it provides an implicit commentary on the soul talk format as a cultural site in which group solidarity and group boundaries were recreated and sustained. The fictional scene in question is that of the group's final gathering, after they had all contributed their written fragments to the communal diary they had decided to compile. In hushed excitement, they gathered for a reading aloud of the diary as an ultimate and final gesture of spiritual sharing. At one point, Elisha, an older, highly educated, and beloved member of the group, was reading a deeply tormented and erotic confessional piece composed by one of the girls in the group, Shoshana. This ecstatic reading was suddenly interrupted by a piercing cry for help that came from the Arab village nearby. Bistritsky describes this scene as follows:

> At that moment, when Elisha reached that point [in the text], a piercing scream rose from the night, a scream like that of Eve in the last moment of labor, or like that of a person bitten by a snake, the ancient enemy. It seemed that the voice was coming from the Arab village which was closest to their yard. The scream vibrated in the air and did not stop. But those seated there did not turn their heads, did not move, only their backs responded as to the touch of a knife.
>   Elisha did not stop his reading. Shoshana's torments are greater than any other, let all other pain be submerged by the pain of our sister Shoshana! The voices of pain surrounded the seated group—they were attentive to the pain of their sister, which was laid out in front of them, while the voice of another pain, dull and ancient, nudged them from behind.[72]

The group remained seated in a circle, immersed in their reading. They continued to read even when crowds of frightened Arabs began to bang at the gate, calling for help. The watchman opened the gate and learned that the third, youngest wife of Said Sheikh, the village patriarch who had been their benefactor and frequent visitor, had been bitten by a snake. The Arabs were asking for a carriage and a person to accompany their trip to the Jewish hospital in the nearby town. The group did not budge, not even the delicate young pioneer named Uri, who had developed a special relationship with Said Sheikh. Torn between their immersion in the spiritual experience of the ritual of reading on the one hand and the call for help on the other, the group members chose not to attend to the Arab woman's painful predicament. For them, Shoshana's pain prevailed because it was part of the group circle they had formed, while the Arab woman's pain did not belong in it; she was an outsider. Unable to break away from the group, they felt they couldn't heed the Arab woman's call "because it is here where you belong, in this circle, within the domain of the group's pain."[73]

The group did not even notice that the watchman, Franz, had left his guard, took a cart, and accompanied the Arab woman to the hospital in town. Completely self-absorbed, they did not know how many hours he had been gone from his watch. The reading was followed by spirited dancing, another central practice of group solidarity. Then their sense of group ecstasy was shattered by the sound of a gun—it was Franz, who was the only group member who had not been lured by the relentless grip of group spirit. He had grasped the moral implications of their choice, and could not tolerate his position of insider-outsider and the knowledge that came with it. He committed suicide. Franz had understood that the group's immersion in their trance-like reading had led them to a point of morally unacceptable self-absorption.

The solidarity-building mechanism of the ritual talk and the reading of the diary as an extension of it created a wall between the group and the world outside it. This was a profound insight—the realization that group togetherness has its moral pitfalls, that the group boundaries that enclose members also shut out those who do not belong and whose humanity and very existence may consequently be violated. Franz's suicide, sacralized by his choice to wear the festive blue shirt he reserved for special occasions, was indeed a moment of rude awakening for the group. They seemed to have grasped its implicit message of reproach. Inconsolable and torn apart, they ended up burning the precious pages of the communal diary one by one in a flagrant and painful gesture of textual desecration.

As I read it, Bistritsky's rendition of the saga of Bitaniya Ilit brings out an aspect of the "intimate group" experience that is even darker and less obvious than the coersiveness highlighted by David Horowitz. It speaks to group members' self-centered blindness to the reality and humanity of others, those who do not belong in its circle. The group's lack of responsiveness to the Arab woman's plight indicated that in the utterly self-enclosed world they had constructed there was no place for human compassion that would extend beyond group boundaries. The life of their Arab neighbors—their cultural "others"—had no reality and entailed no moral claim in and of itself. An outsider's tragedy, it was no more than a momentary, irksome interruption of the group's inner process. It took the death of their comrade, who committed suicide in protest against this incredible scene of group oblivion, to jolt them out of their self-absorption. *Days and Nights* ends on a note of disillusionment, with the burning of the diary, followed by the smashing of the dining-room bell whose sounding symbolized the possibility of the soul talks. These two painful gestures of renunciation were a troubled admission of the failure of the group's communal vision.

The group scene of spiritual self-absorption accompanied by oblivion to the existence and plight of the Arab neighbors further complicates the depictions of Arab-Jewish relations that appear in other parts of the novel. In *Kehiliyatenu* the issue of Arab-Jewish relations in Palestine had barely figured in the group members' written fragments. Although the diary is dedicated to the memory of pioneers who died either on the way to Palestine or after arriving there, the Arab-Jewish conflict is not thematized. *Kehiliyatenu* is a text concerned with the internal communal conversation of the self-absorbed group of Jewish pioneers.

In *Days and Nights,* on the other hand, issues of intergroup relations between Arabs and Jews are elaborated in a number of ways. The book contains detailed accounts of group members' responses to the traumatic loss of their first leader in the very first days of their six-month stay at the Bitaniya Ilit encampment. This loss hovers over the text in which Arabs are simultaneously romanticized as natives who are an integral part of the local landscape and seen as potential enemies. In another central scene in the novel, two of the group members are caught in the Arab riots during a trip to the city of Jaffa. One of them is killed, an event that revives the trauma of their loss of their beloved first leader.

These two losses and the sense of danger attending intergroup relations between Arabs and Jews more generally are central elements in Bistritsky's depiction of the group's life, much more so than a reading of *Kehiliyatenu* alone might suggest. At a time when many Jews felt that the Zionist project brought "a people without a land to a land without a people," as the well-known adage had it, Bistritsky was among those who had a more realistic, less romantic, view of the situation. His sober account of the acute intergroup strife that was developing in Palestine of the 1920s was only slightly attenuated by images of cooperation and mutual liking that were conjured through the story of Said Sheikh's attraction to the group, and particularly through the description of the tender father-son relations that developed between him and Uri, one of the group members.

As suggested, however, Bistritsky's final scene of the group's reading aloud ritual offers a critique of Arab-Jewish relations from yet another angle. It points to the in-built blindness attending processes of group formation, including nation-building projects. Bistritsky pointed out that this blindness went hand in hand with the pioneers' striving for a life of dialogue, a life that would fully express the humanity of group members to each other. This scene relentlessly posed the question of how the noble strivings for authentic dialogue could be reconciled with the group's callous treatment of those who were outsiders to it. The critique implied in this question was an early artistic statement that the choice to overlook the humanity of Arab neighbors, even if an incidental byproduct of the group's self-absorption and inner-directedness, would ultimately undermine the realization of the group's communal dreams. In fact, I believe that the novel's most powerful message was the warning that group solidarity could not be sustained without proper attention to intergroup relations. By foregrounding the issue of Arab-Jewish relations in a variety of ways, Bistritsky's novel suggested that the attempt to divorce the Israeli-Jewish Zionist pioneering project of nation-building and self-making from its larger political context was untenable.

The foregoing discussion of the different venues and modes in which the saga of Bitaniya Ilit has been contested indicates that it has played a much more complex role in Israeli collective memory than its nostalgic inscriptions in Hashomer Hatza'ir official lore might suggest. The lofty accounts of the soul talks as ecstatic moments of dialogic sharing were, in one way or another, subverted by testimonies of the acute difficulties individuals experienced in seeking to participate in the group exchanges; by critical accounts of the spiritual tyranny through which the soul talks were sustained; and by the moral misgivings that came with the realization of the human costs attending the group's self-absorption. These themes reemerged as central in further treatments of the Bitaniya Ilit saga in later years, and we shall return to them in the discussion that follows.

Indeed, when *Days and Nights* was first published in 1926, Haim Nahman Bialik, the national poet of Hebrew revival, commended it highly, saying that this book would be rediscovered some fifty years later, when a need to revive the vision of Zionism would arise once again. This cultural moment would involve a "vision of the revival of Israel not only as a Jewish state—but of a revival of the Jewish people as a form of redemption."[74]

It took some fifty years for the dialogic spirit associated with the soul talk ethos to be "resurrected" in particular locations and forms on the Israeli cultural scene. A closer look at some of these reappearances of the soul talk spirit in real-life reenactments and in fictional depictions on stage and in film reveals the continued relevance of the cultural tension between inwardly directed group solidarity on the one hand and attentiveness to intergroup relations on the other—between words and deeds. These tensions reemerged forcefully in well-known reenactments of the soul talk ethos which took place in the context of the soldierly conversations organized by the kibbutz movement following the June 1967 war between Israel and its neighboring Arab states.

These reenactments of the soul talk format, which addressed issues related to military rather than settlement activities, were marked by a shift from a focus on a spiritual quest toward a concern with ethical dilemmas and questions of patriotism. They constituted a cultural site in and through which the Israeli pioneering ethos and its attendant national values have been renegotiated over the years. The cultural continuities as well as the cultural shifts these reenactments reveal will hold our attention in the following pages.

REENACTMENTS: *THE SEVENTH DAY* AND AFTER

In the fall of 1967, shortly after the Six Day War, a book titled *Si'ah Lohamim* (Fighters' Talk) appeared on the Israeli cultural scene and soon became a runaway bestseller. The book inscribed a series of dialogic encounters among members of kibbutzim from around the country, who had fought in the war. Its English translation was published in 1970 under the title of *The Seventh Day*.[75] The group discussions recorded in this book dealt with participants' experience of the war and the personal meanings it held for them. They were excerpted from some thirty oral discussions held in various kibbutzim, which involved some 140 participants in all. The discussions were initiated by a group of young kibbutz intellectuals and educators, who had been active in the area of youth education in the years preceding that war. Before the 1967 war they had formed ideological discussion circles among members of different kibbutz movements in order to discuss issues related to kibbutz life, and, in particular, their stance toward spiritual matters and toward Jewish tradition. They gathered around the literary-philosophical magazine *Shdemot* and were known as the *Shdemot* Circle. This 1960s version of the tradition of philosophically and existentially oriented group dialogues came to be referred to as *tarbut hasihim* (the dialogue culture).[76] Not surprisingly, perhaps, a number of the core members of the group, who served as moderators of the 1967 dialogues and participated in the publication effort inscribing them, were later also involved in reviving the saga of Bitaniya Ilit in the 1970s and 1980s.[77]

The 1967 dialogic encounters were established with the specific purpose of sharing experiences and feelings related to the 1967 war. The impetus for forming these circles of talk had to do with the sense that there was a sharp contrast between the obvious despondency experienced by many of the fighters who had come back from the war and the public euphoria that swept across the nation at what was perceived as the miraculous victory of the Israeli army over the combined forces of Egypt, Syria, and Jordan. For most of the young men participating in these dialogues, the 1967 war was their first encounter with the battlefield. Initially, many of them felt exhilarated by the opportunity to take an active part in such a high-profile national endeavor. As members of a generation born after the great moments of the Zionist nation-building era, they had felt somewhat marginalized. Before the outbreak of the 1967 war many of them welcomed the opportunity to become part of a momentous history-making effort associated with national defense. A participant in one of the circles of talk, who later became a right-wing activist and West Bank settler, Yoel Bin-Nun, articulated this generational sense of frustration thirty years later in a conversational circle designed to reflect back on these earlier dialogues: "The frustration we felt—since the ingathering of the Jews had already been accomplished, and the swamps had already been drained and the roads had already been constructed, and the state had already been established and the Palmah [prestate elite underground unit] had already done its fighting. Even about the retaliatory acts against the Arabs [peulot tagmul] I had already read as a teenager."[78]

Against these initial expectations of generational redemption through participation in the war effort, the encounter with the realities of the battlefield was excruciating. It was a trauma for which the myths of combat heroism this generation had grown up with had not prepared them. These young kibbutz fighters had been raised within a society and an educational system that stressed humanistic values, respect for human life, and equality. Many of them were deeply shaken by their war experience, having come face-to-face with the dark excitement of battle on the one hand and the horror and futility of war on the other. These feelings were aggravated for some by the further moral misgivings triggered by the fighters' contact with the civilian Palestinian population in the West Bank and the Gaza Strip, which had been under Jordanian and Egyptian rule since 1948. These were the first days of the Israeli army's new role as an occupying force, and the soldierly conversations gave voice to moral dilemmas that would become much louder, more emotional, and more contentious in years to come.

These probing and confessional dialogues were clearly—if implicitly—a latter-day version of the early pioneers' soul talk model. This model of group dialogues provided a culturally sanctioned discursive format for the expression of the fighters' inner torments and moral questioning in a supportive group climate. While in its earlier version the soul talk format was associated with the ideal of the "intimate group" and the production of small-scale communities of dialogue, the group discussions following the 1967 war were held in the context of well-established kibbutz communities, whose boundaries were somewhat blurred in an attempt to enrich their dialogic potential. This "culture of dialogue" also resonated with the radical spirit of the 1960s that had become another available model with reference to which invocations of young people's experiences could be cast in the aftermath of the 1967 war.

Like Kehiliyatenu, The Seventh Day was quite heavily edited and organized around thematic sections, which delineate the war experience as a kind of rite of passage, and include "How It Began," "Into Action," "Ordeal by Fire," "Generation to Generation," "At Home," "Jerusalem," and "Facing the Future." The book first appeared as an internal publication of the kibbutz movement some three months after the war, in October 1967, and sold some 20,000 copies to every kibbutz family at production costs. Though it was originally intended for internal distribution only, word got round the country, and a further edition of the book was produced and sold within weeks. Reviews and extracts from the book were printed in the national press, and it became obvious that the interest in it went far beyond the confines of the kibbutz movement itself. After some deliberation, and against fears concerning the effects of commercialization, a general edition was issued and sold to the public at large. Like *Kehiliyatenu* in its own time, *The Seventh Day* triggered greater interest than anticipated. It, too, gained the status of a cult book, selling more than 80,000 copies over the years. It was also translated into several languages, including English, French, Russian, and Yiddish.[79]

The book contains a series of group dialogues held around the country, each by a different set of young kibbutz members who had taken part in the war. In sharing their experiences as fighters in the 1967 war, participants in these encounters candidly gave voice to their traumas, sense of loss, and moral dilemmas in a way that was quite unheard of in Israeli public discourse. This personal discourse of troublesome emotions and dark premonitions went totally against the grain of the many "victory albums" that dominated the post-1967 war publishing scene. Reflecting on these soldierly dialogues thirty-five years later, author Amos Oz, who was a member of the editorial team and one of the facilitators of these discussions, described the subversive stance taken by participants in this venture:

> There was a feeling that the Messiah had arrived, of incredible glibness. And I wanted to shout: "Stop dancing on the rooftops." True, victory is better than defeat, but already then I felt the victory is a disaster, not only for them, but for us, too. I understand that we were heading into a conflict that might only end with nobody left, not only with the Arab world, but with the Islamic world. I had a tremendous need to stick a pin into the euphoria.[80]

This retrospective account echoes some of the fears voiced immediately after the 1967 war by participants in *The Seventh Day,* who were appalled to find themselves in the position of an occupying power and sensed that the occupation would breed further hatred and would lead to further wars and more victims on all sides. By providing a glimpse into the private regions of the fighters' thoughts, misgivings, and feelings of insecurity, these soldierly dialogues became the first widely accessible cultural site in which the Israeli military ethos was publicly negotiated and to some extent subverted. While not all participants challenged the taken-for-granted assumptions underlying Israeli military goals and practices, they all wrestled with them in one way or another in the context of these group encounters. The dialogue groups provided a supportive, even "therapeutic," climate in which a range of feelings and ideological positions could be articulated and explored, and in which even radical departures from the mainstream Israeli consensus were given voice. They also undermined the heroic image of the tough and victorious Israeli combat soldier that was widely promulgated by both the victory albums and the mainstream media coverage of the war.

Muky Tsur, the editor of the 1988 edition of *Kehiliyatenu,* was also one of the participants in *The Seventh Day.* In the summing up discussion held in Tel Aviv, after the material which formed the book had been collected and partially edited, he said, in words that echoed the early pioneers' spiritual yearnings, their search for "vital symbols," and their faith in the possibility of new forms of dialogue:

> We need some sort of spiritual concourse, something different from the usual institutionalized forms of meeting. A genuine meeting of minds, a frank and wide-ranging discussion on many intellectual levels. We must give some depth to life in order to open up new horizons before we reach the stage of decision. Such a discussion could save us from the vicious circle of courage in practical affairs combined with superficiality and timidity in spiritual matters. One can see the danger that empty iconoclasm and obstinate conservatism will between them prevent a genuine renaissance with its roots in reality.[81]

In an interview he gave upon the republication of *Kehiliyatenu* in 1988, Muky Tsur further reinforced the line of continuity between his involvement in the post–Six Day War dialogic encounters and his later immersion in the commemoration of the saga of Bitaniya Ilit:

INTERVIEWER: There is some continuity between this collection [*Kehiliyatenu*] and *The Seventh Day,* which you have also edited, after the Six Day War.

TSUR: There is a connection. The very medium of conversation, and then written conversation. There is also a continuity in the self-questioning tone. It is certainly part of the story, in both collections.[82]

The line of continuity between these two sets of inscribed group dialogues, which were set apart from one another by nearly fifty years, clearly relates to their shared spirit of soul-searching and self-disclosure and to their enactment within the enclave of a small group setting. In both cases, these dialogic moments held the promise of spiritual connection among participants, grounded in the sharing of crucial life experiences and conducted in the intimacy of a face-to-face encounter. The themes discussed in these dialogues went to the heart of participants' existential concerns as they related to pioneering life and its spiritual meanings in the one case, and to military engagements and their emotional and moral dimensions in the other. In both cases, too, despite expressed fears concerning the consequences of publicity, the oral dialogues were inscribed and disseminated much more broadly, providing a conversational model for alternative ways of speaking, thinking, and feeling.

The participants in the fighters' talks were described by Henry Near in his introduction to the English translation of the book as an elite group of Sabras, whose social status implied patriotic devotion. Their patriotism was expressed as an attachment to the land of Israel as the national ancient homeland of the Jewish people. It also expressed itself as a faith in the kibbutz ideology of social justice and its attendant belief that one could sustain a viable communal order without forfeiting members' individuality. Perhaps it was due to their privileged social position and their status as combat soldiers in Israeli society that the participants felt they could risk creating spaces in which personal feelings and alternative formulations could be heard.[83] The larger context of postwar euphoria did not encourage the open expression of the private emotions and moral questionings that became the centerpiece of these encounters. But this particular group felt that "spiritual reckoning" *(heshbon nefesh)* of a different kind was needed at that point in time, and the feeling was strong enough to propel dozens of young kibbutz members to participate in the circles of talk created for this purpose. Near described the process by which these dialogic circles were formed:

> In the summer of 1967, a small group of young kibbutzniks met to discuss the possibility of recording in permanent form the effect of the Six-Day War on their generation. . . . They knew what the war meant to the younger generation in the kibbutzim, because they were of that generation. As they said later: "We felt within ourselves the need to hear each other, to talk to each other, to open up a dialogue of heart and mind. We wanted to explain

to ourselves and to our comrades what had happened to us in those six short days [of war] that lasted so long."[84]

The moderators of the talks formed an editorial board, and the audiotapes recording the group dialogues were transcribed. Technological progress, which now allowed for the spontaneity of oral speech to be preserved, had changed the nature of the process of textualization, and the communal diary was transformed into an edited collection of inscribed conversations as a textual collage. The process of editing involved the identification and isolation of recurrent themes to be included in the final text. Furthermore, appropriate segments taken from kibbutz journals, diaries, and letters were added to the edited text (as was later the case with the 1988 edition of *Kehiliyatenu*). Despite the fact that members of the editorial board included writers, editors, and educators of recognized stature, they sought additional reinforcement and asked two more experienced people to join them in their venture: Abba Kovner, a kibbutz member, veteran author, and well-known spokesman of Holocaust survivors; and Colonel Mordechai Bar-On, Chief Education Officer of the Israeli army and scholar. With the help of small grants from the kibbutz movement and the Workers' Union *(histadrut)*, as well as release time from their own kibbutzim, leading members of the group traveled from one kibbutz to another, organizing and recording informal dialogue groups that discussed the Six Day War experience. As word about this dialogic venture spread around the country, similar groups sprang up in every part of the kibbutz movement. The spirit of the discussions held by these many groups was described by Near as follows:

> This was a generation talking to itself, a true dialogue, with no thought for the outside world. . . . The method of discussion was, on the whole, a form of free association, usually sparked off by some general question from the interviewer. Sometimes the interviewer had his own special interest and even his own axe to grind. In these cases, the tables were often turned, and the interview became a many-sided discussion, a confrontation of several points of view. But, whatever the starting point, a number of themes returned again and again in virtually every discussion. "Dialogue opens that which cannot be opened in any other way," wrote Martin Buber. Such dialogue is the core of *The Seventh Day*. (*The Seventh Day* 5)

The *Seventh Day* volume was dominated by the experience of war, its horrors and excitement alike. The dialogues inscribed in its pages became a site for the expression of previously unarticulated private feelings, the negotiation of fundamental moral values, and the airing of ideological positions regarding core aspects of participants' lives. The most salient feature of these dialogues, however, was their focus on the speakers' complex emotions about the war—the fear of being killed or injured, the disgust or morbid attraction at the horrible sights, the intensity of male bonding, the anger at the unbearable loss of comrades-in-arms, the survivor guilt experienced in the face of others' death, coupled with the relief at being alive, and the sense of futility at the ruin and destruction that engulfed them. As we shall see in the next section, these emotional themes, rather than the acts of war described in the more commonplace popular war annals, made up the main substance of this book.

FIGHTERS' DIALOGUES AND THE LANGUAGE OF EMOTION

The fighters' dialogues inscribed in *The Seventh Day* involved a degree of self-disclosure and expressivity that was quite unusual among Israeli fighting men. Israeli military culture, like that of other nations, is characterized by a masculinist ethos of "toughness" and a premium put on emotional reticence. Israeli directness of style, as the section on *dugri* speech will bring out, did not usually involve self-disclosure and emotional openness of the kind encountered on the pages of this book. The participants in these talks affirmed the profundity and complexity of the war experience through their willingness to probe their emotional responses in an explicit manner, often in conjunction with the war anecdotes they recounted.

Many of the moderators' questions were direct probings into the fighters' feelings about different aspects of military combat. The moderators' questions sometimes related to particular emotions (for example, fear), or to particular moments in the chronicle of war (for example, the moment of entering into battle). Participants' responses invoked a broad range of feelings, both positive and negative. They were formulated in very personal terms and were associated with particular experiences. At the same time, they were also couched in a generalized idiom of patriotism and comradeship-in-arms. Even when testifying to very personal feelings, speakers often inserted a "we all felt that way" clause, generalizing beyond their individual case and assuming a shared structure of feeling within their combat unit. The most poignant parts of the fighters' talk were also the more subversive ones vis-à-vis the mainstream public discourses of heroism and conquest. That they were cast in the candid language of private emotions and personal experience made them particularly powerful. The following are a few examples that illustrate this point.

Thus, in response to the moderator's question "Were there times when you were afraid?," Asher, who served in the army as a doctor, responded: "It's not just fear, it's a complex feeling with all these factors in it. Yet the moment you go into action all these feelings disappear and you just function automatically. I can tell you when I was frightened, though—when four Migs strafed us. This time I felt that I had had it" (66).

In another group discussion, Shai, a twenty-seven-year-old lieutenant, the second-in-command of a paratroop unit during the war, also spoke about the fighters' fear and its overcoming: "The fear goes right through you, especially in the hours just before the fighting starts, from the very minute you know you've got to fight, right down to the second the attack begins. That's when you're most afraid. You don't know exactly what's in store for you but you know it's going to be dangerous. I remember looking around me and wondering which of us wouldn't return. Which of us would be wounded. And I'm sure they all felt the same way" (79).

Another intensely explored emotion was the feeling of inconsolable loss at the death of one's comrades. The same paratroop officer, Shai, discussed it as follows: "I remember that after the battle our most immediate concern was how many dead we had and what state the wounded were in. I can still see the faces of the boys after the attack on Um Katef, as we waited for the helicopter to come and to evacuate the wounded, and they weren't happy faces. They didn't exactly look depressed, but you could see that everyone was upset about the casualties" (81).

Negative feelings such as fear and rage at being caught up in overwhelmingly difficult combat situations sometimes led to a physical sense of nausea. A particularly powerful and candid expression of the sense of horror triggered by the war experience appeared in an anonymous interview one of the fighters gave to a kibbutz journal shortly after the end of the war. Excerpts from this interview were then included in *The Seventh Day* under the heading "I never want to go back there." The interviewee vividly recounted his intense emotional reaction to killing at close range. Unable to forget the scene, he simultaneously acknowledged its sickening, dulling, and dehumanizing effect, but also its power to produce in him anger and hatred:

> But as we went on fighting, I began to care less. For the whole three days that we fought I was sick and vomiting, but it meant less and less to me. All my friends were going down and I grew madder and madder. I wanted to kill them, all the time that I didn't want to see them. I wanted to get a wound and get out; that's what we all wanted—anything to get out. . . .
>
> As we grew angrier, we stopped being human beings. You start out shouting, but by this time, we were all just machines for killing. Everyone's face is set in a snarl and there's a deep growl coming from your belly. You want to kill and kill. You grow like an animal, you know—no, worse than an animal. (90)

Another participant in the round of talks, Yoram, expressed similar feelings of rage and nausea, which overcame him every time he heard the call for help "stretcher bearer!" a call which made him physically sick after the first phases of the battle:

> One of the things I forgot to mention before was a real physical reaction I had every time they shouted "Stretcher bearer!" . . . My stomach would tighten up. I didn't feel angry with anyone in particular. It was fury with the whole world. Together with a feeling of despair and exhaustion. You know it's just like in books—actually writers have had centuries of experience in finding the right words for it—every time there was a shout of "stretcher bearer" I felt like throwing my Uzzi down on the ground, screaming curses and sitting down right there, and saying, "Count me out, I'm not playing any more." (120)

He nevertheless continued to run around and bring stretchers, trying to help as best he could, demonstrating a recurrent theme in participants' talk—the sense of dissociation between actions and feelings, which no emotional labor could bridge, and which was given voice through the bodily language of somatic reactions.

The first encounter with death in the battlefield—of one's comrades or of enemy soldiers—is repeatedly addressed and is described as a self-transforming moment of deeper realization. Gad, who fought in the tank corps, said:

> We were all quite pleased about things at first. When we entered Khan Junis the people started clapping us, and there were white flags flying. Then suddenly we started seeing the first of the dead.
>
> When you see one of the ones who's caught it, you curse the whole damned war. You wonder why it's got to happen, why you've got to shoot. I started thinking about people; it seemed awfully strange at first. In the

beginning you deliberately don't aim very accurately, it's awfully difficult to make yourself shoot. Then you do, and you get used to it. I remember how amazed we were at how much we'd changed. What have I got against an Arab? Even if I see that he's got a gun. I don't know, it's awfully strange. You shoot at him, you know he's a man, that he's got a family, that he's married. It all goes fine right up to the moment that you see someone dead. That's when we began to curse the war. (99–100)

In a similarly candid statement, a participant in another dialogic encounter, Amnon, highlighted the dissociation between the moment of action and actors' retrospective evaluation of it. He responded to the moderator's question about whether he felt a cheapening of human life as a result of all the death and horror they had come upon, saying:

The value of our own life didn't lessen, not even during very critical moments. The fact that we began to kill without being bothered by it all—retrospectively, this was an appalling experience. At first it was grim in itself. Later—how can I put it?—the enemy stopped being a person. He became just a thing opposite us. . . . But I don't think the value of life lessened because of this. People were horrified at themselves, at how they'd been able to kill. (120)

In a similar spirit of relentless self-scrutiny and a refusal to adopt a heroic posture, the anonymous fighter whose interview was cited above foregrounded the effect of combat activity itself, refusing to claim any essential character traits, and suggesting how rage and courage become intimately linked in these highly charged battlefield situations: "You don't just pick courage up from nowhere: the enemy gives it to you. You see your own boys dying around you, your friends, and you get mad" (88).

Indeed, although so much of the fighters' talk deals with private emotions, questions of responsibility and blame, right and might, loom large in the discourse of *The Seventh Day*. Some accounts were cast in terms of localized responses to particular incidents on the battlefield, while others addressed the basic Zionist agenda of settling Palestine. In discussing these issues, Nahman, an educator, acknowledged the essentially tragic dimension of Zionism as a political agenda that mandated that the Jews' return to their ancient homeland would entail the uprooting of the Palestinian inhabitants of the land. He acknowledged that force was the determining factor, not agreements or goodwill. For him, as for many Israelis, as we shall see, the conclusion was an acceptance of the rule of force and the need to be strong:

> When we were talking about the war in the dining-hall on Friday, I said
> that for me one of the toughest of my experiences was coming to a certain
> intellectual conclusion: right goes along with might. In other words, right
> without might is meaningless. And anyone who wants right to be something
> more than simply an abstract idea—anyone who wants to live by that
> right—has got to be strong. That's the law of our times. It's cruel; but all
> I can do is regret it. And I'm not prepared to have a bad conscience if I'm
> compelled to implement that right by force, because I haven't any other
> course of action. (172–73)

A less confident note was sounded by Tamar, the wife of one of the
fighters, one of the few women who participated in these rounds of
talk. She reflected about the burden of educating children toward war,
and instilling in them the spirit of self-sacrifice that was so warmly
extolled by some of the speakers. She resonated with the sentiment
raised by author Amos Oz in a group discussion held in Hulda, where
he questioned the need to retain control of the Wailing Wall in Old
Jerusalem that had been conquered in the war, saying he was willing
to visit it as a tourist if such renunciation could save human life (186).
Wrestling with her misgivings about the basic Israeli claim that this
was a war of "no choice," Tamar said:

> Some people have already fought four wars. How can you bring people up
> that way? It's one big contradiction in terms. Sometimes the thought steals
> into your mind: perhaps it would be better to give up this country, to do
> away with one war in the world, to get rid of one war area. I don't know.
> Sometimes I really had rebellious thoughts; in the shelter, for example, as
> I held my two weeks-old baby in my arms I wondered whether this was
> really necessary. (112–13)

Perhaps the clearest way in which the moral tension created by the
Six Day War experience played itself out was through the uses speakers
made of Holocaust imagery in attempting to make sense of the war situation. Most references to the Holocaust were spoken out of a deep sense
of identification with Jewish victimage during the Holocaust period, as
a way of accounting for speakers' acute fears. The prewar waiting period, in particular, when most reserve units had been called to duty,
with its attendant anxieties and sense of helplessness, invoked deeply
ingrained Holocaust-related anxieties inscribed in people's collective
or personal memories. There were participants, however, who used
Holocaust imagery to express their moral torments with regard to the
injustices perpetrated on Arabs, which made the victory less than sweet,
generating complex feelings about it. Menahem, who participated in
a group discussion held at Kibbutz Ein Hahoresh, spoke to this issue,

describing his feelings at the sight of Palestinian refugees he met on the road:

> I felt uneasy about being a victorious army, a strong army. If I had any clear awareness of the World War years and the fate of European Jewry it was once when I was going up the Jeriho road and the refugees were going down it. I identified directly with them. When I saw parents dragging their children along by the hand, I actually almost saw myself being dragged along by my own father. This was perhaps one of the immediate experiences that brought an association with the war years. It wasn't so noticeable in times of action, but just at those moments when we felt the suffering of others, of the Arabs, against whom we fought. This was perhaps the tragic thing, that the identification had to be with the other side, with our enemies. (216–17)

Thus, the dialogic circles inscribed in *The Seventh Day* provided a format and a context for the articulation of the personal and the communal dimensions of participants' war experience. These dialogues were modeled on the early pioneers' soul talks and reflected the unique sociohistorical context of the post-1967 war period. As we have seen, they addressed the complexity of the war experience—as an ultimate test of character and nationhood as well as in terms of the heavy human costs it entailed. There were participants who echoed mainstream Israeli ideologies that supported their sense of rightfulness and celebrated "positive" patriotic feelings. They saw the war as promoting such values as brotherhood-in-arms, commitment to the common cause, mutual trust, coping in situations of hardship, a readiness for self-sacrifice, and courage. These values anchored a battleground ethics of leadership and personal example (encapsulated in the phrase "follow me!").

While acknowledging these values, many speakers expressed negative feelings associated with the war experience. Some, as we have seen, agonized over its brutalizing effect and the routinization of horror. They candidly described such feelings as an overwhelming impulse to take revenge for a fallen comrade, a morbid desire to feast their eyes on the sight of corpses, or a general sense of inner hardening produced by the close contact with death and the brutalities of the battlefield. Speakers furthermore voiced powerful and often conflicting emotions such as the desire to participate in active fighting coupled with the fear of battle, feelings of shock at the death of friends, and the sense of guilt attending the relief they felt at their own personal survival. They were also obsessed with the question of their feelings toward the Arab enemy, professing to feelings of hatred, which they felt went expressly against their humanistic inclinations and moral stance. While some admitted to feelings of hatred toward the enemy in general, others professed to hating only particular enemies, such as the Syrians who had tortured Israeli prisoners of war.

Other participants took pains to deny any feelings of hatred, revenge-seeking, or battle enthusiasm, claiming to have unwillingly fought a "no choice" war that was imposed on them by the enemy leadership. In later years, this attitude of the reluctant fighter, which was quite prevalent among participants in these dialogues, came to be criticized as evasive and self-righteous, and was given the label "shooting and crying" *(yorim ubokhim)*. This phrase was used to critique the fighters' attempt to dissociate the perpetration of violent actions from the need to stand up to their consequences. It hinted that all these soul searchings and self-recriminations were a strategy for shirking responsibility for one's actions.[85]

The Israeli public's obvious interest in this volume suggested that these soldierly conversations had in fact touched a raw nerve. To many, the direct and honest way in which participants dealt with the darker aspects of the war experience was indeed a welcome counterpart to the mainstream cultural conversation. In many ways these conversations upheld the humanistic heritage of the Zionist enterprise through the fighters' wrestling with moral issues and their expressed distaste for the use of force and for the horrors and violence of war. This volume of inscribed conversations triggered some uneasiness. It offered an alternative to the self-aggrandizing, triumphant notes that engulfed Israeli society by foregrounding the dark side of war in a moment of military bravado.

Yet its broad appeal suggests that the voices in it did not in fact challenge the public consensus about the ultimate justifiability of the war or, indeed, its overwhelming mystique. While the conversations brought out the futility and anguish of the battlefield experience, they did not undermine the militaristic ethos in which they were grounded. By and large, combat activities were still depicted as largely ennobling moments by the participants. The dialogues themselves were, indeed, a further indication of the fighters' noble feelings. The courage they showed by putting their thoughts and feelings into words was regarded as a further badge of honor. Much as they dwelt on the horrors of war, the conversations contained in *The Seventh Day* did not leave readers with the feeling that the soldiers participating in them were likely to respond negatively to a call to take part in future wars. In fact, they served to help augment what George Mosse has referred to as "the myth of the war experience" that "led to the search for a 'new man,' hard as steel, who found his identity in the camaraderie of battle."[86] The myth of the war experience in this case was constructed around a less hardened image of the "new man," one whose feelings and moral sentiments played a role in his experience of soldierhood.

Needless to say, the conversational focus on battlefield experiences, from which women were excluded, served to both privilege and punctuate men's life-world and point of view. Indeed, very few women participated in the talks (although the fifteen-member team of discussion facilitators included four women) and the voices of women were included in the volume only very marginally and in a way that largely reinforced the focus on men's experiences of violence, death, and male-bonding.

As in the case of the communal dialogues inscribed in *Kehiliyatenu,* a major role for women in these groups, when they did participate, was that of a facilitative presence in the expression of men's experiences. As group facilitators, they asked questions from an outsider's stance, inquiring what went on in the soldiers' heads during war in a way that underlined their lack of firsthand knowledge of the battlefield. They repeated anecdotes they had heard from other fighters in other conversations, making clear that they did not claim narrative authority. They also facilitated the men's talk by acting as an appreciative audience, giving voice to wonder and admiration at the stories of courage, hardship, and coping they were told.

On some occasions, women's voices were heard in a more autonomous way, as participants in the larger experience of the war; they spoke as the wives and mothers who took care of the home and the children while the men were away and they were left in kibbutzim that suffered heavy shelling, or as the few noncombative soldier-girls who inadvertently found themselves in the front line. Thus, one of the conversations inscribed in the volume was specifically concerned with the wartime experiences of women who inhabited kibbutz Tel-Katzir, where they spent six days in the shelters due to the relentless Syrian fire directed at the kibbutz. It is the only conversation in the volume dominated by women's voices and concerns. They spoke of the fear induced by the sounds of shelling, of the hardships of the prolonged stay in the shelters, of moments of panic induced by a sense of isolation, and of the children's shock at the destruction they witnessed on the kibbutz grounds when they were finally allowed to go out. They also spoke of a heartwarming sense of shared responsibility and mutual support both within the kibbutz and between kibbutzim. To the facilitator's direct question as to gender differences in responses to the war, one participant, Berela, answered: "The girls are less communicative. The boys generally stand around and talk—amateur strategists. When a girl comes past, she contents herself with just listening to what they're saying. I think each of the girls thought about it, but they didn't talk much."[87]

At least some of the women's silence can be attributed to their sense that they saw things differently than men, and that their unexpressed thoughts might turn out to undermine the widely accepted, male-dominated perspectives they were surrounded by and which they felt they could neither support nor subvert. The openness of the group encounters allowed some of them to give voice to their deep-buried ideological doubts. Thus, Tamar, whose misgivings about the very necessity of fighting the war were cited earlier, subsequently undercut the forcefulness of her protest at the prospect of endless wars by proclaiming the war to be justified in retrospect. But it was not a wholehearted statement, as she admitted that she might have felt differently if her husband had not come back. Her personal conclusion, expressed in an idiom of fear and potential loss, harmonized her position with the widespread sentiment that elevates women's role as mothers in Israeli society, as motherhood is seen as a contribution to the nation: "Really, perhaps we need lots and lots of children—we've just got to go on having children."[88] In another encounter, Nurit sounds a subversive note, marking her distance from the Israeli military ethos, as she similarly questions the inevitability of war as an ongoing fixture of Israeli existence. She says: "I've often asked myself what would have happened if we really did finally achieve peace here. It's interesting that, as I see it, if the Arabs really do want to finish us off, then the best thing they could do would be to make peace with us."[89]

There were a few young women who accidentally found themselves in the battle zone, an area from which women were usually evacuated. One of them, Ayelet, shared her experiences in a group discussion that included both men and women. She was quite aware that her presence there was fortuitous and though she shared the men's experience of exposure to the sights of war, she knew she was not there to fight. Like some of the men, she reported a sense of emotional numbing that overcame her at the sight of corpses and at the nearness of danger. Even at the time of her retrospective account, she was reluctant to delve into the memory of the battlefield experience and use the occasion of the group conversation to make sense of it for herself, as many of the male soldiers did. Perhaps this was because, unlike the men's meaningful presence on site, the girls' presence had no meaning, and Ayelet felt that "if I or another girl were to be hit it would be a pointless death, we hadn't come to fight and our death here wouldn't help anyone. It wasn't such a pleasant thought, that you might die here by mistake." [90]

We see, then, that some of the women's voices went further than the men's in casting doubt on the personal as well as the collective meaning of the war experience. Yet taken together, in the context of the male-dominated cultural conversation that fills the pages of *The Seventh Day*, these voices remained largely muted and became incorporated within the patriarchal order signaled by the book. Clearly, this book made a considerable contribution to upholding the aura of the battlefield as the ultimate experience by foregrounding its various facets to a degree that went above and beyond the sagas of conquest found in the victory albums. The myth of the war experience was further complicated by the positions expressed in these soldierly conversations, not subverted by them. The positions expressed in them were a far cry from the explicit political protests voiced by soldiers in the wake of the 1973 Yom Kippur War, or the 1982 Lebanon War, even though they may have opened the door for the more radical, dissenting pacifist voices that followed these later military engagements. In later years, open, sustained public protest and various manifestations of conscientious objection became much more common.

FROM COMMEMORATION TO MORAL CHALLENGE

As the years went by, the Six Day War experience became eclipsed by the wars that followed it. They included the highly traumatic Yom Kippur War of 1973; the troubling military and moral position of the Israeli army as an occupying force in the West Bank and Gaza since 1967; the 1982 Lebanon War and the subsequent Israeli occupation of Southern Lebanon; the Palestinian uprising that began in 1988 and was renewed in 2000—to name but the major landmarks of Israel's troubled political-military history. The "victory albums" that were so prominent on the Israeli scene in the months following the 1967 war turned into a sad reminder of the euphoric celebration of survival and conquest that swept the country at the time. For many, they became a bitter ironic commentary on the Israeli condition of never-ending strife and conflict—the "tragedy of Zionism," as it was benevolently called even in the pages of *The Seventh Day*.

The self-critical, more vulnerable voices of the participants in *The Seventh Day* thus became an emblem of the emergence of an alternative sensibility that was traceable to the days following the Six Day War itself. As such, not surprisingly, *The Seventh Day* became once again an instrument of collective self-reckoning. It was increasingly colored by an irreconcilable nostalgia for the yearnings and dilemmas of a past not yet tarnished by these many layers of trauma and guilt. Primary occasions for the emergence of such commentaries were commemorative invocations of *The Seventh Day* on anniversaries of the Six Day War. These took the form of radio discussions or printed articles in kibbutz publications as well as in the national press. The ritualized retrospective commentaries were in many ways as much occasions for reassessing the present as they were reappraisals of the spirit of *The Seventh Day* itself. Again, as in the case of the soul talks of pioneering days, the dialogical encounters inscribed in *The Seventh Day* became subject to ongoing reinterpretations and revaluations.

A year following the Six Day War, in June 1968, a group of young people from Kibbutz Ein-Shemer met to discuss two topics: their feelings about the war "a year later," and their views of the kibbutz from the standpoint of members of the second generation. Like the dialogues that formed the basis of *The Seventh Day*, these dialogues were recorded, transcribed, and disseminated within the kibbutz movement and eventually appeared in a book titled *Bein Tzeirim* (Among young people).[91] They roused considerable interest in kibbutz circles and were discussed in the kibbutz press, but also reached the wider public when segments of these talks appeared in the national high-brow daily *Ha'aretz* and became the topic of more wide-ranging commentary.[92] The article in *Ha'aretz* was provocatively titled "The Hashomer Hatza'ir Youth Question: Is There a Justification for the State of Israel?" It gave voice to a range of the more pointed views expressed by the participants in this talk concerning the human cost attending victory in war, the nation's ability to withstand further wars, the erosion of kibbutz ideologies, the search for a new social vision, the belief in spiritual values, the injustices perpetrated against the indigenous inhabitants of Palestine, and the concern about the ways in which Israel's role as an occupying force would affect the future image of the Israeli army.

The Ein Shemer encounter was a clear reenactment of the interactional format of the earlier soldierly soul talks, replicating their searching, introspective spirit. It addressed personal experiences, moral issues, and questions of meaning. Obviously colored by the recent experience of war, which made the search for a meaningful life all too urgent, the discussions held by young kibbutz members addressed basic ideological and social themes. They questioned their choice to make the kibbutz their home and way of life, their links to Judaism and to the Jewish people as a whole, their intergenerational relations with the founding generation of the kibbutz, and their visions for their personal and collective future. Participants felt that as the inheritors of the Socialist Zionist vision of the kibbutz, they had come to a point where they needed to engage with the aftermath of the war and with its implications for their own lives as kibbutz members, Israeli citizens, and Jews in as truthful and profound a manner as they could.

A special note of urgency was added to the additional rounds of dialogue organized in the wake of *The Seventh Day* when participants realized that their feeling that the 1967 war was the last they would have to fight for Israel's survival and security had been delusional. The ongoing War of Attrition in the Sinai brought home the fact that the cycle of violence, which had engulfed the country, was by no means over. The heavy toll in terms of soldiers' lives on the southern front coupled with the moral dilemmas generated by the military occupation of densely populated Palestinian areas in the Gaza Strip and the West Bank had by then become a source of great concern.

For participants in these kibbutz encounters, this dialogic format appeared to offer a viable means of addressing the myriad spiritual and moral issues they were facing. As was the case with the early pioneers' soul talks, the self-disclosive and highly expressive nature of the discourse in these exchanges became a symbol for the ability to move individuals out of their self-imposed silence and depression and engage them in a communal ritual of liberating talk. Not surprisingly, these latter-day recyclings of the soul talk format reinvoked the basic cultural tension between "words" and "deeds," pitting expressivity and spirituality against a problem-solving, pragmatic, down-to-earth approach. We have seen that this tension had been central in discussions of the soul talk ethos in the 1920s. This thematic continuity was attended by a continuity of style between the earlier dialogic encounters of the 1920s and the later ones of the 1960s, as is indicated in the following commentary: "From the point of view of its sincerity of expression, openness and willingness to explore one's inner-truth to its very core—the Ein Shemer volume was identical to *The Seventh Day*. Once the silence was broken and the participants started talking—it appeared that all the inhibitions that stand in the way of a person's desire to disclose in front of others were removed."[93]

In a warm critical response to *Bein Tzeirim*, Israel Ring exhorted readers to pick up this book "without delay." His response focused specifically on shared speech forms that gave the talk inscribed in this volume the recognizable flavor of "kibbutz speech"—that is, speech that is nonstylized, somewhat cryptic, and oriented to the inner dealings of a group with its own distinctive set of concerns, presumptions, and value orientations. He describes these dialogic encounters as constituting spiritual, life-giving acts, which are uniquely suited to the task of giving voice to the young generation's experiences and existential probing:

> It turns out that the unmediated, non-planned encounter is (a) Almost the only possibility to make many of the young people of the kibbutz talk about essential topics. (b) It is almost the only possibility for young people to go beyond limited side comments and give voice to a sustained stream of responsible thought. This way they can at least attain an open and profound presentation of the problematic involved; and at times, they can fumble toward some responses. It would not be an erroneous conclusion to say that the dialogue form is particularly suitable for the task of overlaying a familiar, shared social world with a tentative intellectual search.[94]

Other commentators, however, did not share the same enthusiasm for these dialogic encounters. They took issue with particular emotional or ideological positions expressed in them. For some, the separation between Zionism (as a secular enterprise) and Judaism (as a religion) did not make sense, as to them Zionism was an expression of Judaism. Others rejected the young participants' pursuit of self-actualization in the form of a career-oriented education and professional enhancement, claiming that it subverted the collectivist and egalitarian ideals of the kibbutz. Others still objected to the expressions of collective guilt found in some participants' reflections on the wrongs perpetrated by the Zionist movement in uprooting the local Palestinian population.

Beyond the substantive controversies raised by specific topics addressed in the commentaries on *Bein Tzeirim*, they pointed to the expressive limitations of these talks, which were modeled on *The Seventh Day* and were shaped by the immediacy of their response to the drama and trauma of participants' war experience. The emotional discourse of self-disclosure that felt appropriate in the wake of the 1967 war came to be viewed as an inadequate discursive form in later years, when the need to move into a more pragmatic and deliberative mode of discussion became pressing.

Comments that directly addressed the dialogic texture of these talks rather than their contents could be heard in the early 1970s. Open critiques of the dialogic, highly expressive, and confessional form of the young people's talk appeared in the press. An example of such a critique was found in an article that called for a move from confessional dialogues to deliberative discussions. In comparing the two books of inscribed conversations, *The Seventh Day* and *Bein Tzeirim,* the commentator felt that the former spoke in a much more poignant voice, addressing a very special moment in Israeli history—a generation's raw encounter with the horrors of war. But he also acknowledged the commonalities between the exploratory and confessional tones of these two texts. Recognizing the value of this form of talk, he also pointed out its limitations:

> The confessional talks, which are very common in youth movements, are nice and good and healthy at a particular stage of growing up, but when young people stay too long at this stage, the phase in which they spend their time wondering about the nature of life and about self-actualization, it is a sign that they are being held back in their spiritual development. This stage of existential probings, with all the "trials and tribulations" associated with them, must lead to the further stage of integration into the realities of life and the larger society, the acceptance of public responsibility. . . . We expect the confessional talk to grow into a deliberative discussion.[95]

Another commentator similarly raised questions about the appropriateness of the expressive dialogic format of the inscribed talks for the consideration of ideological and moral issues. He felt that this self-centered style mainly revealed immaturity and lack of responsibility for what is said and for responding to the words of another. He refused to consider speakers' emotional outpourings as a form of "authentic dialogue," and further questioned the value of disseminating these exchanges in written form, saying:

> There's no question about the sincerity of the doubts, misgivings and criticisms that are expressed in this volume. The question is only whether this form of expression and publication should be cultivated, even if it is considered to be for "internal consumption" only? Consider: if the volume is designed to encourage reflection and generate argument, there's no room for deliberate sloppiness, a faulty style, and unfounded, rigid statements; and if it is designed to cultivate a new form of encounter and exchange

through living dialogue—what is the point of publishing the protocols of these talks for the wider public?[96]

The failure of *Bein Tzeirim* to match the riveting emotional power of *The Seventh Day* confirmed the extraordinary impact of the earlier volume, but also brought to light the limitations of its expressive idiom. The shift from expressive talk to rationally oriented discourse designed to serve the goals of discussion and deliberation was felt to necessitate different ways of speaking. The call for a move to a more reasoned mode of discourse about the war and its meanings, or about life in the kibbutz, as a form of political action, was left unheeded. In fact, for years to come, participants in such circles of talk would be allowed to give uninhibited expression to their feelings and doubts. But it was increasingly recognized, too, that this expressive outlet, which was grounded in the ability and willingness to separate emotional responses and moral reflection from the world of political action, had no more than a cathartic role to play in their lives.

In subsequent years, when dialogic encounters modeled on *The Seventh Day* became routinized as part of commemorative occasions, the question of their larger consequences was raised again and again with an increasing sense of unease and self-recrimination. In language that echoed the cultural tension between the categories of words and deeds, retrospective accounts of these post-1967 war soldierly talks presented very different perceptions of the meanings of these dialogic encounters than originally attributed to them. These retrospective readings followed different directions. Some claimed that these dialogues served as a premonition—"a writing on the wall"—anticipating the problems that would lead to the outbreak of the 1973 war, which was in many ways even more traumatic than the 1967 one. Others thought that these talks marked the erosion of Labor Zionism and kibbutz ideology, which eventually led to the political "turnabout" *(mahapakh)* of 1977, when for the first time the Labor movement lost the elections and the right-wing Likkud party, headed by Menahem Begin, came into power. Others saw in *The Seventh Day* the seeds of the sensibilities that later led to the emergence of the Peace Now movement. Others still identified in these same sensibilities the roots of the Israeli-Jewish peace camp's moral limitations.

In retrospect, the 1967 soldierly dialogues triggered harsher criticism as well. Some claimed that it was only within an ideational system in which values and sentiments could be plausibly divorced from action that fighting could continue to be thought of as moral even while the fighting soldiers themselves expressed qualms about the ethics of the missions they fulfilled. The repeated discussions of the virtue of killing one's enemy without feeling hatred was considered a similarly curious disavowal of the personal-emotional roots of one's actions and the reality of their consequences. Yet retrospective accounts of these soldierly dialogues reinforced their original framing as nonpolitical in intent. As Amos Oz put it thirty-five years after the events, "To the interviewees, who were kibbutzniks, we said that the book was not meant to be politically programmatic. It wasn't about the distinction between left and right, and we did not deal with the issue of whether we would remain in the [occupied] territories forever. We were dealing with feelings and humanity."[97]

Another central line of discussion involved an extended meta-communicative debate about the promise and limitation of dialogue as a communicative form. In one soldierly conversation, which took place a couple of years following the publication of *The Seventh Day*, the role of dialogue and its dubious manipulation within a politics of counterpolitics was discussed with particular force. Yoni, who believed in dialogue as a viable communicative form, saw the importance of dialogue as a context in which social problems could be articulated and discussed. Uri, who distrusted the cathartic focus of the 1967 dialogic encounters, considered them to be a distraction from the need to formulate a viable line of action. Interestingly, as the argument proceeded, it turned into a discussion of basic cultural assumptions about the act of speaking and the proper line to be drawn between words and deeds. Yoni refused to draw such a line, arguing for a view of speech as a form of action; Uri, on the other hand, subscribed to the mainstream Israeli cultural view whereby speech and action are essentially opposed. Their exchange illustrates how crucial beliefs about speech provide a grounding for broader ideological positions:

YONI: Today speaking is a form of doing! A great deal of our doing is accomplished through speech. What does the economist of the kibbutz do, speak or act? In the social sphere, too, all action finds expression in speaking. Where's the line here?

URI: No doubt at the practical level there's no borderline between saying and doing. You speak—so that things get done. But in principle there's an essential difference! Doing means a change in people's behavior with regards to their relationships—not a change in talk. Take for example the kibbutz general meeting [*asefa*]. Except for griping [*kuterai*], the second generation does nothing about it. They simply don't come to the meetings!

YONI: Perhaps the form of the dialogic group discussion offers an alternative, or a potential for change in the general meeting? New contents for the meeting?

URI: The idea you suggest, of the discussion group, has been around for years. . . . The talk in the discussion groups is a distraction from actual doing, they go in parallel lines that never meet.

YONI: If the talk has no value *as talk*—it will have no impact on our life and our decisions. We want to bring back the moment of dialogue to particular communities.[98]

The speakers finally agreed that the distinction between words and deeds needed to be maintained with reference to economic matters. Yoni insisted, however, that in social matters the lines between words and deeds are essentially blurred, that talk itself is a form of action, and that much of social and political life is carried out in talk. Most significantly from the standpoint of this study, however, was the fact that in concluding their discussion they invoked the specter of *Kehiliyatenu* as a way of making sense of the particular dialogic moment they were wrestling with. Uri, like the detractors of the early pioneers' soul talks, was only willing to concede the value of talk that functioned in an instrumental vein, that helped reach a common goal by leading to joint action. Yoni, like the proponents of the soul talks of yesteryear, saw great value in the exploratory and contemplative role of speech in shaping personal goals that can then be shared with others. Thus:

YONI: Can you point to shared goals and interests in the kibbutz? In *Kehiliyatenu* your approach could have worked, because they had a common goal. Members of the kibbutz today live in a society of opposing interests, and these oppositions need to be clarified! And that's what the dialogues did. Clarified differences—and tried to find a common denominator.

URI: That's it! The attempt to revive *Kehiliyatenu* through dialogic encounters was doomed to failure from the very start, because the participants had no common goal! The moment you limit yourself to the clarification of ideas, you discover differences that are unbridgeable. . . .

YONI: On the contrary, the dialogue clarifies ideas and conceptual differences in order to achieve a common ground.

URI: And what common ground do you want to achieve?

YONI: A shared life, a life of togetherness, the kibbutz as a commune, that's what I want to achieve.[99]

In an interview he gave in 1977, on the tenth anniversary of the Six Day War, Muky Tsur similarly addressed the question of the practical and political implications of the post-1967 war dialogic encounters. In so doing, he too addressed the question of the role and the efficacy of talk. He recounted that after the traumatic Yom Kippur War of 1973 he held a series of discussions with fighters in that war, saying that their comments in these dialogues were even more provocative and controversial than those of the 1967 dialogues. Yet this time participants began to question the efficacy of the confessional talk format, wondering whether it had any power to change reality.

This attitude was different from the one he encountered in leading discussions as part of the 1967 *The Seventh Day* project. The latter volume appeared at a time when people still believed that things could change, that the 1967 war would be the last round in the Israeli-Arab conflict. This belief was defeated by the outbreak of subsequent wars. Muky Tsur spoke of his and others' profound disappointment with the power of speech to change reality following the 1973 war. He therefore chose not to publish the dialogues he recorded in its aftermath. The interviewer in this 1977 commemorative article, journalist Aharon Bakhar, pushed him on this point, trying to clarify Tsur's views about the link between individual expression and political action, about personal ethics and politics. Tsur claimed that this link was tentatively made in the 1967 dialogues and needed to be further cultivated through dialogue. The vision of dialogue sketched by Tsur was, not surprisingly, highly reminiscent of the early pioneers' soul talk ethos:

BAKHAR: You say you were aware of that link, and that the problem attending it had only intensified. Would you say you did anything to articulate it?

TSUR: I think that one of the most important accomplishments of this volume has to do with the fact that we created a living link with people, we tried to listen to what they thought and felt—and to give them voice. Communication is the lever—if you believe in a person's moral ability to act, and you believe in the individual and you know how to make contact with him, listen—you made a significant step. Many people feel a terrible loneliness and helplessness just when their consciousness is raised, when they have the desire to express themselves, to say what they think and feel, and then they're overwhelmed with information or propaganda and nobody bothers to ask them: Just a moment, what do you think? What do you feel? What do you want? . . .

I think that we should revive the institution of the conversation, of dialogic encounters which enable one to converse and listen to another.[100]

Having reiterated his firm belief in this vision of dialogue, Tsur conceded, however, the essential limitations of the encounters that formed the basis of *The Seventh Day*, particularly their reluctance to explore larger structural and moral issues. Bakhar claimed that this reluctance led to the ineffectiveness of these dialogues as politically relevant statements. He pushed Tsur on this point:

BAKHAR: Perhaps you recoiled from making a political statement?

TSUR: It seems to me that in those days we believed that if we had to choose between politics, which is a professional and rather empty endeavor, and a meaningful life of reflection on Judaism and Socialism, then we would choose the second option without any hesitation. I believe we did not realize that it is in the very distinction between these two domains that the problem lies. In this respect, *The Seventh Day* has sinned. The sin was mainly in the feeling that creative thought had no place in politics, which is an utterly closed field both in terms of its subject matter and in terms of human relations.

On the other hand, I must say that for me personally *The Seventh Day* triggered a desire to say what I think, to dare, to express myself, to share my thoughts with others. I began to give voice to my feelings because of this experience, and I think I am not alone. *The Seventh Day* opened the hearts of many who had been silent for many years.[101]

This discussion seems to have clarified the links between the culturally constituted dichotomy of words and deeds as interpreted within this particular context. In this version of the Israeli vision of dialogue, words were associated with individual expression, a desire to connect with others through self-disclosive verbal gestures rather than engaging in political action. The book thus marked a domain of counterpolitics grounded in individual needs and sustained through expressive outlets. Its enormous popularity indicated that many Israelis felt they could recognize themselves in this self-reflective talk. Yet accusations of self-righteousness suggested that some identified its problematic standing.

In 1987, around the twentieth anniversary of *The Seventh Day*, a gathering was held of some of the participants in *Bein Tzeirim*, the sequel to the 1967 volume of inscribed dialogues. In this exchange, the question of the political implications of these dialogic encounters was tackled again. One of the participants, Doron, claimed that *The Seventh Day* began to shape a sensibility that later led to open protest and resistance. The interviewer, author and journalist Rubik Rosenthal, questioned this claim head-on:

RUBIK: You talk about commitment [*ikhpatiyut*], and I'm asking does the protest come out of the book? The book doesn't give voice to protest but rather to self-questioning, to the participants' inner conflicts. And the question is, really, if alongside what you call commitment, *The Seventh Day* did not leave us with a form of self-questioning that replaces our concern with changing reality.

DORON: I'll respond with one sentence: Before *The Seventh Day*, they shot and did not cry, that's all. When we look at the War of Independence [1948] and the Sinai Campaign [1956], they shot and didn't cry. In *The Seventh Day*, that's the new thing and the main message, people also wanted to cry. Not that they said there that you shouldn't shoot, but something inside was roused. It is true that *The Seventh Day* was not essentially a protest. It contained self-questioning, conflict, but there was protest as well, between the lines you can find lots of it, things that earlier could never be found in Israeli war literature.[102]

It seems that by 1987, following not only the War of Attrition and the Yom Kippur War, but also the 1982 Lebanon War, Israel's military entanglement in South Lebanon, and its continued occupation of the West Bank and Gaza Strip, subdued protest spoken "between the lines" was not felt to be good enough. Avishai, another participant in this discussion, addressed this feeling by trying to explain why only four out of the many more participants invited to that reenactment of the 1967 dialogic encounter took the trouble to come. He said: "I have the feeling that we, those who participated, who took part in the making of *The Seventh Day*, are a generation of unfulfilled promises. . . . The volume contained a promise that eluded us, that we did not fulfill, and therefore people have the feeling that it is recycling the same things once again, and it's not authentic any more, and it will make no difference."[103]

In another commemorative article, published in 1992 in marking the twenty-fifth anniversary of the volume, Muky Tsur reconstructed *The Seventh Day* from the standpoint of the 1990s as an early testimony of the downfall of the image of the Sabra, which will be further discussed in chapter 2. By that time, the Sabra image had lost its cultural lure as a model of the native Israeli New Jew:

> Muky Tsur says today that *The Seventh Day* marks the beginning of the end of the Sabra version of machoism. The dialogues fractured the cult of silence and subverted the stereotype of the fighter with a tough exterior who hides within himself the sensitive soul of a poet. The surprised responses of many of the old-timers in the kibbutzim proved how totally imprisoned they were in this stereotype. The surprise had to do with the "revelation" that their sons had souls! Sensitive, searching souls in the hearts of the tough fighters.[104]

In this encounter, too, however, the claim was made that participants in the dialogic encounters of the post-1967 war did not translate their inner conflicts and newfound sensibilities into a viable political-moral program. They failed to make their way into leadership positions, leaving a spiritual and leadership void that was later filled by the right-wing religious messianic settlement movement of Gush Emunim, the Bloc of the Faithful. In fact, one of the dialogic encounters held after the 1967 war involved a group of religious soldiers who gathered in "Merkaz Harav" yeshiva, and whose talk reflected the seeds of the spirit of the Bloc of the Faithful, which led the way to the expansionist West Bank settlement movement of the 1970s. This encounter was not represented in *The Seventh Day*, allegedly for technical reasons. It was published separately some six months later in the journal *Shdemot*.[105]

In an interview held on the occasion of the thirty-fifth anniversary of the 1967 war, the book's editor, Avraham Shapira, admitted that its exclusion from the book had, in fact, been deliberate, and that he felt that he could not give voice to the positions and feelings expressed by the religious-Zionist fighters "for moral reasons."[106] These positions were widely at odds with the soul-searching and humanistic misgivings that marked the text's orientation as a whole, and members of the editorial team who were either present at the discussion or read its transcript were horrified at the militaristic chauvinism, mystical nationalism, and inhumane spirit that permeated the religious fighters' talk. They were completely untouched by the moral pains and dilemmas associated with the war and the subsequent occupation of civilian territories that had led the participants in *The Seventh Day* to engage in self-probing discussions. Some fifteen years later, Amos Oz described a highly disturbing encounter with the future leaders of the West Bank Settlement Movement in a book of essays, saying:

> The kibbutzniks among the participants left the meeting perplexed and grieving. It was not only because of the euphoria among the yeshiva students, the ecstasy over the Wailing Wall and Biblical sites in the West Bank, the talk of victory and miracles, Redemption and the coming of the Messiah, though all this was a totally foreign language to us. . . . After the victory there was some agonizing among us. Values, ideals, conscience, world view—all of this made it impossible for us to ignore the implications of having become an occupying power. . . . All of this was, for us, a shock and a source of agonizing moral dilemma, but not one of the men from Rabbi Kook's yeshiva understood the pain, the moral problem, or that there was any problem at all. We met up with total insensitivity. . . . The insensitivity of the yeshiva students appeared to us—and in the interests of honesty I will use sharp words—to be crude, smug and arrogant, power drunk, bursting with messianic rhetoric, ethnocentric, "redemptionist," apocalyptic—quite simply, inhuman.[107]

The editor's reluctance to include this very different conversation in the compass of the book has certainly contributed to the ideological coherence of its message, but it has also prevented the book from conveying the kind of complex picture that its inclusion would have allowed. Including this religious-national voice would have pointed toward the two opposing political paths taken by the 1967 fighters' generation. *The Seventh Day* signaled the emergence of the Peace Now movement, whereas the Merkaz Harav discussion signaled the emergence of Gush Emunim—the two movements that have marked the poles of Israeli-Zionist political discourse, which has centered on dilemmas of occupation and settlement, since 1967.

Israel's ongoing involvement with wars and military struggles has made *The Seventh Day* and the "dialogue culture" associated with it an available discursive model which was periodically invoked in later

years. There were many other sporadic occasions on which the dialogic encounter format was revived in discussing fighters' experiences
of subsequent military engagements—such as the Lebanon War that
broke out in 1982,[108] or the Intifada, the Palestinian uprising that broke
out in late 1987.[109] Fighters' talks on these occasions, too, involved an
ongoing cultural negotiation of the tension between words and deeds,
between speaking and acting. These discussions, often published under the heading of *Si'ah Lohamim* of one sort or another, appeared in
press accounts of conversations with military men in which journalists
solicited fighters' perspectives of the battlefields in which they found
themselves. As Nurit Gertz points out in her analysis of the journalistic
coverage of the Lebanon War in its early phases (1982), conversations
with fighters in the battlefield gave expression to the moral qualms and
feelings of guilt of young Israelis "who had been nurtured on humanistic values but did not adhere to them during the war."[110] She indicates,
however, that when torn between the pull of the humanistic ethic to
which they gave eloquent expression and the requirement to take military action, the desire to take part in action had the upper hand:

> The fighters' deliberations and moral qualms that seem to be divorced from
> their acts, are actually closely connected to them. They license these acts
> and provide an apology for their commission: "We're not bloodthirsty—
> just the opposite." In this way the soldiers establish their position for the
> humanistic ethic within the bounds of which they express the other view
> reflected in their actions: "But if it's war, we didn't volunteer for combat
> units [in order] to stay at the rear. If it's war then we want to be at the
> front."[111]

Gertz furthermore shows that the same tension seeped into the accounts of journalists who covered the war, for some of whom, too,
action triumphed over words as they contrasted "the army's dynamic,
active deeds and the 'futile' talk that characterizes the home front. Such
comparisons express the writers' scorn for the 'passive babblers' and
'bleeding hearts' who engage in moral musings without understanding
the real war."[112]

In some cases, participants' comments in such conversations suggest that the existential misgivings about the futility of war expressed
in 1967 had turned into concrete objections to the use of military force
in solving the Arab-Israeli conflict. They indicate that Israel's heavy
reliance on military force in handling that conflict, and the policing
tasks combat soldiers are required to fulfill vis-à-vis the civilian popu-

lation as part of their service in the Occupied Territories were becoming an intolerable moral burden. A participant in the 1989 "commanders' dialogue" among officers who served in the Intifada, segments of which were published in the daily *Ma'ariv*, expressed his disaffection by drawing a comparison between the post-1967 situation and the Palestinian uprising (Intifada) that broke out at the end of 1987. The 1967 war appears to be an object of nostalgia in his account:

> The dialogue then [1967] referred to a war which enjoyed full consensus, a war that was imposed on us. The waiting period before the war created a feeling of real threat, a feeling that we were bound to go to war. The quick end filled us with joy. Everything was much more naive then, even the sadness was a happy one. In fact, there was no real moral dilemma. We had no doubt that we were defending our very existence. . . . Today we're in a completely different situation. We're not the army that extricated itself from a highly threatening situation, and saved the country. We are an army whose task is to restore order, to quell riots in the very heart of a civilian population. We're in a war that offers no quick victories, there are no victories at all. We are required to do things that are completely at odds with the political convictions of most of us. Very difficult moral dilemmas. A very great contrast to the dialogues of those days.[113]

A similar level of disaffection was expressed in a discussion among veteran commanders, who had served in the Occupied Territories in 1991 and had been involved in accusations of inhumane conduct toward the Palestinian population. This discussion also came under the heading of *Si'ah Lohamim*, and participants were quite open in expressing their concern that the kind of service soldiers were performing in the Occupied Territories had a morally corrupting effect on Israeli youths.[114]

The introspective discourse of emotions sprinkled with moral qualms that characterized the soldierly dialogues following the 1967 war was gradually replaced by increasingly tortured discussions of ethical dilemmas associated with the social demand to fight in a war of choice and to routinely engage in acts that go against one's conscience and desires. Even the high priest of the Israeli cult of dialogue, Muky Tsur, who promoted emotional openness as intrinsically valuable, addressed the importance of the moral dimension in the retrospective reenactment in 1997 of the original 1967 dialogues published in *The Seventh Day*. On the occasion of this thirtieth anniversary of these encounters he said: "In my opinion, emotional openness can encourage free thought, on condition that the person who immerses himself in this trance of emotional openness, basically knows that this does not release him from a moral standpoint. It is no release from thinking, casting doubts, misgivings, and making decisions."[115]

Indeed, the issues discussed in *The Seventh Day* are still at the center of Israel's moral dilemmas at the time of this writing, perhaps most clearly apparent in the voices of dissident soldiers who refuse to serve in the Occupied Territories, whose words often echo the pain and moral misgivings voiced by participants in *The Seventh Day*. However, as stated in an article published after the dissolution of the Oslo process and the outbreak of the Al Aqza Intifada in the fall of 2000, the gulf between "shooting" and "crying" has become greater than ever before. The article is titled "Today there are those who shoot and those who cry," and it heralds the fall of the image of the sensitive fighter whose tears somehow redeem his acts. It suggests a deep social division between the doers and the talkers in the face of moral dilemmas that have changed little over the years "the occupation, historical justice, attitudes toward the enemy, the limits of power."[116] Despite the persistence of these moral issues, participants in the original dialogues felt that attempts to replicate the original soldiers' conversations would be ultimately futile in the Israeli social scene of the turn of the third millennium. Israeli society was too fragmented and conflicted for authentic dialogue to be enacted and for the open emotional expression and moral deliberation found in the original fighters' talks. In Muky Tsur's words: "Discourse as a therapeutic process can succeed only if there is trust in the process of conversation. . . . Today conversations are so photogenic, so expected, that they can't do for people what *The Seventh Day* has done. Even the soldiers' voices from Lebanon were individual voices, unaccompanied by a unifying tune."[117]

The polemic against the spirit of the two volumes of inscribed dialogues that followed the 1967 war, and the subsequent reenactments of their format in later years, calls to mind the kind of objections initially raised against the soul talks of the "intimate groups" of young pioneers in the 1920s. As in the case of the participants in *Kehiliyatenu*, the participants in *The Seventh Day* and *Bein Tzeirim* were seen by some as dangerously "spiritual" and self-absorbed, as "bleeding hearts" who posed an unwelcome challenge to the task-oriented and goal-driven spirit of the pragmatic kibbutz movement and the nation in arms. The voices that were marginalized in the 1920s reemerged some fifty years later, for a moment weaving once again a sense of promise, harking back to the early pioneers' dialogic vision.

What appeared as a daring expressive idiom in the late 1960s became increasingly criticized in the years to come as a self-righteous and self-serving wallowing in tears. It was claimed that it permitted Israeli fighters to continue acting in ways that went against their basic sense of humanity and keep their conscience clear by "crying" after the shooting was done. Some claimed that by smoothing over the dissonance they experienced, they were prevented from moving into full-fledged political protest, exchanging mere words for actual deeds. Others felt that the post-1967 "dialogue culture" was a necessary step toward the formation of the more peace-oriented sensibility that shaped many peace movement efforts in later years. Whatever the case, the commemorative reenactments of the soldierly dialogues have become semi-institutionalized occasions for both nostalgic and bitter reflections about Israel's ongoing involvement in war and military occupation, and about its national mission.

As I have tried to show, these contemplative occasions always had a metacommunicative component to them, serving as discursive sites for the reassessment of the role played by words in the conduct of social life. In the early pioneering version of the soul talk ethos, the polemic about words and deeds was a central element in the cultural conversation of the day. The enmeshment in introspective, confessional dialogic encounters was felt to pose a threat to the youngsters' ability to engage in the pragmatic and political work of nation-building. It distracted them from what could be counted as deeds. In its later version, when deeds were interpreted in conjunction with war and combat and some of the basic assumptions informing it ceased to be shared, words and inner feelings were not seen as a distraction from deeds but as a way of avoiding their moral consequences.

Young Israeli fighters of the 1960s, for whom the *Seventh Day* volume became a cult book of sorts, were regarded as "doers," especially in view of their willing participation in national security and war efforts. Yet, unlike the generation of fighters that preceded them, at least some of them had become "troubled doers," torn by doubts and inner torments concerning the justification and the conduct of war. The moral dilemmas surrounding war and conflict became clearer and sharper as the years went by, and the fighters' introspective language of emotion was increasingly replaced by explicit and elaborate moral arguments. In retrospect, as we have seen, some participants in the dialogues of the 1960s believed that these open exchanges and their extraordinary reception when published in book form had paved the way for the peace and protest movements that followed the 1973 Yom Kippur War. Others, frustrated with the inefficacy of these protests—evidenced by the repeated wars in years to come and by the continuing Israeli occupation of the West Bank and Gaza Strip—saw in the "shooting and crying" syndrome the seeds of the Israeli peace camp's inability to stand up resolutely to governmental war policies they opposed. As we shall see in the next section, however, the few who did stand up to those policies and publicly expressed their refusal to serve in the Occupied Territories did so by reenacting their own version of the fighters' talk format.

BETWEEN MORAL CHALLENGE AND POLITICAL ACTION

The moral and ideological dilemmas facing Israeli soldiers in the third year of the Al-Aqza Intifada, the Palestinian uprising that erupted in the fall of 2000, seem as intractable as those faced by their parent generation, by the soldiers who fought in the 1982 Lebanon War and by those who served in the Occupied Territories during the first Intifada of 1987–1993.

Confronted with these moral dilemmas, a small number of reservists have chosen the path of "selective refusal"—refusal to serve in the Occupied Territories—and a small number of eighteen-year-olds have chosen the path of draft refusal. While some of the youngsters have claimed to be pacifists, saying their act of refusal is morally and not politically driven, the reservists who have had long stretches of combat duty behind them were quite explicit about the political nature of their appeal. The veteran refusal movement named *Yesh Gvul* (There is a limit/border), which was established in 1982 by soldiers who refused to take part in the Lebanon War,[118] revived its public support for this "selective refusal," which they claimed was an original Israeli invention.[119] A newly formed group of reserve soldiers publicized their refusal to serve in the Occupied Territories under the title *Ometz Lesarev* (Courage to refuse).

Members of both movements openly challenged the equivocal rhetoric of the "shooting and crying" syndrome and the half-hearted opposition to governmental policies it entailed. They did so in a language that echoed some of the critiques of *The Seventh Day* at the time of the book's first publication. At this political-historical juncture, words were mobilized in the hope of counteracting what mainstream

Israeli society viewed as the epitome of collectively oriented deeds. Members of these dissident groups expressed their refusal to participate in state violence, attempting to propel alternative lines of action that would eventually bring a change in governmental policies vis-à-vis the occupation of the West Bank and Gaza. These acts of resistance became more and more visible in terms of the moral and political challenge they mounted against the prevailing political consensus. They were publicized through paid ads in the press, journalistic coverage of on-going vigils and demonstrations, court actions, and the monitoring via the Internet of the repeated prison sentences many of the refusers were required to serve.

Along with the newly established network of high school seniors, three hundred of whom put their signatures to a letter of draft refusal, known as *Mikhtav Hashministim* (Seniors' letter), the two groups, *Yesh Gvul* and *Ometz Lesarev,* sounded a note that consistently challenged the status quo even though spokespersons for the military and a large part of the Israeli public have downplayed this challenge as marginal and ineffective. It was precisely because they embodied a fundamentally alternative moral stance through their unwillingness to actively partake in the occupation and the violence associated with it that a considerable effort was made to marginalize them in public opinion. The signatories on the statements of selective refusal formulated by *Yesh Gvul* and *Ometz Lesarev* number well over a thousand at the time of this writing. This is clearly far less than those who serve out of conviction or a sense of duty, but also less than the (undocumented) number of reservists engaging in what is widely called "gray refusal" *(seruv afor)*—the non-ideological evasion of service by claiming ill health, traveling abroad, failing to register a change of address, and so on.

Probably the most visible attempt to challenge Israeli occupation policies by the very people called on to keep them in place dates back to January 2002, when the *Ometz Lesarev* group, then numbering more than a hundred reserve soldiers serving in combat units of the Israeli army, published a letter in the elite daily newspaper *Ha'aretz,* stating their refusal to serve in the Occupied Territories on moral grounds. For each of the reservists who signed the letter that came to be referred to as "The Fighters' Letter" (*Mikhtav Halohamim*), the decision to sign involved a great deal of chutzpa—courage to refuse, a phrase that has become their special slogan and gave the group its name. They cast the refusal to participate in military action in the Occupied Territories as the ultimate form of action and as the only moral path open to them. Not claiming to be pacifists, their refusal to serve was restricted to service in the Occupied Territories and expressed their willingness to serve inside Israel's 1967 borders. They considered military service as an occupying force in the midst of a densely populated civilian territory as irrelevant to the army's mission of self-defense and as inevitably leading to and legitimizing unethical conduct. Aware that their act of refusal violated deep social convictions (as well as the law), they were willing to accept the social sanctions and prison sentences that faced them.

In their letter, the young men calling for courage to refuse cast their motives and decisions in explicit and elaborate moral terms, fundamentally challenging the social consensus that required unquestioning acceptance of the call to arms and the ethical considerations that gave it force. The letter said, inter alia:

- We, combat officers and soldiers who have served the State of Israel for long weeks every year, in spite of the dear cost to our personal lives, have been on reserve duty all over the Occupied Territories, and were issued commands and directives that had nothing to do with the security of our country, and that had the sole purpose of perpetuating our control over the Palestinian people.

- We, whose eyes have seen the bloody toll this Occupation exacts from both sides.

- We, who sensed how the commands issued to us in the Territories, destroy all the values we had absorbed while growing up in this country.

- We, who understand now that the price of Occupation is the loss of IDF's human character and the corruption of the entire Israeli society.

- We, who know that the Territories are not Israel, and that all settlements are bound to be evacuated in the end.

- We hereby declare that we shall not continue to fight this War of the Settlements.[120]

This letter, like similar ones by high school graduates and reserve soldiers published earlier, caused an uproar and started a public debate about morality, war, and citizenship. The debate, which was kept alive by the media at different levels of intensity for several months, revolved mainly around the issue of the right to refuse in a democratic society. Articles, opinion pieces, letters to the editor, and interviews with conscientious objectors, draft resisters, and their various supporters and opponents created an ongoing exchange over the issue of refusal, focusing on the legitimacy of this stance rather than on the moral distress expressed by many of the refusers through their personal stories. Clearly, the discussion of military service in the Occupation was moving away from the emotional focus of the soldierly talks of earlier times and focusing more explicitly on moral dilemmas and political action.

For a short time in early 2002, it seemed that public opinion was shifting; polls indicated some 30 percent of the public supported the refusers' choice, even though it was strongly criticized by the military and political leadership and some of the press. However, after the Israeli reoccupation of the West Bank in April 2002 (following a series of horrendous suicide bombings), and especially the controversy surrounding the military operation in the Jenin refugee camp, the support dwindled. What had seemed to be a growing social movement became increasingly viewed as a marginal group of "bleeding hearts." While more and more people signed the petition, and more and more of them served first-time and repeated prison terms, the political impact of their act of resistance remained negligible.

At a certain point the Courage to Refuse group, who initially sought to address the Israeli public only, decided to influence public opinion outside Israel as well, particularly (but not only) targeting Jewish communities in the United States and Europe, who overwhelmingly support Israeli governmental policies. They created a worldwide Refuser Solidarity Network and sent representatives on speaking tours to European and North American campuses and Jewish groups. On May 5, 2002, one of the group's members, Rami Kaplan, was featured in a much-discussed *60 Minutes* episode on CBS. On September 12, 2002, in an attempt to revive their public drive within Israel, the Courage to Refuse group organized a public event in a well-known Tel Aviv theater hall, Tzavta, titled "*Si'ah Lohamim* 2002" (Fighters' talk 2002), which not only invoked the mythical 1967 fighters' talks, but also included the participation of some of the 1967 war veterans, who had taken part in the original soldierly discussions that were later published in *The Seventh Day*.

The public invitation to this event referred to it as an opportunity to both listen and speak, highlighting the testimonial, personal dimension of the act of refusal, which tended to remain submerged in the public debate over its legitimacy. The invitation said that the event would feature eyewitness reports: "Reserve officers and soldiers, who came back from the Territories, talk about what they did and what they saw." The topics to be covered included concerns associated with the act of refusal: the price to be paid, mainstream social attitudes toward refusal to serve, and arguments justifying this choice. A report in *Ha'aretz*, which appeared a few days later, suggested how far this public reenactment of the soul talk format had come from the soul talks of the 1920s and the 1960s alike once it lost its "intimate group" aura. What was supposed to be an occasion for open dialogue, with people who came both to speak and to listen, turned into a highly intolerant "conversation of the deaf." Invoking the 1967 war precedent, this newspaper report concluded that "a book will definitely not come out of it," and that the organizers had learned their lesson. They decided to go back to the original format and hold only closed meetings, which would be published later if they were felt to have indeed generated true dialogue. A sixty-three-year-old veteran of the 1967 war, Shai Hulda'i, pointed out the difference between social attitudes toward the Courage to Refuse group in 2002 as compared to the acceptance of the challenge mounted by participants in the 1967 fighters' talks, which did not encourage a refusal to serve. He said: "We came from the heart of the consensus, we were even heroes. We were kibbutzniks, we felt that things that came from our hearts came from the people's heart. People even liked the fact that we appeared uncertain and full of inner torments. This is not the case with today's refuseniks, who are outside the consensus, even though I consider them our conscience, our Emil Zolas who call 'J'accuse.'"[121] It may have been this sense of social marginalization that led to the failure of the Tzavta event, encouraging a discourse that was exclamatory rather than questioning, with well-packaged television talk show–style statements dominating the talk and no space allowed for the kind of questioning and debate over the positions expressed that would render the occasion more truly dialogic.

A stock-taking article published in the weekend magazine of *Ha'aretz* at the end of 2002 summarized the refusers' experience as one of "sobering up." The article did not claim that the dissidents changed their minds about their act of refusal (as did some high-ranking army officers) but that they had come to realize that the overall impact of their movement remained negligible.[122] The subtitle of the article stated that the refusers' initial confidence that 500 signatures on their letter would bring about a revolutionary change in governmental policy was not borne out. Even though many of the refusal campaigns made a point of stating their opposition in terms that would simultaneously reaffirm their commitment to the state (for example, by using slogans such as *mesarvim lema'an hamdina*—refusing for the sake of the state), they were effectively marginalized by mainstream Israeli society.

In some respects, the debate about the refusal to serve in the army became a bitter intergenerational dialogue that both invoked and rejected the moral ambivalence of the parent generation's "shooting and crying" syndrome. Claiming to represent an unequivocal moral stance, the dozens of youngsters gathered in support of the prisoners of conscience outside the military prisons where more than two hundred of them were incarcerated during 2002, or in demonstrations held in various city centers, pointed to the familiar "shooting and crying" syndrome, chanting with great relish the rhymed "Not shooting, not crying / Refusing to be occupiers" (*lo yorim, lo bokhim / mesarvim li'hjot rotzhim*). The challenge they posed was not only to the right-wing government whose policies they abhorred. In this chant they challenged what has come to be called the "disoriented left," mainly of their parent generation, that—following the outbreak of the Al Aqza Intifada—had "gone to the right" and both publicly and privately expressed harsh criticism of the refusers' decision not to serve.

Even though the public reenactment of the soul talk format in the Tzavta event may not have been a great success, by establishing support networks for would-be refusers, vigils, demonstrations, petitions in the daily press, and continued presence in court hearings dealing with refusal, the various refusers' groups have grown into a small, loosely organized community of several hundred like-minded and dedicated supporters who participate in the struggle against Israel's official occupation policy. In the spirit of the times, they have effectively used the Internet to mobilize their supporters through active lists and elaborate Web sites that allow them to further consolidate and disseminate their message.[123]

The refusers' Web sites provide a virtual space in which they and their supporters can congregate and engage in an electronic soul talk of sorts. The hypertexts that make up these Web sites present users with complex, multivocal, and ideologically driven statements of the refusers' points of view. These texts combine public declarations, such as the refusers' initial statement, press articles written by them or about them, background information in the form of official reports by human rights groups, statements of support by academics and others, as well as personal statements by some of the signatories on the letter that launched the group and is the backbone of this Web's virtual discursive space. On the Courage to Refuse Web site, close to sixty of the more than five hundred reserve soldiers who signed their names to the group's joint letter also posted personal statements. These statements are personalized accounts of the reasons, experiences, and arguments that led to the writers' act of refusal. Some are declarative in tone and structure, giving voice to the authors' unequivocal moral stance against service in the Occupied Territories; some are argumentative, presenting well-reasoned justifications for the refusers' stance. In many cases, the refusers' well-crafted arguments are presented in explicit or implicit dialogue with their various opponents. At times, they are directly formulated as counterarguments to frequently heard objections to the act of refusal. In many cases, the arguments are sprinkled with testimonial narratives dramatizing the refusers' encounter with the reality of the Occupation, thereby offering another layer of justification to the argumentative edifice cumulatively constructed by these statements.

The personal statements amplify the moral protest voiced by the letter they all signed and the other public statements made by members of the group and their supporters. They often concretize the general statements about the corrupting effect of the Israeli occupation on fighters whose military service involves a systematic violation of the basic human rights of more than three million Palestinians. Each of the statements gives voice to its author's refusal to continue to partake in the day-to-day maintenance of this generation-long oppression of the Palestinian civilian population. The personal testimonies often chart the path of growing unease and moral awareness of the writers, which led them away from the heart of the Israeli consensus to their current position as marginalized refusers. While each statement reflects its author's own distinctive experience and point of view, they all similarly reject the equivocation implied in the "shooting and crying" syndrome of the previous generation of Israeli fighters. Indeed, some of the authors explicitly fault their parents' generation for allowing the occupation to go on for thirty-five years, leaving to their offspring a legacy of violence, oppression, and unresolved guilt.

One such statement, which could easily be multiplied in its general contours yet usefully highlights the intergenerational dialogue surrounding refusal, was made by Asaf Oron, a reservist with the Giv'ati

Brigade. It is an autobiographical account of his military experience, beginning with the day of his draft (in 1985), through successive periods of reserve duty. Having joined the military straight out of high school without any hesitation, like the vast majority of Israeli youngsters, seventeen years later Oron found himself "in a head to head collision with the army, while the public at large is mocking me [him] from the sidelines." Describing his repeated encounters with the civilian Palestinian population during his military service, both in terms of events and sights he was witness to and in terms of the inner dialogue they generated in him, he recounts several steps of consciousness raising, which eventually led to his change of heart and moved him from the position of "the perfect occupation enforcer" to the one of conscientious objector. Attuned to the intergenerational dimensions of the strident public debate about refusal, he frames his statement as an attempt to overcome what he calls the "conversation of the deaf" concerning the refusal to serve in the Occupied Territories. Adding his voice to this debate, he points to the conflicted parental message of universalism sprinkled with tribalism (or vice versa) that he feels is responsible for the ambivalence and ambiguities that have given rise to the impossible current situation that Israeli soldiers are entrapped in: "Our parents' generation lets out a sigh: we've embarrassed them yet again [by refusing to serve]. But isn't it all your fault? What did you raise us on? Universal ethics and universal justice, on the one hand: Peace, liberty, and equality for all. And on the other hand: 'The Arabs want to throw us into the sea,' 'They are all crafty and primitive. You can't trust them.'"

The refusers' personal statements on the Courage to Refuse Web site and the discussion forum included in it make it possible for a new culture of dialogue to emerge. As in the case of the fighters' talks of 1967 (and after), which the refusers invoke through their denunciation of the "shooting and crying" syndrome, these statements focus on military experience and its emotional and moral ramifications. The electronic soul talks on this Web site provide an arena in which dissenting voices enter into dialogue and resonate with unusual clarity as well as a renewed urgency. The draft resisters and refusers of the turn of the twenty-first century conduct part of their struggle in cyberspace. Whereas face-to-face public discussions of refusal as a strategy of resistance may be fraught with tensions, the Web sites the refuser groups have put together provide a virtual space where arguments and stories can be freely offered and attended to.

These electronic soul talks—much like the original soul talks of Bitaniya Ilit—are textualized in the form of a hypertext, whose authors and readers reach out to each other in the safety of their enclosed virtual spaces, creating a patchwork of both expressive and deliberative individual contributions. This electronic version of the soul talk format is continuous with the soul talks of yesteryear in that they echo the unique combination of steadfast commitment, soul-searching, and communal boundaries we have come to associate with the other dialogic sites discussed in this chapter. While broadly addressed to the public at large and readily accessible on the Web, the site remains largely an in-group conversation for members of the group. In both form and content this electronic soul talk holds a conflicted relationship with the dialogic moments of the Israeli past. It replicates the format of the pioneers' and fighters' soul talks, yet it rejects the legacy of moral equivocation the refusers attribute to the "shooting and crying" syndrome associated with the 1967 fighters' talks.

The soul talk format is one major path through which the spirit of Bitaniya Ilit has been kept alive over the years, combining homage and critique. Another path involves the migration of the legacy of Bitaniya Ilit into the rather rarified realms of art and academic scholarship. Scholarly treatments of the soul talk ethos have been woven into my foregoing discussion. The next section turns our attention to Israeli drama, which is the major artistic context in which the spirit of Bitaniya Ilit has been thematized, rearticulated, reexamined, and disseminated between the 1970s and the 1990s. Exploring some poignant artistic reenactments and retextualizations of the soul talk ethos, I will discuss how the quest for authentic dialogue has further shaped Israeli cultural conversation during those years.

THE SOUL TALK ETHOS IN ISRAELI DRAMA

The saga of Bitaniya Ilit has become inscribed in Israeli collective memory through various processes of textualization. These include firsthand testimonies and memoirs written over the years by participants, inscription of reenacted soul talks in such texts as *Si'ah Lohamim* and its offshoots, and fictional treatments, such as Nathan Bistritsky's *Days and Nights*. The early fictional accounts contributed significantly to the crystallization of the myth of Bitaniya Ilit in the 1920s and 1930s. The later invocations of the saga of Bitaniya Ilit in Israeli theater, which marked the revival of interest in this myth as predicted by Bialik fifty years earlier, attested to the ongoing search for the roots of the communal dream that has made this saga a powerful cultural metaphor. Theatrical retellings of the saga of Bitaniya Ilit, or dramatic allusions to it, became occasions for exploring the great changes that have taken place in Israeli society over the years.

The dramatic invocations of the pioneering saga of the 1920s in Israeli drama can be traced to the period between the 1970s and 1990s. They point to a search for cultural continuity with the pioneering era and, simultaneously, constitute allegories of sociocultural change. In what follows I discuss three plays written by three different playwrights, each of which invokes the saga of Bitaniya Ilit in one way or another. The first and best known is Yehoshua Sobol's play *Leil Ha'esrim* (The Night of the Twentieth), referring to the twentieth day of the month. It was first produced by Haifa Municipal Theater in 1976 (and again by Habimah National Theater in 1990). Sobol's play takes Bitaniya Ilit as its setting and draws heavily on the text of *Kehiliyatenu,* using this early pioneering saga to address concerns that were relevant to contemporary audiences.

Sobol's play and the problematic it addresses were dramatically engaged by a play written by Hanan Peled that was produced in 1989 by the Khan Theater in Jerusalem. This play, titled *Hevre* (Buddies), dramatizes the pioneering myth of group solidarity in the context of the 1980s state-sponsored Jewish settlement project in the Galilee, a region of the country that is densely dotted with Arab towns and villages. Peled's play highlights the changing contours and moral meanings of settlement activities and the ideology surrounding them in 1980s Israel through intertextual allusions to Sobol's play. Finally, Moti Lerner's play *Ahavot Bitaniya* (The loves of Bitaniya), which was produced for television in 1994, takes as its setting the opening day of the (fictional) settlement museum commemorating Bitaniya Ilit. This play offers its own take on the saga of *Bitaniya Ilit.* I will treat these plays one by one, considering them both for their shared themes and for their distinctive contributions to the construction and deconstruction of the myth of Bitaniya Ilit in Israeli collective memory.

In Search of Cultural Roots: *The Night of the Twentieth*

The 1976 Haifa Theater production of Sobol's dramatic reconstruction of the saga of Bitaniya Ilit has become a cornerstone of Israeli drama. In fact, this play was the vehicle through which most Israelis were first exposed to the saga. This became evident when *Kehiliyatenu* was republished in 1988. For example, an article titled "The Torments of Hashomer Hatza'ir," which heralded this event, carried the following subtitle:

> You have seen *The Night of the Twentieth*, now you can read the original. The *Kehiliyatenu* collection, written by the members of Bitaniya Ilit out of the social pressure cooker in which they were being cooked with Freud, Buber, Socialism, Eroticism, was published this month by Yad Ben-Zvi. Group dynamics in the spirit of Hashomer Hatza'ir when it was really young. Meir Ya'ari and David Horowitz were empowered there, others broke down and went back to mummy in Europe; one committed suicide.[124]

In Sobol's play, as this citation suggests, the soul talk format became reinterpreted in the increasingly familiar language of psychology as a form of "group dynamics." Journalistic accounts of the play's production made a point of mentioning the group process that was part of the actors' rather extended period of work on the play under the leadership of director Nola Chilton. During this period they lived as a commune in the artists' village of Ein Hod.[125] As part of this group process they also met some of the participants in the Bitaniya Ilit venture, who were then in their eighties. In a sense, the audience too became a vicarious participant in the group's intense inner dynamics, often responding with great enthusiasm to the viewing experience. In the words of Dov Bar-Nir, which echo those of other reports: "The audience did not cease to clap, and most importantly—did not budge, as if it wanted more and more, that the plot should go on indefinitely. I know no greater compliment than this."[126] The story of the play, as rendered in both Hebrew and English in the program of its 1976 production, ran as follows:

> The story of a group of *halutzim* [pioneers] from Austria and Galicia, first comers of the 1920s. The group of young people, who had arrived in the land only a few months before, is passing its last night in a temporary camp on a mountain in Lower Galilee. It is 3 a.m. and the youths who have spent the night dancing and singing, have lain down to rest on the packed baggage, and are now waiting for the lorries which will take them to their permanent settlement. Repose, however, not to mention sleep, is quite beyond them.
> A manic urge to confess, to expose inner selves and a terrible thirst for human contact, takes hold of the young men and women and moves them to question, to communicate and to act upon each other all the things which until this night had been repressed and blocked inside them.

> And so, in heightened clarity or, perhaps, in greater confusion, the group
> sets out to face the future.[127]

This night of confession and bitter confrontation is an artistic reconstruction of the legendary night in which one of the group members,
David Horowitz, challenged Ya'ari's leadership position in the group.
In the play it was the night of the twentieth of October 1920, depicted
as the very night before the crucial pragmatic and symbolic act of establishing a new settlement was to take place. From the play's opening
lines, this act of settlement was colored by a strong sense of danger and
moral torment. Descending from their mountaintop camp to the valley
allocated for their settlement was not an easy move. The group members discussed the anticipated resistance of the Arab peasants, who for
generations had been cultivating the fertile land of Mansurin that the
Jews had recently purchased from rich Arab landowners. They were
obviously reluctant to give up their homes and source of livelihood.
This acute awareness of the inevitable linkage between the Jews' settlement and the dislocation of the Palestinians frames the play as a whole,
clearly speaking to the sensibility of the 1970s rather than to that of the
1920s. Indeed, in an article published by one of the veterans of Bitaniya
Ilit, Yedidyah Shoham, after he viewed the play, he pointed out:

> In one important detail I take issue with the playwright and join the neg-
> ative criticism on this matter. The pangs of conscience and doubts about
> driving away the Arab tenants of the land did not preoccupy the [Jewish]
> newcomers in those days. . . . It may be the case that the problem of up-
> rooting the Arabs preoccupies the author and his friends in the 1970s—but
> it did not concern the youngsters who were waiting around with their pack-
> ages on *The Night of the Twentieth* and it was not the issue they discussed
> and over which they clashed. This is a disturbing note, because contrary to
> the play as a whole, it is untrue and sounds artificial, as if it was stuck on
> to what is happening on stage.[128]

The ideological debate surrounding this vexing issue is articulated, for
example, in the following exchange between Akiva and Ephraim, two
of the characters in the play:

AKIVA: We will settle the land and above our heads there will wave a
flag with the word "blood" inscribed on it.

EPHRAIM: This is an argument that belongs to the past.

AKIVA: To the future, Ephraim, to the future.

EPHRAIM: The question was resolved before we even came to the land [of Israel].

AKIVA: We are not responsible for what the previous generations have done. But tomorrow we will settle the land, and our first deed will be a deadly fight with the Arab tenants.[129]

Some of the group members try to postpone the act of settlement. They claim, rather vaguely, that they are not spiritually ready to commit themselves to the new way of life in the new place, and ask for more time in which they can discuss the kind of society they want to create. Moshe, who is the group's most consistent advocate of the need for intensive engagement in soul-searching and spiritual reckoning, grounds his plea to postpone the act of settlement in the moral implications of the Zionist project. Rather paradoxically, he seeks to justify the material dispossession of the local Arab tenants by cultivating a utopian vision of spiritual and moral perfection grounded in shared community. In his words: "We are going to live there in place of the people who have been living there until now. We are coming to inherit their place. If we content ourselves with exchanging their justice for ours, we will be disgusted with ourselves. We can do it only on one condition: that we establish a society with the highest of values."[130]

These spiritual and moral yearnings are utterly foreign to Ephraim, who expresses the voice of rationality and pragmatism, invoking the need to comply with the decision that the pioneering group establish their new settlement without delay and in compliance with the "politics of settlement" imposed from above. More profoundly, however, he rejects the self-probing spirit of the soul talks as detrimental to the mission they have set out to accomplish—the goal of becoming resolute "doers," saying: "I just want one thing: to release myself from inner contradictions. To go. To do."[131]

Ephraim thus clearly echoes the fears expressed by the pragmatically oriented critics of both the early pioneering days and of the post-1967 war period concerning the potentially debilitating effect of talk and discussion on the pioneers' or soldiers' ability to carry out a collective mission. Indeed, the play's closing lines are a verdict on the limited power of language that the author puts into Ephraim's mouth: "What words destroy words cannot correct, let's leave it to the future."[132]

This concern with the problematic of inner fortitude on the one hand and outwardly directed ruthlessness on the other—and the link between the two—was also a reflection of the social-moral climate of the mid-1970s. These issues became more explicit and more central in response to the trauma of the 1973 Yom Kippur War. The play's ending suggests that the misgivings voiced by Moshe are dismissed and the act of settlement is to be undertaken as planned. Ultimately, the Zionist consensus over the priority of pragmatic and "iron fist" settlement activities is upheld and the land of Mansurin, we are led to understand, becomes the site of conquest and blood.

It was the trauma of the 1973 war that gave rise to the playwright's desire to examine the core of the Zionist project. A former member of Hashomer Hatza'ir, he considered the saga of Bitaniya Ilit to be at the root of the Israeli ethos. Indeed, in an interview he gave on the eve of the play's production, parts of which also appeared in the program of the 1990 version of the play, Sobol indicated his motivation for making this saga the theme and vehicle for his drama:

> The youth movement socialization and the experiences associated with it are for me, to this day, a rich ideational and emotional background. My position about what is going on in Israel right now, and the questions I ask myself with regards to the basic problems related to our life and existence in this land, have their roots in the education I received in the youth movement. One of the strongest experiences I remember from when I was a 17-year-old member of Hashomer Hatza'ir has to do with discussions and explorations undertaken in preparation for getting the movement's "veterans' sign" [semel bogrim]. Every member who was a candidate for this sign had to expose himself to the evaluation of the group and make a personal confession in front of it. For me it was always a riddle: Where did this practice of making such personal confession in public come from? In the 1950s people in Israel didn't yet talk of "group dynamics" and we knew this practice had profound roots in the youth movement tradition.[133]

This youth movement nostalgia was, however, overlaid with concerns relating to the Israeli situation in the 1970s. The extent to which the themes and dilemmas addressed in the play were indeed anchored in the trauma of the 1973 war is suggested in an interview Sobol gave in 1985 to a special supplement dealing with "the theater and Israeli society" issued by the daily *Yediot Ahronot*:

> During my reserve duty in the Yom Kippur War I was very preoccupied with the question of where the process of deterioration of Israeli society had started, the process of self-alienation. I looked for it in the roots of the establishment of the pioneering society in Israel, and so I came upon the saga of Bitaniya. Working on it I realized that Israeli society grew out

of crisis situations from the very start. There's a legend about there having been an idyllic, heroic era. This is fake. What attracted me about the material on Bitaniya was the fact that it was a group that experienced a deep crisis. I read the group's diary. That's how *Leil Ha'esrim* was born.[134]

Sobol further indicated that it was David Horowitz's memoir *My Yesterday*, published in 1970, and the cultural conversation stirred by Meir Ya'ari's animated response to it in a series of articles in the daily *Al Hamishmar*, that first suggested to him the idea of writing a play about the Bitaniya Ilit group. He also felt that the saga of Bitaniya Ilit had been repressed in Israeli collective memory, even in the memory of those who participated in its making, because it was such a powerful reminder of the pioneers' unfulfilled utopian dreams. The sources he used included texts that have already figured in this chapter, such as *Kehiliyatenu* and Bistritsky's *Days and Nights*.

On another level, beyond the search for cultural roots in foundational moments, the play's intended message had to do with basic yearnings for a meaningful life and the doubts and tribulations associated with them. The issues raised in the play were of existential import to Israelis at the time of the play's production no less than at the historical moment depicted in it. In the words of Rachel Shklovsky:

> Sobol's *The Night of the Twentieth* speaks both to nostalgia and to a gossipy sense of curiosity, but it also speaks to an authentic questioning of the logic of our existence in this land. It is a play about people in search of an identity written for a society in search of its identity. . . . There are indeed many among us—young and old alike—who ask the most basic questions: What are the goals toward which our life should be directed? What's the meaning of being a Jew today? And what does it mean to be an Israeli? And is it worth it?[135]

The sense of continuity with the existential predicaments of the early pioneers and those of the audiences addressed by the play went hand in hand with viewers' nostalgia for the spirituality of these pioneers' quest for authentic dialogue. Another commentator pointed out:

> What differentiates those people of Bitaniya Ilit from us is first and foremost their profound need to understand things to the last, to reflect about themselves and their world, to seek truth without worrying about accepted conventions. The bitter argument we see on stage is revealed as a surprisingly contemporary argument.
>
> It's the argument between the desire to find the answer to human existence through a search for self-understanding, self-reflection and an analysis of the forces that motivate us as human beings and a focus on the

objective, social role played by Zionism, settlement and us as bearers of these societal values. Perhaps today we would speak of it as a "quality of life" issue, perhaps as the question of the moral essence of the State of Israel.[136]

The many ways in which the dilemmas discussed by the pioneers anticipated the basic predicaments of kibbutz life, and Israeli life more generally, were specified by yet another commentator, who saw in the play an attempt to deal with basic cultural dilemmas that have beleaguered the Israeli cultural experience for many years:

> In this collective confession you will find, at their roots, all the life problems of kibbutz members, and of Israeli citizens, over the years: questions pertaining to the individual and the collective, Eros and sex, the ambivalence of love and hate, the loneliness of living in an isolated spot at the end of the world set against the deafening noise of urban life, freedom and obligation, the ephemerality of life as against routinization and continuity, dream and reality—all that distinguishes between rootedness and uprootedness.[137]

In 1990, Habimah National Theater decided to undertake another production of *The Night of the Twentieth*, which was by then considered an Israeli "classic." An article that anticipated the play's production indicated the double-layered complexity of this artistic endeavor, saying: "This will be a two-pronged project, addressing both the myth of Bitaniya Ilit and the myth of the first production of *The Night of the Twentieth* in Haifa Theater."[138] The renewed encounter with the saga of Bitaniya Ilit through Sobol's theatrical version of it was marked by a multiple sense of cultural continuity—between the play's setting in the 1920s and its two moments of production and reception—the Israeli landscapes of the 1970s and the 1990s. Some of the commentary on the play addressed the thematic threads linking the pioneering saga of the 1920s and the cultural juncture in which Israeli society found itself in the 1990s. For example, in an article titled "*Leil Ha'esrim:* The End Is the Beginning," a commentator pointed out:

> When Yehoshua Sobol time traveled to 1920, to Bitaniya, on the eve of the establishment of permanent settlement by a group of Hashomer Hatza'ir youngsters of the third aliyah, he wanted to tell us that in that beginning the end was already to be found. The materials that make up the unending search for an Israeli identity free of the Jewish diaspora, and at the same time rational and humanistic—were already there, in that visionary morning. The cracks in the moral justification to appropriate the land were already formed at the height of Zionist zeal. The totalitarian elements on the one hand, and the mystical ones on the other, were already laid out in

that highly demanding communal setup. They were already revealed then, in *The Night of the Twentieth*. Desperation was mingled with hope already then. It was the underlying element of the intimate group.[139]

The commentary about the second production of the play thus dwelt on continuity, often making it a point of departure for a larger generalization about the "Israeli situation" writ large. The theater critic Elyakim Yaron wrote: "Today, too, fourteen years after it was first produced, Sobol's play continues to touch all the central existential problems we face in this country."[140]

Another commentator pointed out the shared dialogic threads that link the early pioneers' soul talk ethos and the therapeutic ethos that had come to permeate Israeli society in the 1990s:

> In this country there have always been and there still are situations of the *Leil Ha'esrim* variety. The collective confession has indeed been replaced by professional and well-organized "group dynamics," the soul talk by the psychiatrist's couch, the collective meal by the various forms of mass media, but the "tension of perpetual becoming" is still felt and is pushing toward integration at various levels between one crisis and another.[141]

In some ways, then, *The Night of the Twentieth* and the cultural conversation it occasioned in the wake of the highly traumatic 1973 war had a comparable function to that of *The Seventh Day* in the wake of the 1967 war. In both cases, there was a turning toward the saga of Bitaniya Ilit. The soul talk dialogic format was both reenacted and textualized. It came to serve as a cultural resource through which the existential predicament of the present moment and the essential tension between spiritual yearnings and pragmatic, anti-spiritual forces could be addressed. In an article published in 1974, around the time he was contemplating the writing of the play, Sobol indicated: "My claim is that as a public, as a society, we experienced and are still experiencing the disintegration of the mental framework that shaped Israeli society in the years between the Six-Day War and the Yom Kippur War. Hence, the incessant talk and the heavy silences, and between them—shared by both the talkers and the silent ones—lies a sense of despair."[142]

In this same article, Sobol bitterly criticized the post-1967 infatuation with the concrete traces of Jewish life in Israel that followed the conquest of the West Bank—the Wailing Wall, Rachel's Tomb, Hebron, to name but a few. Contrary to received opinion, he refused to enshrine them as spiritual sites. In fact, embracing the spiritual vocabulary of religious circles, he turned it upside-down, in an attempt to undermine what he considered to be the highly dangerous messianic spirit that had spread among right-wing circles and within the wider Jewish population as well. For him, the Israeli expansionist ideology did not express an authentic attachment to sacred sites but was a form of land-grabbing, an expression of anti-spiritual forces—utterly profane and self-interested despite the religious garb in which they were clothed. Instead, he pointed to the saga of Bitaniya Ilit as an example of authentic, deep-felt spiritual expression.

In *The Night of the Twentieth,* then, the Arabs are neither invisible nor a mere inchoate, threatening presence, as they tend to be in *Kehiliyatenu.* They are also vaguely associated with a moral burden.[143] At the end of the play, and the rise of a new dawn, as the pioneers get ready to leave their mountaintop site and go down to Mansurin, they know that their act of settlement is likely to implicate them in a bloody fight, but they also express the hope that they will redeem this inevitable beginning through future-oriented, spiritual acts of communal creativity. Thus, Sobol's response to the fundamental moral question of the rightfulness of the Jewish settlement enterprise in the land of Israel is given in spiritual and utopian rather than moral terms. As clearly expressed by the more visionary voices in *The Night of the Twentieth,* the justification for subordinating the rights of the Arabs to those of the Jews lies in the latter's ability to implement their utopian vision of a cohesive community of equals whose members strive for a personally and communally meaningful life.

In this view, the possibilities of a future conceived in internal-communal terms override the morally reprehensible appropriation of Arab lands that Jewish settlement entails. In the future-oriented, spiritualized vision of the play, morally questionable acts toward outsiders to the national group can be eventually redeemed, or at least retrospectively justified, by reference to the utopian possibilities that gave rise to them in the first place. Like *Si'ah Lohamim,* then, Sobol's play inserts a moral dimension into the discussion of the Israeli predicament. As in the case of the soldierly talks, however, it does so in a rather apologetic and inconclusive way. As we shall see, it is only with Hanan Peled's play, *Hevre,* which was written in the late 1980s, that the full moral significance of privileging the inner circle of "we-ness," interpreted in both social and spiritual terms, over the fundamental rights of those outside this circle, is given head-long dramatic treatment.

That Sobol's vision still had its poignant moments of reprieve in the 1990s was brought home to me when on Friday, January 22,

1993, the popular weekly televised news magazine of Israel's public television broadcasting corporation, Yoman Hashavúa, presented the story of a group of eighteen-year-olds, members of the Labor-Zionist Hano'ar Ha'oved youth movement, who had recently formed one of six "urban communes." The trigger for the formation of these new "intimate groups" was their members' exposure to Sobol's play *The Night of the Twentieth,* which the youngsters had performed as part of their drama activities and then decided to reenact in real life by forming new communes. They told the interviewer of the struggles they were having with their parents, who considered their children's dream of an ideal community an anachronism and tried to talk them out of their social experiment. The youngsters consistently rejected their parents' persuasive campaigns and their offers of financial support. As in the days of Bitaniya Ilit, the public response to these groups involved neither full endorsement nor outright rejection. While this new communal project was described with more than a tinge of amusement in that television program, it also celebrated—once again—the naivete and enthusiasm of youth, giving the story national exposure on prime-time television. The starry-eyed youngsters, like their forebears of the 1920s, ardently believed that their enactment of an "intimate group" vision would hold "forever," as one of them said. Their engaging optimism was depicted against the background of a widespread recognition of the enormous gap between the pioneers' communal dream and the reality it had bred.

In the 1990s, when Sobol's play was reproduced by Habimah Theater, these utopian hopes, while clearly able to re-engage the viewing public, were already being painfully questioned. Indeed, the full meaning and dramatic power of the next two plays I discuss, Hanan Peled's *Hevre* and Moti Lerner's *Ahavot Bitaniya* lie in their recognition of the futility of these hopes as well as in their critique of Israeli society's insistence on recycling them.

PARABLES OF CHANGE

Hanan Peled's *Hevre* (1989) and Moti Lerner's *Ahavot Bitaniya* (1994) both address the early pioneering saga as a drama of moral decline, but in very different ways. They both use it mainly to bring out the changing contours of Israeli society from the perspective of the disillusioned heirs of the pioneering ethos. In their dramatic form, both plays reenact the "group dynamics" format used in *The Night of the Twentieth.* But they differ considerably in their plots: Peled's play is about a pathetic, essentially dishonest attempt to enact a latter-day version of the saga of the "intimate group," whereas Lerner's play is about an equally pathetic, highly questionable attempt to commemorate the Bitaniya Ilit saga. Both the attempt to revive the pioneering ethos of the 1920s in the context of the 1980s and the attempt to dignify it through documentation and commemoration in the context of the 1990s culminate in a bitter recognition of how untenable this saga is as a model for the present and how questionable the pioneers' vision of a community of dialogue was in the first place.

Group Intimacy Revisited: Peled's *Hevre*

Hevre is set in a fictional new settlement *(mitzpe)* on top of a Galilean hill in the late 1980s. The term "hevre," which is central in Israeli semantics of social relations, denotes a loosely defined yet close-knit group of friends. Members of such a friendship network enjoy a sense of belonging to specified individuals with a shared relational history who are bonded through feelings of group solidarity, or *gibush* (crystallization).[144] The play shares many thematic and structural threads with *The Night of the Twentieth*. It is therefore a valuable resource for exploring the further career of the pioneering ethos invoked in the earlier play. Specifically, *Hevre* explores the syndrome of the individual who is dependent for his or her sense of self and well-being on his affiliation with a group (a sense of "we-ness"). Its most intriguing aspect is the exploration of the troubling relationship between the role of group solidarity within the Zionist ethos and the moral dilemmas associated with the uprooting of the Arab inhabitants of the land.

Like *The Night of the Twentieth*, then, *Hevre* is about the making of a new home in a new place. In both plays there is an acute awareness of the wider geopolitical context in which these acts of settlement take place and in both there is explicit recognition of the conflict over the land that the Jewish settlement inevitably generated.

Moreover, both plays involve some version of a group psychodrama and are constructed around the portrayal of processes of group dynamics within a small, isolated group of individuals who are thrown into an emotionally intense situation of "sticky" togetherness. In both plays, too, the group consists of seven members, one of whom fills the role of charismatic and provocative leader. In *The Night of the Twentieth* the group was about to descend their mountaintop encampment and establish a new settlement in the fertile valley below. In *Hevre*, on the other hand, the settlement to which Haggai, the group's convenor and leader, wanted to attract his childhood buddies was perched on the top of a hill, a site whose advantage lies in the possibility of spatial control over a region densely populated with Arab inhabitants rather than in the possibilities for agricultural cultivation. This is but one of many reversals in terms of which the meaning of *Hevre* is constructed through implicit intertextual references to *The Night of the Twentieth,* a link that was explicitly recognized by critics of the play who commented on how reminiscent it was of *The Night of the Twentieth.* Thus, Michael Handelsaltz said:

> This performance has the flavor of the original Israeli theater of the 1970s. Something like an updated and revised version of Sobol's *Leil Ha'esrim.* Sobol's play depicted a group of youngsters, who considered Zionism a solution to their inner-torments, as they were preparing to come down from the mountain and face the Israeli reality, including its cost in human life. Hanan Peled's *hevre* are about to climb the mountain: an Israeli arms dealer, who is running away from his enemies around the world, brings his friends together so as to resurrect the sense of "togetherness" that was lost with the implementation of the Zionist dream.[145]

And another critic, Shosh Avigal, similarly commented:

> This is a talk-centered play that is reminiscent of Sobol's *Leil Ha'esrim.* A group of young people in their early thirties, the myth of the *hevre,* meet in a new settlement *(mitzpe)* in the Galilee, weigh the suggestion to move there, to "Judaize" the mountain within the green line [designating the pre-1967 war border], to explore a new quality of life, engage in a hypothetical discussion of other existential options, a different Zionism. A weekend of group dynamics, as if disengaged from the country and the Hezbollah, but in the background there are small-scale subversive acts that served as reminders that one cannot completely disregard the surrounding reality.[146]

And Miri Paz said: "The structure of the play reminds one of the success formula of *Leil Ha'esrim.* Both plays deal in completely different ways with people who are losing their way and are in search of a new way. *Hevre* takes itself less seriously, more ironically. It does not deal with soulful idealists and intellectuals but with run-of-the-mill individuals who have lost not only their way but their soul as well."[147]

Thus, Haggai, the group leader, who attempts to revive the myth of group bonding by having all his *hevre* (buddies) join him in the new mountaintop settlement he wants to establish, expresses his desire for group solidarity in a stark metaphor: "I am talking about . . . this feeling that you are complete . . . only when you are part of the *hevre* . . .

that's what I felt abroad . . . like people whose legs have been amputated and they feel the pain in their toes. . . . Do you understand what I'm talking about?"[148]

Haggai's yearnings for group togetherness represent the triumph of the structure of feeling that had fueled the pioneering social project—the desire to merge the individual and the group, as expressed in the well-known saying cited at the end of the play—"All for one and one for all" (kulam bishvil ehad/ehad bishvil kulam). He articulates a personal sensibility described in one commentary as a desire to belong to some exclusive circle, even if temporarily: "In their own eyes, the hevre are always a little special, elitist. The need to conquer the wilderness, to absorb immigration, that you may agree with sometimes—and also to fight Arabs together and to be a 'crystallized' military unit, one for all—all these helped, under pressure, a 'melting pot' it was called, to subordinate the individual to social authority and the group of hevre."[149]

The saga of Bitaniya Ilit, as we have seen, was about the attempt to spark group feelings among like-minded individuals who could touch each other's souls. It was about dialogic encounters that could engender shared understandings and commitments. It was about participants' engagement in confessional talk, merging individual experience with group feeling in a future-oriented social utopia. The "group dynamics" enacted in Hevre harks back to shared youthful experiences that bind individuals together through ties of friendship. The plot of the play tells the story of the reunion of a group of people who used to be close "buddies" (hevre) and who have not seen each other for six years, since their early twenties. Haggai, who summons them all to the isolated new settlement in the Galilee, has recently returned from several years abroad, where he has made a good deal of money in international arms trade. He and his pregnant wife have decided to take part in the government-led Jewish settlement effort in the Galilee. They invite their "buddies" in order to talk them into leaving their city life behind and move to the new settlement. Haggai's persuasive efforts echo the traditional Labor Zionist intertwining of settlement mythology, love-of-nature rhetoric, and myths of group bonding. However, as noted, the group bonding he seeks to revive is anchored in a nostalgic attachment to childhood and youthful memories, not in the relational possibilities of the present moment. In the course of their weekend encounter, Haggai tries to manipulate his "buddies" into accepting his detailed proposal for the establishment of a communal settlement, where they would each pursue their own lines of interest and yet foster the togetherness he so yearns for.

His persuasive campaign involves cajoling his guests, making arrangements behind their backs, misinforming them about the situation with the Arabs of the region, and hiding the fact that he is being pursued by the International Police for his involvement in some shady arms deals. The "group dynamics" generated by the reunion into which they have been manipulated by Haggai brings out old wounds in the relationships between group members. It also highlights the many disappointments of their current lives and the lack of real contact most of them feel toward one another in the present.

The encounter is, in addition, punctuated by the external geopolitical circumstances that Haggai has unsuccessfully tried to disguise from his visitors—the fact that the land on which the settlement is being built has been confiscated from the inhabitants of nearby Arab villages, and that this land appropriation for "national purposes" is strongly opposed by its previous owners. Several incidents indicate that the attempt to ignore these circumstances would not work—one of the women is stoned and injured while driving on her way up, the house generator is rendered dysfunctional by the deliberate insertion of sugar into its engine, which results in the electricity being cut off. Finally, Haggai kills an Arab who infiltrates his yard. It is only in this final scene of the play, when he solicits his friends' help in covering up his crime and burying the body of the Arab, that he manages to mobilize their loyalty and galvanize the group around him. The Israeli myth of group solidarity and militarized "cult of friendship" is thereby reduced to a mafia-like, collusive bonding of participants in a criminal cover-up.[150]

In this pain-filled rendering of the Zionist settlement mythology, the bonds of shared faith, the ties generated by collaborating in a joint venture, and the reciprocal commitments of brothers-in-arms are all transformed into the bonding of criminal collaboration. The broader message of this scene was not lost on the play's viewers. As Boaz Evron put it:

> It quickly turns out that the *hevre,* who are tied to each other like an undifferentiated knot, also resent and despise each other underneath the cloak of the solidarist collective. All this idea [of reviving the group], all this knot, would have exploded if the one who generated it had not killed a Bedouin he found hiding in his kitchen, and it is not clear if he did so out of self-defense. Now they can't leave. The beautiful mountain they inhabit

has turned into a trap and a prison. Their solidarity is now constructed upon the crime they must all hide, because the feeling of loyalty to the *hevre* is stronger than any moral principle, even stronger than an understanding of what is good for them, for each one of them, personally.

This is, of course, a heart-rending parable about the nature of the State of Israel today, in which the only solidarity left rests on the sense of partnership in the disenfranchisement of others.[151]

The abundant use made by the play's characters of cultural cliches, including the words of well-known patriotic songs, generates a playful scene of linguistic familiarity. Yet the play's ironic, self-aware dialogues only add to the bitterness of the scene and to its obviously harsh implications for the assessment of the Israeli pioneering project. This feeling of bitterness is only exacerbated by the play's implicit intertextual relations with *The Night of the Twentieth*. The sense of anticipation and promise that attended the pioneers' ecstatic preparations for the establishment of their settlement in Sobol's play is counteracted by the deceitfulness and disillusionment that accompany every step of the settlement activities discussed in Peled's play. Rather than striving to build an exemplary society, an effort that in Sobol's play is claimed to justify the injustice done to the Arab inhabitants of the land, the Zionism of the 1990s, as presented in Peled's play, harbors no ideological illusions. It is upheld by a fugitive from international law, who cunningly harnesses the rhetorical traces of Israeli settlement mythology in planning a fake communal enterprise at the expense of his Arab neighbors, whose rightful existence he refuses to acknowledge.

In this play, collective action becomes the convenient fig leaf of self-interested individuals in a highly fragmented and profit-driven society. The nostalgia for in-group solidarity becomes the breeding ground for further deceit and injustice. While Sobol's play leaves viewers with a sense of separation between the pioneering group's inner process and the settlement activities they are about to undertake, including the impending fight with the local Arab landholders, Peled's play suggests an inseparable link between the failure of group bonding, the unattainable magic of the inner circle, and the injustices perpetrated upon the group's external "others"—in this case, the insensitivity to the rights and the plight of the local Arabs. In that respect, Peled's play comes closer to the insight attained by Bistritsky at the end of his novel *Days and Nights*, in the scene that punctures the uplifting moment of the ritual reading of the group's communal diary. The play's final scene of guilty solidarity is hailed by the ironic statement of one of the group members: "Unity is stronger than death. Again we have proved to our-selves that we are a united and 'crystallized' group that can overcome any difficulty and remain whole."[152]

As they each finish doing their part in covering up the killing of the Arab—digging the grave in which his body is to be buried, rubbing off the blood stains—they all gather for a final sing-along, the ultimate enactment of group solidarity. Unlike all their former attempts to sing together harmoniously throughout the play, which are either aborted by external distractions or subverted by self-irony, this time they are successful. The choice of the song the playwright puts in their mouth in this final scene is quite telling as it hints at the state of blindness or "unseeing" that is the pioneers' ultimate sin. This song, written by the poet Nathan Yonathan and titled *dugit shata*, is a well-known lullaby about a small sailboat, all of whose sailors have fallen asleep. It asks how the boat can reach the shore safely if these sailors don't wake in good time. This is a question many Israelis ask themselves in metaphorical terms as they look at the reality around them.

Pioneering as Heritage: Lerner's *Ahavot Bitaniya*

The questions raised for viewers of the television play *Ahavot Bitaniya* are similar in tenor to the ones raised by *Hevre*, and they address the demise of the pioneering ethos in an equally compelling fashion. The focus of this play is on the internal reality of the collectivist ethos of the kibbutz and on its unfulfilled promises. The play is set in a veteran kibbutz in the early 1990s on the day of the opening of the fictive Bitaniya Museum, which is designed to commemorate the old-timers' early pioneering years. The plot revolves around the figure of the charismatic leader of Bitaniya Ilit (Harari in the play, clearly modeled on Meir Ya'ari) and his family members: his wife of many years whom he had met in Bitaniya; his elder son, whom Harari had boycotted for twenty-five years for having chosen to leave the kibbutz and move to the city to become a television professional; his younger son, who stayed on the kibbutz and is making efforts to preserve the legacy of Bitaniya in his role as educator and museum-maker; his grandson, who has moved the kibbutz on the path of industrialization and privatization; and other members of the family and the kibbutz, who offer additional commentaries and points of view.

Like *Hevre*, *Ahavot Bitaniya* maintains intertextual relations with *The Night of the Twentieth*, clearly using the same materials that Sobol had used in writing the earlier play. Commentators pointed out the line drawn between Sobol's and Lerner's plays:

> With a certain pain the drama returns to the nostalgic regions of Zionist mythology—in order to dismantle them. But this dismantling is not done out of glee but out of a sober look, against the background of an intergenerational gap and many changes in Israeli society. . . . The point of departure is Bitaniya, which has almost become a legend, and had won many hearts and enchanted many people. The playwright Yehoshua Sobol invoked it in his famous play *Leil Ha'esrim,* and since then Bitaniya has become a symbol for an extraordinary form of pioneering, and the group of young men and women have become an Israeli myth. But Lerner and Chaplin [the director] do not return to Bitaniya of yesteryear, which overlooked the Sea of Galilee and where far-flung dreams were woven. The drama takes place many years later.[153]

When asked about his reasons for choosing to deal with a topic so successfully treated by Sobol, the playwright responded that he was driven by a curiosity to explore how the beginnings invoked in *The Night of the Twentieth* would fare when viewed from the standpoint of the 1990s. He put it this way:

> In the beginning it bothered me that Sobol had already dealt with this topic, and the choice to deal with the eighty-year-old Bitaniya people stemmed from the fact that he had dealt with them in their twenties, and here the difference stands out—in the bitterness, in the cynicism, in the cumulative life experience. In *Ahavot Bitaniya,* I tell the story of a parental couple in their eighties, last remnants of the group headed by Meir Ya'ari and David Horowitz, that made their transient home on the hill of Bitaniya facing the lake of Galilee in 1920. In my script I try to explore the meaning of the Bitaniya experience at a distance of 60 years, to understand how the attempt to build a utopian society based on maximum openness, on love, on mutual commitment, on public rituals of confession that left no private space for the individual, what kind of influence this fanatic experience had on this specific family and on the kibbutz movement as one looks at it in retrospect. The play looks at the family and shows how all the fanaticism and the relentless demand to give priority to collective considerations over the needs of individuals generated dismal relationships within the family, including the second and third generations, until it falls apart.[154]

In Lerner's television play, whose tentative title was originally "Confessions" *(Vidu'im),*[155] the opening day of the fictive Bitaniya Museum is significant at a communal level, as an ultimate gesture of respect for the exploits and accomplishments of the pioneering generation. It is also significant on a familial level since Harari's elder son is scheduled to come to the kibbutz with a television crew in order to report on the museum opening ceremony and the story behind it. He hopes that this will enable him to reconnect with his father and attain some measure of reconciliation with him. This does not turn out to be an easy task. Harari is a sick and disgruntled old man in a wheelchair, whose behavior is as despotic in old age as it apparently was when he acted as leader of the pioneering group in Bitaniya Ilit. The other old-timers on the kibbutz testify to the scars he left on them with his relentless, rigidly ideological demands, and his wife and children testify to the heavy cost his family has paid for his uncompromising, disproportionate commitment to collective values. As the play unfolds, we learn of the bitterness of his wife, the excommunication of his elder son, the broken family of his younger son, whose conflict with his own son reproduces an intergenerational battle that Harari has himself modeled.

The renewed encounter with the son who has left the kibbutz brings back all the bitterness of the rupture that has driven him away. The father-son relations are interpreted within a patriarchal frame that highlights loyalty and obedience rather than love and respect. Harari accuses his son, the first-born of the kibbutz, not only of disloyalty to the kibbutz ideals but also of setting a bad example for his peers and thereby directly undermining his father's position of authority in the kibbutz.

That Harari interprets his relations to his son in terms of power and dependency rather than trust and love is indicated by his response to his son's desire to renew their contact after the many years in which they have been estranged. During those years, we learn, his wife felt she had to lie to him when she went to visit their son in the city. The scene of reconciliation he half-heartedly allows himself to be coaxed into is full of rancor and bitterness. Unable to face his guilt in sacrificing his family to his rigid version of kibbutz ideology, he accuses the son of bad faith, blaming him for the bad blood between them and interpreting his well-intentioned visit as a deliberate insult:

> Reconciliation is what you want? Here is my reconciliation. Give me your hand and I'll shake it. . . . You could have come twenty-five years ago. Why didn't you come? Why did you wait till today? I'll tell you why you waited. You waited until I wouldn't be able to stand on my own feet, and I would need your shoulder to lean on. You waited until my tongue would dangle out of my mouth and I would be unable to move it. You waited until I would be like a baby in a wheelchair, without teeth to bite my bread on, and your mother would feed me a mashed tomato with a spoon, and wipe

my face with a towel. This is the moment you waited for. Now you come with your television, like a Napoleon, and walk around the kibbutz as if you have conquered Moscow. You won? Tell me, you won? Time has won, not you.[156]

These and other statements made by various characters in the play suggest that both the family and the kibbutz community were held together by an intricate web of power struggles, feelings of mistrust and disappointment, as well as unfulfilled yearnings for the warmth of human contact. Thus, while the fictive Bitaniya Museum has been designed to house the pioneers' visions of communal bonding and the concrete traces of an intimate group whose life was ostensibly dominated by love, trust, and solidarity, the play itself in fact reveals a scene of animosity, intrigue, and deceit. Harari's fragmented family colludes in protecting him from the changing reality around him by deceiving him about the many innovations the kibbutz has introduced, which violate basic principles of sharing and equality in kibbutz life. They practice censorship on his reading of newspapers, coach his visitors about what information can and cannot be revealed to him.

The outright lies and half-truths that pervade the characters' lives in the play stand out with particular starkness when set against the vision of spiritual bonding and authentic dialogue cultivated by the myth of Bitaniya Ilit. The spirit of Bitaniya Ilit is both invoked and interrogated by scenes in which kibbutz youngsters are seen rehearsing segments from *Kehiliyatenu* in preparation for the museum opening ceremony under the tutelage of Ehud, Harari's younger son. Ehud has been successful in recruiting the youngsters to his effort of orchestrating the spirit of nostalgia that informed the establishment of the museum in the first place.[157] Thus, despite the fact that the multiple layers of deception surrounding the idealized image of pioneering days become more and more evident as the play proceeds, and some youngsters openly express their skepticism about it, the myth of Bitaniya Ilit does not quite lose its hold. As one of the teenage girls in the play puts it: "For me the most important thing about Bitaniya was the truth. They were preoccupied only with themselves and with their sense of truth. And because of the confessions there were no lies. There were no manipulations, they had a feeling of purity. And when there is such a feeling you have no sense of disgust and you can really love. I wish we could love like that in such a pure way."[158]

Most of the youngsters caught by the television camera nod in agreement on hearing these words, affirming the message of love and truth this girl projects on their mythologized elders. This naive affirmation cannot but sound an ironic note when heard against the denials and recriminations of the old-timers, who reject the glorification of the past promoted by the official line of museum-makers. Even Ehud, Harari's younger son and the teacher of these youngsters, who has worked so hard to preserve the memory of Bitaniya Ilit in the new museum, eventually comes to recognize the questionable status of this saga. Asked by the television crew to articulate the relevance of the spirit of Bitaniya to present concerns, he finds himself entangled in platitudes and self-contradictions: "The lesson I draw from the experience of the Bitaniya group is that you cannot impose love on a group, as father perhaps believed. Love develops only in a climate of openness and free choice, within a set of humanistic values, in recognition of individuals' personal emotions, and by encouraging expression in creative ways. I do not think the Bitaniya experiment has failed." [159]

That the story of Bitaniya Ilit might not be the beautiful saga of spiritualized sharing some want to believe is most clearly expressed by Harari's wife, Haya. Toward the end of the play, in an outburst designed to contain Harari's peremptory command to summon the obviously reluctant people of the kibbutz to attend the opening ceremony of the museum, she says to him:

> Nobody wants to hear you. Nobody wanted to hear you at all. You forced yourself on us. Like an evil tribal witch who intimidated everybody through his magic. Whoever refused to listen to you, was driven away. Whoever didn't want to obey you, was ex-communicated. Now you have no more rabbits to pull out of your sleeve. Now we can finally see the truth. And the truth is that it was all a lie. People will live here just the way they want to live, not as you preach to them. You yourself can't live the way you preach. [160]

Yet neither his wife's reprimand nor the revelations about the current state of the kibbutz are able to quench Harari's desire to lead his people in the path he had envisaged in his prime. Even in his state of obvious decline, helplessly pushed around in his wheelchair, he cannot let go of his visionary posture. His farewell speech at the ceremony bears all the marks of his relentless ideological zeal. Thus, facing the few elderly kibbutz members who took the trouble to come to the ceremony held in the Bitaniya Museum open yard, Harari makes a final appeal for the communal values that govern the kibbutz ideal, lamenting the changes that have taken place in kibbutz life. He calls for a renewal of the soul talk spirit that would bring back the sense of purpose and the spiritual fervor that filled the pioneers' hearts in early days. Using the familiar parlance of early pioneering days, he unsuccessfully attempts to revive the idiom of times past: "I turn to you today, perhaps for the last time in my life, we have to call a meeting, to talk, to discuss. We came here to create a new person, free, without walls inside him, or between him and others. . . . We came to redeem ourselves, to create a new world." [161]

Most of the elderly respond to his speech and to his call for a moment of spiritual reckoning with an obvious lack of interest. However, outside of the dramatic framework, in real life, a few old-timers who had shared the Bitaniya Ilit experience were still alive. They were intrigued by this new dramatic portrayal of their past on television. Interviewed for a kibbutz publication following the airing of Lerner's play in April 1994, they confirmed that the uncomplimentary depiction of Harari accorded with their memories of Ya'ari's leadership style. [162]

Harari's speech, like the few old-timers who gathered to listen to it, are both in and out of place in the ceremony, straddling a fine line between the museum display and the reality encompassing it. Harari's opening question, "What is the kibbutz?"—spoken seventy years after it was originally raised in numerous soul talks—remains unanswered by his rambling speech. Indeed, the two documentary projects around which the play is constructed—the museum-making project led by Harari's younger son, and the television documentary prepared by his elder son—provide contrasting responses to it. The fictive museum was designed to enshrine the spirit of Bitaniya Ilit as part of a nostalgic heritage industry. The television documentary sought to highlight the past conflicts and disappointments that animated the familial drama around which the play unfolds. Both the dreams of the early pioneers, which the museum is designed to preserve and celebrate, and the bitter reality they engendered, as reflected in the trials and tribulations of the Harari family filmed by the television crew, thus become part of the saga of Bitaniya Ilit as it is refracted in its myriad tellings and retellings, retextualizations and reenactments.

Ahavot Bitaniya, unlike *The Night of the Twentieth*, revisits the saga of Bitaniya Ilit, but not by examining the life-world of the early pioneers as did Sobol's play. Somewhat paradoxically, this play is an allegory of social change despite its focus on a moment of commemoration. This commemorative moment is, in turn, destabilized by the camera's gaze, whose documentary efforts penetrate behind the scenes of the museological facade, revealing the dark secrets visitors would never find within the museum walls. The play is thus not only a meditation on continuity and change, on the missed opportunities and unfulfilled promises of a troubled past, on the precariousness of intergenerational transmission. It is also a highly reflexive, self-conscious meditation on the act of telling itself.[163]

A Road Not Taken: The Soul Talk Ethos as Cultural Alternative

The saga of Bitaniya Ilit marks "a road not taken" of the Zionist project—not taken, but not quite forgotten either. Until the 1970s, when it was resurrected in personal memoirs and in Sobol's play, *The Night of the Twentieth*, it was only vaguely familiar within kibbutz and Labor youth movement circles. Pragmatic versions of the Zionist project triumphed over the spiritual alternative proposed by the vision of a community of dialogue encapsulated in the saga of Bitaniya Ilit. Even the "intimate groups" of Hashomer Hatza'ir pioneers that promoted the soul talk ethos in the early 1920s turned to Marxism several years later. The Labor Zionist project became decisively formulated in an idiom of agency and deeds—expressed in acts of conquest, settlement, and combat.

Apparently, spiritual Zionism, the soul talk ethos, and the nonpolitical communal project that the early "intimate groups" were associated with were felt to be unsuited to the nation-building project at hand. From the very start, as we have seen, the soul-searching spirit of the early pioneers' communal dialogues met with suspicion and censure, and came to be considered part of a passing, youthful adventure. The vision of dialogue articulated by the saga of Bitaniya Ilit was abandoned. In years to come, the early pioneers' openness and confessional mode were exchanged for the directness of the offspring of the pioneering generation, the "straight-talking" Sabra, native-born Israeli Jew, whose style was marked by self-assurance, assertiveness, and a pragmatic attitude rather than soul searching and spiritual strivings.

The reenactment of the soul talk format in the context of dialogic encounters involving soldiers who fought in the 1967 war, and the reinvocation of the pioneering saga of Bitaniya Ilit in a range of theatrical performances following the 1973 Yom Kippur War and the military engagements in Lebanon and the Occupied Territories through the 1980s and 1990s, were responses to the traumas of the various battlefields in which young Israelis found themselves during those years. At least for some Israelis, the soul talks provided a cultural model for the arts of open conversation and group bonding. They also served as a site for the exploration of the roots of the communal dream such encounters had spun and for its subsequent decline.

The painful exploration of cultural roots touched upon the utopian underpinning of the Zionist enterprise. Following the battle of words between Meir Ya'ari and David Horowitz in the early 1970s, the negotiation of the meanings of the Bitaniya Ilit foundation mythology took place mainly in the public arena of theatrical production and in the cultural conversation generated by it. As the years went by, the artistic invocations of this unusual settlement saga became less nostalgic and increasingly critical of the basic values and possibilities of the Zionist project. Sobol's *The Night of the Twentieth* resurrected the soul talk ethos and gave it a good deal of cultural prominence, but it ultimately affirmed the pragmatic, down-to-earth version of Zionism. This mainstream version of the Zionist project prioritized "deeds" over "words" as these were expressed in acts of settlement and in military victories.

The plays produced in the late 1980s and early 1990s, *Hevre* and *Ahavot Bitaniya*, both engaged and rejected the nostalgic strand of Sobol's play. *Hevre* is a bitter statement about the moral legitimacy and conduct of the Jewish settlement enterprise. It also undermines the communal utopia cultivated by social Zionism by subverting the myths of group solidarity and friendship. *Ahavot Bitaniya*, like *Hevre*, highlights the corruptive consequences of the pioneering ethos for Israeli society—in particular, the deceptions generated by claims to truth and authenticity and the material wrong created by claims to spirituality.

In writing about Israeli drama in the late 1970s, literary scholar Gideon Ofrat has pointed out that "the pioneering era has turned into a psychological trauma for Israeli society. It is an obsessive historical experience: Israeli playwrights can't help but return again and again to this primary experience, to that wonderful childhood. . . . The pioneering experience has turned into the measure of identity for Israeli society—the Israeli playwright criticizes the Israeli present through repeated comparisons with this glorious chapter."[164]

The exploration of the soul talk ethos as a quest for authentic dialogue, which has been undertaken in this chapter, may have been similarly motivated by this Israeli obsession. It has involved a textual archaeology that started with *Kehiliyatenu* and other testimonies of the early pioneers' attempt to enact a community of dialogue. It has taken us through a discussion of *The Seventh Day* as a textualization of the dialogic encounters organized by and for some of the offspring of these early pioneers following the trauma of the 1967 war. It has culminated in the consideration of theatrical performances that have reinvoked but, in recent years, mainly parodied this vision of dialogue in addressing the moral dilemmas and social disappointments that beleaguer Israeli society today.

The saga of Bitaniya Ilit has been inscribed in Israeli collective memory by particular individuals who acted as "pioneer impresarios" of sorts in holding up the memory of this saga as an unfulfilled cultural alternative. Nathan Bistritsky and Muky Tsur have been two of the most active cultural agents whose publishing and writing activities have helped preserve the memory of this pioneering mythology. Others have been the playwrights, chief among them Yehoshua Sobol, who have given this saga a new life through their art. As we have seen, many more artists, critics, journalists, and commentators have been part of the cultural conversation that has surrounded the story of Bitaniya Ilit.

I would like to propose that this range of cultural activities involves a "politics of counterpolitics," which is set in the field of cultural production and is constructed as separate from the sphere of political activities as usually defined. These activities have resulted in a range of cultural products in the form of publications, performances, and journalistic and academic writings in which the saga of Bitaniya Ilit features in one way or another. These texts and performances, as well as the cultural conversation surrounding them, have served to keep alive the cultural memory of the "intimate group" as a nonpolitical, communal alternative, and of the soul talk format as a discursive possibility that carries spiritual and perhaps moral, but no practical political implications.

The shift from the cultivation of the soul talk ethos as an all-encompassing way of life to its reincarnation in the form of therapeutic discussion groups or theatrical productions half a century (and more) later marks a change in its meaning as well as in its performative scope. In Bitaniya Ilit, the nocturnal dialogues became a privileged site in which a problematic merger between self and community was sought through the performance of confessional talk. The goal in this case was to explore the possibilities of a "life of dialogue" as a nonpolitical

alternative to prevailing forms of social organization. It was a counterpolitics in that it proposed a different, more spiritualized, path for
the accomplishment of Zionist goals. In the case of *The Seventh Day*,
the dialogic encounters held by and for soldiers who had fought in the
1967 war were also performative arenas in which personal feelings of
grief, loss, and horror, as well as the pointed moral dilemmas associated
with the conduct of war, could be displayed and explored.

That these encounters took place in a social-political context in
which victory and military prowess were universally celebrated further contributed to their status as alternative social enclaves removed
from the public sphere of political action yet offering a personal and
moral commentary on it. The goal of these dialogic encounters was
to reintroduce personal voices and moral reckoning into a collective
conversation whose triumphant notes pushed such voices aside. The
theatrical performances invoking the Bitaniya Ilit saga have transposed
the discussion of the roots and consequences of the Zionist agenda to
the realm of fiction, that place-out-of-place where life's most fundamental concerns can find their profoundest articulation. The goal here
was to reexamine contemporary social realities through the lens of this
particular chapter of Israeli pioneering history. As we have seen, these
stage-performed dialogic encounters served to simultaneously revitalize
and undermine the collective memory of the pioneers' soul talks and
the cultural meanings attending them.

Thus, the soul talk ethos in its various manifestations has been
widely disseminated in a range of cultural forms—through layers of
textualizations that mixed nostalgia with moral misgivings and cultural
critique. Somewhat paradoxically, these nostalgic yet highly troubled
imaginative recreations of an idealized image of a community of dialogue have retained their place in the Israeli cultural conversation
through the construction of mass-mediated imagined communities of
contemporary readers, theater-goers, museum visitors, and television
viewers. The promise of a life of dialogue among members of "intimate
groups," though clearly ensconced in the regions of myth and nostalgia,
continued to reverberate in some corners of Israeli culture in the early
1990s. By that time it carried the mark of a lost possibility.

The staged performances of the soul talk ethos, while keeping
its memory alive, were also a bitter admission of cultural defeat and
the demise of the spiritualized-humanistic version of the Zionist enterprise. Clearly, the New Jew has not emerged in the image of the soul-
searching pioneer of the 1920s, and the "group eros" dominating the

early pioneers' communal vision could not provide the kind of bonding they desired. This mainstream version of pioneering foregrounded pragmatic, instrumental values associated with nation-building as a cooperative social and political venture, not a communion of souls. The New Jew was thus forged in the image of the tough-minded, action-oriented, native-born Sabra, whose straight-talking style, natively known as *dugri* speech, encapsulated the newly emerging ethos of pragmatism and activism of Israeli nation- and state-building. If the soul talk ethos marked a road not taken for the Zionist venture, then the Sabra's assertive style, which was grounded in a rhetoric of agency and activism, marked the main road of the much-celebrated first generation of native Israelis. It is to the exploration of this pragmatic ethos of doing things with words, and to its articulation in the form of a culturally distinctive and "named" way of speaking, that I now turn.

Chapter 2

Confrontational Dialogues
The Rise and Fall of *Dugri* Speech

THE SABRA AS STRAIGHT TALKER

The image of the straight-talking Sabras, the sons and daughters of the Zionist pioneers discussed in the previous chapter, has occupied a central place in Israeli nation-building mythology.[1] The term "Sabra," which literally denotes a local cactus bush and its thorn-covered fruit, was applied metaphorically to Jewish children born in Palestine during the British Mandate (roughly, between the early 1920s and late 1940s). These youngsters' formative years were spent in the prestatehood educational system and in other socializing contexts such as the Zionist youth movements, where the mythic image of the native-born New Jew, the Sabra, was cultivated. "Sabra" itself was an outsiders' term, mainly used by members of the Sabras' parent generation, whose national aspirations involved the emergence of a New Jewish person in a new kind of Jewish society. A nonmetaphorical and less myth-laden term used to talk about the first generations of Jewish children in Zionist Palestine was the expression "yelidei ha'aretz" (those born in the land of Israel/Palestine). It was the latter term that was usually employed in the Sabras' own self-designations.

The construction of the new Jewish identity encapsulated in the image of the Sabra was a cultural project of monumental proportions in the early days of Zionist settlement. This project of cultural invention became particularly pressing when the first generation of native-born children came along. The particular meanings and values that were to be woven into the image of the New Jew were a matter of both explicit and implicit cultural negotiations. So were the social practices—including ways of speaking—through which this image would be socially constituted. A concerted effort was made to establish a particular image of the Sabra, the Israeli-born New Jew, as the centerpiece of mainstream Hebrew culture. This effort was part of what Kimmerling describes as "the attempt to create a hegemonic national identity, dominated by a bureaucratized monocultural system."[2]

The rise and fall of Israeli straight talk, natively known as *dugri* speech, is thus one facet of what Kimmerling calls "the invention and decline of Israeliness."[3] Just as the invention of Israeliness is associated, inter alia, with the emergence of *dugri* speech, its decline is marked by the fall of *dugri* speech in the increasingly multivocal Israeli society. From a communication angle, the growing pluralization and fragmentation of Israeli society has meant a diversification of its speech norms and ideologies. This section, then, offers a communicative angle on a well-recognized process of sociocultural change associated with the story of the production and negotiation of "Israeliness." That speech is so deeply implicated in this culturally central process of change is a point of special interest to scholars concerned with understanding the interplay of communication and cultural life.

The emergence of the Sabra as a cultural type involved a double-layered self-distancing move. As part of the Zionist revolutionary ethos, the new Sabra style involved the rejection of diaspora ways of being and acting (an orientation known as "the negation of the diaspora" *[shlilat hagola]*). In particular, the Sabra image involved a rejection of the image of the effeminate and spiritualized diaspora Jew as depicted most clearly in antisemitic portrayals of European Jews.[4] Pursuing Western, post-Enlightenment masculinist values of agency, practicality, and autonomy, the Sabra's quest for authenticity lay in energizing moments of confrontation and social action rather than in the spiritual possibilities of the early pioneers' quest for genuine dialogue. Indeed, even if secondarily, the emergence of the Sabras' style of straight talk was also a response to the pathos-filled style of the pioneering generation, which found its clearest expression in the soul talk ethos discussed in the previous chapter.

According to the "New Jew" ideology, the Israeli Jew was to be everything the Diaspora Jew was not. In communicative terms, this cultural gesture of refusal implied the rejection of ways of speaking associated with Jewish diaspora life, with European bourgeois culture, as well as with the pioneering alternative enacted by the soul-searching youngsters in Bitaniya Ilit. As depicted in Zionist ideology, diaspora Jews' ways of responding to life's exigencies, and especially their ways of interacting with the non-Jewish world, were marked by a sense of restrictiveness, defensiveness, and passivity as an adaptive mechanism. Traditionally, Jews recognized the value of using speech adroitly as a way of coping with a potentially hostile environment. Furthermore, Jewish talmudic tradition colored Jews' disposition toward *pilpul,* an elaborate form of discussion that involved a recognition of the complexity and many-sidedness of issues, the inherent ambiguity of human affairs, and the role of confrontation and debate in clarifying issues.

Notably, both the early pioneers' and the Sabras' attempts to distance themselves from diaspora ways of speaking retained the cultural focus on language as a locus of cultural self-definition. The formers' soul talk ethos was as logocentric as was *dugri* speech, yet it promoted expressive rather than deliberative and realist discourse. The expressiveness of the soul talks drew its cultural inspiration from Jewish-Hasidic roots as well as the anti-bourgeois youth movement spirit rather than from the modernist, pragmatic ethic underlying the Sabra's straight talk, which privileged nonmanipulative openness, simplicity of expression, and explicitness of purpose.

For the Sabras, as compared to their parent generation of early pioneers, the struggle to shed an unwanted identity became less central. Yet having rejected "anything that smacked of the diaspora," as this was sometimes expressed, left them with no clear behavioral models. They no longer nurtured the cultural richness of their Jewish roots, nor were they so obviously burdened by their constraints. Their central challenge became the task of creating and sustaining a credible cultural image for themselves with little to draw on from the older generations. At the same time, they carried with them traditionally Jewish interactional preferences such as the use of conflict as an intragroup resource.[5] In this culture-making project, mimesis was largely replaced by partial inversion as the most easily accessible strategy for constructing the new Jewish identity and its symbolic-linguistic articulation in a distinctive style that would project and reaffirm the image of the Sabra in everyday social exchanges.

The difficulty involved in translating this cultural task into communicative practice is expressed in an autobiographical novel written by a legendary soldier-girl of the Palmah, a leading prestate underground combat unit, Netiva Ben-Yehuda. The book tells the story of the months preceding the official outbreak of the War of Independence from the point of view of an arch-Sabra.[6] The Sabras, she wrote, were left with the unusual cultural burden of having to invent themselves: "Clearly they could not think of everything a person needs, a member of a new people, if we were to start everything from scratch. For example, they could not invent for us the accent we were going to have when we came to speak English, or what our hand-gestures were going to be like."[7] Her vivid account of the first generation of Sabras suggests that they were at least partially successful in this task of cultural self-invention. She points out an enormous difference between the Sabras, the so-called first-generation-to-redemption, and the newcomers to the land who were born in the diaspora. It was a difference manifested in style of dress and behavior, as well as in speech. In fact, in one of my conversations with her, the author attributed the emergence of the Sabras' *dugri* way of speaking to their desire to set themselves apart not only from their parents' generation but also from the new immigrants, who began to arrive en masse in the late 1940s, and who were felt to be "tainted" by their past diaspora experience.

Clearly, the grip that the Sabra image had on the communal imagination has far exceeded the numerical weight of the Sabras in the budding Israeli society, especially since the advent of the mass immigration in the late 1940s and 1950s. In fact, although the term "Sabra" applies officially to Israeli-born Jews in general, it has been used mainly to refer to a subset of them—to the sons and daughters of immigrants of European origin who were bred in the spirit of the negation-of-the-diaspora that dominated the Zionist ethos until well into the 1960s. As a group, the Sabras became culturally dominant in the years preceding the establishment of the State of Israel and through the first decades of its life.[8] The prominent status this image enjoyed for many years invariably became a mechanism of social stratification and cultural exclusion. The most obviously excluded group of Israeli-born Jews, who were constructed as marginal to the nation-building ethos, were native-born Israelis of Middle Eastern and North African heritage, usually referred to as Sephardi or Mizrahi Jews. Women were marginalized, too, given the masculinist values encapsulated in the image of the action-oriented, assertive yet tight-lipped, and straight-talking Sabra. Over the years, however, the status of the Sabra as a cultural model has been repeatedly challenged. The two social dramas I discuss below point to the kinds of cultural negotiations that have accompanied challenges to the Sabra ethos vis-à-vis demands for social inclusion on the part of these two marginalized groups.

Although by now the Sabra image has lost much of its lure, it was for many years a recognized symbol of mainstream Israeliness. The use of the term *Sabra* to denote the native Israeli Jew is itself worthy of comment. In citing the most widespread explanation for this linguistic choice, Elliot Oring says that the sabra fruit of the prickly pear cactus-like bush "is a metaphor for the native personality. Like the prickly pear, the native born is sweet and gentle within, but only to those who understand how to penetrate the tough and thorny exterior."[9] Like Oring's account, and like most others one encounters, the following self-description echoes many Sabras' identification with the outside/inside dimensions highlighted by the prickly pear metaphor: "Like our fruit, the Sabra, we are prickly outside. We often seem rude, though. But deep inside, we, too, have our conscience."[10] This metaphorical reading is oblivious of the cultural role of the Sabra bush as a symbol of tenacity and connection to the land in Palestinian culture. Borrowed from local Arab vernacular, the word *Sabra* has become a cornerstone of an internal Jewish-Israeli cultural conversation.

Given the centrality of language as a symbol and tool in nationalist agendas in general, and in the Zionist project in particular, it is no wonder that the overall search to construct a new Jewish identity involved the crystallization of a distinctive, recognizable way of speaking, natively known as *dugriyut*. Indeed, through all my discussions of *dugri* speech with native speakers of Hebrew, they consistently associated it with the image of the Sabra and the cultural problematic attending its "invention." "To speak *dugri*," as one of my informants succinctly put it, "is to act like a Sabra." Similar comments about Israeli directness of style, or *dugri* speech, are frequently encountered in discussions of the Israeli scene by both insiders and outsiders to it. References to Israeli straight talk, or bluntness, or forthrightness—to mention differently colored alternative labels—are a routine part of the metadiscourse about Israeli discourse.

Although it has become increasingly problematic in its assumptions and deployment, the mythic figure of the straight-talking Sabra is part and parcel of the Israeli story of nationhood. It is still occasionally invoked in interpersonal and public settings although not as frequently as during the initial period of this research, in the early 1980s. At that time, portrayals of members of the nation's political and social, male-dominated elite that appeared in the daily press or in magazines made frequent references to their *dugri* style. These portrayals clearly drew on widespread understandings of the cultural positioning of the Sabra subculture at the time, and also served to reconfirm its positive valence. In what follows I cite examples that support the inseparable link my informants invariably made between the Sabra image and the *dugri* way of speaking. These examples will also help me flesh out the texture and meanings of speaking *dugri* as a culturally situated expressive idiom.

The first example invokes *dugri* speech in a way that clearly links it to an action-oriented, pragmatic orientation and a preference for deeds over words. It sketches the figure of a well-known senior officer in the Israeli Defense Forces, Binyamin Ben-Eliezer, who has since served as Minister in both Rabin's and Barak's cabinets, and was Minister of Defense in Sharon's cabinet as well as the leader of the Labor Movement. This description appeared on the occasion of Ben-Eliezer's departure from military life and his entry into politics: "He speaks *dugri*. It is easy to get him to talk. His hawkish views are well-crystallized. His sentences clear, sharp. . . . Commitment to the task at hand is for him the highest of values. . . . His advice: in place of empty words—a lot of deeds."[11]

This descriptive idiom has seeped into portrayals of Israeli public figures in some of the foreign press, too. Thus, comments made in an obituary for former Defense Minister Moshe Dayan, the first and perhaps foremost Israeli soldier-turned-politician, which appeared in the *International Herald Tribune*, echo the descriptions of Sabra personalities in the Israeli press. They blend elements of the pioneering ethos ("Jewish peasant") with an account of the Sabra style: "He called himself a Jewish peasant but to millions around the world, Moshe Dayan was a symbol of Israel—proud, straight talking, defiant and instantly recognized by the black eye-patch he always wore."[12]

A less enamored view of the *dugri* style could also be found in press portrayals in the early 1980s. Thus, for example, a portrait of the late Mota Gur, a former Chief of Staff who became politically prominent in the Labor movement during the 1981 election campaign, is ambivalent in its depiction of the Sabra interactional style. It highlights the Sabra's rough edges, but at the same time it acknowledges the potential attractiveness of the Sabra image for voters. The Labor party, having lost the national elections in 1977, is described in this article as eagerly looking for "a savior in the image of a Sabra," a description the late Mota Gur seemed to fit at the time: "He is a former chief-of-staff, a Sabra who speaks Hebrew without a foreign accent, dynamic, speaks *dugri*. Many like him just because of these characteristics, his lack of rhetorical flair, his terrible roughness, the fact that he is a through-and-through Sabra, a native-born and not a foreign transplant."[13]

Several years later, another portrait of Mota Gur, written by a different journalist, drew a comparison between him and Ariel Sharon, also a former General turned politician, who has held many prominent positions and as of this writing is Israel's Prime Minister. This portrait mentioned that during their military careers, both Gur and Sharon were in the habit of "saying *dugri* whatever they thought, and paid for it dearly more than once."[14]

Another article describes Mr. Tulipman, an enterprising figure in security affairs and a former director-general of the national power company. His angry resignation, following a stormy meeting with that company's board of directors, was narrated in the press with reference to his characteristically Sabra *dugri* style. Indeed, the incident, which took place in a civilian public sector sphere—like others of its kind— became an occasion to interrogate the appropriateness of the *dugri* speech style in a world in which it had become vulnerable. The following account reads somewhat as an apologia for the straight-talking Sabra:

> He is a man of the direct approach, the *dugri* speaking style, high principles and an inner honesty which he applies both in his personal and his public life. An old friend of his defines him as a person who is sensitive—and inflexible, who ranks high on "Sabra toughness." The leader of the workers' union in the company rejected the suggestion that Tulipman was a tough and uncompromising director-general, offering a most favorable valuation of his Sabra manner: "Right, he is a Sabra manager, with all the good qualities this implies. Simple. *Dugri*.[15]

More recently, both the campaign and the political commentary surrounding the election of Ehud Barak as Prime Minister in May 1999 have underscored Barak's avowal to uphold the legacy of the late Prime Minister Yitshak Rabin, who was assassinated in 1995 by a right-wing opponent of his peace initiative. For those familiar with the Israeli scene, Barak's election meant not only the possibility of a resumption of the peace process but also the promotion of a contemporary version of the Sabra image and the meanings associated with it. In his dealings with the Israeli public, Barak invoked his own version of the straight-talking Sabra, presenting himself as resolute and forthright yet attentive to his addressees' feelings. Thus, unlike Rabin, who had bluntly dismissed the position of the West Bank Jewish settlers, he acknowledged the legitimacy of their fears of uprooting when he initiated political negotiations that involved discussions of possible withdrawal from the Golan Heights or the West Bank. The sense of forthrightness Barak sought to convey during the election campaign was underscored by many of his supporters. For a while, he also persuaded the Palestinians of his resolve to pursue "Rabin's legacy." Thus, Palestinian chairman

Yasir Arafat reportedly said to Yosi Beilin, then Minister of Law: "Ehud is *dugri, dugri*. In this respect he is like Rabin, and therefore I am optimistic about the future. I feel that you can believe this man. With him I know where we are heading."[16] However, the most obviously poignant and nostalgic invocation of the Sabra image and the *dugri* speech style appeared in the press following the assassination of Rabin in 1995. At that point in time, the *dugri* speech style had momentarily regained some of its magic power and was frequently invoked in nostalgic constructions of Rabin's mythic image of the legendary fighter and straight-talking Sabra, who exudes uprightness and inspires trust. Rabin's straightforward, unadorned speech style was appreciatively and profusely mentioned in obituaries published after his assassination, whereas its rough edges, which had triggered at least some criticism in his lifetime, were forgotten. Indeed, of all Israeli politicians—quite a gallery of *dugri* speakers, as suggested by the above examples—it is the figure of Rabin that has been inscribed in Israeli collective memory as the epitome of the *dugri*-speaking Sabra, the man who never hesitated to say what he thought and who always meant what he said. Thus, for example, in an article written by journalist Doron Rosenblum on the thirtieth day following Rabin's assassination, the author attributed a *dugri* flavor to Rabin's leadership, calling it "three years of *dugri*— straightforwardness, bluntness, the sharpening of the edges."[17]

The particular interactional texture of this *dugri* regime was specified by another journalist, who wrote of Rabin with intimate affection a few days following the assassination:

> It is amazing how this timid red-head with his *dugri* Hebrew symbolized for many people so many different things, since there is no one image of Rabin: For the young generation he may have symbolized a father figure, the man who looks after them, makes peace on their behalf. For the older generation he may have symbolized the figure of the lost son, that well-known and highly familiar mythological Sabra, who managed to win wars and come back from them unhurt.[18]

And a few days later, in an article titled "He Spoke His People's Language," the same author further elaborated upon Rabin's use of language and his interactional style:

> Yitshak Rabin was our first and only Sabra Prime Minister. He was born in Jerusalem, educated in the agricultural highschool Kadoorie and was a fighter and commander in the Palmah [prestate underground units] and Zahal [Israel Defense Forces]. It is there that he formed his worldview and

it is there, too, that his language, field of associations and images were shaped. His style was a mixture of the Hebrew of the [British] Mandate period, Palmah-style comradeship *[hevremaniyut Palmahnikit]*, and military *dugriness [dugriyut zahalit]*. They said that he was not eloquent, that he spoke with mistakes, that his speech was blunt and sharp, that his syntax was deficient and his vocabulary limited. And so he was the first Israeli Prime Minister who actually spoke his people's language. . . . He was direct and hated flowery language, his words always reflected his heart *[piv velibo tamid hayu shavim]*.[19]

The commemoration of Yitshak Rabin thus became an occasion in which to sound an appreciative note regarding the authenticity of the *dugri* style in a world felt to be increasingly dominated by manipulativeness and deceptiveness. These nostalgic invocations were spoken with more than a tinge of exasperation at the post-*dugri* cultural and political climate in which deliberate ambiguity, intentionally elaborate and vacuous statements, upbeat cliches, copyrighted populist assertions, and unbridled flattery appeared to be the order of the day. These latter expressive forms were cited as indicators of a new cultural ethos dominated by the public relations industry and its manipulative tenets, which had come to supersede the Sabra ethos of personal integrity, interpersonal accountability, and straight talk.

Thus, writing in conjunction with the third anniversary of Rabin's death, in an article that also included a straightforward critique of Rabin's accomplishments as a leader, another journalist explicitly contrasted him with Benyamin Netanyahu, who won the elections in 1996, saying: "Unlike Netanyahu, Rabin was straight as a ruler, perhaps too straight for a politician. His Sabra *dugriness* and the credibility he exuded were what gave him the electoral edge over Peres."[20]

The frequent association of the *dugri* style with military personas, many of whom have become prominent politicians, is not incidental. Informants frequently mentioned the military arena as the cultural site where the Israeli scene of meaningful action and the directness of style appropriate to it find their quintessential place. With the shift of cultural focus from settlement activities to military exploits, or the increasing over-layering of the second on the first, the image of the *dugri*-speaking Sabra-warrior replaced that of the pioneer. In fact, this image was still invoked with reference to military leaders long after it had been proclaimed anachronistic in most other quarters. Yet, even though the Sabra subculture has become only one of the many subcultures of modern Israel, traces of this style can still be found in the form of habituated speech preferences, in the context of nostalgic references, or as part of counternostalgic critiques.

Although no longer dominant, the *dugri* ethos must still be considered as part of the overall patchwork that constitutes Israeli culture today. This is so even when contemporary Israelis engage in cultural self-distancing moves vis-à-vis the Sabra image and the *dugri* style as they reconfigure their cultural identities in post-*dugri* terms. Indeed, Israeli culture, like "the culture of any society at any moment is more like the debris or 'fall out' of past ideological systems than it is itself a system, a coherent whole."[21]

As we shall see in the discussions that follow, the *dugri* ethos has become an increasingly marginalized and contested cultural possibility. However, before we attend to the ways in which it has been contested and changed, we must try to understand the proverbial directness of Israeli Sabra speakers with reference to the cultural world in which it has emerged. I will do so by "exoticizing" the Sabra ethos within the context of an ethnolinguistically oriented study that foregrounds the meanings and values associated with *dugri* speech as a culturally named way of speaking. This way of speaking has become a verbal "key symbol" in Israeli Sabra culture that "in an ill-defined way, is crucial to [its] distinctive organization."[22] My first move, then, will be to try to tease out the cultural meanings of *dugri* speech as they were formulated and interpreted by cultural members themselves, in other words, as considered "from the native's point of view."[23]

This internal look will be supplemented by views presenting cultural alternatives. I will consider challenges to the dominance of the Sabra model of personhood and its attendant values and meanings. These came from many directions and in many guises: religious Jews have rejected the secularization that attended the Sabra vision; Middle Eastern and North African immigrants have rejected the obviously European flavor of the cultural project of self-transformation that promised to turn them into Sabra-style New Jews by effacing their distinctive ethnic origins; the growing bourgeoisie as well as many younger Israelis have rejected the collectivist spirit of the Labor Zionist ethos; women have had more of a say in shaping Israeli cultural sensibilities and challenging its masculinist flavor. For many different reasons, then, many Israelis experienced a deep sense of discomfort in dealing with the roughness of style associated with the *dugri* interactional code. My account will, therefore, involve a consideration of a wide range of changing attitudes and cultural practices in Israeli society that are traceable to the shifting place of the Sabra culture.

Outsiders to the culture, most significantly many of the Arabs with whom Israelis have interacted over the years, have also experienced a sense of stylistic unease in their contacts with *dugri* speakers. On top of the well-known political tensions and power struggles between Arabs and Jews in Israel/Palestine, I believe there are cultural grounds for miscommunication between members of these two groups that can be brought to light through a study of the vicissitudes of *dugri* speech. Although clearly secondary to issues of power and control in the broader scheme of things, they are nevertheless well worth elucidating. I will do this by comparing the Sabra *dugri* ethos with the ethos of *musayra,* which names a culturally focal way of speaking and acting among Arabic speakers.

The juxtaposition of the cultural styles encapsulated within the notions of "speaking *dugri*" on the one hand and "doing *musayra*" on the other is instructive in understanding the potential for miscommunication between Arabs and Jews as they routinely interpret each other's ways of saying and doing. My account will therefore probe into the meanings of *dugri* speech as a group internal interactional code associated with the Sabra subculture, yet it will also attempt to recapture the challenges it has met in and through contacts with those considered (or constructed as) outsiders to it. In what follows, I will attend to instances of what Kenneth Burke has termed "style gone wrong" as he highlighted the intercultural significance of conversational directness as a dimension of style, saying: "A plain spoken people will distrust a man who, bred to different ways of statement, is overly polite and deferential with them, and tends to put his command in the form of questions. . . . They may even suspect him of sneakiness. He, conversely, may consider their blunt manner a bit boastful, even at times when they are almost consumed with humility."[24]

In Burke's terms, then, this study is concerned with the Sabra's "drama of character" as stylistically articulated, as well as with the possibility of "style gone wrong" in encounters between Sabras and cultural outsiders of various kinds. Tracing the change processes which have resulted in the loss of dominance of *dugri* speech as a cultural style suggests a shift in cultural orientation, whose details can be appreciated once we have sketched the meanings associated with *dugri* speech in Israeli Sabra culture. It is to this task that I now turn.

THE CULTURAL MEANINGS OF *DUGRI* SPEECH

A consideration of the cultural meanings associated with *dugri* speech as a symbolic form will be our first step in unraveling its changing place and significance in Israeli Sabra culture. It is by invoking the cultural meanings associated with the employment of *dugri* speech that speakers enact the image of the Sabra and mitigate the social costs attending its confrontational edge.

The symbolic meanings of *dugri* speech, as discussed below, have been inductively derived from my reading of the extensive data I have accumulated through sociolinguistic interviews with both members of the Sabra culture and outsiders to it. I have also gathered anecdotal data derived from everyday interactions and press accounts and a number of carefully selected literary sources. Not surprisingly, *dugri* speech as a symbolic form shares many of the meanings and values that can also be traced in more deliberately constructed cultural productions associated with the Israeli nation-building era, such as collective myths, reinterpreted traditional festivals, newly formed rituals, and so on.[25]

The meanings and values associated with *dugri* speech provide a cultural warrant for the employment of a way of speaking that challenges the Goffmanian assumption that all interaction is grounded in a rule of considerateness—a rule that requires interactants to abide by the unspoken agreement to maintain each other's "face" in communicative exchanges.[26] Goffman considers this to be the ground rule of all interaction. *Dugri* speakers obviously violate it by speaking their mind in a confrontational mode. One wonders how a style defined in terms of the violation of such a basic interactional rule could have gained such symbolic force. The answer, I maintain, is to be found at the level of language ideology—through a consideration of the cultural meanings members ascribe to this form of talk and the view of language it implies.[27]

The term *dugri* has always been considered a slang term. Like many other slang words in Israeli Hebrew it was borrowed from Arabic.[28] As Elliot Oring has pointed out with reference to the Arabic word *chizbat* (lie), which was used to label a native-Israeli oral tradition during the prestate years, the Arabs were then regarded as the behavioral model for the native Israeli Jews. They were felt to be part of the local landscape in a way the newcomers from Europe could not possibly be.[29] Arabic words were borrowed from Arabic speech along with Arab mannerisms and customs. It is, therefore, interesting to note that the term *dugri* has undergone a considerable semantic shift on its route from Arabic to Hebrew. The occurrence of a meaning shift is a common phenomenon in language borrowing. This point is abundantly illustrated in Sornig's study of lexical innovation, where he specifically underlines the prevalence of borrowing in the development of slang, the prevalence of semantic shifts in lexical innovation, and the socio-cultural roots of such shifts.[30] For our purposes, the particular direction this shift has taken in the case of the word *dugri* is highly instructive, since it brings out some of the meanings and values that are central to the Sabra culture as well as points of difference from Arab culture.

The Semantic Journey of *Dugri*

The word *dugri* is explicated in the popular dictionary of Hebrew slang compiled by authors Dan Ben-Amotz and Netiva Ben-Yehuda. It is said to be derived from Arabic and to have two meanings:

1 Speaking straight to the point, for example: "I'll tell you *dugri*, I can't stand your face"; or, "There stormed in the courageous young man with his *dugri* and embarrassing way of speaking."
2 A label for an honest person who speaks straight to the point, for example, "He is always *dugri*."[31]

According to my Arabic-speaking informants, the word *dugri* is not considered a pure Arabic word but is borrowed from Turkish. It is etymologically related to the Turkish word *dogru,* which, as several interviews with native speakers of Turkish have persuaded me, is generally used the way *dugri* is used in Arabic. *Dugri* speech in both Hebrew and Arabic usage denotes verbal conduct that adheres to the norm of truthful expression, a norm that has been argued to be fundamental to human society.[32] *Dugri* utterances, however, constitute different types of communicative acts in the two languages. In both of them, speaking *dugri* names a linguistic performance that would fall under the rubric of the "bald-on-record" strategy in Penelope Brown and Stephen Levinson's model of politeness strategies.[33] That is, it refers to talk that is truthful, informative, relevant, and clear in its expression. The *dugri* speaker in either language thus tells the truth, avoids beating around the bush, and speaks to the point. However, the cultural meanings attending such talk as an embodiment of the "bald-on-record" strategy in these two languages are quite distinct, and must be recaptured with reference to the larger cultural context in each case. In Israeli Hebrew, *dugri* speech encodes reports of subjective experiences, thoughts, opinions, and, to a much lesser extent, feelings. In Arabic, however, *dugri* utterances are reports of the speaker's knowledge of what has happened. In claiming to speak *dugri*, an Arabic speaker claims to be imparting true information, facts about an objective reality "out there." This is a central meaning shift that is specifically related to the way *dugri* has come to figure in colloquial Hebrew.

Furthermore, there has been a narrowing in the application of the term *dugri* in Hebrew. In Arabic it is used both literally to denote straightness (for example, a straight line or a straight road) and metaphorically as an attribute of a person who is *dugri* (roughly, honest and honorable), or of speech, as in "speak the *dugri*" (in other words, tell the truth, don't lie). Only the metaphorical usage has been imported into Hebrew. In this restricted sense, the term *dugri* can be used as an attribute of either a person (as in "He is *dugri*"), a way of speaking (as in "Speak *dugri*," i.e., in a straightforward way), a speech event (as in "a *dugri* talk"), or a human bond (as in "a *dugri* relationship," implying a relationship in which *dugri* speech is the rule). In its use as an attribute—functioning both adjectivally and adverbially—the word *dugri* in Hebrew can thus be said to color or structure the interpersonal domain: it is uniquely concerned with persons and their interrelations as behaviorally manifested in and through speech. At the same time, in Hebrew, unlike in Arabic, the word *dugri* has been nominalized, turning it into a noun, *dugriyut*, which denotes a speech style, i.e., the property of speaking in a *dugri* manner (as in "I like/don't like his *dugriyut*").

Another more subtle difference concerns the cultural meaning of *dugri* speech in Hebrew as compared to Arabic. The difference can be briefly summed up as follows: although both my Hebrew-speaking and Arabic-speaking informants explicated the term *dugri* as referring to the quality of honesty, to Hebrew speakers it meant honesty in the sense of being true to oneself, being sincere, whereas to Arabic speakers it meant being true to the facts. *Dugri* speech in Hebrew involves a conscious suspension of face-concerns so as to allow for the free expression of the speaker's thoughts, opinions, or preferences in cases in which they might pose a threat to the addressee's face.

To attenuate the confrontational edge of such statements, they may be prefaced by metapragmatic phrases that draw attention to the directness of the talk, as in prefixing one's utterance with a phrase containing *dugri* ("I'll tell you *dugri*, I didn't like the way you put it," or "Let me ask you *dugri*, why don't you like her?"). These kinds of prefixes might occur in conversation-initial position in casual exchanges and are not necessarily associated with conflict situations even though they point to a clear violation of face-concerns. Even an interactional encounter that is labeled as a "*dugri* talk" and can be characterized as an agonistic ritual encounter is not affectively colored by anger but rather by assertiveness and determination, as will be further elaborated on below.

The purpose of speaking *dugri* in Arabic is to represent faithfully factual information that the speaker may be tempted to either conceal or embellish. Thus, a young unmarried Arab woman said she had "spoken the *dugri*" with her parents when she told them she had gone to Tel Aviv to join a student demonstration without letting them know. She explained: "I could have told them that I had stayed at my girlfriend's home. But I thought in the long run it is better to speak the *dugri* to them." When I asked my Arab informants about a prefix in Arabic that would be analogous to "I'll tell you *dugri*" in Hebrew, they produced a construction that was slightly but tellingly different; it often took the form of a request: "*Beddak eddugri?*" ("Do you want the *dugri*?"). Here, as in the former example, *dugri* functions as a noun, not an adverb of manner, describing the way things are said. An utterance of this kind may occur in disputes and is not likely to appear at the opening of an exchange. In a conflictual situation, one can legitimately suspend the general rules of prudence and tactfulness that underlie the customary use of indirect forms of discourse. These cultural rules reflect the highly valorized Arab ethos of *musayra* (meaning roughly "to go along, to humor, to accommodate oneself to the wishes of others"), whose contours and meanings will be further elaborated below.

In Hebrew, *dugri* speech is contrasted to lack of sincerity, hypocrisy, talking behind one's back, or, at times, the indirectness associated with evasiveness and diplomacy. In Arabic, speaking the *dugri* stands opposed to concealment in an attempt to mislead, or, alternatively, in the service of *musayra*. What stands in the way of truth-speaking in the Hebrew *dugri* mode is oversensitivity to face concerns, interpreted as lack of courage and integrity. What stands in the way of truth-speaking in the Arabic *dugri* mode is the high value placed on smoothness in interpersonal encounters as well as on the ever-present temptation to embellish the facts for rhetorical purposes in the service of self-interest.

It is therefore not surprising that some of the *dugri* utterances given by my Arab informants could not be characterized in Hebrew by the term *dugri*. For example, one Arab informant, who was a teacher, cited her use of *dugri* in a confrontation with her husband in which she defended herself, saying: "I am speaking the *dugri*. It did not happen the way you've been told." Commenting on her use of *dugri* in this case, the teacher explained: "It is my class and I know better than anybody else what goes on there." That is, she referred to her speech as *dugri* to underline her credibility as a witness, as someone who has access to the facts.

A different meaning of Arabic *dugri*, which is not shared by its Hebrew counterpart, relates to "fairness" or "impartiality" in judgment or in the treatment of others. An example illustrating this usage was given by a teacher who told me that she had been asked by her principal to serve as judge in a contest between two classes. He accompanied his request with the comment: "But you must be *dugri* between them." He warned her against the temptation to favor one class over the other. Similarly, another informant noted that a parent must be *dugri* among all the children, not favoring one over the rest. The construction "*dugri* among" is not acceptable in Hebrew, and *dugri* is never used in the sense of "fair." However, most interestingly, the English word "fair" has penetrated colloquial Hebrew (as have many other English words, English having replaced Arabic and Yiddish as the main source of language borrowing in contemporary Hebrew slang). Initially, it was used only with its English meaning, but more recently it has also come to be used in place of *dugri*. Thus, rather to my surprise, some of my younger informants used "I'll tell you fair" in discursive contexts in which I, as well as many of the older informants, would have used "I'll tell you *dugri*."

Moreover, what appear to be analogous uses of *dugri* may have completely different meanings in Hebrew and Arabic utterances. Whereas in Arabic the sentence "He is *dugri*" means that a person generally tells the truth impartially, in Hebrew it means that the speaker tends to be direct and straightforward in expressing his noncomplimentary thoughts or opinions, or that he or she takes the liberty to invade the addressee's privacy in asking a direct question. In Arabic, *dugri* speech is viewed not as a matter of style but of content, whereas in Hebrew it is definitely a matter of style (associated with particular types of communicative effects). This accounts for the fact that speakers of Arabic could not accept the utterance "He speaks *dugri*, but he is a liar," judging it to be self-contradictory. Some speakers of Hebrew said it could be accepted: *dugri* could be interpreted as referring to how things were said, not to what was being said.

In sum, for speakers of Arabic, speaking *dugri* implies the choice of a speech mode primarily involving a set of conditions that apply to the content of the message. The use of this mode must always be strategically weighed against the demands of *musayra*. For Sabra speakers of Hebrew, on the other hand, *dugriyut* is a culturally defining way of speaking—that is, an informally crystallized, valorized, interactional style whose use carries implications for members' identity claims.

In its passage from Arabic to Hebrew, the term *dugri* has, thus, undergone a meaning-shift on a number of dimensions: it has become specialized in its application to the interpersonal domain only; it has come to denote a speech style, and as such, it is associated with the notion of sincerity rather than of truth in the sense of correspondence with external (or internal) facts or in the sense of possessing the required evidence.

The idea of sincerity, which has emerged as central in the foregoing cross-linguistic comparison, is only one of the meaning clusters associated with the colloquial Hebrew version of *dugri* speech. *Dugri* speech as a symbolic form is associated with five analytically distinguishable yet obviously related clusters or dimensions of meaning. Often these meaning dimensions were explicitly verbalized in informants' spontaneous talk in such statements as "He is *dugri*, he is sincere," or "He talked *dugri*, he was not afraid to speak up," "A *dugri* person is natural," and so on. Otherwise, I was able to abstract them from metacommunicative talk about the *dugri* way of speaking and from a consideration of actual instances of *dugri* speech. In what follows, I consider them one by one.

The Rhetoric of Agency

The first set of meanings associated with *dugri* speech in spoken Hebrew has to do with agency, determination, daring, courage, forcefulness. These mark *dugri* speech as an idiom of defiance associated with concepts of inner strength and an activist orientation. None of these notions were mentioned by speakers of Arabic in discussing the role of *dugri* speech or *dugri* speakers in their speech communities. I will henceforth refer to this dimension as the *rhetoric of agency*.

As discussions of the Sabra image routinely indicate, assertiveness and forcefulness of expression are important dimensions of style associated with the cultural construction of the New Jew.[34] Agency and inner strength have emerged as central to the meaning of *dugri* speech as well. In this context, speaking *dugri* implies knowing one's mind and having the courage and confidence to state it in a straightforward and resolute fashion. Informants often contrasted this projection of courage and forcefulness with the stance of hesitancy and defensiveness attributed to diaspora Jews.

The symbolic affirmation of an assertive, fearless, and confident speaking style had clearly gendered overtones. The image of the New Jew was cut in a Western male image—self-assured, uninhibited, forceful, and decisive in his orientation to life. It was a basically masculinist style associated predominantly with the earthiness of the farmer-pioneer on the one hand and of the fighting spirit of the combat soldier on the other. Indeed, as mentioned, over the years the image of the *dugri* speaker became more and more closely linked to the straightforward, pragmatic, and clipped style of the military parlance of professional soldiers. While such men continue to hold prominent positions of power in the political and public service arenas, my forthcoming analysis of the Ori Or Affair, a scandal that involved a former General-turned-politician, suggests far-reaching changes in the cultural positioning of the *dugri* ethos even where these military figures are concerned. These changes, I will argue, are inextricably linked to the decline of the culturally dominant Sabra Ashkenzi ethos associated with Jews of European descent and to an increasing recognition of the multicultural nature of the contemporary Israeli social scene. As will be further exemplified in the forthcoming discussions of the *dugri* interactional code and the *dugri* ritual, the rhetoric of agency is a defining feature of *dugri* speech.

The Attitude of "Antistyle"

The attitude of "antistyle" is another central element in the Sabra *dugri* ethos. Implied in this attitude is the view that stylistic embellishment involves affectation and lack of spontaneity. It finds its expression in a preference for plain, clear-cut, and straightforward talk. The "plainness" of *dugri* speech is not an absence of style but rather a stylistic option, which is anchored in the contrast between the categories of "words" and "deeds." The cultural polarity between these two categories relegates "words" to "mere talk," as is indicated by the proliferation of metalinguistic terms in colloquial Hebrew that denote some form of "blabber" (such as *birburim, palavrot, patpetet*). Deeds, on the other hand, denote the realm of agency, effectiveness, and commitment.

Within this scheme, the valorization of *dugri* speech involves a preference for effective, matter-of-fact, and, hopefully, productive instrumental action. It implies a rejection of the "high rhetoric" modeled by the first generation of Zionist pioneers and visionaries who invested themselves in ideological formulations and pathos-filled proclamations. The elders' explicitly ideological stance was rejected by the Sabra generation of "doers" and dubbed "Zionism in quotes" *(tzionut bemerkha'ot)*. Considered by the young generation of "realizers" as a form of Zionist hypocrisy, this phrase referred to the practice of preaching Zionism—using pathos and high-blown expressions—rather than realizing the call for concrete, productive, manly work in and for the land of Israel. Hence, the Sabras' impatience with verbosity, eloquence, and elaborate expression, and their dread of the glib tongue, a dread that was as proverbial as their thorniness.

The crucial point for our purpose here is that this cultural conception implies an overall devaluation of speech. Crafted speech thus becomes a negative symbol, standing for lack of productive action. The investment in speaking comes to signal a failure to contribute to the accomplishment of communally cherished goals with the full commitment and effectiveness of men-of-deeds. This pragmatic, narrowly instrumental orientation, the emphasis on practical ends—*takhles* in Yiddish, a word borrowed into Hebrew slang as well—was also a rejection of what was perceived to be the ineffectual spirituality and emotionality of diaspora Jews.

A rather touching illustration of this attitude of "antistyle," which colored the speech of male-fighters in the prestate underground units of the Palmah, is presented humorously as self-acknowledged rhetorical ineptitude in Netiva Ben-Yehuda's autobiographical novel *1948— Between Calendars*. In the opening anecdote of the book, she tells about the day the United Nations voted for the establishment of a Jewish state. She was riding a bus as one of a group of soldiers on their way to their newly designated posts, having just completed a military training session that had kept them out of touch with current events for several weeks. On the way, they happened to run into a limousine carrying Golda Meir, and she passed on the great news about the "outbreak of the State" to their young commander, a quintessential Sabra. He felt he had to dignify the moment by saying something appropriately ceremonial to his soldiers, but found himself at a loss for words. Completely disoriented, he urged his aides:

> I am telling you, I have the feeling we must tell something to the guys, and I'm telling you we must do something. We can't leave it just like that, with nothing." And he kept saying: "But what does one say at such a moment?" And he kept pressing: "Sasha, you've read books, you're an all-round egghead, what did others say when a historical moment suddenly landed on them?" And he kept crying: "Just my damned luck. If we only had one of those professional speech-makers here, at least one, why does it have to happen just to me? What do I know about ceremonies, I?"[35]

As we see, the expressive difficulties completely drenched the commander's exultation at the greatness of the moment. He managed to make a short speech, concluding it by explicitly contrasting words and deeds: "I want to say one more thing. Perhaps this was not a great speech. But what does it matter today—speeches. Today what matters is who does what. We're done with 'See, see how beautifully he speaks!' So that's it. So on we go. There's no time. . . . Yes. And good luck with the state!' "[36]

His soldiers, attuned to his groping for an appropriately ceremonial form, recognized his predicament and were both amused and respectful of the "super-human" efforts he made "to match his speech to the historical moment."

This example illustrates the cultural force of the attitude of "anti-style," as well as its felt limitations. However compelling it is for members of the Sabra culture, there are moments when "plain" speech is experienced as inappropriate, and a yearning for greater verbal sophistication is acknowledged. In a similar vein, the author—a paradigmatic *dugri* speaker if ever there was one—at one point laments Israelis' disdain for the noninstrumental aspects of life, their inability to indulge in the playfulness of high culture: "All the things that are important to people in the large world—we have no time for it. We have no patience for the trivialities, the subtleties, the fine distinctions, the gentle differences, the sophistication—for all those things that are called 'culture' in the world. With us—there's not a trace of them."[37]

As I will elaborate later, in discussing the *dugri* ritual we are not dealing simply with the traditional difference between ceremonial and nonceremonial speech.[38] Rather, what is at issue is a difference between two distinct ceremonial idioms. Instrumentality is treated in expressive terms and *dugri* speech constitutes the ceremonial form appropriate to the occasion. Its very plainness provides an expressive vehicle for the self-assertion of cultural members, and thereby a ritual reaffirmation of the Sabra image. In some contexts, such as the historical moment described by Ben-Yehuda, where communal events call for a celebratory idiom, one that embodies more of the artistry and flamboyance of a consciously stylized attitude, the Sabra may well find himself at a loss for words.

My discussion of the attitude of "antistyle" may seem familiar to readers of American prose. Lanham's remarks on American norms of expression bring out some interesting analogies as well as differences between the Sabra and the American versions of the attitude of "antistyle."[39] In both cases, the notion of style is associated with affectation and lack of sincerity, whereas the valorized form of expression, "plain talk," is associated with clarity of expression as an aspect of a moral conception, a "responsibility dialect" on the one hand, and a utilitarian, pragmatic attitude on the other.

There are two notable differences between these versions of straight talk, however. First, the assumed penchant for plain, spontaneous speech in the United States involves a degree of politeness that falls short of the direct, blunt character of *dugri* speech. Secondly, whereas the central contrast in the Sabra ethos is between words and deeds, the central contrast in the American ethos of "plain talk," as described by Lanham, is between words on the one hand and ideas and concepts on the other. Israeli *dugri* speech is about pragmatic instrumentality; American "plain talk" is about the transparency and clarity of transmission. In both cases, the end result in terms of cultural stylistic patterns is a deemphasis on the poetic function of the lingual means, an emphasis on language as a tool. In both interpretations, words are—ideally—to be looked through and not at.

In her insightful analysis of the politics of style in British journalism and other forms of writing as it relates to the norms of "plainness" as a stylistic recommendation, Deborah Cameron points out that "arguments about plain versus more elaborate language have typically arisen in the context of broader moral, ideological and political debates."[40] She further notes that the transparent style that constitutes "good writing" in contemporary English is in fact a complicated construct with multiple symbolic meanings: "Depending on the circumstances and purposes for which it is recommended, it [plain style] can be a populist or anti-elitist gesture or a mark of the writer's good taste, a proof of 'authentic' moral virtues such as honesty and sincerity or a sign of the painstakingly acquired craft skills in which professional writers and editors take pride."[41]

Cameron's detailed analysis of the shifting cultural meanings associated with the aesthetic of plainness in English writing brings out the ideological underpinnings and contextual specificity of "plainness" as a stylistic regime. This line of thinking is supported by my analysis of the attitude of "antistyle" as a multifaceted and culturally embedded stylistic option.

The Accent of Sincerity

For many of my informants, the *dugri* way of speaking is the communicative counterpart of being sincere or being "true to oneself." The term often used was *shalem im atzmi* (whole with myself), pointing to the self-integrity of the person who speaks his or her mind. Another, more literary, expression sometimes used to designate the *dugri* person was *piv velibo shavim* (his mouth is equal to his heart), designating the absence of pretense in social intercourse. *Dugri* speech is also frequently interpreted in terms of the notion of *kenut* (sincerity), which similarly points to the social requirement to give public expression to one's personal thoughts and inner feelings. That is, *dugri* speech, as it is conceived by native speakers of colloquial Hebrew, is intelligible in a cultural world in which the quest for genuine dialogue clearly combines a personal and a social inflection.

Genuine dialogue within this framework does not privilege the tentative process of self-exploration and self-discovery like the one that constituted the early pioneers' soul talks. Rather, *dugri* speech constitutes a discursive vehicle for social action. It is a tool for the expression of deeply held positions and attitudes that links individuals to their public roles. By making their voices heard, *dugri* speakers engage in a remaking of their social world. They do so by reasserting (rather than discovering) their "true self." The quest for genuine dialogue in this case is a search for a public space where personal voices can be freely heard in the context of socially meaningful action. The *dugri* speaker does not engage in a socially alienated search for an authentic self that stands opposed to public roles. Rather, he or she seeks to reinstate a lost symmetry between self and society by transforming both.[42]

The idea of sincerity has been central to Western philosophies out of which grew modern notions of personhood. In an important sense, then, the *dugri* way of speaking finds its credence in the larger matrix of modern Western culture. The concept of sincerity, understood as the congruence between avowal and actual feeling, is predicated upon an interpretation of the notion of the *individual* or *self* as it evolved in the Western world after the Renaissance with the advent of humanism. It has been subject to different interpretations in various European cultural traditions, ranging from sincerity as a form of soul-searching and self-disclosure (as in the pioneers' soul talks or in the American notion of "communication") to sincerity as encoded in *dugri* speech—as an assertive, no-frills, action-oriented, communicative style. As Lionel Trilling pointed out, the ideas of sincerity and authenticity are historically situated. It was only at a certain point in history that people began to think of themselves as intrinsically precious, as something they "must cherish for [their] own sake and show to the world for the sake of good faith."[43]

The Sabra culture's receptivity to the spirit of modern Europe is understandable in view of the fact that the process of secularization that started in Jewish communities throughout Europe at the end of the eighteenth century (associated with the Jewish Enlightenment movement *[haskala]*) was inspired by modern European cultural trends.[44] Thus, the Sabra as New Jew was a product of modernity. Presumably, if the Sabra had been invented at a different point in history, the new Jewish identity and Sabra expressive values would not have been woven around the notion of sincerity and the broader ideational context of which it formed a part. This context, as discussed with reference to the early pioneers' soul talks, included European back-to-nature revolutionary ideologies, such as the German youth culture revolt,[45] and the influence of the Russian populist movement.[46] These movements inspired successive generations of Zionist pioneers who adopted the cult of sincerity, naturalness, and simplicity in various contexts and forms.

An early expression of the ideologically oriented concern with style as related to Israeli speechways is found in the writings of A. D. Gordon (1856–1922), a laborer-philosopher of the early pioneering era whose teachings and personal example greatly influenced the Israeli Labor movement. Gordon emphasized the role of speech in both reflecting and shaping the nation's spirit, and suggested guidelines for what may be viewed as a language planning program on the level of style. Not surprisingly, his formulation contained an outright rejection of decadent European ways of speaking. He argued vehemently for the abolition of deferential address terms, underlining their corruptive impact on the immediacy of human relations. Echoing the ethos of sincerity, he contended that instead of adopting European ways of politeness, the Jews of Israel should introduce into their speech "true, internal politeness deriving from a pure source—from the pure heart and simple soul—politeness which makes no recourse to fancy expressions either in speech or in writing."[47]

Gordon's reference to "internal politeness" brings to mind the introspective mode of authenticating experience that was part of the early pioneers' soul talk ethos (of which he had direct knowledge). But just as in that case, the commitment toward self-making through the enactment of some version of authentic dialogue was socially embedded in a wider social matrix colored by the social injunction to be true to oneself. In both cases, in the pioneers' soul talks and in *dugri* speech, dialogue is a locus of authenticity within the context of an egalitarian, collectivist ethos. Yet despite the threads of similarity between these styles, Sabra *dugri* speech marks a shift from the combination of inner-directedness and interpersonal openness associated with the soul talk ethos. *Dugri* speech epitomizes the paradoxical position of the individual whose search for authenticity, or commitment to the revolutionary project of self-making, becomes socially encoded and mandated as part of a cultural style. In this case, this search is reinterpreted in terms of the spontaneity and naturalness of the sincere individual, whose project of self-making is both a gesture of cultural revolt and a communal venture.

The Ethos of Naturalness

A fourth set of meanings associated with Hebrew *dugri* speech has to do with the notions of naturalness, earthiness, simplicity, and spontaneity associated with the image of the New Jew. I will refer to this dimension as the *naturalness* cluster of meanings. The ethos of naturalness is constructed around the polarity of "nature" and "culture," and has arisen as a counterstatement to what was seen as Jewish bookish tradition on the one hand, and the decadence of bourgeois, European urban culture on the other.

Like the accent of sincerity and the attitude of antistyle, the ethos of naturalness is also rooted in European back-to-nature philosophies that were inspired by the work of Jean Jacques Rousseau (1712–1778)— his protest against the corruptive force of culture, and his promulgation of the ideal of the noble savage. In his prize-winning essay "A Discourse on the Moral Effects of the Arts and Sciences," Rousseau claimed that sincerity and strength were central qualities of the natural man.[48] I have chosen to treat these clusters separately for analytic purposes since they have emerged as distinct, variously emphasized and valorized clusters of meanings in the talk of my informants. The rhetoric of agency, for example, has received a particular cultural coloration in *dugri* speech; the idea of autonomy and strength associated with it has to do only secondarily with the vitality of the natural man and was interpreted primarily with reference to the experience of Jewish victimage.

Mary Douglas's discussion of the role of classification in the construction of the social order provides a helpful terminology with which to formulate the link between a revolutionary cultural orientation and the cultural meanings subsumed under the naturalness cluster.[49] In seeking to free oneself of prevailing classifications that define a no longer acceptable cultural scheme, revolutionary orientations tend to capitalize on the symbolic contrast between culture and nature and to emphasize the "nature" end of this dichotomy. Hence, the emphasis on simplicity, spontaneity, and earthiness. Hence also the inarticulateness and terseness, the distrust of language, which, as a primary tool of classification, becomes the symbol of it.

Indeed, the Sabra culture's elevation of the ethos of naturalness helps to account for some of its central values and for some of the major behavioral displays found in it. The stress on naturalness accords with an emphasis on the elemental, basic, instrumental, survival-oriented necessities of life and with a rejection of the complexities and frivolities of high culture.

The Spirit of Solidarity

Dugri speech, despite its confrontational tones, is associated with the spirit of group solidarity, which I propose to interpret with reference to Victor Turner's notion of *communitas*—the counterstructural, undifferentiated, and egalitarian social relations that link together participants in ritual or backstage contexts of in-betweenness and marginality.[50] The mode of directness, which defines *dugri* speech, can be seen as a routinization of symbolic expressions whose circumstantial and ideational roots are traceable to *communitas*-related contexts. With the domestication of spontaneous *communitas,* the particular symbolic forms generated in it are infused into the mainstream of social life and become part of its approved style, encapsulating the culture's code of living, its ethos, and its worldview.

Dugri speech seems to be a product of both an ideology of *communitas* and a historical phase of social fluidity and lack of structure that was typical of the life circumstances of the early pioneers and their offspring, the first generation Sabras, who, in turn, actualized the spirit of solidarity in their own way. The emotional sharing associated with the spirit of *communitas* marked the solidarity and camaraderie of the youth movement experience. It also permeated the esprit-decorps of paramilitary units in the prestate years (notably the Palmah units), and later the ethos of choice combat units in the Israeli army. Indeed, Turner's list of the properties that contrast liminal spaces of *communitas* with social-structural arenas calls to mind central aspects of the Sabra ethos as discussed by Oring in relation to the Palmah.[51] Both Turner's and Oring's accounts include such properties as directness, simplicity, naturalness, and spontaneity. These echo the cultural meanings associated by my informants with the *dugri* way of speaking.

Studying liminal spaces involves an expansion of sociolinguistic research to encompass not only structural but also "interstructural" social contexts, whether they are spontaneously emergent or deliberately constructed. The study of *dugri* speech thus addresses a dimension of human interaction that has wide-ranging applicability across cultures. Indeed, ethnolinguistic accounts that single out the directness dimension of style are quite common.

The special flavor of *dugri* speech pertains to its role as a confrontational style that is used to invoke a sense of authentic dialogue and thus reaffirm the Sabra culture's "semantic of identity." As we have seen, this version of straight talk has little to do with a quest for factual truth, with an urge to self-disclose, or with notions of "speaking rights" that seem to anchor the directness of mode in various forms of American speech.[52] They have a localized coloring that should be borne in mind as we take a closer look at *dugri* utterances and at *dugri* speech events in the sections that follow.

THE *DUGRI* INTERACTIONAL CODE

By referring to *dugri* exchanges as "confrontational dialogues," I have tried to capture their double quality as at once agonistic and solidarity-oriented. The directness and openness of the *dugri* style mark it as a cultural locus of authenticity within a conception of communication as action, as a means to social coordination. The *dugri* code is not a cultural site through which a communion of souls can be accomplished as were the early pioneers' soul talks. John Peters, inspired by John Dewey's philosophy of communication, highlights the importance of the pragmatic conception of communication that is clearly embedded in the *dugri* mode, referring to it as a form of "pragmatic making-do in community life."[53]

In this view of speech as a form of concerted action, as a way of participating in the creation of a collective world, confrontational talk may acquire particular meanings. Indeed, straight talk that goes under the label of *dugri* speech is culturally constructed as an idiom of participation in a social world in which disagreements can be aired, information is shared openly, and a basic sense of mutuality and trust prevails. It is a world in which individuals are not afraid to speak their minds rather than keep silent or engage in "behind-the-back talk." Confrontation in this scheme of things does not signal a disruption of social relations but rather the ultimate test of a community of purpose and action, whose members are not threatened by the openly expressed opinions of others even when these contradict their own. It is in this sense that *dugri* exchanges become ritualized confrontational dialogues.

Goffman's discussion of expressive regimes can help to understand the role of *dugri* speech as a "ceremonial idiom."[54] This ceremonial idiom is enacted through ritual-interactional gestures that affirm participants' public self-image, or "face." This interactional work, which Goffman terms "facework," is a pervasive feature of everyday interaction. It involves the mutual protection of social images through the recognition of two basic "face-wants": The desire for *autonomy*, that is, the wish to be unimpeded by others, which underwrites the politeness of *nonimposition;* the quest for *solidarity,* that is, the desire to be appreciated by others and connected to them, which underwrites the *politeness of approval.* Taking interactional measures to protect their own face, speakers manage their presentation of self, their *demeanor,* trying to avoid embarrassment. Performing gestures that protect one's interlocutor's face, conversational partners convey considerateness and *deference* toward each other, attempting to avoid offense. Verbal acts that violate either the rules of demeanor or the rules of deference constitute social offenses. To avoid social disruption, such violations are therefore often mitigated in a variety of ways either in the course of their enactment or in retrospect, through corrective action.

Penelope Brown and Stephen Levinson have applied Goffman's discussion of facework in their seminal model of politeness phenomena.[55] This model is designed to account for the mitigating devices interlocutors use in protecting each other's face from violations of face-wants. These violations are referred to in their model as Face-Threatening-Acts (or FTAs). Some threats to one's interlocutor's face relate to the politeness of nonimposition, as in the case of performing directive speech acts, when the other's autonomy is infringed upon by being told what to do. Other threats involve the politeness of approval, when one fails to display a generally expected level of solidarity through signs of agreement, acceptance, or like-mindedness.

The Brown and Levinson model is grounded in a view of actors as rational agents, systematically delineating the linguistic realizations of politeness strategies within a cross-linguistic perspective. It posits a universal concern with face yet at the same time provides a language for describing and accounting for cultural differences in interactional style. Notably, this model focuses on "the universality of rational action devoted to satisfying others' face wants."[56] In Goffman's terms, it thus deals with the politeness of deference, with ways in which speakers address the face-wants of their interlocutors in displaying cooperativeness, not with the politeness of demeanor. The notion of demeanor, which relates to the speaker's own comportment and self-presentation, is not addressed in their model. It becomes crucial, however, when one's goal is to study speech as a form of identity construction, as a cultural display of a localized version of personhood. Given the central role played by *dugri* speech as an idiom of cultural self-making, as a vehicle for the construction of the Sabra image, issues of demeanor must figure prominently in its analysis as a way of speaking.

The account of *dugri* speech in face-work terms implicates two levels of analysis, which refer to the social and to the cultural dimensions of speech conduct. In social-situational terms, the performance of a *dugri* utterance constitutes a threat to the interlocutor's face, as it is used to signal disagreement, suggesting that the desire to speak one's mind overrides the desire to secure approval. In saying, "I'll tell you dugri, I have a different take on this," the speaker explicitly foregoes the opportunity to convey agreement. He or she could have wrapped up the disagreement in terms that would more clearly suggest a desire to maintain shared ground, as in saying, "I see what you mean, but I see this differently."

In cultural terms, however, within the context of the *dugri* ethos, a speaker's directness of style, which involves a willingness to violate the social norms governing the politeness of approval, is taken to be a sign of a more embracing solidarity. It is a solidarity grounded in a shared cultural commitment to the meanings and values of the Sabra ethos, which serve as warrants for the use of straight talk (the strategy of speaking bald-on-record, in Brown and Levinson's terminology).[57] Thus, the face-violations involved in employing the *dugri* mode are part of the in-group language that signals solidarity. They are not considered face-threatening-acts in the way they might be interpreted in other cultural contexts. The analytic approach employed here for the study of *dugri* speech, therefore, draws on Brown and Levinson's face-work model as well as extends it in some ways.

Even though *dugri* speech is a culturally coded version of the bald-on-record strategy, as described by Brown and Levinson, the explicit use of the term *dugri* in prefacing an utterance (as in the aforementioned "I'll tell you *dugri*, " constructions) in fact functions so as to mitigate its face-threatening force. This use of the term *dugri* as an indexical sign, or "indicating device,"[58] in what I call "explicit *dugri* utterances," is highly instructive. A closer look at such utterances can help us elucidate some of the subtler ways in which *dugri* speech performs its communicative functions.

Explicit *Dugri* Utterances

The employment of explicit *dugri* utterances defines the interactional context in which they occur as involving a conscious, hopefully consensual, suspension of face-concerns that would normally be expected to hold. Such utterances articulate speakers' metacommunicative judgments regarding the directness of their talk in a spontaneous, explicit, and structurally recognizable way. The study of *dugri* utterances, whose intended directness is made visible by the use of a *dugri* preface, can therefore provide a source of data that supplements the data obtained from observations of talk that I or my informants have intuitively identified as *dugri*.

The "I'll tell you *dugri*" prefix can be followed by speech-acts expressing thoughts and opinions. They are not articulations of emotional states, although they are inherently subjective speech-acts whose purpose is to ascribe a judgment rather than to deal with questions of truth and falsity.[59] These judgments are perceived by the speaker to contradict those of the hearer, and their verbalization is accompanied by a defiant, confrontational tone. As one informant colorfully put it, on hearing "I'll tell you *dugri*," she feels as if an internal alarm has been sounded, and she slips into a combative mood, ready for a confrontation. The contentious tone attending the use of "I'll tell you *dugri*" relates to the assumed disagreement between speaker and addressee, not to the actual content of the utterances. Typical examples of such devices are prefixes that appear in the following:

1 "I'll tell you *dugri*, this is getting too technical for me."
2 "Tell me *dugri*, what do you want me to do?"
3 "You can ask me *dugri*, I've got nothing to hide."

The very choice of using an indicating device to preface a straightforward statement suggests a recognition of the addressee's face-concerns, as compared to the employment of unmitigated *dugri* statements or questions. The particular choice of *dugri* rather than some other possible form of mitigation invokes the cultural meanings associated with this particular term. Specific *dugri* utterances provide a specific warrant for the violation of the addressee's face-wants, mobilizing the symbolic dimension of the term "*dugri*" as a speech sign to legitimate the interactional transgressions it apparently involves. They therefore provide an intriguing example for the intermeshing of these two levels of meaning in the use of a single speech sign. By attending to both the symbolic and the indexical dimension of *dugri*, we can learn not only what it means but also how it means to its users.

The particular flavor of explicit *dugri* utterances can be elucidated by comparing them to straight talk that is not encompassed within the *dugri* frame, such as statements framed by "I'll tell you the truth. . . ." Statements using the latter indicating device (such as "I'll tell you the truth, this is getting too technical for me") do not share the indexical meaning of *dugri* as a speech sign—its punch-like, action-impelling communicative effect within the situational context in which it is enacted. What, then, is the difference between saying

"I'll tell you *dugri*, this is getting too technical for me"

and saying

"I'll tell you the truth, this is getting too technical for me"?

As I will try to show, these two indicating devices signal subtle differences in the kind of mitigation function that accompanies the use of what the speaker perceives to be a straightforward statement. These differences can be pointed out with reference to the two levels of analysis mentioned earlier: the level of social-situational meanings and the level of cultural meanings. At the level of social-situational meanings, both these indicating devices reflect the speaker's concern with face: they prepare the addressee for the forthcoming face-threatening act, thus facilitating his or her maintenance of demeanor. On the level of cultural meanings, however, they differ in that each provides a different warrant for the performance of the face-threatening act.

Utterances containing "I'll tell you the truth" do not involve a stance of disagreement or a challenge to the other's position. Rather, they are markers of self-disclosure. In disclosing discrediting information about oneself, the speaker fails to uphold the public self-image he or she would like to claim. As noted, the use of "I'll tell you *dugri*" mitigates a potential threat to the addressee's face and is oriented to matters of *deference,* in Goffman's terms. On the other hand, the use of "I'll tell you the truth" mitigates a potential threat to the speaker's own face and is therefore oriented to matters of *demeanor.*

This suggests that even in contexts in which both devices could be appropriately used, they would not be interchangeable. Although in using either of these devices the speaker appeals to the notion of authenticity as a warrant for the performance of a face-threatening act, each device reflects a different focus and a different interpretation of this overarching warrant. In neither case are they interpreted as an appeal to the factual rendering of information. Rather, they signal different interpretations of the *social* meaning of the utterance involved. Clearly, in speaking *dugri,* one also reveals something of the self, whereas self-disclosive acts can be impositions on the hearer. It is precisely because these possibilities exist that the speaker's choice of indicating device serves to orient the addressee toward a particular interpretative path. In the case of *dugri,* the focus is on straight talk despite possible offense to the hearer. In the case of "I'll tell you the truth," the focus is on openness despite possible risk to the speaker.

In using an explicit *dugri* utterance, the speaker cannot readily assume that straight talk is acceptable, but he or she may test this possibility by using the *dugri* indicating device, thereby creating a social context in which straight talk is appropriate. This observation is reinforced by informants' comments concerning constraints on the use of explicit *dugri* utterances in different kinds of encounters. In talk with intimates, using the *dugri* indicating device is felt to be out of place, as the conditions for straight talk are assumed to be unequivocally there. In encounters involving considerable interpersonal distance, when total strangers meet, and it is clear that no solidarity may be appropriately invoked, an explicit *dugri* utterance cannot be used to redefine the situation as one in which straight talk is called for. For *dugri* to perform a creative function sociolinguistically speaking, it must be employed in contexts where the shift to a "backstage" communicative code is appropriate. Usually, such a transformation is accomplished rather smoothly. At times, however, a speaker may misjudge the relational context, and the attempt to redefine it may be aborted. This was the case in a comment I overheard an older person make to a younger one: "Don't start this *dugri* business with me. I'm not your buddy."

In the terminology employed by Michael Silverstein, the *dugri* indicating device functions as a *creative* rather than as a *presupposing index*. As a creative index, it redefines rather than merely reflects the social situation by making implicit aspects of the ongoing interaction explicit and overt. In Silverstein's terms, creative indexes are most important when "the occurrence of a speech signal is the only overt sign of the contextual parameter, verifiable, perhaps, by other, co-occurring behaviors in other media, but nevertheless the most salient index of the specific value."[60]

Some uses of the *dugri* index are more creative than others, depending on whether other signals of shared affiliation are present in other forms (such as dress, posture, or other nonverbal behaviors), and on the extent to which the speaker can assume such an affiliation. When no other comparable signals exist and interpersonal distance is great, the use of such an indicator carries its greatest creative force, and is interpreted as an indication of the speaker's desire to decrease social distance. In attempting to do so, the speaker legitimates the use of the *dugri* code by emphasizing what he or she shares with the addressee rather than what sets them apart. In cases in which other signals are present, and/or the speaker perceives himself or herself to be on familiar terms with the addressee—though not close enough for the unchecked use of "backstage" language—the indicator serves a less creative function. It acts more as a social reminder than as a context-defining element. Notably, some informants claimed that the use of the "I'll tell you *dugri*/the truth" indicating devices tends to rouse their suspicion, suggesting to them that the speaker is manipulative and insincere. As several of them put it: "Someone who needs to declare that he is *dugri* is probably not really *dugri*." In these cases, the indicator clearly fails to accomplish its creative function.

As was suggested earlier, the analysis of *dugri* utterances—whether explicit or not—must take into account two types of meanings: social and cultural. From the standpoint of social-situational meanings, *dugri* utterances are claimed to pose a threat to the addressee's face. This is felt to be warranted by the high cultural value placed on the speaker's self-assertion on the one hand and on the uninhibited flow of social information that characterizes close-knit, solidary social units on the other. Thus, from the standpoint of cultural meanings, *dugri* speech is both speaker-focused and communally oriented.

Within the Sabra ethos, the *dugri* way of speaking has acquired symbolic value in the display and affirmation of character. When appropriately employed, *dugri* speech affirms both a sense of self and a sense of communal participation. Indeed, refraining from speaking *dugri* when this is warranted would be self-diminishing—a failure to uphold the public self-image a proper Sabra would want to project. This would, at the same time, prevent the generation of the sense of community and trust that uninhibited, direct, yet solidary, expression can be hoped to create. Thus, despite their recognition of the bluntness of their *dugri* talk, some of my informants expressed annoyance at people who were not able to respond to it graciously and were visibly hurt by its blunt edge. Taking a *dugri* comment as an insult is not only a failure to act like a Sabra, it also aborts the speaker's attempt to play out this cultural role appropriately.

More poignantly yet, in discussing *dugri* speech with self-proclaimed quintessential Sabras, those who claimed they would speak *dugri* under any circumstances, I came to realize that their understanding of this version of straight talk was strongly colored by their culture-specific interpretation of the meaning of "facework" itself. Echoing the cultural meanings associated with *dugri* speech (as discussed earlier), they said that in speaking *dugri* they displayed respect for their conversational partner as a person who was strong and forthright enough to accept *dugri* comments and to function within a *dugri* relationship. People who have to be "treated with silk gloves," as some informants put it, cannot command true respect. Within this interpretation, it is in refraining from *dugri* speech that one displays lack of respect for the hearer. That is, paradigmatic *dugri* speakers do not disregard the hearer's face wants, but they interpret the interactional dance Goffman refers to as "facework" within a culture-specific framework that privileges the stamina of those who can engage in unadorned, *dugri* exchanges. Within this interpretive framework, respect, rather than considerateness, is the issue, and both demeanor and deference are measured in terms of interactants' willingness to engage in straight talk. Thus, the case of *dugri* speech indicates that speech communities vary not only in terms of the specific norms governing "facework" but also in terms of the weight and specific interpretation they assign to "facework" in organizing members' social interaction.

The foregoing analysis has demonstrated that explicit *dugri* utterances, as tokens of *dugri* speech, serve many interactional functions in terms of both the social and cultural meanings of the statements in which they are embedded. As speech signs, *dugri* indicating devices emphasize the speakers' concern with face. The analysis of these devices, I have argued, requires an extension of the Brown and Levinson model of politeness strategies in order to accommodate issues related to the speaker's demeanor. The case of *dugri* speech suggests that the ethnographic study of ways of speaking must go beyond the investigation of devices and strategies and acknowledge the role played by cultural meanings and speech ideologies in the shaping of culturally focal speech styles.

Whereas *dugri* utterances may occur sporadically in casual conversation, coloring the relational context to a greater or lesser degree, on some occasions they actually define the speech situation, producing a speech event type referred to by cultural members as "a *dugri* talk" *(siha dugrit)*. Having elucidated the main features of the *dugri* interactional code, I now turn to an exploration of "*dugri* talks" as culturally distinctive speech events whose study can deepen our understanding of *dugri* speech as a ceremonial idiom.

THE *DUGRI* RITUAL

A *dugri* talk is not just any encounter in which the *dugri* idiom is employed or in which utterances indexed as *dugri* are exchanged. A *dugri* talk is a distinct type of speech event with a sequential and motivational structure of its own that can be viewed as a verbal ritual (see below). Thus, although a *dugri* talk implies *dugri* speech, speaking *dugri* does not necessarily imply the staging of a *dugri* talk. Indeed, informants clearly distinguished between the two, making repeated references to encounters they described as "*siha dugrit*." In considering a *dugri* talk as a speech event, I will move beyond the single utterance or single speech-act level of analysis and examine larger discourse units and their episodic and ritual structure.

Several typical enactments of the *dugri* ritual appear in my data under the heading of "*siha dugrit.*" They involve interactions in the workplace—that is, in an organizational context that clearly relates to the social modality of *societas*, with its system of differentiated roles and statuses. In one case, an engineer in his early thirties told me at some length about a *dugri* talk he initiated with his boss. He started what he described in retrospect as "*siha dugrit*" by declaring: "I want to speak to you *dugri*. I don't like the way this department is being run." In another case, a young faculty member of approximately the same age (whom some of his colleagues had independently identified as a *dugri* fellow) initiated what he referred to as "*siha dugrit*" with one of the senior professors in his department just as he was being put up for tenure, criticizing the way things were run. He prefaced his list of complaints by saying that he wanted to voice his opinion before he got tenure so that no one could say he had been afraid to speak his mind before his job was secure. The forthcoming analysis should clarify what these two men were up to.

Another example of what I would call "a *dugri* ritual" to which I myself was witness brought home to me its compelling force in a most vivid way. It took place during a meeting between a group of university faculty and representatives of the Ministry of Education who had sought the academics' assistance in setting up some new extracurricular programs for elementary school children. In previous meetings, there had been some fundamental differences of opinion between a number of these academics and the ministry people on the nature of the proposed programs and the kind of involvement expected from the academics. The meeting opened with a lengthy conciliatory speech by a ministry representative in which he acknowledged the validity of the academics' view that educational efforts should be directed toward the improvement of regular schooling, but pointed out the constraints under which the ministry was operating. These had led them to plan the proposed programs. He expressed the need to bridge over differences and reach a working consensus.

One of the university professors, a first-generation Sabra, who had initially demanded a principled discussion of the cooperation proposed, changed the tone of the encounter by initiating a version of the *dugri* ritual. Using blunt language and a confrontational tone, she argued that the university should not play the role of educational contractor for the ministry and should become involved only with programs that called for and permitted the exploration and rethinking of educational issues and policies. She said that as long as children's regular schooling was allowed to be meaningless, there was no point in establishing extracurricular programs. She stressed that she had no problem helping those programs in her field of expertise and would do so if asked, but refused to share in the pretense that anything of substance was being done for the children. She concluded by saying that she would not lend her name to something she did not believe in.

This event provided me with a live, prototypical example of the *dugri* ritual as it will be characterized later. Its initiator, who was familiar with my work, turned to me shortly after the event and, half triumphant, half embarrassed, said: "Well, there, I gave you an example of a *dugri* ritual." Neither she as initiator nor I as peripheral participant had been at all self-conscious while this was happening, but both of us readily recognized the ritual dimensions of the exchange after the event, and could discuss our interpretation of it in the terms employed in the forthcoming analysis.

Notably, unlike the tenure situation, this case did not involve a clear-cut hierarchical relationship but rather an attempt to prevent the incorporation of the academics into the educational establishment. It was a ceremony of discord, performed in the culture's legitimizing idiom: the idiom in which one's personal integrity and one's shared cultural world are reaffirmed. The use of *dugri* speech here, as in all other cases of its ritual enactment, served to counteract what in the Sabra culture is considered the tendency to gloss over interpersonal differences in the service of a false, superficial consensus, a concern with harmony in interpersonal relations at the expense of dealing with basic issues and matters of principled opinion. In a way somewhat reminiscent of the interactional texture of some of the early pioneers' soul talks, despite the discomfort caused by its confrontational tone, the *dugri* ritual was experienced as a moment of true contact, of unmasking, and was received as both legitimate and appropriate even by participants whose own style was a far cry from *dugri* speech.

I am not claiming that participants consciously recognize the ritual dimensions of a *dugri* talk. What I propose to do is to apply the ritual metaphor to encounters referred to by my informants as "a *dugri* talk" so as to shed some light on what I perceive to be its ritual dimensions. In what follows, I show that the *dugri* ritual manifests a recognizable pattern of symbolic actions whose function includes the reaffirmation of participants' relationship to what can be considered a culturally sanctioned "sacred object"—their self-identity as Sabras. A *dugri* talk can be seen as providing a context in which the meanings and values associated with *dugri* speech are encapsulated and dramatized. In particular, it is a context in which the image of the Sabra as the dauntless, committed, and sincere New Jew is reaffirmed through a ritualized test of verbal confrontation.

Thus, despite the discordant note associated with it, the *dugri* ritual manifests the functional nature of conflict as an integrative force in the life of individuals and groups. As Simmel has pointed out, conflict no less than cooperative social engagements should be conceptually distinguished from indifference and a refusal of contact.[61] The agonistic behavior that constitutes the *dugri* ritual is perceived by members of the culture as a sign of authentic engagement and commitment. Frequently used native terms for this motivational pattern would be *me'oravut* (involvement) or *ihpatiyut* (concern for others or for public issues). As conduct that is both self-assertive and communally oriented, it is contrasted with indifference, with self-absorption, or with anti-social behavior. Both indifference and self-absorption signal alienation from one's social world. Enactments of the *dugri* ritual therefore provide reassurance that one is socially engaged.

THE FORM AND FUNCTION OF A *DUGRI* TALK

The forthcoming account of the *dugri* ritual offers a variant of Dell Hymes's well-known schema for the study of speech events, which was proposed as a heuristic input for ethnographic descriptions. It includes the following components: message form, message content, setting, scene, participants, ends (further divided into goals and outcomes), key, channels, instrumentalities (or forms of speech), and norms of interaction and interpretation.[62] These categories, though analytically distinguishable, often blend into each other in the description of actual speech events, as is the case at various points in the following account.

Participation Structures and Interactional Norms

Although the *dugri* ritual marks an interactional shift of gears that results in the social leveling of the participants, this does not imply that there is an interactional symmetry between them. In fact, the ritual is organized in terms of two clearly differentiated interactional roles. The first is the role of the initiator, the person who has a protest to voice and who defines the situation as calling for the enactment of the *dugri* ritual. The initiator challenges the addressee's position by expounding his or her views. This role involves personal choice and therefore implies a measure of self-expression. The second is the role of the respondent, the person whose position or paradigm is being challenged. The ritual is primarily the initiator's; the respondent's role is secondary. The latter contributes mainly by being attentive to and accepting of the initiator's attempt to stage his or her "drama of character."

The poignancy of the *dugri* ritual is greatest when the initiator has less power than the addressee in social-structural terms (for example, the employee compared to the boss in the workplace), and when no appeal can be made to institutional rights so as to warrant outspokenness. When the ritual is initiated by the more powerful person in such a relationship (e.g., the boss in the workplace), its enactment implies that the initiator either cannot or refuses to appeal to his or her institutional power. Whether a person's place in a hierarchy precludes outspokenness, or whether a person is unwilling or unable to mobilize his or her power-based right to speak, the *dugri* ritual is a culturally available format for sidestepping the bounds of *societas*. The confrontational encounter provides an arena for the assertion of character. At the same time it is softened by the spirit of solidarity upon which it is modeled. Its ritual containment prevents it from radically affecting participants' structural relations outside of the ritual framework, while it provides a forum for the airing of discontent and for affecting future action.

Thus, participants in the *dugri* ritual must be linked through suspendable social-structural bonds, but at the same time they must share the Sabra interactional code that serves to ritually invoke the spirit of *communitas* within the context of the *dugri* talk. In contacts between Sabras and outsiders to the culture who are neither familiar with nor inclined to accept the *dugri* idiom, the staging of the ritual is felt to be utterly inappropriate. A context in which the re-creation of *communitas* through direct, confrontational, *dugri* speech is neither intelligible nor legitimate is that of diplomatic encounters. In fact, one of the informants often contrasted the term *dugriyut* with the notion of "diplomacy." Diplomatic encounters probably stand at the farthest remove from *dugri* talks. Diplomacy with its air of caution, tentativeness, and stylization can hardly accommodate the *dugri* speaker's preference for a clear-cut, unambiguous, confrontational idiom. When this is forgotten or deliberately ignored, the result can be confusing as well as disconcerting. An example of such an occasion involved a meeting between former General and later Prime Minister

Ariel Sharon with American Special Ambassador Philip Habib during the 1982 Lebanon War, when Sharon was Minister of Defense. On that occasion, he seemed to have stretched the directness of the Sabra style beyond its customary bounds, taking it outside the boundaries of the speech community in which it finds its legitimacy.

Thus, a news headline in the evening paper *Ma'ariv* reported that "Habib needed medical treatment after a talk with Sharon." The subheading consisted of an anonymous citation stating that "Habib was on the verge of a heart attack," apparently as a result of the fact that "Sharon employed a tough, resolute and blunt style." The body of the article stated: "The protocol of the Habib-Sharon talk indicates that, indeed, it was not a routine conversation. The minister of defense, in his open and direct way of speaking, told the American intermediary what was on his mind, given the lack of progress in the negotiation which costs Israel human lives."[63]

In fact, this conversation triggered a diplomatic incident as well as puzzlement at Israel's intentions and, apparently, a misinterpretation of its political stance. Although he had been invited to Jerusalem by Sharon on Begin's behalf, Habib seemed to have interpreted Sharon's straight talk on that occasion as a signal that Israel had despaired of the diplomatic effort. In this as in other communicative contexts, the way things were said carried more weight than their actual content. Thus, in the English-language daily newspaper of the same day, the *Jerusalem Post*, Wolf Blitzer reported that the American ambassador to Israel, Mr. Lewis, had complained to Prime Minister Begin on behalf of the U.S. government of Sharon's brusqueness with Habib. The Prime Minister apparently endorsed both the positions put forward by Sharon and the straightforward style he had employed.

We see, then, that the *dugri* ritual involves the suspension or reinterpretation of societal norms of "facework" and the adoption of an alternative set of interactional norms. These alternative norms are predicated on a cultural ideal of personal worth and on a culture-specific interpretation of the nature and role of "facework." The performance of the *dugri* ritual is governed by two complementary interactional norms:

1 The initiator, having defined the situation (to himself/herself and to others) as involving a rhetorical exigency, is expected to initiate the *dugri* ritual in an attempt to motivate the addressee to correct it.

2 The addressee, at the same time, is required to accept the *dugri* approach in good spirit and to refrain from interpreting it as a personal affront.

As we have seen, and as will be further illustrated later on, outsiders to the culture who do not share this normative code may either misinterpret it or reject it outright.

The Speech Situation: Setting and Scene

A *dugri* talk is a somewhat formal event and has to be set up in terms of time and place. It is not initiated casually. Typically, the initiator informs the addressee that he or she wishes to have a talk and will wait for an appropriate time or place to be suggested. This occurs when he or she is willing to oblige the addressee by limiting participation and conducting the talk in an inner office or some other private space. When this is not practicable (as in the aforementioned meeting between academics and Ministry of Education personnel), the ritual is enacted in a public domain, in view and hearing of other participants, who become an audience for the initiator's self-dramatization no less than the addressee.

My informants' characterization of the psychological scene of a *dugri* talk, as one calling for corrective action, protest, or challenge, marks it as a rhetorical situation in Lloyd Bitzer's terms.[64] A social situation can be described as rhetorical when it is interpreted as involving a rhetorical exigency—a situation which calls for a corrective rhetorical act. It is a rhetorical exigency because it is believed that it can be positively modified and that this modification requires or is assisted by the use of discourse. Thus, in order for a member of the culture to initiate the *dugri* ritual, he or she should:

1 Define the situation as involving a rhetorical exigency, that is, as requiring a remedy to be achieved through discourse.
2 Define the addressee as a rhetorical audience, one of a category of persons who can be influenced by discourse and become mediators of change.
3 Feel a moral obligation and commitment to interpret the situation as one addressed to himself or herself.
4 Feel that he or she has the right to confront the addressee in demanding the correction of the situation.

The initiation of the *dugri* ritual, then, can be regarded as a rhetorical move that is "a fitting response to a situation which needs and invites it."[65] It is predicated on a sense of communal participation interpreted both as an obligation and a right to have one's say and to influence one's social world in the direction one sees fit. This was revealed most clearly when informants repeatedly cited two contexts in which they would not stage a *dugri* talk. The first context involved situations in which speaking *dugri* was felt to be ineffective, "would make no difference," or "would not change anything." The second type of context involved situations in which the informant felt he or she had no stake. People said they would not bother to speak *dugri,* let alone initiate a *dugri* talk, if they did not care whether things would change or not. The *dugri* ritual provides a way of articulating one's sense of commitment and a context for the self-dramatization of the person who is prepared to speak up. Therefore, even when the initiator does not really hope that much can be accomplished through the enactment of a *dugri* talk, it is nevertheless not considered futile. Rather, it is perceived to serve as a link in a change-producing chain of action by signaling division and lack of consensus.

In the context of the *dugri* ritual, the disagreements are not only acknowledged but also intensified by the initiator's refusal to gloss over fundamental differences for the sake of maintaining the appearance of harmony, to "plaster" over the issues *(letaye'ah)*, as the prevailing metaphor has it. There is no expectation, however, that the ritual confrontation would lead to the resolution of these differences. In fact, those who reported about *dugri* talks they had initiated indicated that they would have been embarrassed if the addressee were to readily concede and declare a change of opinion. This would have meant that the initiator's "drama of character" had exceeded its stage. Immediate resolution thus implies a misjudgment, because to overdramatize one's "character" implies loss of face no less than to efface it.

The Ritual Message: Contents and Functions

The *dugri* ritual is a multifunctional affair. Its purposes (or ends) pertain to the participants' psychic life, to their definition of their social task, to their construction of their cultural identity, and to their communal affiliation. As noted earlier, in terms of its content, the *dugri* ritual involves the initiator's protest against a state of affairs the addressee upholds, or, as is often the case, is in some way responsible for. The situation protested against may be formulated as an issue related to the public good or to one's personal or group interest. In either case it tends to be cast in ethical terms and to deal with basic tenets and principles of moral and social life. The protest against "the way the department is being run," for example, was thus a way of challenging undemocratic management procedures, and the criticism of a university department was presented as a defense of academic standards.

In fact, differences of opinion that cannot be readily dealt with in discussion between the participants would not be proper candidates for a *dugri* ritual. This ritual, like the "griping ritual" I have studied elsewhere,[66] is not a problem-solving session, although it takes problematic issues as its topic. Whatever the subject of the *dugri* ritual, its underlying theme is the tension between dissensus and affiliation: the initiator, through an act of protest and self-assertion, disassociates him- or herself from a given structural or personal relationship while at the same time asserting a deeper affiliation of a more basic and a more compelling nature.

The form in which this tension is expressed and resolved seems to be rooted as much in traditional Jewish culture as in a revolutionary communal orientation. The actualization of the individual in and through communal affiliation is a longstanding theme in Judaic culture.[67] A traditional ritual context in which this conception is dramatized is that of public prayer, whose symbolic structure has been insightfully analyzed by Prell-Foldes.[68] Jewish public prayer, and the *dugri* ritual in its very different but structurally parallel fashion, both demonstrate the possibility of interweaving individuality and communal orientation in constituting members' sense of self. The early pioneers' soul talks, as we have seen, constitute another arena socially structured by this kind of fusion.

For the initiator, the enactment of the ritual has a clear cathartic function. It provides a ritual context in which to release pent-up frustrations with respect to one's social place or social relationships. It is generally felt that for the initiator the main outcome of the ritual is a sense of increased confidence and control, the satisfaction that goes with self-assertion, with not being "afraid to speak up." For the addressee, particularly in those cases in which he or she has power over the initiator, the *dugri* talk is a cultural channel through which to obtain social information that may otherwise remain unavailable. At times, the *dugri* ritual can also allow for the redefinition and clarification of social positions. From the communal point of view, the *dugri* ritual reaffirms participants' cultural identities and shared affiliation.

It encapsulates the whole spectrum of cultural meanings and values associated with *dugri* speech and suggests a model—more for than of—the ideal person and authentic human relations.

The Shape of Talk

The explicitness and clarity of expression associated with the *dugri* interactional code are also manifested in the form of the messages conveyed in a *dugri* talk. Speech exchanged in such talks avoids ambiguities and elaborate expressions that might render interpretation less immediate and clear-cut. In staging a *dugri* talk, the initiator ritually triggers a sequence of events propelled by a *dugri* statement that is a violation of interactants' implicit agreement to maintain their own and each other's faces. This breach dramatizes the possibility of a cultural paradigm that involves a reinterpretation of the notion of face and suggests an alternative mode of human bonding. The breach is not the outburst of the person blowing his or her top or the recklessness of rebels burning bridges behind them. Rather, its intensity is contained, encased in a ritual framework. The social drama that is triggered by such a breach does not develop beyond its initial crisis phase—nor is it expected to. The agonistic ritual fulfills its function precisely by creating and culturally locating a state of crisis that remains unresolved. It thus both indexes the existence of conflict and capitalizes on it, suggesting the possibility of change within a culturally sanctioned framework.

There is a generally recognized pattern in the sequence of symbolic acts comprising the *dugri* ritual. As noted, a *dugri* talk tends to be prearranged in some way, often through the initiator's suggestion. The initiator may indicate that the discussion falls into the category of a *dugri* ritual by saying: "I want to/I must/let me speak to you *dugri*," or "I want to be sincere with you," or the like. This use of the *dugri* index has a clearly creative function. It establishes a ritual context within which straight talk is culturally sanctioned. The addressee briefly signals agreement to enact the *dugri* ritual by indicating that the initiator can proceed. Most of the event consists of the initiator's protest; the addressee may make some counterclaims, but not vigorously. His or her position is well known; it is the challenge to it that is the issue.

It is in confrontational situations that a person's ability to act is brought to a head. Therefore, looking for a fight is a common way to test and reaffirm one's actional potential. In a sense, the *dugri* ritual as an agonistic ritual genre provides a safely circumscribed context for such a test. In making his or her protest, the initiator of the *dugri* ritual dramatizes the choice of action over restraint and acquiescence. The ritual thus provides a generic form through which members can reaffirm the cultural value attached to action that for them spells mastery, strength, and autonomy—hence, dignified survival.[69]

The ritual, when successfully accomplished, is terminated with a sense of relief, sometimes verbalized by the initiator's statement that "I have done my part" and the addressee's reply "Okay, I've heard you." At times, participants may express gratitude for the enactment of the *dugri* talk (such as "Thank you for your frankness" or "I appreciate the fact that I could be frank"). This last step helps to take participants back smoothly into the realm of *societas,* implicitly reaffirming the interactional norms applicable to it.

Since the *dugri* ritual is typically associated with spoken, face-to-face encounters, it also involves directness in the sense of unmediated communication and immediacy of contact. There are interesting nonverbal concomitants to the enactment of this conversational ritual that involve the display of a stance of resoluteness and sincerity—such as eye contact and a well-controlled, tense posture. Both in its movement and in its verbal thrust, speaking *dugri* can be metaphorically regarded as a punch: it is direct, strong, and quick. Thus, a person who projects a resolute or sincere image in his or her verbal behavior, but whose nonverbal behavior is felt to undermine this claim, is not judged credible in the attempt to enact the *dugri* ritual.

Similarly, a person who projects sincerity but speaks hesitantly and in a low-key manner, or whose posture is relaxed and noncommittal, is not likely to be judged as properly enacting the *dugri* ritual either. These considerations came up frequently in discussions of the *dugri* quality of various public figures who are mainly observed on television. Informants listed a variety of specific nonverbal displays that disqualified a person from being considered *dugri*. These included mostly postural tendencies such as fidgeting or shifty eyes.[70]

In terms of its feeling-tone or affective coloring, the *dugri* ritual can be characterized as an emotionally charged speech event: it is dominated by a sense of "something important being at stake," as one informant put it, and also by the intensity accompanying confrontational exchanges. Despite the opposition and confrontation involved, the tone is one of contained, rather stylized, somewhat impersonal anger. It differs significantly from the outburst that tends to accompany conflicts grounded in the clash of personal interests and contrasting desires.

Since the ritual roles of the participants are asymmetrical, they differ in the tone accompanying their respective performances. The initiator, as noted earlier, has to exude an air of resoluteness, sincerity, and defiance. The addressee must maintain his or her composure and accept the initiator's protest, projecting the image of the forthright person who is prepared to take criticism "without becoming personal about it," as one person put it. Thus, both participants, in their own way, pay homage to the image of the person of character.

In sum, an ideal *dugri* speaker should both speak *dugri* when this is called for and respond to *dugri* speech addressed to him or her in a fitting manner. Some of my informants made biting comments about Sabras who speak *dugri* but recoil when such speech is addressed to them. *Dugri* speech, then, especially as enacted in the *dugri* ritual, generates a dialogic moment that is both confrontational and cooperative in orientation, and whose expressive function is to affirm shared identity and membership in the Sabra culture.

The image of the authentic Sabra is thus communicatively constructed out of this distinctive type of confrontational dialogue. As a model for ways of being an Israeli it has been disseminated in myriad ways during its years of cultural dominance, especially through literature and popular culture. From the very first, newcomers to the land were expected to learn to be like, act like, and speak like Sabras. Netiva Ben-Yehuda described the coercive nature of this dissemination process in her aforementioned autobiographical book *1948—Between Calendars,* to whose more detailed consideration I will turn in the next section. As she put it, new immigrants got a clear-cut silencing message: "If you can't speak like us, then shut up."[71] Thus, the *dugri* ethos, like all cultural codes that serve an identity function, such as the soul talk ethos discussed in the previous chapter, is about exclusion no less than about inclusion.

Ben-Yehuda's retrospective account, written three decades after the events narrated in it, provides a further, more self-aware, layer of dissemination for the image of the *dugri*-speaking Sabra. It presents a complex portrait of the Sabra world, one that is offered as a corrective to the eulogizing that had been typical of the literature depicting that generation. As I will show, the publication of the novel constituted a public reenactment of a *dugri* ritual, transmitting its dialogic qualities through the printed page. In what follows, I analyze this publicly enacted ritual in terms of Victor Turner's notion of a social drama, a normative rupture that eventually leads to a state of reintegration. I then attend to another conflictual public event through whose unfolding the *dugri* code became widely disseminated and renegotiated. My second "case study," the Ori Or Affair, culminated in a schism. The cultural negotiations surrounding these two public occasions demonstrate the promise as well as the precariousness involved in the dissemination of the *dugri* ritual across time and social space.

The *Dugri* Idiom in Social Drama

The cultural negotiations surrounding *dugri* speech and the Sabra image became publicly visible in conjunction with two events that can be illuminated within the analytic framework proposed by Turner's processual unit of a social drama, which was discussed in the introduction to this book. Turner has pointed out that the study of social dramas is particularly rewarding since conflict brings into view fundamental aspects of society, which normally remain submerged. In such conflict situations, people find themselves taking sides "in terms of deeply entrenched moral imperatives and constraints, often against their own personal preferences."[72]

The following discussion of two publicly visible social dramas as they relate to the employment of *dugri* speech further helps to explore the ways in which the *dugri* speech style has been implicated in cultural contestation and in cultural change. If my account is persuasive, it may also have more general methodological implications for the study of ways of speaking and the attempt to relate them to larger cultural concerns. From the standpoint of cultural analysis, I try to show that just as our understanding of the texture and structure of the *dugri* ritual was enhanced by considering it in relation to the notion of social drama, so our understanding of particular public events, which manifest the phased structure and oppositional nature of social dramas, can be enhanced by considering them with reference to the *dugri* code and its ritual functions.

Let me, then, turn to an examination of two public events whose interpretive reading forms the substance of my argument. The first involved the publication in 1981 of what was then considered a provocative autobiographical novel by Netiva Ben-Yehuda, *1948—Between Calendars*. The novel relates Ben-Yehuda's experiences as a fighter in the Palmah assault units during the months preceding the Israeli Declaration of Independence. The other event, known as the Ori Or Affair, occurred in July 1998. It involved a political scandal that followed a controversial public statement made by former general and member of Parliament (Knesset), Ori Or. This statement was highly offensive to Middle Eastern and North African Israeli Jews, especially targeting Jews of Moroccan descent.

Both these events, the publication of Ben-Yehuda's novel and the Ori Or Affair, which took place almost two decades apart, constituted cultural sites in and through which *dugri* speech, and the meanings and values associated with it, became publicly visible and visibly negotiated. They each constituted a symbolic trigger to a social drama, as evidenced by the public debates that followed them. A consideration of the public controversies they engendered brings out the shifting contours of *dugri* speech.

The forthcoming summary of these events and the public conversation surrounding them are not designed to give the full range of possible interpretations or to evaluate any of the actions or views that formed part of these public dramas. My goal is a more modest one: I consider these events as public occasions in and through which the code underlying *dugri* speech and the cultural meanings associated with it became highlighted. If my account makes sense, I will also have shown that in the twenty years that spanned these two events, and commensurate with the radical changes in the standing of the Sabra image, the *dugri* idiom has lost much of its force and even some of its intelligibility on the Israeli cultural scene.

Dugri Style as an Art of Speaking:
1948—Between Calendars

Netiva Ben-Yehuda's novel, the first in a sequel of personal reminiscences of the 1948 War of Independence, was published in 1981, thirty-three years after the events narrated in it.[73] It had a great impact on Israeli readers, sold several editions, and occupied a respectable place on the bestseller list. It drew many critical responses by both critics and lay people, and its author became even more of a public figure than she had been before. In an article written about the author following the book's publication, the journalist Tamar Avidar expressed many readers' response to the book when she said that "it is a landmark—both in its style of writing and in its myth-debunking and norm-shattering function."[74]

In this chapter I treat the publication of the novel as a rhetorical act that became part of a rhetorical event whose unfolding reveals the processual nature of a social drama. In both content and form, the novel constituted a breach: a breach on the level of cultural norms, a stab at taken-for-granted national myths, as well as a breach on the level of literary canon. Most interestingly from the standpoint of this study, the novel was advertised by its publisher as employing "colloquial, fluent and *dugri* speech." Indeed, readers, critics, and the author herself confirmed this description in many references to the novel's style, underscoring both its linguistic features and its social-functional properties.

I therefore claim that a full account of the novel's rhetorical impact must take into consideration the meanings and functions of *dugri* speech as an expressive symbolic form. My first step is to examine in some detail the breach phase involved in the publication of the novel and the motivations underlying it. Understanding what the breach consisted of, we can then appreciate what the crisis phase was about and can trace the social drama through its redressive and reintegration phases by examining the public debate that followed its publication.

The information given on the jacket of the book about its author and protagonist is minimal. It states the date and place of her birth and mentions the schools she attended and her military service. Her coauthorship of a popular dictionary of Hebrew slang is also mentioned. This superficial description, which does little more than establish the author as a Sabra, stands in sharp contrast to the regnant terms with which she has been described in accounts of the War of Independence, where she is noted for her unusual exploits, for which the Arabs came to call her the "yellow-haired devil." Indeed, many Israeli readers of the early 1980s did not have to be introduced to the author, who was well known for her pursuits in the field of language—as an outspoken proponent of vernacular Hebrew—no less than for her wartime exploits.

The author became famous following an ambush of an Arab bus in which she took part as a fighter and killed a considerable number of Arabs singlehandedly and at close range. She came to be the bane of the Arabs of the Galilee, and a "wanted dead-or-alive" advertisement was published by a Syrian newspaper that offered a handsome reward for her. During the years since the War of Independence, she has refrained from giving public expression to her experiences either in writing or in journalistic interviews. She has, however, attracted public attention because of the battle she has been waging against the linguistic establishment on behalf of spoken, colloquial Hebrew. In the mid-1990s she broached a new career as host of a late-night call-in radio program in which she swaps nostalgic stories and personal experience narratives with her callers, many of whom are obviously familiar with the Sabra world of yesteryear (none of these exchanges falls into the therapeutic category of call-in radio discussed in the next chapter).

In interviews given after the publication of the novel, Ben-Yehuda expressed her distaste for the image of the "yellow-haired devil" that had stayed with her through the years. She deeply resented the inflated images of the Palmah fighters and the glorification of war so commonly found in accounts of the period by the "heroic writers." They, she alleged, spent the war in sidewalk cafes in Tel Aviv and had no notion of what it actually meant to be one of those nineteen- or twenty-year-old youngsters, whom she describes on the jacket of the book as "our dear cannon-fodder," who ran about in the muddy battlefields and turned the politicians' words into a reality "with their young bodies and meager breath."

In presenting the events from the standpoint of pawns in the war, Ben-Yehuda sought to modify the way in which the war was represented in the public discourse. Thus, rather than the image of a "yellow-haired devil," her account brings forth the image of a perplexed girl whose experience in the battlefield left her guilt-ridden and disoriented rather than victorious and proud. She felt that the war experience would never leave her, that she was "marked for life." She was both the killer and the kill, sacrificed by society to do the dirty job involved in "making history." Yet at the time she could not stay away from the battlefield even when she had a chance to do so.

This feeling was further intensified after an incident in which she was sent to command a battle she did not think had a chance and lost one of her best soldiers in it, extricating the others with great effort. Surprised to find that her own commander refused to take any responsibility for the incident, she blamed herself for not having spoken up and refusing to comply with the order in the first place—the *dugri* speaker had betrayed herself and her mission by keeping silent just when straight talk was so urgently called for. Following this incident, she experienced a nervous breakdown. She ran away to Tel Aviv only to find herself on the way back to her unit just a few days later, "on the run from running away." She was torn between a sense of deep estrangement from the ideology that required her to be what she did not want to be and could not be—a tough, remorseless, unquestioning woman-fighter—and the overwhelming emotional grip that same ideology had exerted on her. Throughout the book and in her interviews, Ben-Yehuda repeatedly said that the image cast for her and for her comrades by her parents' generation was untenable, that the people who had spun the mythic image of the Sabra out of the depths of their own fears and anxieties had no idea what it amounted to in terms of the flesh-and-blood reality of their own sons and daughters.

Ben-Yehuda's feelings and conflicts about the Sabra fighter identity—which is as central to the book as it is to the culture in general—are clearly brought out in her account of the events following the ambush of the Arab bus that earned her the fearsome reputation that stuck to her through the war. I believe this incident constitutes a critical moment in the book, the moment at which she awoke to the reality of war and found herself questioning her most cherished values and beliefs.[75] Most tellingly, to her this traumatic experience was a profoundly existential moment, articulated in the idiom of the Sabra's quest for a livable identity. From the standpoint of her newly acquired awareness, her inner doubts as to whether she could become anything like the mythic New Jew could not be dispelled. The only answer she could give to herself as she tried to come to terms with the full implications of her heroic deed remained disturbingly equivocal: I can and I cannot.

The author's two reported attempts to articulate her thoughts and feelings at this critical point in the book, the moments following the ambush on the bus, can be structurally regarded as precursors to the act of writing the novel years later. Her account of what she tried, but failed, to say then can give us some insights into her motives in writing and publishing the book. Using the culture's accent of sincerity, she relates experiences that echo the main dilemma of her generation, the first generation of Sabras: Who will the Sabra, the new Homo Israelicus, be?

The first of Ben-Yehuda's two unsuccessful attempts to speak up after the bus incident involved her meeting with Saul, a member of a kibbutz and a friend of her parents. He was elated at the success of the soldiers' mission, and, seeing her grim looks, pulled her aside and asked her what the matter was. She told him she was upset because he wanted her to feel proud of what she had done, blurting out: "People were killed, so I don't want to be proud of myself." At this he grabbed her by the shoulders, held her at a distance, took his time and shouted:

> F-o-ol! F-o-ol! Idiot. Like all of them. What will you all amount to? . . .
> Don't start talking like that, do you hear? Wipe those foolish thoughts

from your head, do you hear? These are the thoughts of a weak, miserable people. Do we want a normal people here? Do we want to stop being miserable Diaspora Jews? Weaklings? So among other things we have to invent the Jewish hero. . . . A strong person, free, liberated, who can take a gun in his hand and kill those who want to kill him, before they do, do you hear? If you can't be like this, then you are either a woman or a damn Diaspora Jewess![76]

As he was shouting, Ben-Yehuda felt that he was panicking at the thought that the First Generation to Redemption would not fulfill their parents' expectations after all, and she drew her conclusions, which came to be shared by more than one generation of close-lipped Sabras: she should have remained silent and prove to herself, to Saul, to the whole world that the New Jew existed. That's what she should have done—however hard, however lonely it was going to be: "Whatever goes around in your mind—God forbid, don't let a word of it come out, not even one syllable. One must be strong, overcome everything, and strangle any desire to pour out one's thoughts. One should be strong, and stronger and yet stronger. And the strong one doesn't speak. The strong one—keeps silent."[77]

Note the ironic twist here: to be the long-hoped-for Jewish hero, as strong and fearless as the ideology commands, one must not dare question the accepted ideology. To be strong in this case was not to be the assertive *dugri* speaker, but rather to keep one's thoughts to oneself. So she abided by the unwritten rules and kept her thoughts to herself, sensing that others were doing the same. And in their silence, they all helped to uphold the dream of the strong Jew who could take it, who could do it, who would not let history repeat itself. Note, also, how deeply gendered Saul's image of the Sabra as the New Jewish hero was. Not living up to this heroic image would cast her either as a non-Sabra or as a woman, both of them equally despised options in his mind. Or even worse, it would cast her as both—a "damn Diaspora Jewess"—the ultimate, unacceptable "other" of the Sabra ideal masculinist image.

Her urge to articulate her distress and puzzlement, however, was not silenced by Saul's outburst. She still felt that someone from the parent generation had to hear her and realize what was happening to their offspring, because "all our lives they urged us to go forward, but they don't know what this means."[78] So she composed a letter to her father, Barukh Ben-Yehuda, who was the principal of Herzeliyah high school and a well-known public figure in prestate years. In the letter she asked him, as she had asked Saul, not to take pride in the success of her mission when he read about it in the newspaper. To her the knowledge that she had killed people was nothing to boast about; she said she found that at the moment of killing, the word "enemy" lost its meaning and enemies became human beings. So in her letter she felt compelled to reiterate in exasperation: "I am sure there is something bad here, very bad, a terrible crime, an injustice. To us and to them. To everybody."[79]

But, then, perhaps remembering the panic she had sensed in Saul's reaction, she went on to reassure her father that he had nothing to worry about, that she would not fail him: "I will go on doing what I have to do, like all of us here, we the young 'realizers'; there's just one thing I want to say: if you knew it was like this, why didn't you tell us? And if you didn't know—you should know now. And then you can reconsider the whole thing."[80]

This letter, which was never sent, encapsulates her predicament. Inwardly torn, she could neither fully accept nor fully reject the role of the new Jewish hero. This attitude calls to mind the moral questioning and profound ambivalence accompanying military action revealed in the fighters' soul talk–like gatherings after the 1967 war, as discussed in the previous chapter. In neither case did the self-questionings lead the speakers themselves to "reconsider the whole thing" and possibly resist future calls to arms. Rather, in both cases they opted for the strategy that has come to be labeled "shooting and crying."

The author's solution was no solution for a member of the Sabra culture. Doing things she did not believe in went against the culture's fundamental values of integrity and sincerity. At this juncture, two clusters of meanings associated with the *dugri* mode and the Sabra identity clashed: inner strength and sincerity. To be strong she had to become insincere, and her outspokenness revealed her weakness. Ironically, as she testified in the book, she felt that "she had done her part" after writing this letter (and before failing to send it), rather than after successfully completing her military mission. It seemed to her that in speaking *dugri* more than anything else, she could become an agent and a full participant in her cultural world and reaffirm her sense of self.

Now, with the publication of the book, the story whose telling started thirty-three years earlier was finally brought to a conclusion. Rather than a call for help, however, it was now a testimonial to the fallen, the many close friends whose lives had been sacrificed in the war. She felt her survival entailed a pledge to tell the story of the war as they had seen it, "with all the shit," and as an antidote to the glorified accounts of the battlefield that were circulated over the years.

Ben-Yehuda told an interviewer that after the war, she saw that none of the books that came out told the true story of the war as she knew it. So she approached some of the writers of the Palmah generation and asked them: "Why don't you write your book in a *dugri* way?"[81] The book she finally wrote was thus offered as a counterstatement, as an attempt to correct the public conception of the 1948 war—and of what war is like in general—in the hope that it would serve the cause of peace. In an interview with journalist Dan Omer, she asked: "How did it happen that American public opinion stopped the Vietnam War? Who can guarantee that books that started with Remarque and then Norman Mailer did not affect the people's thinking about the waste and hopelessness of wars?"[82]

Thus, through its testimony to the past, the book offers a protest with the hope of affecting the present and the future. The author stated that after the 1973 Arab-Israeli War she had to face a young generation that was turning to her with the same accusation she had directed toward her father: "If you knew, why didn't you tell us?" So she sat down to tell her story, addressing it to the soldiers of the traumatic 1973 war, the generation of her own daughter.

Indeed, the book is intensely addressed. In the introduction the author presents her dialogic conception of her work, insisting that it is neither art, nor history, nor memoir: "Actually one can say that the book is an interview. As if someone, unseen, who knows nothing about 'then,' asks me questions throughout the book, and more questions, and asks again and again, and the whole book consists of the answers I give—*in speech.*"[83]

In fact, the front cover of the book shows a startling painting by Ben-Yehuda's daughter of a nude Israeli paratrooper—identified as such by his boots and the paratroopers' wings pressed to his bare chest—in the posture of the crucified Christ. It was painted following the 1973 war. Ben-Yehuda told me she had insisted on using that painting on the book's jacket. She had placed the original in front of her while writing the book and it was to him, to this mute interviewer, this anonymous successor of hers, this contemporary sacrifice, that her "spoken" answers were addressed.

Although the book was addressed to the younger generation, it naturally interested members of the author's own generation, and many of them responded to it in a variety of ways. Some of the responses highlighted an additional aspect of the myth-debunking thrust of the novel, which members of the author's generation were apparently more sensitive to than other readers: the author's questioning of the widely held picture of the Palmah as an enclave of *communitas*-like relations.

Thus, in his review of the book, the literary critic Dan Meron underscored the significance of the author's clear, sensitive depiction of the Palmah social scene, which challenged accepted accounts of the Palmah spirit as characterized by a unique quality of human relations, comradeship, and deep emotional ties. As the critic noted, the social world of the Palmah fighters, as depicted by Ben-Yehuda, was, on the contrary, "marked by a lack of intimacy—social, intellectual, emotional, and even sexual. A genuine interchange, when it occurs, is something of a small miracle."[84]

The scene of alienation and social differentiation depicted by the author subverts the Palmah's mythic image of an all-encompassing group spirit. The existence of moments of profound camaraderie is not denied, but these are described as emerging in the midst of a highly routinized and differentiated social world, whose inhabitants are both held together and kept apart by social-structural arrangements. In fact, the author's description of Palmah culture is an interesting account of the routinization of *communitas,* which is accompanied by increasing stylization. The many rules of conduct that became associated with the Palmah ethos and its symbolic expressions are found throughout the book. A reviewer, Dalia Shhori, summarized some of them, indicating what was involved in being a proper Palmah member:

> Knowing what to say at the right moment. Not showing any weakness. Being "in" *(ba'inyanim)*. Acting out the tough guy. Behaving like an Arab so as to appear like a native Israeli. Laughing at foreigners (newcomers and those not born in Israel). Disrespecting one's elders ("old" commanders who had passed the age of thirty). Doing everything for a friend. Dressing simply and modestly, but according to clear and well-defined rules. Not nominating oneself for an important job. Ignoring sex.[85]

Thus, the routinization of ideological as well as spontaneous *communitas* produced a social world of structure sprinkled with the symbolic elements of solidarity and permeated with a longing for its spirit. It is in this interplay of increasingly routinized structures and persistent elements of *communitas* that the two scenes grounding the novel—the then and the now—find their shared texture.

The most salient feature of the novel is its colloquial, fluent style.

Unlikely as it may sound, I can readily confirm a comment made by more than one interviewer: "She writes exactly as she speaks and speaks exactly as she writes."[86] The spontaneity, immediacy, and directness of her written speech are mentioned repeatedly by reviewers and readers, whatever their responses to it. Some take the style for what it claims to be, whereas others see it as a stylized form rather than straightforward, uninhibited expression.

The crucial importance of the style for the author was brought out by her account of her battles with publishers in earlier years in which she fought for the legitimization of colloquial Hebrew as the language of literary expression. She both identified with the style and used it to identify herself. It is an inseparable part of the message of the book. By introducing colloquial, spoken, *dugri* speech into literature, Ben-Yehuda endowed it with a degree of legitimization beyond anything it had known before.

Most of the comments made on the book's style, whether by those who approved of it or those who did not, noted a basic "fit" between the style and the content; the style was regarded as metonymically related to the scene, an apt vehicle for conveying the flavor of the Palmah experience. For example: "It seems to me that this combination creates a very lively language, wonderfully expressive, which stands out in the correspondence between content and style, a correspondence which contributes a great deal to the evocation of the distant period in which the events occur."[87]

Granting the style's important role in evoking the scene of the Palmah, I nevertheless would like to argue that it plays a much more complex role in this book. The employment of *dugri* speech here raises many questions, given the earlier characterization of it as involving an identity-function in the Sabra culture. Earlier in this chapter, I claimed that the use of *dugri* speech reaffirms the cultural identity of the speaker as a proper Sabra, a New Jew—the very identity the author finds she cannot fully embrace, as a woman and as a person. In fact, I believe the main message of the book is its disconfirmation of the Sabra myth. If my analysis of the *dugri* way of speaking is correct, the use of the *dugri* idiom to say things such as "I am probably a diaspora Jewess" is, indeed, a contradiction in terms. Thus, the author paradoxically uses the patriarchal idiom of cultural affirmation to disconfirm the very identity the idiom has been forged to celebrate.

As noted, my reading of the book and the circumstances of its publication have led me to see it as a public enactment of the *dugri* ritual. Like all such enactments, it gives expression to the problem of identity that is so central to the Israeli cultural experience. Unlike more mundane enactments of the ritual, however, it is both explicit and implicit. The explicit message that critiques the Sabra image contradicts the implicit message that affirms it through stylistic choice. It seems to me that the tension between the novel's explicit and implicit messages—the first given in its substance, the second in its style—is essential to its overall meaning and effect.

It is precisely the lack of "fit" between the author's explicitly expressed "burden" and the work's stylistic structure of "unburdening" that makes us so acutely aware of the poignancy of the Sabra's problem of identity and its unresolvable nature. In the *chizbat* oral tradition of the Palmah, as Oring has argued, it is the structure of humor (appropriate incongruity) that tells us that the cultural identity of the Sabra is inherently paradoxical, since it encompasses the two incompatible identities of the Israeli-born and the diaspora Jew.[88] Somewhat similarly, Ben-Yehuda's *1948—Between Calendars* tells us that paradox is an essential feature of the Israeli identity by disconfirming the Sabra mythic image through its very idiom of cultural affirmation. Perhaps such a radically subversive statement could have only been made by a woman, a native-born who was never really invited to become a full-fledged member of the masculinist Sabra culture in the first place.

I believe, however, that the conflict between the novel's explicit and implicit messages not only alerts us to the author's problem but also indicates what to her seems to be the direction of its solution. Her resolution of the paradox lies in her attempt to reinterpret rather than totally reject the image of the dauntless Sabra. Playing on the notions of strength and weakness, she claims the right to be strong enough to acknowledge her weakness. She applies the resolute *dugri* form normally used to express firmly held opinions and beliefs to voice her doubts and indecision. In so doing she violates one level of cultural norms and yet affirms another, apparently more vital, level.

If "to speak *dugri* is to act like a Sabra," as one of my informants put it, then the writing of this book is an act of an arch-Sabra. Ben-Yehuda is a Sabra, a New Jewess, because she can speak *dugri* (despite the fact that she is a woman). In the public drama of *1948—Between Calendars* she has used her culture's resources in a new and startling way—to confront the values and meanings presupposed by its ritual idiom. As on all occasions in which *dugri* speech is appropriately employed, she has done something *for* her readers by doing something *to* them. A comment she made during one of our conversations is for me a poignant summary of the book's intended impact. "This is not a book," she said, "it is a scream."

My discussion so far has been an attempt to delineate the nature of *1948—Between Calendars* as the product of a rhetorical act, an act involving a breach on a number of levels. On the level of content, it was a breach in that it blatantly disconfirmed the accepted image of the Sabra as an eager and dauntless fighter and refuted the picture of boundless solidarity as a central feature of the Palmah spirit; on the level of form, it was a breach in that it violated the accepted canons of literary style by reverberating with spokenness and in that it used the Sabra's *dugri* idiom to interrogate the Sabra image.

The many responses to the novel indicate that in 1981 the author already had the audience she felt she did not have right after the 1948 war. I suggest that the acceptance of her explicit message was greatly facilitated by the novel's style. By that time, the book's readers, like the author herself, refused to accept the Sabra myth at face value, yet were similarly reluctant to give it up completely, at least as a reminder of past longings and dreams. They willingly joined the author in her rebellious desire to reshape and redefine this shared cultural image. They joined her in asserting that they refused to assert themselves. Caught in this cultural double bind, they were even willing to echo Ben-Yehuda's equivocal, paradoxical verdict on the mythic image of the New Jew—it is and it is not.

Thus, it seems to me that the ritual invocation of the *dugri* idiom functioned here as it does in all enactments of the *dugri* ritual: it made the author's message more palatable by implicating the reader in its ritual framework. Not all readers were so lured, however. Some had difficulty accepting the novel's breaches and responded angrily to them. One woman, in a letter to the editor, accused the author of grossly distorting the image of the Palmah,[89] as did some of my informants in private conversations.

Other unfavorable responses by readers involved an attempt to invalidate the author's testimony, or at least minimize its representative value. Some of the people I talked to about the book, who had themselves served in the Palmah, said that the book did not really reflect the Palmah experience, that it presented a very personal point of view, the unrepresentative responses of an "individualist." Netiva Ben-Yehuda, they said, had always been different. However true and sincere her account was, it reflected her own psychology and not a widespread cultural problem. Reframing the testimony in those terms was a strategy designed to limit its claims.

The crisis that followed the breach after the publication of the novel was rather mild. It looks even milder in retrospect, at a point in time when revisionist historians have gone so far in recasting Israeli collective memory. The crisis was not allowed to escalate, so that the redressive acts applied were, accordingly, rather mild, too. This was partly due to the fact that the controversy was related to events that belonged to the distant past. It was also due to the fact that the drama in question involved a literary work and could be relegated to the realm of art (mere play), in contrast to real-life political dramas such as the Ori Or Affair.

In talking to Ben-Yehuda, I felt she was both pleased and annoyed by the public attention she had received. She told me she was tired of the numerous useless interviews she had let herself be dragged into. Yet she did not reject the attention of the media. As we listened together to a radio interview she had given some time earlier, I felt that she was savoring the relived experience. Although she muttered that she didn't know why she was taking part in "all that festival," I felt I could offer a guess: the "festival" had an obviously redressive function. It was part of the processual logic of the social drama in which she played the major role. Refusing to take part in it would have amounted to preventing the social drama from proceeding toward its closure in the final reintegration phase, which appeared to have naturally followed.

Whether this was because the times were ripe for her protest, or because of the manner in which it was voiced, or the way in which the drama unfolded, or for all of these reasons combined, there were many unmistakable indications that the reintegration phase had been reached. Let me mention just a few: Ben-Yehuda became a popular speaker in the army and was often invited to speak before young soldiers; she told me with satisfaction that her book was used as a graduation gift for soldiers of the Nahal troops (successors of the Palmah in many ways); and, above all, this book was just the beginning of a large-scale autobiographical project. These were indications that the author's protest and manner of renegotiating the Sabra ethos had found a niche in the cultural patchwork that came to constitute Israeli public life.

In considering this social drama, we traced a gradual process of disengagement from the Sabra image. It reflected a spirit of self-questioning that originated within the very core of the Sabra culture itself. The gradual fall of the Sabra image from the heights it enjoyed up until the late 1950s or early 1960s, however, had a great deal to do with social processes that were external to native Israeli culture, especially the growing heterogeneity of Israeli society. Following the establishment of the State in 1948, the mass immigration of the first decade of statehood more than doubled Israel's Jewish population, and the country became an immigrant society par excellence.

For a couple of decades, the small group of Sabras of European extraction retained its status as a cultural elite. This position of social advantage became translated in terms of military, political, and civilian careers, keeping the Sabra ethos and *dugri* style alive in some influential domains of the Israeli social scene, especially in military and political circles. However, even in these contexts it became increasingly contested in the 1990s. This was indicated by the scandal triggered by Ori Or's remarks that touched on interethnic relations in Israel, which were described by some as *dugri* and by others as racist. The scandal that came to be known as the Ori Or Affair hints at what has become of the *dugri* idiom in a society where cultural diversity could no longer be ignored, and social exclusion buttressed by the demands for a monolithic interactional style no longer held their sway.

Dugri Speech and Israeli Identity Politics: The Ori Or Affair

On July 29, 1998, the morning paper *Ha'aretz* published an article by a highly regarded journalist of Moroccan extraction, Daniel Ben Simon, which was based on an interview with Knesset Member and former General Ori Or.[90] The political uproar caused by the publication of this interview will provide the substance of the second *dugri*-related social drama to be analyzed here.

The title given to Ben-Simon's article was "Ma sliha, eize sliha" (roughly, "What pardon, forget the pardon"). It referred to the famous public apology extended in the fall of 1997 by Ehud Barak, then leader of the Labor movement and later Prime Minister, to Israeli Jews of Middle Eastern and North African origin. These Jews of Muslim lands, who are variously referred to as Sephardim, Mizrahim, or, in English, Oriental Jews,[91] have been subject to stereotypical and denigrating treatment. Barak's apologetic speech was made in the name of generations of members of the Labor Party (of which he was a relatively new member). The Israeli Labor movement had been established and dominated by Jews from Eastern and Central Europe and their descendants. It has traditionally had much difficulty in incorporating into its membership Israel's Oriental Jews, who make up close to half of the country's Jewish population and by far the larger part of its economically deprived working- and lower-middle-class strata.

The speech sought to counter the ongoing sense of alienation and antagonism that Oriental Jews harbored toward the Labor movement, whose position of power was consolidated in prestate years and during the first three decades of statehood. The political parties constituting this movement have long represented the social and cultural hegemony of Jews of European descent, Ashkenazi Jews. They continued to do so to some extent even after 1977, when the right-wing Likud Party led by Menahem Begin and strongly supported by Oriental Jews, won the elections for the first time. The significant political change that followed was largely attributed to the resentment felt by many Oriental Jews toward the Labor establishment and its Orientalist attitudes toward non-European Jews. The latter were depicted as primitive, backward, irrational, and overemotional in a way reminiscent of European stereotypes of the Arab world more generally.[92] The Jews from Muslim lands considered the Labor establishment responsible for the suffering and humiliation they had experienced during their immigration and adaptation to life in Israel, and for their ongoing social marginalization and economic deprivation.[93]

Barak's conciliatory move was designed to acknowledge past mistakes and bad judgment in order to overcome what he described as the emotional barrier between Oriental and European Jews, which had such dire consequences for the Labor movement. This was an open recognition of the role of ethnicity in Israeli social life as well as of the role of psychological and emotional factors in its political organization.

Implied in the rationale offered for this attempt at historical reconciliation was the contention, later explicitly stated by Barak and others, that the Labor Party, when it was in power, had erred at a symbolic level even while it had in fact done much more than the right-wing Likud Party to improve the lives of Oriental Jews in practical terms. Emotional factors such as hurt feelings were claimed to stand in the way of giving proper recognition to Labor's effective contributions to immigrant absorption and nation-building, of which the newcomers from the Orient were major beneficiaries. Labor's rival, the right-wing Likud Party, especially under the leadership of the late Menahem Begin, was claimed by Labor members to have succeeded in wooing many Oriental Jews to its support through emotional manipulation, using inflammatory rhetoric in the service of identity politics yet contributing little to their material welfare.

Labor's accusation was grounded in the culturally constructed polarity between words and deeds that is central to the *dugri* ethos. Barak's apology suggested a reversal of the values attached to the words/deeds binary, not its challenge. This was pointed out by *Jerusalem Post* writer Herb Keinon, whose article on this issue was subtitled, "By apologizing for indignities caused *Sephardim* [Oriental Jews], Ehud Barak shows he recognizes the primacy of words over action."[94] The apology, as a gesture of reconciliation, thus marked a first step in the renegotiation of the meaning configuration associated with *dugri* speech. It gained further resonance when officially ratified as a resolution by Labor Party delegates in their much-publicized subsequent assembly in Netivot, a southern "development town" populated by Oriental Jews. This public gesture turned out to be highly controversial and elicited a great deal of commentary in the press and electronic media. While supported by some as a sincere and courageous political move, it was criticized and questioned by others as an electoral gimmick. Barak's critics considered it a pretentious and groundless statement, particularly since it was spoken by a newcomer to the Labor Party in the name of the party's long historical lineage.[95] Some long-time Laborites, most of them of European descent, felt the apology was utterly misguided and reflected neither their intentions nor the positive and important role they had played in "immigrant absorption" during the early years of the state, when the mass immigration from Muslim lands poured into the country.

Many Oriental Jews, too, were skeptical of Barak's apology, with its focus on emotional issues rather than concrete action. They claimed it reinforced Orientalist stereotypes of Jews from Arab lands as "emotional" rather than protecting their rights as equal citizens. They demanded that the apology be backed up by actual "deeds." For example, they wanted to see an effective move to increase investments in their children's education; measures taken to overcome the increasing rate of unemployment in "development towns" and other areas were many Oriental Jews lived; both legal and practical action that would result in improved housing conditions. Interestingly, few commentators dwelt on a particular comment made by Barak in the course of his apologetic speech that seems highly significant to me: his rejection of the ideological view held by former generations of Labor movement activists that a New Israeli person could be produced. This idea, so central to the

Zionist ethos, was now pronounced by Barak to have been a misconception. He claimed that it contradicted the value of cultural continuity with the Jewish past and the legitimization of ethnic diversity among Israeli Jews.

Apparently, however, this implicit vindication of cultural pluralism and political correctness in its Israeli version did not rub off on MK Ori Or, Barak's close political associate. Or's controversial remarks owed more than anything to the ideological stance of the quintessential Sabra, the straight-talking New Jew whom Barak had proclaimed a historical error. As a friend and political ally of Ehud Barak, Or had much to say about the apology speech and the issue of ethnic diversity. He initiated an interview with journalist Daniel Ben Simon to discuss the latter's book on the 1996 elections in order to clarify his position on the traditionally troubled relations between the Labor party and Oriental voters, whose political preferences and involvement were the topic of Ben Simon's book. The article in which Ben Simon reported on his interview with Ori Or foregrounds the latter's expression of disappointment with the offshoots of Barak's "apology speech." Or explicitly blamed the Mizrahi politicians (particularly those of Moroccan origin) for the failure of Barak's symbolic gesture. The journalist, on his part, stressed that Or had been having difficulties with politicians of North African extraction for some time. His disaffection extended to prominent members of his own party, whom he had publicly accused of undermining Barak's authority and of exploiting ethnic feelings of discontent among their followers in subverting Barak's position.

What is most interesting from our point of view is that Or attributed these political difficulties to ethnically based differences in interactional style and emotional makeup, claiming that he couldn't talk to politicians of Mizrahi extraction in a straightforward manner and express his real thoughts for fear that they would react emotionally and irrationally to his direct approach. He said: "The problem is I can't talk to these people the way I talk with others, who are *more Israeli in their character*. Every time you say something, they immediately jump and are offended and begin to lose control. They have sensitivities and problems of honor *[kavod]* and as a result you can't have a *normal conversation* with them" (my emphasis). He attributed his inability to be straightforward with Oriental Jews to their refusal to accept criticism, to their tendency to read an ethnic slur in every word they didn't like, and to indulge in endless "honor games." In addition to repudiating the manipulative emotionality of Oriental Jews, Ori Or also spoke of their "tribalism" as a problematic form of solidarity, one that is a world apart from the comradeship found among members of the close-knit group of military men that he himself belonged to and cherished. To him this spirit of comradeship-in-arms was not only the epitome of fellow-feeling but also the essence of "Israeliness." Finally, according to Or, the problem was not only an emotional but also a cognitive one. He claimed that a lot of this had to do with the fact that Oriental Jews, especially Moroccan Jews, are cognitively restricted and have "no curiosity to know what's happening around them and why. When I appear before them, I see they have no interest in listening, understanding and getting to know what's good and what's bad. And this is distressing because it hurts not only them but Israeli society as a whole."[96] Taken together, Or's statements, which might have gone unchallenged in earlier times, violated the sensibilities associated with the late-1990s Israeli version of political correctness. They constituted a breach of the unspoken interethnic decorum in Israeli public discourse and as such marked the first phase of the social drama that ensued. The public scandal triggered by Or's statements constituted the second, "crisis," phase of the social drama, which was comprised of a series of further accusations and counteraccusations. Indeed, the ethnocentric and exclusionary spirit of Or's comments gave rise to many angry responses and much brow-beating. The outrage was shared by Jews of Oriental and European extraction, and by members of the Labor Party and its political rivals.

There were many calls demanding Ori Or's resignation as a way of signaling the party's recognition of the breach that led to this scandal. Ehud Barak, Or's political patron, responded by rejecting Or's "generalizations," emphasizing that the country's strength lies in its ethos of equality. He was reported to have initiated Or's resignation from public life, but refused to actually enforce it.[97] Eventually, Or was not made to resign but was officially suspended from all the positions he held in the party and as a member of parliament. Seeking redress, Or subsequently undertook a journey across the country, especially to "development towns" populated by Oriental Jews, in order to apologize to those who may have been hurt by his words. A little over three months afterward, the Labor Party voted to restore Or to all the positions he had held before the scandal, a move that was accompanied by another round of media coverage and commentary, perhaps a little more cynical than the first. Yet during the election campaign that followed, Or was effectively marginalized and eventually disappeared from the political scene.

Barak's initial response appeared to many party members to be too indecisive and lukewarm and he was accused of privileging his longtime personal friendship with Or over the party's interest and the public good. While Barak spoke of unacceptable generalizations, others within the Labor Party and outside it were much more ready to condemn Or's statements as racist. One commentator said:

> The desperation one feels on hearing Ori Or's statements is not just due to their content but to the encounter with the ignorance, lack of cultivation and blindness that populate the spiritual, moral and cultural world of one who appears to be the most perfect embodiment of the Israeli Sabra—salt of the earth, member of the Labor party, former General, former deputy minister and chair of the Security and Foreign Affairs Parliamentary Committee. How exactly did the Israeli Sabra become an Afrikaner?[98]

Some did not consider Or to be a racist, but saw him as insensitive and stupid enough to make an inexcusable political error. Others, of course, responded with a series of partisan outcries, most notably Prime Minister Netanyahu, who made his criticism of Ori Or's statements the center of his parliamentary speech the day on which the interview was published. He used the incident to distract attention from the no-confidence vote his government was facing on that same day.

Ori Or's response to the many angry accusations leveled against him was part of his engagement in redressive action. During this phase of the social drama, in which he attempted to clarify his stance and clear his name, the *dugri* code came to occupy center-stage once again. In fact, Or did not try to explain or justify the positions he expressed in the interview, which others considered racist. Rather, he presented himself as the straight-talking, military man, an image he counterposed to that of the glib-tongued politician. He prided himself on having had the courage to give expression to attitudes that many others among the Israeli populace harbored as well, but did not have the forthrightness and courage to voice.

This argument was stretched to such a point that Ori Or demanded to be given credit for forcing a thorny issue into the open, making it part of the Labor Party's political agenda. The much-needed public discussion that he generated, he claimed, was one that many before him had tried to suppress at considerable cost to the Party. Speaking of himself in the third person, he said:

> The issue of the relations of the Labor movement with Mizrahi [Oriental] Jews did not begin with Ori Or and will not end with him. This is testified

by the fact that this article triggered the first ever discussion of this issue within the Labor party that lasted six hours. This means that Or was right after all. Ori touched a difficult question, which people had refused to discuss thoroughly, and yesterday, for the first time in the history of the Labor party, it was discussed thoroughly, and it was I [Or] who asked for this discussion, nobody else.[99]

Or's argumentative response triggered a larger debate about the role played by Israeli ex-generals in political life. Thus, in an article titled "The Civilian Option," where he argued against the prominence of ex-generals in Israeli politics, journalist Gideon Levy offered a critical commentary on the kind of personal background they brought with them to the political sphere, which he characterized as infused with ethnocentrism, self-celebration, and a manipulative use of the image of the straight-talking, pragmatic Sabra. In Levy's words: "In a reality where self-interest and manipulation lead the way to the top, no less than in any civilian organization, military men pride themselves on not being 'politicians,' on being honest and 'saying what they think'— without 'the nonsense and complexes you find in politics,' in Or's words. Is roughness a value, or are we talking about bluntness and lack of sensitivity?"[100]

Ori Or's line of self-defense was thus a complex one: he apologized for his statements in the famous interview, saying he had been misunderstood; he vehemently rejected all accusations that he entertained racist attitudes; and at the same time he prided himself on having had the courage to be *dugri* enough to give voice to views everybody else preferred to "shove under the rug."

While this somewhat confused line of defense did not help much, and accusations of racism continued to flow, other voices sounded a different tune in the midst of the widespread public censure. There were those who supported Or's interpretation of his statements as involving *dugri* speech, offering alternative accounts that, just like Or's own self-defense, focused on the act of speaking up rather than on the contents of the talk. Some commentators, such as poet and columnist Nathan Zach, remarked that Or's problem was not the content of his statements but the fact that he chose to make them despite their obvious lack of popularity, since "the state of Israel and Israeli society can tolerate anything but the truth." And, depicting Or as the quintessential *dugri* speaker, he accused him of naivete rather than racism. In Zach's analysis, Or had been naive enough to think that he could express himself freely in a climate dominated by the newly imported spirit of "political correctness," which stifled any attempt at open argument and discussion. Seconding Or's claim that what he wanted was to bring up the thorny, rarely discussed topic of the Labor Party's failure to reach the hearts of Oriental voters, he supported Or's claim that he "said what so many—on both sides of the non-imaginary [political] line—think, but will never dare to say." [101]

In addition to those who commended Or for saying what others feared to express, still others rejected the "political correctness" of those who attacked him, branding it as hypocrisy. One commentator commended Or for not patronizing Oriental Jews by being overly protective toward them. In this interpretation of Or's interview, which comes close to the original understanding of the *dugri* stance within Israeli Sabra ethos, Or's *dugri* statements reflected his respect for Oriental Jews rather than his denigration of them. This view was eloquently expressed in an article written by a woman of Oriental extraction, Tami Shemesh-Kritz, which was published in the daily *Ma'ariv*. Its subtitle ran "Ori Or spoke to us as equal and strong people. Instead of embracing him, we joined his attackers." In the article she explained: "Anybody who read the article, and not just the headlines, could see how much Or wanted to speak to Oriental Jews as equals, as confident people who can listen to things they reject. He sees us as strong enough to be told things that hurt us; and if we weren't so immersed in defending our lost honor, we would recognize his helplessness and weakness as opposed to our own strength."

She continued to express her annoyance at the patronizing behavior of most Ashkenazi Jews, Barak's apology included, and suggested: "It's time the Oriental Jews cease to convey the vulnerability of a poor kid who needs to be protected. I can be laughed at, looked down upon, ridiculed. That's the price of true equality." [102]

The most interesting and double-edged argument formulated in the course of this debate, it seems to me, was related to the *dugri* stance Or claimed for himself. Both he and many of his supporters upheld his *dugri* act as a token of personal courage and respect for the other. His supporters thus accepted his self-description as the Sabra who speaks *dugri*. Or's detractors similarly confirmed his self-description as a straight talker who says what he means and means what he says, yet condemned him for the content of his statements, emphasizing that these were no slip of the tongue—that he was a racist and the mouthpiece of others like him. Both sides to the argument thus saw Or as a representative of a larger group of like-minded people. This was all the more reason to either condemn or defend his position, depending on the critic's point of view.

Or's removal from his public functions and his ultimate marginalization were ways Labor leaders sought to distance themselves from him and to bring the story to a close. Even though this distancing move was initially only half-hearted, soon afterward a Labor-led government was formed that included Shas, the religious orthodox party of Oriental Jews, many of them of Moroccan heritage, and did not include Or. Shutting the door behind Or and the scandalous air trailing after him was a way of marking out the "sayable" from the "unsayable" in the Israeli public sphere of the late 1990s. At that point in time, the public needed to be protected from the *dugri* speaker's impulse to "say it all."

The Ori Or Affair suggests that the affiliative promise and exclusionary potential of the *dugri* code have made it a distinctive cultural vehicle through which the "Israeli ethos" is currently constructed, contested, and renegotiated. That the *dugri* idiom was perceived to be associated with Israeli identity at the turn of the third millennium was indicated by a survey in which respondents listed *hutzpa* (impertinence) and "directness without politeness" as the two leading characteristics of the "ordinary Israeli."[103] Yet the process of cultural contestation involving the *dugri* code and the Sabra ethos has become increasingly visible on the Israeli public scene. The cultural changes associated with the erosion of the *dugri* idiom have more subtle manifestations as well. An exploration of the changes I consider most significant to the understanding of the shifts in the Israeli ethos of directness follows next.

TRAJECTORIES OF CULTURAL CHANGE

The diminishing consensus surrounding the cultural position of the *dugri* speaker has been associated with two very different processes of sociocultural change. Both of these processes—each in its own way—indicate a rejection of the realist, responsibility-oriented idiom of *dugri* speech, suggesting cultural-discursive alternatives to the Sabra's straight talk. I will refer to them, respectively, as "the softening and the roughening of *dugri* speech." The terms *softening* and *roughening* are not intended to imply a coherent process moving in two opposite directions but rather to convey the uneven fluctuations of Israeli expressive style in the last few decades between increasing harshness on the one hand and increasing tentativeness and hedging on the other. These various cultural trends, which reflect the growing diversity of Israeli society, share a greater emphasis on the expressiveness of talk as an emotive display, yet each seems to have affected Israeli expressive culture in different ways.

Notably, however, the greater multivocality and diversity of styles in Israeli society, which have worked to undermine the standing of *dugri* speech as a communicative ideal, have had little effect on intercultural contacts between Arabs and Jews. In concluding this chapter, I will therefore point out the significance of cultural divergence in communicative style between Arabs, who cherish the ethos of indirection natively referred to as "doing *musayra*," and Israeli Jews, for whom *dugri* speech represents a cultural preference. I believe that despite recent changes in the cultural standing of the *dugri* ethos, intercultural encounters between Arabs and Jews in Israel (and elsewhere) may still be significantly colored by the contrast between the speech symbolism associated with speaking *dugri* and doing *musayra*, respectively.

The Softening of the *Dugri* Mode

The affective display of tentativeness with respect to one's own speech through the use of a variety of mitigating devices has been referred to as "the softening of the *dugri* mode." This style is associated with the construction of the "thornless Sabra" *(tzabar bli kotzim)*, a social designation that plays on the prickly pear metaphor introduced earlier. In an interview, a middle-aged Sabra described it as follows: "I used to be very *dugri* when I was younger, but now I've grown up, I've mellowed. I'm careful not to go with my head against the wall. My friends, we've all grown up you could say. We are Sabras but without so many thorns." There are two aspects to this softening process—one has to do with social changes, the other with changes in views of personhood. Social changes are related to the growing recognition of the interpersonal costs attending the potential bluntness of the *dugri* style in an increasingly heterogeneous and hierarchical society, many of whose members never shared the value system that warrants the use of *dugri* speech in the first place.

Calls for a better quality of life, interpreted, inter alia, as greater considerateness and politeness in interpersonal contacts and in public debate, support this orientation. One linguistic manifestation of this trend involves the proliferation of such relational terms as *yahas* (attentiveness toward the other), or the term *lefargen* (to be happy with or for the other), as they and their derivatives are deployed in everyday parlance. These terms denote interpersonal behavior that concretizes the notion of interpersonal support. The term *yahas* refers to humanizing gestures of attentiveness and considerateness. Susan Sered and Ephraim Tabory found it to be central to the discursive construction of illness and treatment narratives by breast cancer patients, but it is widely used in other settings as well.[104] The term *lefargen* extends the notion of social support beyond contexts of trauma or disaster to encompass everyday contexts that invite pleasure in the accomplishments and well-being of others. It signals a positive attitude that can counteract potential feelings of envy in an increasingly competitive world whose base of human solidarity is threatened by the relentless pursuit of personal interest.[105]

In fact, many of the references to *lefargen* or *yahas* in everyday talk are lamentations about lack of support and considerateness *(lo mefargenim; ein yahas)*. The frequency of such complaints suggests that even though people's expectations are often thwarted, there is greater cultural emphasis on the value of supportiveness in interpersonal life. Gestures of friendliness and human recognition are explicitly valued even in their absence, perhaps supplanting ideologically driven identity displays and invocations of communal feeling. The rise of the interpersonal is probably one way in which the shift from a collectivist to an individualistic ethos, as it is often referred to by students of Israeli society, finds concrete expression.

The other cultural change signaled by the softening of the *dugri* mode has to do with changes of emphasis in ways of conceptualizing persons. More specifically, these involve a reinterpretation of the notions of sincerity, openness, and resoluteness, which are central to the Sabra identity. In fact, the softened version of *dugri* speech seems to hark back to the introspective, openly emotional, and spiritually oriented flavor of the early pioneers' soul talks. This shift indicates a growing ability to acknowledge the volatility of emotional experience and give expression to personal feelings rather than focus on self-assertion and social commitment, which have been at the core of the *dugri* mode. It seems that the shift toward interpersonal focus and an introspective stance has been reinforced by the increasing influence in Israeli culture of the Western therapeutic ethos (as will be further discussed in the next chapter). In fact, some younger informants, especially teenagers, surprised me by interpreting the term *dugri* with reference to self-disclosure and intimacy, and a couple of them specifically invoked the notion of soul talks, interpreted as a heart-to-heart dyadic conversation, in explicating the notion of *dugri* speech.

This cultural refocusing is also related to a newfound tolerance for tentativeness, lack of resoluteness, and self-questioning, a discursive attitude that is especially noticeable in the proliferation of the use of hesitation signals and hedging devices, such as *kaze* and *ke'ilu* (roughly, discursive equivalents of the English "like"), which have first appeared as generational markers of young speakers, but have by now become a staple of casual Hebrew conversation.[106] This process of cultural change has thus given rise to new cultural emphases and has legitimized the exploration of uncharted expressive stances. I believe that it has been facilitated by its flexible incorporation within a reinterpreted version of the native Sabra notions of directness and sincerity.

As noted, however, the overall Israeli scene has been colored by contradictory cultural pulls. The increasing concern with interpersonal relations and personal worlds has at the same time been accompanied by greater license for violence and brute force in everyday conduct. This is manifested in a shift from a premium placed on assertiveness to an anxiety over aggressiveness. I refer to this change as the roughening of the *dugri* mode, to which I now turn.

The Roughening of the *Dugri* Mode

The roughening of *dugri* speech refers to forceful expression that foregrounds issues of power over such values as cooperation and harmony in the conduct of interpersonal life. I would propose that the roughening of the *dugri* mode is a communicative correlate of the power-orientation that grounds Israeli militaristic values and what Kimmerling calls its metacode of "security in Israeli culture."[107] In the interpersonal domain, it is epitomized by the communicative style known as *kasah*, a slang term that implies a forceful, aggressive verbal blow aimed at one's interactional partner. The term *kasah* and its various derivatives (especially the verb *lekase'ah*, or the noun *kisu'ah*) are commonly found in everyday parlance and in the press. Apparently originating in the soccer field, it has become an integral part of the Israeli metacommunicative lexicon. This term can, in fact, be heard much more frequently than the term *dugri* in contemporary Israeli speech. The metaphor underlying the style of *kasah* is that of boxing; hence, the expression "*kasah* without gloves," which underscores the ruthlessness involved.

Indeed, although a *dugri* encounter could be unpleasant and even threatening for the person addressed in the *dugri* mode (as in "I'll tell you *dugri*, I don't like the way things are going around here"), the speaker who invokes the *dugri* frame is making an appeal to shared values of sincerity, forthrightness, and solidarity, thereby legitimating the face-threat involved. Not so with the deployment of the *kasah* style. Forceful speech marked as *kasah* does not carry the attenuating impact of a shared, legitimating code. Rather, it is interpersonally directed as a put-down, unmitigated by the invocation of a cultural frame that might warrant its aggressiveness. *Kasah* as brute force tends to be associated with the growing factionalism and radicalization of Israeli social life, which implies an absence of a consensual system of symbols and meanings.

A poignant invocation of the notion of *kasah* that involved a commentary on Israeli society as a whole appeared in an article by Gideon Samet, which lamented the lack of sensitivity shown toward the elderly. The author claimed that this was the mark of a society that is dominated by an aggressive, *macho* style and that "has so strongly integrated into its lexicon the term *kasah*."[108] Interestingly, the entry for *kasah* in the second volume of the dictionary of Hebrew slang by Ben-Amotz and Ben-Yehuda acknowledges the use of the term only in reference to physical violence. In this dictionary, the entry for *kasah* is defined as "A violent fight involving blows and beatings." The dictionary definition refers to physical violence only, but the examples given there suggest that the term may be used with reference to verbal violence as well: "She is a member of Hashomer Hatza'ir and her older brother is in *Eretz Israel Hashlema* [The Whole Land of Israel, a right-wing movement]. Don't ask what *kasah* goes on in that home."[109]

As far as I can tell, *kasah* is systematically ambiguous in its reference to physical or verbal violence. At times, the context clarifies the meaning of the term, as when a TV debate is reported as "a televisual *kasah*" *(kasah televizioni),* or when physical political violence in the city of Hebron was reported in the weekly *Koteret Rashit,* whose front cover carried the words "Days of *Kasah*."[110] In other cases, the meaning may remain ambiguous. Thus, when someone reports an attack or altercation, using "He went down on her *kasah*," or "There was *kasah* there," there is no way of telling if words, blows, or both were exchanged. In these contexts it may not really matter much—the words exchanged are as violently intended as the blows. At the time of this writing, I believe *kasah* is mainly used in colloquial Israeli Hebrew to denote verbal violence.

Several informants described *kasah* as a corrupt, degenerate version of the *dugri* mode, mainly in discussing the limits of *dugriyut.* I have noted comments explicitly contrasting these two styles, most commonly, "This is not *dugri,* it's already *kasah.*" These comments were intended to distinguish between the two styles, which are sometimes felt to blend into each other. I am not claiming, however, that the style of *kasah* is an outgrowth of the *dugri* mode. I do suggest that this style and the ethos to which it gives expression—unpalatable as both may be to many Israelis—have become competing forces in Israeli culture and are linked through a conflation of terms and rhetorical appeals to similar-sounding cultural values. Both *dugri* speech and *kasah* style valorize forceful expression and the direct approach. Thus, in what seems an almost imperceptible shift in meaning, the Sabra's drive toward autonomy and agency is reinterpreted in terms of unbridled license to exercise force. Power of intimidation rather than fortitude and strength of character become the measure of all things.

Clearly, the softening and roughening of the *dugri* mode are incompatible, and both reflect widely acknowledged trends in contemporary Israel. They are equally incompatible with the ethos underlying *dugri* speech in one important sense: neither the retreat to a purely interpersonal domain nor the construction of a public domain in which brute force reigns supreme can support the self-focused yet communal and solidary orientation that marks the distinctive meaning-complex underlying *dugri* speech.

The foregoing account has delineated the vicissitudes of *dugri* speech as they are inscribed in the metacommunicative lexicon of Israeli speakers, in contexts of both interpersonal and public utterance. These shifts in the meanings and uses of *dugri* speech, like all subtle changes in cultural style, usually proceed largely undetected. As we have seen, the decline of the Sabra ethos, the *dugri* mode, became a frequently used marker of cultural identity and a particular version of personhood, whether invoked in a nostalgic or critical vein. At times, it became the center of explicit attention. The social dramas discussed earlier exemplify occasions of open, often conflict-laden, negotiations of speech norms in which the notion of *dugriyut* plays a central role. Other occasions in which the problematic of Israeli cultural communication style has been openly and forcefully addressed fall under the category of phenomena identified by sociologists as "moral panics."[111]

I therefore conclude my discussion of these changes by exemplifying how media-manufactured moral panics have singled out Israeli cultural communication style as a focus of criticism. While social dramas encapsulate genuine occasions of cultural negotiation, moral panics mobilize the authority of the media to introduce an alarmist note and a profound sense of cultural unease into the public sphere. A consideration of some recent examples of such media-induced moral panics in relation to the demise of *dugri* speech can shed further light on the current state of Israeli straight talk.

From Social Drama to Moral Panic

In a study concerned with the moral panic generated in Britain with reference to the teaching of grammar in schools, Deborah Cameron defines this concept as follows:

> A moral panic can be said to occur when some social phenomenon or problem is suddenly foregrounded in public discourse and discussed in an obsessive, moralistic and alarmist manner, as if it beckoned some imminent catastrophe. . . . In a moral panic the scale of the problem is exaggerated, its causes are analyzed in simplistic terms, anxiety about it climbs to intolerable levels, and the measures proposed to alleviate it are usually extreme or punitive.[112]

As scholars have pointed out, moral panics do not erupt but are constructed as such by the mass-media as part of its agenda-setting role. The media establish something as an issue, a problem, or indeed, a crisis situation, and then dramatically intensify the public's concern with it through widespread and repeated coverage, galvanizing public attention and arbitrating public opinion on the particular issue. I find it both curious and intriguing that moral panics surrounding Israeli communication style are repeatedly manufactured by the Israeli press. While I think this fact deserves a more sustained discussion than I can give it here, I will exemplify the role of the press in generating style-centered cultural panics whose analysis can throw further light on the vicissitudes of *dugri* speech. The elite daily paper *Ha'aretz* has played a leading role in such discussions of cultural style, particularly through extended coverage in its weekend magazine. Over the years, it has offered a range of articles, either the product of one journalist or the collaborative work of several, in which self-deprecating and self-distancing discussions of communication style have become sites for cultural self-definition and for the creation of group boundaries and social distinctions.

Issues of interpersonal politeness and interactional appropriateness have been central to these folk-communicative accounts, which are often cast in an implicitly comparative framework vis-à-vis other "more civilized" nations in the West. Lamenting the degradation of Israeli speech style, these articles constitute a discursive site for the renegotiation of Israeli identity as it is produced in and through talk. These discussions of communicative style are divorced from the social and political context of the country's life and are presented as involving a cultural trait symptomatic of a more encompassing yet unexplained climate of moral malaise. The following analysis exemplifies the kind of metacommunicative discussions elaborated in such articles, which sketch the image of the "ugly Israeli" as projected through "uncivilized" forms of talk.[113]

On September 24, 1999, the lead article in the weekend magazine of the high-brow Israeli daily, *Ha'aretz*, which took up eight full pages, was titled "Big Mouth," and its cover page carried a grotesque and vulgar drawing of a huge, wide-open, screaming mouth topped by widely open nostrils, both in strong colors of red and purple.[114] The picture was punctuated with the big-lettered title of the article itself, "Big Mouth," and in smaller letters its theme was elaborated with the following words: "The public discourse in Israel is flooded with unbridled and politically incorrect expressions uttered by men of fame who enjoy a high status. Who are the biggest mouths and why do we forgive them?"[115]

This article provides a public arena for cultural self-reflection, one among a myriad of other occasions on which the questions of "who we are and what we look like" become foregrounded in Israeli cultural conversation. In this case, most conveniently from the point of view of the present analysis, Israeli straight talk itself is the focus of journalistic treatment. In terms of my earlier discussion, this meditation on Israeli cultural communication style traces the ascendancy of the style of *kasah* within the Israeli speech economy in contexts of public performance. This article is a site of cultural reflexivity, a discourse about discourse that is also a discourse about Israeli cultural identity. It is a "cultural text" that provides a metadiscursive commentary on the aberrations of Israeli straight talk. The subtitle to the article itself attests both to the disaffection and to the puzzlement that motivate this reflexive move: "An unbridled tongue, verbal provocation, vulgar expressions and politically incorrect slips of the tongue are an inseparable part of public discourse in Israel and have never harmed their owners. On the contrary, they typify key personalities in society, all of them the salt of the earth" (24).

Interestingly, the article combines attention to Israeli speech style as a version of "straight talk" with attention to scandalous moments of unrestrained public utterance of the kind discussed with reference to the Ori Or Affair. In fact, the Big Mouth phenomenon points to a situation in which blunt, even racist, public statements of the kind made by Or did not usually trigger public response, let alone generate a social drama, but rather became incorporated as acceptable communication practices within the dynamic, mass-mediated structure of power and prestige in Israeli society.

The article thus consists of ten portraits of the top Big Mouths in Israeli society, all well-known personalities. Whereas the *dugri* speaker's straight talk, as described earlier, is anchored in a legitimating set of cultural values, such as sincerity, spontaneity, assertiveness, and so on, the Big Mouth is here described mainly in terms of social position and the privileges this position affords. The Big Mouth is overwhelmingly an older, Jewish-Ashkenazi male who is well-spoken, self-confident, and enjoys a sense of self-worth. His combative spirit is anchored not in a desire to fight the system but in a sense of mastery and confidence in his ability to manipulate it. Big Mouths draw attention by annoying people without ever truly relinquishing their hold on the heart of the social consensus. Thus, "they gained their position as people who speak their mind in an uncalculating way, not because they lose their temper and curse around but rather because they have a clear sense of the rules of the game and its limits" (24).

The reasons the Big Mouth strategy works, the article says, have to do precisely with the fact that it is encompassed within a socially consensual frame, which makes the Big Mouths appear more as entertainers than as rebels. They thrive on their readiness to expose themselves publicly and on their ability to project a sense of humanness, which generates a forgiving attitude among members of the public. Big Mouths are nurtured by the media that uses them and, in turn, legitimates their statements and upholds their social status. Thus, the article makes clear, the Big Mouth image benefits its bearers and is tolerated, and even encouraged, for several reasons: "First of all, Israel is a vulgar state and the boundaries of its public discourse are left undefined. Maintaining rules of politeness and diplomacy is perceived as weakness, whereas *dugri* statements, even extreme ones, are appreciated and rewarded. Secondly, the Israeli public has a hard time facing nuances. The public likes its speakers in black and white, not in colors of gray" (24).

These comments bring out the basic features attributed to the Big Mouth image while the rest of the article portrays variations on the Big Mouth theme—the patriot (MK and journalist Tommy Lapid); the narcissist (entertainer and TV personality Dudu Topaz); the misanthrope (artist Yigal Tomarkin); the Don Quixote (lawyer Yoram Sheftel), and so on. As I show in the following excerpts, the different types of Big Mouths mentioned in the above article all provide variously colored public performances of "straight talk" and, at times, retrospective commentaries about instances of infelicitous outspokenness. Dudu Topaz, the entertainer who became a well-known Big Mouth in 1981, when he used a racist label to refer to the Mizrahim, Jews from Muslim lands, attributes his style to his Israeliness, offering the following sociohistorical explanation for its emergence:

> The Israeli generally speaks his mind, with no British understatement. He is much more open than is proper. This is probably some kind of reversal that has occurred among the Jewish people, or the Israeli people, that were for years closed in and had to think of every word they said, and suddenly today there is this thing about saying it all, even in a blunt and exaggerated way. Of course, afterward you get apologies. I don't like it, as someone who has slipped more than once. (28)

The explicit question as to whether Israelis say what they think, which was posed to several of the Big Mouths portrayed in this article, was more often than not answered in the negative. Thus, the prominent Israeli artist Yigal Tomarkin said: "Today, all but a few follow the path of political correctness, all this American pseudo-intellectualism. People tend to think twice [before they speak]" (28). Advocate Yoram Sheftel's response was more provocatively formulated: "The Israeli public is the most cowardly and despicable in the Western globe. It is so cowardly that not only is it unwilling to fight for its country, but it is also afraid to speak its mind." He then added, "It is certainly possible that people see me as someone who says what they think—hence the appreciation they feel for me" (30).

Politician and former Minister of Education Shulamit Aloni, the only woman on the list of ten, presents a similar view, albeit in more subdued language: "In Israeli society there is a cult of consensus. Its im-

age as a society in which people say what they think—as distinguished
from mere bluntness—is unfounded, if we compare it to the USA or to
France, for example. Once, when the society was more restrained and
more united, one could hear the voices of those who cared enough to
confront it. Today everybody takes care of himself" (32).

And national soccer coach Shlomo Sharf, whose abrasive comments have made him the Big Mouth of Israeli sport, similarly rejected
the view that Israelis say what they think, saying, "I don't think people
in Israel say what they think. In Israel people lie more, they are not
more courageous" (36).

Surely, by rejecting the Israeli stereotype of the "straight talker,"
these Big Mouths underscored the uniqueness and special value of
their own outspokenness, much as by embracing this stereotype Dudu
Topaz sought a cultural warrant for his own highly consequential, racist
slip during the 1981 election campaign. Indeed, the public statements
that were responsible for the Big Mouth status of these personages
were often ethnic slurs, yet none of them had any problem discussing
"Israelis" as an overarching category. Moreover, the Big Mouths usually
saw themselves as forthright and outspoken in the spirit of the *dugri*
ethos. Yet, for at least some of them, unbridled bluntness was the name
of the game, which came closer to the style of *kasah* than to the Sabra's
dugri speech.

Notably, Israel's former president, Ezer Weizman, did not fit into
any of these Big Mouth categories. He was labeled "the greatest of all"
and claimed to be "a representative of the good old Sabra *dugriyut*,"
which in his case has yielded well-publicized insults, chauvinistic comments, impatient reproaches, anti-gay slurs in front of high-school
students, and strange, embarrassing impromptu speeches. Upon the
publication of his decision to resign from the presidency, following the
financial scandal he was involved in, a flurry of highly critical articles
of his conduct, including his speaking style, appeared in the press.

Some commentators linked his demise with the fall of the image
of the mythical Sabra. Thus, for example, an article written by a his-
torian and published in the evening paper *Ma'ariv,* was subtitled "The
resignation of President Weizman and the withdrawal from Lebanon
symbolize the end of the mythological Sabra." The author claimed
that Weizman—more than any of the other leaders of his generation,
including Moshe Dayan and Yitshak Rabin—symbolized the essence
of the Sabra myth. Among the reasons he cited for this assessment
were "the directness, the *dugri* quality *[dugriyut],* and lack of [social]

distance that characterized him so well." He went on to say that Weizman's acceptance of ongoing financial support from rich businessmen, a pattern of conduct reminiscent of petty politicians in the *shtetl,* had the effect of "turning the Sabra myth into a greedy, shameless, grotesque figure."[116]

Indeed, even the vulgar drawing of the big, open mouth on the magazine's cover page does not prepare one for the cumulative effect of the blunt statements, racial and ethnic slurs, chauvinistic observations, and outright insults that populate the pages of this article. Nothing was left of the *dugri* speaker's ennobling touch in this bitter text of cultural stocktaking. In this verbal Hall of Mirrors, the image of the self-absorbed yet nobly motivated, *dugri*-speaking Sabra has been transformed into the image of a self-righteous provocateur bent on the verbal belittlement of others. The article, though obviously critical of this image, participates in the media "festival" to which it owes much of its cultural prominence in the first place.

Two years later, on September 14, 2001, a similar large-scale article appeared in the weekly magazine of *Ha'aretz,* which, like the one delineating the portrait of the Israeli Big Mouth, provided a moment of cultural reflexivity whose focus was, once again, Israeli communicative style. It was compiled by a team of senior *Ha'aretz* journalists and entitled "A State of Vulgarity" *(medinat vulgaria).* The large-lettered subtitle states that Israelis live with the feeling that Israel is one of the most vulgar places on earth:

> The coarse, crude and cheap behavior, devoid of any subtlety and sophistication, which knows no boundaries, and shows no respect for the other and triggers an immediate sense of discomfort, has become a mark of Israeliness in and out of the country. It penetrates all aspects of life, can be found in all social groups regardless of gender, place of origin or level of education; it is pervasive among old as well as new elites, and is considered a major cause of the widespread sense of desperation and internal alienation, lagging just a little behind the security and economic situation. People with a particularly high level of good-will may characterize it as an expression of authenticity, directness and intimacy, typical Israeli traits that can be appreciated, but more and more Israelis have a hard time finding comfort in this characterization.[117]

The first contribution in the series of topically related articles, by journalist Uria Shavit, identifies fifteen prominent expressions of vulgarity. The third on the list is called "the vulgarity of the *dugri*" and includes the following account, which ridicules the *dugri* ethos as described earlier: "A common Israeli conception according to which it is permitted—in the name of directness and sincerity—to say everything, everywhere, to anybody. It is permitted to meet an acquaintance in the street, to view her with interest, and to comment: 'Come on, you've put on some weight recently.' It is permitted to hold someone by his sleeve and ask him openly: 'Tell me, how much do you make a month?' "[118]

The examples and reflections appearing in these two articles suggest that the Israeli public sphere, and Israeli social life more generally, have become sites where directness is a highly questionable proposition and where "saying it like it is" is at best an attention-grabber and at worst a rude infringement upon another's personal space. Talking straight in this new scheme of things is no longer a way of participating in a collective, cooperative enterprise, let alone an honorable gesture of self-definition. That straight talk can command such reflexive attention suggests that moral panics over ways of speaking go to the heart of the ongoing and rather tormented quest for a viable Israeli identity.

This is especially the case in view of the unusual triumph of the Hebrew language, which until a century ago served mainly a liturgical function for most Jews, and has now become the main language of everyday life and artistic expression among Jews in Israel. While the use of Hebrew, whose revival as a spoken language was central to the production of Israeli identity, is now a taken-for-granted dimension of Israeli life, the cultural anxieties over language use have migrated primarily to the domain of style and its role as a vehicle for identity display. The question raised through the vehicle of stylistic lamentation is the basic question—what has Homo Israelicus, the New Jew fabricated by and for the Zionist project, turned into? The answer given in the above alarmist articles points to a dread of vulgarity, lack of control, unbridled expressiveness, which seem to be part of the cultural conversation about the interface of language and culture in Israel. Perhaps it points to an Orientalist, European-bred dread of life in the "uncivilized" Middle East, whose impact is sometimes referred to disdainfully by Israelis of European descent as "Levantinization."

Notably, other lamentations often heard on language-related issues involve other signs of cultural-stylistic degradation, notably the disfluencies and hedging represented by such particles as *kaze* and *ke'ilu* (like) that I have mentioned in conjunction with the softening of the *dugri* mode. Originally these hedges were typical of young speakers to the point of becoming a generational marker of youthful defiance, but they have migrated into adult language as well. The tentativeness and inconclusiveness that are read into the frequent use of such expressions in everyday speech are a far cry from the Big Mouth syndrome, although both are critically viewed as signs of stylistic impoverishment. Indeed, the vagueness and inconclusiveness expressed by the prolific use of *kaze* and *ke'ilu* seem to trigger anxieties of another kind—the fear of being trapped in the lack of vitality, overcautiousness, and indecisiveness attributed to the overcivilized, oversophisticated, feeble-willed, and—ultimately—emasculated Western man. When considered in conjunction with each other, the opposing cultural anxieties—the fear of verbal loss of control and the fear of inadequate verbal vitality—suggest a deeper layer of cultural symbolism in which *dugri* speech is currently implicated. While originally, as I have pointed out, it was construed solely in relation to Jewish diaspora existence, it has now also come to stand for the unattained balance between East and West, between chaos and order.[119] The grotesque image of the Big Mouth and the unimposing, hesitant, wishy-washy image of the teenager whose disempowerment is signaled through his or her sloppy speech are both used to invoke moral panics about the nature of contemporary Israeliness.

The foregoing analysis has explored the cultural meanings and interactional functions of *dugri* speech as well as the change processes it has undergone "from the native's point of view." My emphasis has been on the explication of the *dugri* way of speaking in all its particularity as a historically situated phenomenon. As noted, the term *dugri* has been borrowed from Arabic and has undergone subtle semantic shifts in its journey across languages. Although this instance of linguistic borrowing may be read as part of the fascination that Arab culture held for the early Jewish settlers in Palestine who admired it for its flavor of "nativeness," I believe that like other appropriations of Arab customs, such as dress, foodways, or fighting lore, it actually hides more than it reveals about intercultural contacts between Arabs and Jews. The superficial nature of these contacts has been extensively discussed with reference to the literary productions of the early pioneering era in which they were depicted.[120]

Thus, despite the shared etymologies, there is an enormous gap between Arabs and Jews in their culturally focal speechways, and these speak to deep-rooted differences that cannot be easily glossed. Interviews with Arabic-speaking informants have led me to a study of the interactional ethos of *indirectness*, natively referred to as *musayra*, which is as central to Arabic culture as the *dugri* ethos is to the Sabra culture. A closer consideration of what is entailed in doing *musayra* will help me to bring into further relief the particular cultural configuration encapsulated in the *dugri* code as well as the differences between the two codes. As I will argue, these differences are well worth noting as they have far-reaching implications for intercultural communication between Arabs and Jews in Israel.

STYLE GONE WRONG: SPEAKING *DUGRI* AND DOING *MUSAYRA*

"*Musayra*," one of my Arab informants said, "is in the blood of every Arab person." It seems that the indirectness of style associated with the ethos of *musayra* is shared by men and women alike, although there are gender-related differences in the contexts, manner, and norms of doing *musayra*. Trying to explain how the code of *musayra* is acquired, one informant said, "You drink it with your mother's milk," and another said, "It's in the air, you breathe it in." Doing *musayra*, they explained, implies metaphorically "going with" the other, humoring him or her, accommodating oneself to the other's will or desire. It signals a conciliatory attitude, a willingness to compromise one's own desires in the service of maintaining solidary and harmonious social relations. Doing *musayra* carries many potent overtones for cultural members, as do its derivatives such as *musayir*, a person disposed to doing *musayra*. These are terms used in everyday discourse, and are typically invoked in passing judgment on social actors or social conduct.

The traditional notion of *musayra* can be traced to its historical roots in both religious Islamic doctrine and in the high degree of interdependence that characterized the social relations of early Arab communities. Indeed, the art of comporting oneself with social delicacy was praised by pre-Islamic poets, who were keenly aware of the role of such stylized conduct in the maintenance of harmonious social relations within the close-knit tribal group. This cultural orientation received explicit religious legitimation with the advent of Islam, as expressed in the elaborate literary tradition of *adab* (the ways of politeness, etiquette) that flourished from the beginning of the eighth century and was influenced by the cultures of newly Islamicized nations.[121]

Verbal acts of *musayra* can be marked by a sense of *conversational restraint* on the one hand, and *conversational effusiveness* on the other. Conversational restraint is displayed through strict adherence to procedural rules of deference, such as the management of topic shifts and the effort made to avoid topics of potential discord or any form of confrontational talk. It is very much about not saying things or saying them indirectly. Restraint is also exercised in the use of one's voice and the protection of speakers' right to the floor. Thus, loudness is shunned and so are hurried pace and interruptions. Conversational effusiveness involves a variety of interactional patterns that dramatize and intensify interpersonal bonding. These include unlimited accessibility to prolonged verbal exchanges, the effusive use of many layers of greetings, the use of multiple deferential or affectionate forms of address, accentuated displays of attentiveness, and open sharing of personal resources, in both time and effort.

The use of special forms of address in doing *musayra* is a good illustration of conversational effusiveness. For an address form to be heard as involving *musayra* it has to be contextually interpreted as exceeding standard expectations. Thus, doing *musayra* involves more than just following basic rules of social interaction; it involves, as one informant put it, "a norm of going beyond the norms." Addressing one's uncle as "my uncle" would be a minimal form of address, indicating that one is appropriately respectful, but no more. Addressing an uncle as "my father" would, however, be more than respectful—it would signal the intention to highlight a special bond, in the spirit of *musayra*.

Informants distinguished between different types of *musayra* on the basis of social-structural and contextual considerations. The basic code of doing *musayra* involves the *musayra of respect,* which mandates that the person lower in the hierarchy is required to act with *musayra* toward the one higher up: the child to the adult, the woman to the man, the young to the old, the simple villager to the village leader, and so on. Among men of equal status, reciprocal ritual acts of politeness, which are interpreted as articulating *musayra,* mark the absence of claims to status differentiation by the individuals involved. In addition, the doing of *musayra* may be associated with specific circumstances, particularly with contingencies. I refer to this as the *musayra of magnanimity.* Thus, one does *musayra* to a sick child; a man may act with *musayra* when his wife is pregnant; one is expected to act in the spirit of *musayra* toward a stranger in one's community.

A person's ability to engage in verbal conduct that would promote adherence to the ethos of *musayra* in potentially disruptive interpersonal contexts (so as to prevent open, angry disputes) is highly valued. This is the *musayra of conciliation.* Participants in a confrontational exchange may be enjoined by friends to do *musayra* toward each other as gestures of appeasement so as not to allow the conflict to escalate. As long as one's point of honor is not felt to be compromised, the injunction to act in the spirit of *musayra* may serve to restore harmony in social relations on occasions of mild conflict.[122] *Musayra* in such cases is equated with the art of speaking well. Mediation is an important communicative vehicle in such contexts. As one of my respondents described it, each party does *musayra* to the mediator who moves between the litigants' homes and tries to bring about conciliation.

Interest-driven musayra is also very common. This is where personal interests and interpersonal manipulations come in. Indeed, one of my informants referred to it as "the politics of everyday life," and people testified that they had gone out of their way to act with *musayra* toward those whose good will they wished to secure for specific purposes. For example, a man said that for several years he took care to do *musayra* to a woman he would ordinarily not have bothered with because he was interested in her daughter as a possible match for his son. He said that when he chatted with her from time to time he always greeted her profusely, using multiple forms of address as a sign of respect. Other stories involved a local politician who, just before the elections, went out of his way to do *musayra* to the villagers by giving them rides from the bus station on the main road to the village center in his private car, but disappeared from view after the elections.

The code of *musayra* is associated with traditional ways. It implies the recognition of social differentiation and hierarchical relations upheld by the authority of religion. Modernization is claimed to counteract the cultural force of *musayra*, and young people seem to find it increasingly difficult to conform to the demand for other-oriented, concessive behavior. However, even when they admit to this, they usually feel that there is no other way they can act in their own community, and find themselves using the tactics of *musayra* in contexts of intercultural contact as well. For some, such as those whose work or studies bring them into continuous social contact with Westernized Jewish society, the move between cultural worlds may involve code-switching along the directness dimension.

A touching example of generational differences in attitudes toward doing *musayra* was given to me by an informant who was a highly educated professional. He vividly recalled an exchange he had had with his elderly father during which they discussed some marital difficulties the son was experiencing at that time. The father interceded, saying to the son, "*Sayerna*, she is your wife, after all" (act with *musayra* toward her—in other words, make a compromise, don't bring the conflict to a head, try to smooth things over). The son replied in a way that shocked his father to such an extent that he subsequently reminded him of this exchange again and again in later years. The son's reply was: "Precisely because she is my wife I won't act with *musayra* toward her."

Reflecting on that interchange, the son said that our probing into the cultural meanings and uses of *musayra* made him realize that he had applied to the situation of marital conflict a Western cultural logic according to which interpersonal difficulties, especially those experienced with "significant others," need to be addressed explicitly and negotiated by the parties involved. It is through such mutual confrontation that interpersonal bonds can be revitalized and reaffirmed. He said he felt that he would not be taking his wife seriously if he allowed issues to be "pushed under the rug." His father, he explained, expected him to come forth with a show of magnanimity, and interpreted his unwillingness to act with *musayra* on that occasion as a rejection not only of his wife, but also of the binding force of social relations and the family as a locus of order in communal life. Western influence may affect young people's willingness to act with *musayra,* but even in cases in which this ethos is assigned different valuations, there is a basic shared understanding of the intricate working of doing *musayra* as a culturally "named" interactional code.

There are, however, cultural contexts in which doing *musayra* is out of place and may be explicitly suspended. An example of such a case that was repeatedly given by informants involved situations of mate-seeking in the context of arranged marriages. In such situations one seeks information about a prospective match for one's son or daughter and is dependent on the accuracy of facts one can gather about him or her. Since faithfulness to the facts is felt to be of paramount importance in this case, one may hear requests to suspend the code of *musayra* and speak "the *dugri.*"

What is recognized as directness or indirection in various cultural settings involves a different social dynamic in societies with a different history and cultural matrix. The differences relate to social practices, notions of responsibility or commitment, conceptions of truth, ideas of personhood, and attitudes toward interpersonal life. These are central elements in the folk-sociology and folk-psychology of cultural groups, and may lead to miscommunication when not recognized. Juxtaposing the code of *musayra* with the Sabra *dugri* code can provide some insights into why members of the two groups may rub each other the wrong way even on those rare occasions in which good will prevails. Given the foregoing discussions of the Sabra *dugri* ethos and the ethos of *musayra*, I will briefly delineate the major points of potential cultural clash between the two codes.

First, the Sabra *dugri* speaker's assertiveness involves a focus on the speaker's own face, a concern to project the image of a "proper" member of the Sabra culture, one who is expected to speak his or her mind in a straightforward way and is not afraid to do so. The assertive *dugri* mode thus implies a self-centered concern for the speaker's demeanor. It is thus diametrically opposed in interactional orientation to the other-directed mode of *musayra*, where the main concern is on respecting the addressee's face-wants. The coming together of these two orientations—the one constructed around demeanor, the other around deference—can be problematic indeed.

Second, *dugri* speech is motivated by a high value placed on the idea of sincerity interpreted as correspondence between one's inner world and one's behavioral display, as argued earlier. This is a modern Western notion that is not part of traditional Islamic cultures, which accept, and know how to work with, a disjunction between one's inner self and one's public self-image.[123] This sense of disjunction allows participants to maintain a high degree of ambiguity and embellishment in social communication in the pursuit of personal interest and rhetorical flourish even while holding on to the values of truth-speaking and impartiality. Speakers assume they can rely on hearers' dexterity in decoding ambiguities and overstatements. As a result, however, Arab communication patterns are perceived by many Western-oriented Jews to involve a high degree of "fabulation" and inspire little trust.[124] Arabs, on the other hand, often find the Sabra's sincerely expressed opinions exceedingly blunt and disrespectful.

Third, *dugri* speech involves a momentary suspension of the requirements of the immediate social situation and the social relations with one's interactional partners. It invokes, instead, more encompassing relations of solidarity grounded in cultural membership. Doing *musayra*, on the other hand, involves a set of cultural injunctions that are highly sensitive to various aspects of the social situation, such as participants' ages, genders, and degree of familiarity.[125] Solidarity is concretely grounded in the immediacy of social relations rather than involving a transcendental sense of affiliation. These are very different attitudes toward the situatedness of social encounters.

Fourth, speaking *dugri* is associated with an attitude of spontaneity, with the elevation of "naturalness." Doing *musayra,* on the other hand, is associated with the capacity for self-control and the positive value placed on stylization and artifice. In this orientation, it is the "culture" rather than the "nature" end of the culture/nature binary that is valorized. To Arabs, the Sabra speaker's spontaneity sounds like lack of restraint; to Sabra ears, a great deal of Arabic speech sounds affected, manipulative, and even hypocritical.

Fifth, the *dugri* speaker's attitude of antistyle is associated with a devaluation of speech (which is contrasted with action). The ethos of *musayra,* on the other hand, is associated with the high cultural value placed on the Arabic language,[126] with a delight in its stylistic possibilities, which Raphael Patai has called "rhetoricity."[127] For Sabras, this style is overly ornate; for Arabs, the Sabra style smacks of unfathomable literal-mindedness.

Sixth, the use of *dugri* speech is anchored in a social vision that allows for the possibility of creating egalitarian, *communitas*-like social relations. The ethos of *musayra,* on the other hand, is associated with hierarchical social arrangements and is routinely employed in reproducing highly differentiated status and power relations.

Seventh, the *dugri* ethos, especially as articulated in the *dugri* ritual, is agonistic in nature, enacting a tolerance for conflict in the construction of identity and in the creation of a shared communal space. The ethos of *musayra,* in contradistinction, is associated with a strong cultural disposition toward the maintenance of social harmony and the avoidance of open conflict.

Eighth, the directness associated with the *dugri* interactional code implies a preference for nonmediated, face-to-face communication. One expression informants used to characterize *dugri* talk was "straight to the face" (*yashar bapanim*). The *dugri* speaker is perceived as one who takes responsibility for his or her act of speaking and is contrasted with the gossip who circulates unfavorable social information in a backhanded way. Arabs, on the other hand, value the use of mediation and prefer to convey unpleasant social information indirectly in order to reduce the potential threat to participants' face.

When these divergent cultural attitudes are applied to one and the same communicative encounter between Arabs and Jews, it can easily become deflected even in the context of a wholehearted pursuit of a cultural and political modus vivendi. Those Jews for whom *dugri* speech, or vestiges of it, serve as an idiom of self-definition, and Arabs for whom "life demands *musayra*" both have quite a good deal of cultural learning to do in order to communicate with each other in a satisfactory manner. The possibility that such a mutual cultural learning process may emerge seems now as remote as it ever was despite the changes that have taken place both in the cultural standing of the *dugri* code and in younger people's willingness to conform to the code of *musayra*.

Even the recent disaffection expressed by many with regards to the bluntness associated with the *dugri* ethos has nothing to do with the influence of Arabic speechways. Thus, in an article sketching the image of the so-called trigger-happy neo-Israeli, senior journalist Uzi Benziman concluded his rather dark reflections by saying:

> The Israeli ethos has enshrined the values of spontaneity, *dugriness*, and interpersonal immediacy. One of the distorted results of this value system is the speed with which knives are drawn out. Spontaneity is not necessarily lawlessness, and directness does not mean one has the license to be carried away without limits. There is something positive about the language of understatement and about the restrained style by which British and American children are educated. Israeli temperament justifies a special effort in teaching school children the arts of self-restraint.[128]

I find it significant that in weaving his fantasy of a better social world, one governed by self-restraint and interpersonal decorum, Benziman turns to the education of British and American children. Although his disaffection with the *dugri* ethos might have plausibly pointed in the direction of *musayra*, he did not recommend that Israelis be tutored in its arts. I believe that this Western orientation is shared by many middle-class Israelis of European descent who systematically fail to appreciate (or even see) the Middle Eastern culture that surrounds them, either that of Palestinian Arabs or that of Middle Eastern Jews. As my analyses of the early pioneers' soul talks and of the Sabra's *dugri* speech have indicated, Israeli ways of speaking have emerged out of a complex dialogue with European speech-ways, Jewish and otherwise. These dialogic relations often took the form of unselfconscious appropriations and self-conscious rebellions.

The impact of the indigenous Arab inhabitants of the land on the Jewish newcomers to it did not go beyond the much-touted, rather superficial gestures of the cultural appropriation of signs of "nativeness" in dress, food, and so forth. Even in the early years of Jewish settlement, when the Arabs were still romanticized and to some degree emulated, the subtleties of interactional codes and social relations were left out of view. Therefore, it would be as unreasonable to claim that the mythical Sabra has rejected the ethos of *musayra* as to propose that Benziman and other Israelis might learn something from it. So near at hand, the undercurrents of Arabic culture are in fact beyond many Israelis' horizons. The Sabra ethos and the *dugri* code were so obviously constructed within the context of the Jewish-European experience that many Jews from Muslim lands, whose lifestyles as well as communication styles were much more in tune with Middle Eastern codes, felt discredited and marginalized by the unrelenting pressure to conform to the image of the New Jew, Sabra-style. When they either refused or felt unable to undergo the kind of identity transformation this required, they were judged as not Israeli enough in the eyes of Sabras like former MK Ori Or. As the years went by, the hegemonic definition of "Israeliness" was replaced by a growing recognition of the cultural diversity of Israeli society, so that by the late 1990s Or's denigrating comments about Moroccan Jews were not allowed to pass, even when clothed as *dugri*.

Indeed, cultural codes of communication, such as *dugri* speech, are powerful mechanisms for policing group boundaries, signaling who is in and who is out. They are grounded in deep-seated assumptions about proper ways of being, feeling, and relating to others. Cultural styles of speaking embody recipes for living, and changes in the way they are interpreted and valued imply changes in deep-seated sensibilities and identity constructions. Having lost its privileged cultural position, *dugri* speech became one of several interactional options, one that was part of the repertoire of fewer and fewer members of Israeli society. It lost its resonance as marking the possibility of an authentic confrontational dialogue, which harbors the promise of a true meeting of minds, and it assumed the role of a symbol of fallen grace. The Israeli scene was filled with degraded forms of straight talk, exchanges in the style of *kasah*, statements by Big Mouths of one sort or another.

The culturally constructed dichotomy between words and deeds has lost much of its poignancy even though it is still occasionally reinvoked. I have recently encountered it in political and military discourse, such as a reported exhortation by a top military officer to combat soldiers serving in the Occupied Territories to do more and talk less, or in radical left critiques of governmental policies toward the Palestinians that claim that the government uses words to camouflage deeds, not even to replace them, engaging in talk of peace while making war. The image of the *dugri* speaker, in the person of the assassinated Prime Minister Yitshak Rabin, is repeatedly invoked in a nostalgic vein, accentuating the sense of loss associated with the demise of the *dugri* ethos. Thus, in a piece titled "A Man of the Past Century," published on the fifth anniversary of Rabin's assassination, journalist Doron Rosenblum described Rabin in the following terms:

> He did not know how to market himself in front of the camera. He did not belong to e-very-body (*ku-lam*, a populist turn of phrase used by Ehud Barak). He was not even a friend. Certainly not mine and yours. Nevertheless, he was a leader, one of us, and he was also himself. He was a man of the past century, the last one to ride the tide of *dugri* and good faith, which have probably been lost forever.[129]

Even though the authenticity associated with the mythical image of the *dugri* speaker seems indeed lost forever, some version of the direct mode as a coveted locus of authenticity is still an important aspect of Israeli culture. Rather than harking back to the meanings and values associated with the *dugri* ethos, this new form of directness involves emotional openness and accessibility that were not typical of the *dugri*-speaking Sabra. This became clear in commentaries that have accompanied the election of Israel's Minister of Defense, Binyamin Ben-Eliezer, originally from Iraq, to the position of leader of the Labor movement. His victory was attributed to his direct approach, sometimes even by explicitly invoking the *dugri* ethos. Yet commentators did not refer to Ben-Eliezer's directness as involving the opinionated, confrontational edge ordinarily associated with the *dugri* speaker, but rather as involving an idiom of immediacy and emotionality.

In an article published in *Ha'aretz*, Gideon Samet spoke of Ben Eliezer's "warm directness," which he referred to as a *dugri* approach marked by simplicity and a measure of roughness.[130] This approach, he claimed, was at the root of Ben-Eliezer's appeal to the electorate. The *dugri* mode had moved from the position of a hegemonic, self-defining cultural style to become an ingredient in a multicultural repertoire of personally styled ways of speaking and ways of being.

The story of the rise and fall of *dugri* speech is an important chapter in the story of the cultural politics of language in modern Israel. As such, it also tells the story of the politics of Israeli identity.

The rise of the *dugri* ethos was associated with the project of creating a new Jewish identity in the image of the quintessential Sabra, the native-born Israeli Jew. Like much of the new culture in prestate years and in the early years of statehood, this image had its roots in European culture and was part of a nation-building agenda. The process of its production involved homogenizing and standardizing efforts and re-sulted in the establishment of an "Israeliness" scale that dominated the Israeli cultural scene well into the 1970s.

Following the wars of 1967 and 1973, each with its own blend of trauma and victory, the hegemonic Sabra ethos began to lose its grip. One expression of this emerging cultural vulnerability was the introduction of a new politics of identity, whose most important aspect was the increasing cultural power of Oriental Jews who traced their cultural heritage to Muslim lands. The ethnicity-based identity politics that became increasingly prominent on the Israeli cultural scene has been experienced by the Israeli Ashkenazi elite as a destabilizing process of gradual disempowerment. As we have seen, loss of hegemony has given rise to periodic nostalgic invocations of the image of the mythical *dugri*-speaking Sabra alongside occasional harsh self-criticisms that fo-cus on Israeli cultural communication style. Torn between the poles of nostalgia and bitter self-critique, Israelis have tended to experience the story of the rise and fall of *dugri* speech as a story of both promise and loss. Yet, viewed from a different perspective, the growing multivocality of the Israeli cultural scene is not a story of communicative undoing but part of a larger process of culture-making, of which the emergence of the *dugri* ethos was but one chapter. Other ways of speaking and other communicative occasions have emerged as culturally significant over the years.

This brings me to the next "dialogic moment" I have chosen to focus upon in this book. The next chapter will consider late-night call-in radio programs that deal with personal problems as distinctive speech occasions. As mass-mediated speech events, they are grounded in the possibility of dissemination, re-creating "dialogic moments" of a particular kind. Participants in these programs locate the authenticity of their discourse in the personal world of individual emotions and interpersonal relations even while enacting emergent forms of identity politics. One of the two programs I focus on in the next chapter artic-ulates a Western-based quasi-therapeutic ethos that echoes the idea of "communication" that struck me as peculiarly American some twenty years ago.[131] The other program employs a Middle Eastern cultural code of social support that intertwines emotional resonance with practical help. Both use the special features of radio communication in constructing ephemeral communities where "public intimacy" is the name of the game. Both give voice to culturally inflected ways of speaking in a context in which speech codes are simultaneously given and crafted anew.

Chapter 3

Airwaves Dialogues
The Cultural Politics of Personal Radio

THE "DIALOGIC TURN" IN
CONTEMPORARY MEDIA CULTURE

The increasingly important contribution of the media as a key agent in shaping the speech economies of contemporary societies is widely recognized. Anthropologist Debra Spitulnik has highlighted the fruitfulness of studying media-related language use within an ethnography of communication perspective: "The fact that media help to circulate and even canonize a basic repertoire of ways of speaking has implications not only for the social life of language but for the production of culture, ideology and identity. The models of language use in media do not come out of thin air, and they are always inherently ideological."[1] And she continues: "The ability of media to delineate social identities and to function as forums for collective participation is greatly dependent on language use. Social identities (e.g., class, gender, age, ethnicity) of both media producers and media audiences are constructed through a choice of topics, code, register, and style."[2]

Radio is the most distinctively aural medium of mass communication within our contemporary, visually centered, mediascapes. In his study of what he calls "radio texture," Joe Tacchi describes radio listening as a social activity, as a safe environment in which people can cultivate their sense of sociality:

> Radio as a medium is immediate, intimate, and direct. Translating this quality of radio into language, people often speak of it as a "friend," as "company." These terms are used as metaphors to express a particular (and usually unexpressed) relationship with a medium that we are not normally asked to talk or even think about. Thinking of radio sound as textured allows the possibility of considering how it operates, and how people operate within it.[3]

Talk radio is totally dependent on the performative potential and resonance of the spoken word, and is often consumed as a secondary activity while doing other things, such as driving or performing domestic
chores. For many years, radio communication has attracted relatively
little scholarly attention in media studies compared to the considerable
interest in television as a media form. Recent research on the history of
radio, however, has brought out the crucial role of radio broadcasting
in shaping the notion of the audience, in forging an enhanced sense
of subjectivity, and in establishing "media communities" of various
types.[4] Susan Douglas addresses this complex contribution in the following terms:

> One primal experience those born before *and* after the Second World War
> share is lying in bed, sometimes with the covers just barely over the heads,
> listening intently to the box next to us. Maybe it was the darkness, the
> solitude, or being in bed, but the intimacy of this experience remains
> vivid; listeners had a deeply private, personal bond with radio . . . radio
> has worked most powerfully inside our heads, helping us create internal
> maps of the world and our place in it, urging us to construct imagined
> communities to which we do, or do not, belong. . . . Certainly it has played
> a central role, over the last nine decades, in constructing us as a new entity:
> the mass-mediated human, whose sense of space and time, whose emo-
> tional repertoires and deepest motivations cannot be extricated from what
> has emanated through the airwaves.[5]

Radio's intimate tones became even more pronounced in the early
1980s, with the advent of what has been called the dialogic turn in
media broadcasting. This turn involved a movement from one voice
to many voices. Lay people joined media-trained professionals and
experts in "live" radio exchanges in the most directly participatory
mode the media had yet been able to offer at the time. Passive listeners became eavesdroppers by tuning in to the back-and-forth of
other people's conversations, taking sides and even volunteering their
responses. Call-in radio programs, in particular, commanded new
forms of listenership than the casual, incidental listening that had
come to characterize radio consumption as a secondary activity. Gibian's account of the dialogic turn in talk radio registers his surprise
at this "boom in airwaves dialogues": "Who would have believed, a
few years ago, that the call-in talk show and the news-issue debate—
the most raw, humble, primitive forms on the air—would blossom
forth as the hottest media formats for the 1980s, the models for a
wide range of programming now reaching us twenty-four hours a day?

And who can foresee where the audience hunger for voices in dialogue may lead?"[6]

Indeed, this "hunger for voices in dialogue" is one of the products of radio's response to the emergence of television as the dominant medium of electronic communication in the second part of the twentieth century, leading to a revitalization of visions of communication-as-dialogue in a context where communication-as-dissemination dominates, in John Peters's terms.[7] Peters points out that the performative dilemmas associated with communication-at-a-distance were a central issue in the early history of radio, when the question of how the fact that people could be in touch without appearing to each other in person was raised. The attempt to address this question gave rise to what Peters calls "compensatory dialogism"—the development of "new forms of authenticity, intimacy, and touch not based on immediate physical presence."[8] He continues:

> The hunt for communicative prostheses—compensations for lost presences—was vigorous in the culture of commercial radio in the 1920s and 1930s. Broadcasters quickly recognized the risk of alienating the affections of listeners and invented diverse strategies to replace what had apparently been taken away: the presence of fellow listeners, a conversational dynamic, and a personal tone. Commercial broadcasting was quite self-conscious about overcoming the listener's sense of being stuck in a mass audience without mutual interaction or awareness, with one-way flow of communication and anonymous styles of talk. New discursive strategies were designed to compensate for the medium's structural lacks. The aim was to restore lost presence.[9]

The development of call-in radio programs further compensated for the one-way flow of earlier radio talk programs, reshaping the participation structures associated with communication-at-a-distance, offering new forms of intimacy as well as a new arena for democratic participation. Indeed, "dialogic utopias" associated with technological dreams of an open society, whose affairs are run by "town meetings on the air," emerged hand in hand with the development of radio. These were dreams of the dialogic possibilities inherent in communication as a cooperative, communal endeavor, traces of which are found in discussions of the public sphere to this day.[10] Bertolt Brecht, among others, recognized the interactive potential of radio in its first years, long before the call-in format came into place. He spoke of it in idealistic terms as a vehicle for a free, rational, and nonauthoritarian public dialogue. In his essay "Theory of Radio," written in the 1920s, he remarked:

But quite apart from the obviousness of its functions, radio is one-sided when it should be two. It is purely an apparatus of distribution, for mere sharing out. So here is a positive suggestion: change this apparatus over from distribution to communication. The radio would be the finest possible communication apparatus in public life, a vast network of pipes. That is, it would be if it knew how to receive as well as to transmit, how to let the listener speak as well as to hear, how to bring him into a relationship instead of isolating him.[11]

It took some years for this vision of interactive radio to materialize, but today call-in radio programs have become the most common types of airwaves dialogues in media broadcasting. Nevertheless, they have attracted little scholarly attention.[12] Television talk shows, by contrast, have been the focus of a good deal of critical media research that explores their role as a form of popular culture.[13] It is not my purpose to review this body of work here, but I will mention some differences between these two types of airwaves dialogue in my following discussion so as to bring out the special dialogic potential of the radio format. This potential has been underscored by Gunther Kress, when he wrote: "Of all radio-genres that of the talk-back radio approximates most closely to that definitively private genre, the conversation—a genre which, in its formal aspects, encodes equality of power-relations, and uses speech in its most characteristic form. Talk-back radio thus holds out the promise of actual dialogue, of participation, the possibility of private individuals having access to the mass media."[14]

Call-in radio is particularly intriguing as a broadcasting format since it blurs the customary line between producers and consumers of mass-mediated communication. Invited to call in, listeners are given the floor to express their opinions or share their experiences in their own words. The callers are the ones who initiate the radio exchanges. Their personal concerns or opinions make up the program's agenda. I would say that call-in radio has been the most highly participatory mass communication form until the emergence of the Internet (which is restricted to people who have access to computers and have acquired the necessary skill to use the Web). It provides an arena in which consumers participate directly in shaping radio programming in a way that goes even beyond the active consumption of media forms found in the "poaching" activities of media fans.[15]

While this participatory format democratizes the radio as a mass-mediated form, some of the institutional control is retained by the radio—for example, through choice of host, or through the program's placement in the station's broadcasting schedule. Moreover, even within the most open and free-flowing of call-in radio dialogues, the host remains in a position of authority, performing the important role of discourse leader, facilitator, and regulator. Indeed, radio dialogues, like all forms of broadcast talk, are shaped in institutional terms and thus combine self-expression with discursive control.

This, in terms of Paddy Scannell's analysis of "broadcast talk," implies the need to study the dialogic construction of call-in programs by attending to: "(1) the distribution of communicative entitlements, (2) the allocation of participatory statuses and performative roles, and (3) the organization and control of talk."[16] Scannell claims and demonstrates that attention to such details of the social dimension of conversational organization can contribute to a better understanding of the role played by such radio programs as contemporary public forums. Some of my analysis will therefore trace the ways in which the radio hosts construct and regulate their programs' discourse even while attending to callers' deeply felt personal concerns. Participants in both radio and televised dialogues have to take into account an indefinite number of ratified "eavesdroppers," whose presence-at-a-distance must be kept in mind. Paddy Scannell has referred to this feature of airwaves dialogues as the "double articulation" of broadcast talk, meaning its quality of being simultaneously addressed to particular interlocutors and to absent, imagined listeners.[17]

Call-in radio exchanges are "live" in the sense that they are spontaneous and nonrehearsed, reenacting the free flow of everyday conversation in all its spontaneity and immediacy. Television talk shows, in contradistinction, involve considerable staging and well-rehearsed performances in which participants' contributions, particularly those personal confessions so commonly aired on daytime television, tend to become part of a media spectacle through which human misery and social transgression are put on display, commodified, and served to the public as popular entertainment. These televised dialogues have received more criticism than analysis. Some have repudiated their sensationalism, while others have viewed them as having a subversive potential, providing sites for the formulation of a countermythology that highlights major themes and struggles of contemporary life.[18]

Call-in radio programs, although they may invite voyeuristic listenership, are less oriented toward public spectacle and more concerned with an attempt to simulate interpersonal dialogue. In this broadcasting context, absent listeners are eavesdroppers into a private conversation of strangers who sometimes share intimate, introspective, often painful aspects of their lives in the "public intimacy" of the radio exchange. Acting as ratified but nonpresent witnesses, they are free to engage in real-life dramas of human distress to which they may but need not actively respond. Both the stance of controlled engagement and the stance of intrigued noninvolvement have their tantalizing dimensions. They also offer an opportunity to learn about the often hidden aspects of human experience and about possible ways of responding to them. Being limited to vocal exposure, with the absence of visual clues, the anonymity of the caller-narrators in these radio programs can be more easily maintained. This gives callers some control over the degree of their pubic exposure.

Call-in exchanges on radio are temporally anchored in simultaneity, inviting listeners to share in the moment of the talk and in the uncertainty of its unfolding. They are dialogically constructed as "open" texts, forever unpredictable with respect to the voices they call forth and with respect to the direction of the conversational flow. This essential openness and unpredictability are crucial to the production of the programs and to their audience appeal. This quality of the radio exchange accounts for the observation that radio call-ins—unlike television talk shows—tend to preclude both rehearsals and reruns. It also accounts for the fact that radio call-ins tend to be highly localized and nonexportable—unlike television talk shows, such as Oprah Winfrey's, which have become a globalized media product.

The radio hosts' ways of performing their role, no less than the topics they choose to address, serve to weave together a credible and recognizable radio persona that becomes identified with the program over time. Debra Spitulnik, who has studied radio culture in Zambia, has addressed talk radio as a discursive space in which styles are creatively crafted out of culturally available linguistic resources. She points out that style serves as a trademark of particular radio personalities, saying: "The uniqueness of such radio personalities is to a great degree built upon this verbal creativity, a creativity that is at the same time relatively predictable since it is recognizable as personal style."[19]

Radio hosts give voice to their uniqueness as well as reinforce their authority through various forms of discursive display. They circulate recognizable expressive forms and regulate the exchange in terms of length, cutting callers short when they feel it is necessary to do so. They retain initial control over the range of topics raised in their programs by selecting the calls they respond to on air. In Israel and elsewhere, programs are divided between those dealing with current affairs in the public sphere and those devoted to the discussion of personal issues and the sphere of private life. Typical topics on programs concerned with the public sphere, which in Israel are usually scheduled as part of daytime programming, are generally concerned with security matters, politics, or the economy. They may be triggered by a controversial statement of a politician, by a problematic decision of the Supreme Court, by a bureaucratic mishandling of citizens' affairs, and so on. Topics included in programs concerned with the private sphere, which in Israel are usually scheduled as part of late-night programming, involve personal difficulties and interpersonal relations. They are usually triggered by life events and include such issues as marital strife, ways of coping with addictions, parent-child conflicts, and the like.

The question arises whether such radio exchanges can indeed be viewed as contemporary, mass-mediated versions of the quest for authentic dialogue. A more skeptical view of "open communication" would recognize the "dark side" of these airwave dialogues as newly shaped institutional arenas that, while enacting a spirit of dialogue and solidarity, can also become sites of social control. Like the early pioneers' soul talks, these latter-day radio shows are constructed through processes of cultural negotiation in which personal lives are given public resonance; as in the case of the soul talks, personal lives are also under increased threat of social colonization and of expressive regimentation. This was recognized by Peter Gibian who follows Foucault in questioning the validity of the view that more talk means more freedom, or that more dialogue means more equality. He says: "[T]he more subjects we open to dialogue, the more areas of our lives we open to management, re-structuration and control—while at the same time we also multiply the possible points of resistance to that control. Is the 1980s turn to media dialogue an opening for new decentralized personal resistance and expression, or will it simply relocate older mechanisms of power in more subtle, personal and localized arenas?"[20]

Deborah Cameron similarly questions the utopian view of radio dialogues that focus on the personal domain, pointing out that they provide not only expressive outlets but are also sites where individuals' personal affairs are brought into public view and ways of speaking about the self and about interpersonal relationships become modeled and regulated. She speaks to the potentially "darker" side of such media encounters, saying:

Entertainment media, too, especially talk radio and television, now disseminate to a mass audience the idea that being able and willing to talk about
problems, feelings and relationships is inherently desirable. Some popular media formats—notably the confessional talk show—not only provide
continual reinforcement for the basic idea that "it's good to talk," but also
model the correct way of talking about personal experience in some detail.[21]

The analysis offered in the remainder of this chapter highlights the
tension between call-in radio programs as sites of authentic individual
expression and as sites of social control. Indeed, I have chosen to focus
on programs of the "self-help" variety primarily because they make this
tension most visible. Thus, while my analysis will address the dialogic
potential of these radio exchanges, it will also attend to the hosts' attempts to regiment callers' voices, and to callers' rare attempts to resist
a program's implicit discursive and ideological regime. It is through this
multilayered analytic effort that call-in radio programs can be seen as a
cultural arena in which the personal domain is routinely foregrounded
and reaffirmed in a contemporary Israeli public setting.

I see this mass-mediated arena as a cultural site where the much-
discussed shift from collectivist concerns to a focus on individual experience in Israeli society can be traced. Thus, let me note that the
personal sphere is locally constructed and interpreted on these radio
programs largely through narratives of personal distress (rather than
success stories, for example). This shared thematic focus in the construction of the public articulation of personal lives should be kept in
mind even though much of my analysis will be devoted to different
cultural inflections of the discourses of distress and support in Israeli
society.

CONSTRUCTING SELF-HELP RADIO

The emergence of self-help radio in the early 1980s has been described
by Gibian as follows: "Radio's self-help era began with the hiring of psy-
chics, psychologists, real estate experts, sex therapists, auto mechanics,
and so on, to lead endless discussion sessions with an expanding and
avid audience."[22] Call-in radio programs that fall under the self-help
category address individuals' personal problems, desires, and needs.
When they involve psychologists and counselors, they mark a field of
practice sometimes referred to as "media psychology." Initially, psychologists' involvement with the media, most notably in the form of radio
counseling, was criticized as unprofessional and potentially harmful.

With time, attitudes to the professional participation of psychologists on radio and television programs have changed and "media psychology" has gained greater legitimacy, though it is still regarded with suspicion by many professionals, as some rather sharp comments I received during the time I was conducting this study have indicated to me.

Studies of psychological counseling over Israeli radio, which have combined a uses-and-gratifications approach to the study of media with the study of help-seeking behaviors, confirmed that callers and listeners are by-and-large satisfied consumers of radio counseling. Listeners were found to be motivated by a general sense of curiosity, by a desire to gain psychological knowledge. They were interested in enhancing their self-awareness, and in learning from the opportunity to engage in social comparison with others. Callers attested to their improved ability to handle the problems they discussed on the air.[23]

The proliferation of self-help programs concerned with the interpersonal domain suggests that some of the most urgent experiences people wish to share with anonymous others involve emotional issues associated with interpersonal and familial relationships. Yet this does not mean that all such programs involve the participation of professional psychologists or counselors. Some of these programs are hosted by experts and can therefore be included within the domain of "media psychology." Other self-help programs do not involve the participation of certified professionals; rather, they involve "folk psychologists" who provide solace and counsel in their own ways. Their conceptions of personal life and their beliefs about interpersonal relations are not necessarily in line with the middle-class, hegemonic voices that dominate the therapeutic ethos of the "media psychology" programs. Though often dealing with personal problems that are essentially similar to the ones addressed by professionals, their tone and language suggest that they target a working-class and more traditional segment of the Israeli public.

The choice to turn to the radio program is but one of several self-help options available to callers in attempting to deal with their situation. Other options, such as turning to immediate family members or close friends, or seeking professional help from a clinic or a telephone crisis line, are open to them as well. Both call-in radio programs and crisis lines offer mediated sources of social support. By appealing to either, callers avoid the potential costs of disclosure in front of those who are directly involved with their problem, or the stigma sometimes associated with seeking psychological help. A call to the radio or to a telephone crisis line carries no implications for one's ongoing social relationships. When one's problem is selected for inclusion in a call-in radio program, it also gains public resonance and becomes the vehicle for an individually centered communal dialogue.

Given the popularity of self-help radio programs, not all calls to the studio can be responded to on the air. About one out of four or five calls was put on air in the programs I studied. Callers first talk to assistant producers, who receive the calls and provide the host with summary statements of the personal dilemma or life situation they wish to discuss. Criteria for this selection include the nature of the caller's expressed distress, its urgency (in some cases, a telephone line is set aside for urgent calls), as well as audience-related considerations of media production, such as the call's potential relevance and interest to a wider audience.

Beyond the decision to participate in the public arena of radio broadcasting, even if anonymously, the actual participation in radio call-in programs requires considerable tenacity on callers' part. The lines are often busy, and the prospects of actually getting on air are rather slim. Calls are taken an hour before the program starts and through its duration. Usually each program features between seven and ten calls per night, and the calls tend to span between twenty and thirty minutes on average. This means that the ever-present media constraint of time-pressure is somewhat alleviated and an encounter resembling a genuine, unhurried conversation is allowed to unfold.

Callers who are selected for inclusion in the program are called back at some point during the night, when this suits the host's agenda. When a caller is contacted on the air, he or she is addressed familiarly by first name, which both protects anonymity and creates a familiar atmosphere. He or she is then asked to turn off the radio at home so as to obstruct intrusive noises, further enhancing the feeling of being in a conversational enclosure. Callers often testify to being alone when placing a call, whether at home or at a late-night job, or on the road. The radio-phonic encounter thus comes close to a regular telephone conversation, and callers sometimes appear to forget that they are on the air (and sound startled when reminded of it). This and the nocturnal setting of the call-in conversation work to intensify the sense of intimacy that attends such exchanges.

Given the personal topics discussed on these self-help programs, and the callers' special vulnerability, the interactional climate of warm acceptance established by the hosts serves to modify (or perhaps camouflage) their built-in position of authority. It also counteracts the medium's built-in structural lack—its need to compensate for the spatial separation and anonymity of the interlocutors. The emphasis placed by call-in radio programs on the personality of the host enhances listeners' identification with him or her as a simultaneously familiar and distant figure of charismatic authority.

Indeed, many callers openly express an emotional attachment to the host. These positive feelings are often expressed by callers in prefacing their personal stories with comments indicating their admiration for the host, such as: "I love your program," or "I've been listening to you for years," or "I never miss your program," or "I'm sure only you can help me." Such attachment to media figures, who become part of listeners' social and emotional lives, has been labeled as a "parasocial relationship."[24] It is attended by a basic relational asymmetry that frames the call-in radio format—the host addresses anonymous listeners who become one-time conversational partners, whereas the callers address a particular, known host with whose voice quality and radio persona they have become quite familiar.

Donald Horton and Anselm Strauss have addressed the relational dimension of such media engagements with reference to television entertainment. Their account, I believe, applies to the case of these radio programs as well:

> Over the course of time direct and indirect interplay between performance and audience binds them together in a common institution or, better, a common "world" of entertainment which has its own well-understood values and norms of reciprocal behavior derived from the common social matrix, its own history and course of mutual development. Any one program on the television screen is but a single episode, for most viewers, in this history. The relationships built up, and the understandings that sustain them, seem no different in kind from those characteristic of normal social life; and the symbolic processes mediating them are likewise the same, though their operations are modified somewhat by the special conditions of television broadcasting.[25]

Callers' familiarity with the voice quality and interactional style of the radio host, as well as the higher visibility of the radio outlet, may account for the decision to call the radio rather than the telephone crisis line. The host's charisma does not necessarily depend on professional expertise (such as that carried by expert psychologists, for example). Rather, it may be grounded in the host's sympathetic engagement with callers' problems, and in the sense of familiarity generated by ongoing exposure on radio. The host's production of "public intimacy" and the callers' displays of attachment compensate for the condition of "lost presence" that is built into the mediated radio environment.

John Peters's aforementioned discussion of the processes whereby presence is partially restored in mass-mediated contexts attends mainly to the situational dimensions of the exchange. It does not, however, take into account how cultural diversity in interpersonal communication patterns may affect the ways in which both hosts and callers attempt to restore a sense of presence in the context of their mediated exchange. A more culturally oriented analysis calls for greater attention to different ways of accomplishing a sense of presence in a supportive interchange. Such interactional performances are often subject to cultural coloration whether they occur in mediated or unmediated settings. [26] Cultural codes for expressing distress, making appeals, and offering support affect the flavor of the talk on these programs, playing into the hosts' creative construction of their distinctive styles.

Thus, while these programs are closely identified by the hosts' personas, they are discursively constructed in such a way as to appeal to particular segments of their potential audience—people who share knowledge and appreciation of the cultural codes mobilized by the host. Consequently, they also serve to delimit and constrain the program's listenership, creating a sense of community among those who choose to tune in. As Gibian points out, however, this is a paradoxical community, an evanescent community "somehow formed of the most alienated and atomized of listeners—each alone in a car or living room." [27] Ensconced in their private quarters, callers and listeners reach out to each other in word and thought, attempting to overcome their personal isolation. They form an unofficial and fluid "lonely hearts' club" to which anyone can belong by simply turning the radio on. Host, callers, and listeners are spatially separated yet linked in a shared world of talk. They are at once distant and vocally "embodied" through what Mary Louise Pratt has described as the "liberatory pleasure of experiencing the texture of the spontaneous human voice." [28]

The two self-help programs I have focused on in this study share a standard format for Israeli radio programs of this kind—they involve conversations with callers, which are interspersed with musical interludes and interrupted by commercial spots and hourly news updates. The two programs, one hosted by Yovav Katz and the other hosted by Yossi Saias, are shaped by the hosts' personas and the kind of talk they invite and permit. They are also colored by the musical interludes that punctuate the talk. These two programs are aired on the same channel of Israeli national radio, Kol Israel, the highly popular Channel B *(reshet bet)*. This channel also carries a variety of daytime call-in programs that deal with politics and current affairs as well as other types of talk programs on other nights of the week. In recent years, regional radio channels and a variety of pirate radio stations have greatly diversified Israel's radioscape, and a number of these channels have introduced call-in, personally oriented, programs of various kinds, both as part of their nighttime and as part of their daytime programming.

I have selected late-night call-in radio programs involving intimate address as my research site since I view them as a contemporary version of the quest for authentic dialogue in Israeli culture, which in some ways resonates with (while in many ways differing from) the earlier quests for dialogue considered in this book. These airwave dialogues are a distinctive brand of mass-mediated encounters that have gained cultural force through a combination of institutional endorsements and popular appeal. They are discursive sites of cultural production and reproduction where forms of talk and "dialogic moments" provide both *models of* and *models for* ways of speaking about personal and interpersonal life.[29]

No doubt, the nocturnal framing of these two programs is particularly conducive to the kind of intimate engagement and club-like atmosphere they foster. Late-night radio exchanges carry the temporal aura of nighttime liminality and marginality.[30] Set within a nocturnal liminal zone, these programs allow for the special conversations that emerge among those who remain awake "when the whole world is asleep." These hours of the night, removed as they are from the ebb and flow of daily life, protected from the gaze of full public exposure, open the door to confession and self-exploration. They are temporal enclaves in which discourses of vulnerability as well as moments of communion are allowed to emerge.

As events-in-time these programs chart the contours of fleeting "media communities" whose moral boundaries are sustained as well as renegotiated through particular forms of talk. More specifically, these programs foreground and reconfigure the personal and the interpersonal domains in an idiom of dialogic quest. They do so by using forms of talk that blur the lines between the personal and the communal, and thus speak to a profound cultural problematic—the question of the place of the personal in social life and the role of interpersonal relations in individuals' lives.

Within these nocturnal encounters, the telling of personal experience stories becomes a joint discursive production to which callers and hosts contribute in different ways. This joint performance is anchored in a shared understanding of the particular communicative occasion and in mobilizing individuals' expressive repertoires. It is based on the assumption that the caller, who initiates the exchange, has a general notion of the thematic concerns and forms of talk that can successfully claim the hosts' and the listeners' attention during these programs. It is also based on an assumption of immediacy and urgency that propels listeners to call in when they feel hopelessly enmeshed in life problems. This latter assumption sets these call-in radio conversations apart from the television therapeutic talk show format, which tends to be dominated by a more distanced, retrospective mode of sharing personal narratives of hardship and endurance; or, when the immediacy of participants' problems is dramatized, it gets branded as sensationalist.

A particular communicative assumption of radio call-in programs, which is associated with their sense of immediacy, is that the caller's narrative is told so as to demand the host's response (and occasionally also the response of "absent listeners" who are invited to join in). Indeed, since the programs give voice to human suffering, the caller-initiated dialogue is explicitly or implicitly framed as a request for help. This state of affairs obviously reinforces the host's position of power. Indeed, much of the resonance of these programs lies in the emotional acceptance conveyed by the host's response and the sense of empowerment this generates for callers and listeners alike. To effectively communicate his emotional stance to his listeners, the host must use a culturally appropriate expressive idiom that conveys responsiveness and support. I will explore the shape this idiom has taken in each of the two programs under study in the following account.

RADIOPHONIC IDIOMS OF SOCIAL SUPPORT

The call-in radio programs, whose discourse I examine here, are not only about the dilemmas and predicaments of day-to-day social relations; they are also about the healing power of speech. They enact moments of mediated, open, and free-flowing dialogue that, in their own way, give voice to Israelis' quest for personal authenticity. The directness and openness of the talk on these programs come closer to the confessional and self-disclosive ethos of the early pioneers' soul talks than to the opinionated, confrontational idiom of personal responsibility cultivated by *dugri* speakers. Whether informed by the Western therapeutic ethos that elevates the effectiveness of the "talking cure,"[31] or by the age-old Jewish dictum that the worry in a person's heart should find its articulation *(de'aga belev ish—yesihena)* these programs celebrate the resonance of the human voice, or, in Buber's terms, "the spokenness of speech."[32] They highlight the poignancy of oral communication as addressed, as words reaching out from one person to another. They invoke a sense of communion that can encompass the anonymous listeners who stay up late into the night, silently yet attentively hovering around the edges of these radio dialogues.

The two programs I focus on are hosted by two very different radio personalities, Yovav Katz and Yossi Saias, who have each constructed a personal style and a distinctive "radio persona." Each of them has done so in his own way, generating a distinctive and recognizable interactional style with its own special audience appeal. The fact that both hosts are charismatic men serves to color the programs with a sense of self-assured male authority, whether grounded in a folk-model of traditional counseling or in a modernist, therapeutic model. So even though about half the callers are women, and some of the problems they raise are clearly grounded in female experience, they are always refracted through a gendered frame of reference and articulated through the verbal give-and-take with the male host. However, while both these programs provide arenas for the benevolent display of male authority, they differ greatly in terms of the politics of emotions they enact, the nature of their verbal action and the kinds of interventions they allow. As my analysis will show, this difference in ways of performing emotions and displaying attitudes must be understood with reference to the larger social context in which these programs find their credence.

Recent anthropological research on language and emotion has argued for an approach to emotional displays as a form of situated communicative action. Thus, Catherine Lutz and Lila Abu-Lughud propose that emotional discourses be viewed "as pragmatic acts and communicative performances"[33] that are tied to relations of power and sociability. They furthermore describe the goal of the work included in their volume as that of "establishing the pragmatic force of emotion discourse and the social character of emotion by showing how centrally bound up *discourses on emotion* (local theories about emotions) and *emotional discourses* (situated deployments of emotional linguistic forms) tend to be with social issues."[34]

The distinction between the two kinds of emotion talk—discourses on emotion and emotional discourses—is highly relevant to my following account. It captures a major difference between the discourse of the two programs I have studied. The program hosted by Yovav Katz, which gives voice to a Western-type, quasi-therapeutic code stands out in its emphasis on the *discourse on emotions*. This code consists of exploratory, problem-solving talk anchored in explicit emotion-naming practices. It involves a self-reflective play of social perspectives and the promotion of self-distancing moves. A pervasive concern in this discourse on emotion is the issue of emotional management, as expressed in what Lutz has termed a "rhetoric of control."[35]

This rhetoric, which is associated with middle-class, bourgeois culture in both the United States and Israel, points to a view of emotions as dangerous, as threatening to get out of hand. In this view, emotions pose a threat to the rationality and orderliness of the social world and may thus invite chaos. But emotions are also constructed in romantic terms, as life-giving natural forces, which "are currently constituted as the core of the self, the seat of our individuality."[36] This construction of emotions makes them, rather paradoxically, both desirable and dangerous. Hence, within this ideological framework, there is a need to cultivate and control them at one and the same time. This is mainly done by fostering a measure of emotional distance, perhaps the emotive parallel of the aesthetic distance that Bourdieu has described as the hallmark of the bourgeois aesthetic.[37]

The second program whose discourse I explore, the one hosted by Yossi Saias, is equally dominated by emotion talk. Yet it takes the form of predominantly "emotional discourse"—linguistic deployments of emotional displays—rather than explicit discourses on emotions, such as those found in the quasi-therapeutic idiom. In Yossi Saias's program, emotion talk is performed rather than named and discussed, drawing heavily on what I would call (for want of a better term) a "traditionalist" idiom of social support, which is anchored in a basically religious Jewish worldview (even though Yossi Saias himself professes to be non-religious). As we will see, Yossi Saias associates this traditionalist idiom with the cultural world of Jews from Muslim lands—variously referred to as Sephardi Jews, Oriental Jews, or Mizrahim.[38] I am not claiming, however, that this version of emotional ethnicity has its historical roots in the ethos of the Jewish community in Morocco (as recently described within a culturalist framework by Eitan Cohen).[39] Rather than making an essentialist argument concerning the mobilization of a traditionalist Moroccan interpersonal code grounded in an informal ethic of personalized communal involvement, as Cohen does, I will try to show that Yossi Saias uses his program to invoke, play up, and renegotiate habitual communicative practices of social support. Claiming a discursive continuity between face-to-face conversational practices and radio exchanges, he reconstructs an aura of spontaneity and authenticity that invites callers to share their personal needs for material support, companionship, or concrete advice on matters of day-to-day living. The program thus serves as an arena for the construction of particular emotional displays, thereby demarcating a loosely bounded media community of listeners. Some of the distinctive performances of emotionality on the program, and the dialogic relations they hold vis-à-vis the emotional code promoted in the program hosted by Yovav Katz, will be discussed below.

Therefore, within the shared realm of radio broadcasting, and the interactional frame set up by the call-in radio format, each of the programs I will attend to has constructed its own distinctive voice patched out of habitual ways of speaking and in implicit response to other available radiophonic alternatives. The coexistence of these very different voices within one and the same mass-mediated arena is a testimony to the institutionalization of a certain multivocality in Israeli society. I refer to these voices as "idioms of social support" rather than "therapeutic discourses" in order to avoid the common association of the notion of "therapy" with a Western-based tradition of scientific psychology and the universalistic assumptions underlying it.

The perspective I adopt in the following discussion views Western therapy as a cultural discourse on a par with the prescientific, premedical discourses of emotional healing associated with the traditionalist ethos. In this view, the study of psychotherapy as a cultural form is essentially part of the exploration of a group's "ways of speaking." In fact, Deborah Cameron makes this point in criticizing the fact that the 1981 paper I coauthored with Gerry Philipsen on "communication" as an American way of speaking[40] failed to note its intimate relationship to the practices of therapy.[41] This criticism is well taken. Indeed, the link between "communication" as a cultural form of authentic dialogue and the therapeutic ethos became clearer to me only after reading the seminal study by Robert Bellah and his associates, *Habits of the Heart,* in later years.[42] Cameron puts this point succinctly:

I am suggesting, then, that therapy is significant, not because it stands apart from other cultural practices but, on the contrary, because it is an activity in which many of the themes of modern Western common-sense discourse come together. In therapy, commonplace presuppositions about the self and about moral conduct are made particularly explicit (because the self is the overt focus of therapeutic discourse), and these presuppositions are also quite often embodied in explicit rules for speaking. This is why therapy is a good candidate for "technologization." Because its discourse norms are based on beliefs that are also widely held outside the therapeutic context, it is easy to adapt the same norms to different settings and purposes.[43]

The quasi-therapeutic ethos espoused by Yovav Katz gives voice to and reinforces a speech code grounded in a modernist, liberal view of the individual as involved in what Giddens has referred to as the "reflexive project of the self." It is an individual engaged in the cultivation of "pure relationships" that are dependent on communication since they can "no longer be anchored in criteria outside the relationship itself—such as criteria of kinship, social duty or traditional obligation."[44] As Cameron indicates, in the age of pure relationships, the concern with talk focuses much more than in earlier times on "the techniques of mutual self-disclosure—being open, being honest, talking about your feelings, listening 'actively' and sensitively, understanding and making allowances for communication differences."[45] The "traditionalist" code as enacted on Yossi Saias's program is a radio-phonic version of a communally based and religiously oriented mode of supplication, dramatizing both the callers' distress and the host's charisma and empathy through self-narrations and emotional displays.[46]

As I will argue, each of the two programs considered here uses elements of both a traditionalist and a modernist code, combining them in different ways and privileging elements of one over elements of the other at different times. Yossi Saias's style with its predominantly traditionalist flavor encompasses some modernist assumptions as well, such as a claim to personal authenticity, the value of mutual self-disclosure, and sometimes the stress on agency. The modernist therapeutic code that dominates the program hosted by Yovav Katz, while focusing on individual selves and introspective talk, is also underwritten by communal longings and moral commitments, which are associated with relational stability and mutual dependence.

The multivocality that springs out of these cultural convergences and divergences seems to be a truer reflection of the Israeli cultural scene than any of the codes sifted out and taken in its own terms might suggest. The call-in radio arena, with its dialogic openness to popular voices, makes these processes of style formation and conflation both visible and amenable to critical analysis. I would like to claim, therefore, that while these radio dialogues provide intriguing points of access to the study of underlying cultural codes and their communal functions, they are no less intriguing as sites for an improvisational, creative play with loosely distributed cultural resources. Mary Louise Pratt has highlighted the micro-practices that construct such dialogues: "Such micro-practices do not come into view if you look at conversations only as a manifestation of general conventions, models, roles or rules. They do come into view if you look at conversations as events in time, improvisatory events where social meaning and social productiveness cannot be defined in advance but are worked out as the event proceeds."[47]

The elaboration of personal experience stories in the publicly shared medium of late-night radio programs makes them an intriguing research site for exploring the social construction and negotiation of the personal voice in contemporary Israeli culture. In the following analysis, then, I begin with an overview of each of the two programs. Then I move on to a more detailed exploration of some of the interactional dynamics that mark their unfolding, with a view to the ways in which they construct distinctive idioms of social support. Even though the analysis will highlight the distinctiveness of these idioms, it is important to remember that they are deployed in a socially shared arena of public expression. Their playing field is an arena potentially open to the active participation and listenership of all members of Israeli society so that the invisible symbolic boundaries charted by these idioms are simultaneously real and porous.

The two kinds of late-night call-in radio programs I discuss here reclaim a role for dialogue in a mass-mediated context dominated by a dissemination view of communication. In a sense, this reverses the move traced in chapter 1, where I described a cultural project that involved the dissemination of the experience of authentic, face-to-face dialogue through forms of mediation available at the time. Call-in radio is anchored in a mode of dissemination, reclaiming moments of dialogue through the "restoration of presence" in this context of communication-at-a-distance. The ways in which this particular quest for dialogue is carried out, and its implications for our understanding of the Israeli cultural scene, will be addressed in what follows.

GROUP DYNAMICS ON THE AIR

"In the *Third Night Club*, as usual, you are invited to call us and talk about selected personal problems, eh, talk about dilemmas you are facing, life dilemmas, and respond to each other. Together, through such group dynamics of cooperation between us, we will get through the night."[48]

The above comments are typical statements of the kind that standardly launch the *Third Night Club* program hosted by Yovav Katz. Seated in the small radio studio run by the Israeli Broadcasting Authority, Kol Israel, in the heart of Tel Aviv, Katz invites listeners from all around the country to share their personal stories, feelings, and predicaments with him and with a host of anonymous others. What usually follows the program's rather formulaic opening are between seven and ten exchanges involving the host and a caller in dialogue. This dialogue is sometimes joined in by other listeners, either at their own initiative or, more frequently, in response to the host's prompting. The melody announcing the start of the program, right after the midnight news bulletin on Tuesday nights at the time of the research, was a soothing pan-flute tune. It was chosen by Yovav Katz when this program came on air in the wake of the Gulf War in 1991. This tune, and the deep, warm voice with which the host greets his listeners, have become emblems of the program. They are familiar not only to its regular and occasional listeners but also to many of the patrons of late-night news, who catch glimpses of the program as they prepare to go to sleep.

The name given to this call-in program points to its club-like aura as well as to its temporal niche in the station's broadcasting schedule—Tuesday night, the third night of the week. The running time of the programs in my corpus is between 12:15 and 5 A.M. (before recent changes in its scheduling), offering conversations with callers and musical interludes. The host is aided by a production team, whose members he identifies by name at the beginning of each program and again at different points in it. There are commercial breaks and news updates on the hour through the night, as well as musical interludes that punctuate the conversational flow.

The production team includes a musical producer, who has been with the program for a long time, and whose task is to select the songs and tunes that are inserted in between the call-in conversations. The musical pieces interspersed in the program also affect its overall flavor as a radiophonic occasion. The music selected by the musical producer tends toward the international market of light, popular music, including many songs in English and some in Hebrew or other languages. The occasion is sometimes used to introduce listeners to new music the producer likes, but the musical sound-scape is mainly wrought out of familiar and cherished heartwarming tunes that work on the basis of sound recognition. At times, the songs are chosen in such a way as to provide a link to the radio conversations that have preceded them, offering a musical extension or commentary on the substance of the talk. Thus, a call discussing the predicament of coping with life alone may be followed by a song concerned with feelings of loneliness, or a call by a teenager sharing a story of romantic rejection may be followed by a song concerned with the tribulations of first love.

This use of the songs' lyrics is significant as it offers another layer of generalization for the highly personal human stories shared on the air. Not only are they personal stories that other listeners are expected to find relevant enough to their own experience to listen to, they also become stories whose relevance is engraved in the cultural repertoire of popular music (much like proverbs used to offer a communal backdrop to personal affairs). This is quite a remarkable feat on the music producer's part, especially given the studio's rather rudimentary conditions (she has to bring along a necessarily small selection of music discs each time), and the fact that she has to make her choices on the spot. However, this may also suggest that the larger themes tackled on this program fall into a number of predictable categories that construct the emotional lives of radio callers and songwriters alike.

Other members of the production team are two assistants who receive calls in an adjacent room shared with a sound technician and separated from the studio itself by a transparent glass window. In responding to the calls, they use a specially designed form to write down the caller's name, the nickname the caller wants the host to use on air (no use of real names is allowed), such demographic information as marital status, age, occupation, and education, and the latest hour during the night that he or she can be called back should the host decide to do so. The form also indicates whether the caller has been on the program before, and whether he or she would be willing to come on air the following week. The production assistant then writes down a summary of the caller's story as narrated by him or her.

These serially numbered forms are brought into the studio from time to time and the host consults them during the musical interludes, indicating to the production assistants which of the callers he wishes to call back and put on the air. The production assistants affect this selection process through their rendering of the caller's introductory account, which includes their impressions of the caller and his or her verbal skills in an "open comments" section of the written form. In addition, they occasionally make oral recommendations to the host about particular calls, sharing an assessment of their potential interest to prospective listeners or conveying a sense of urgency in the caller's appeal.

Since there are many more calls than can possibly be accommodated in one program, the selection process becomes all the more important. Given its commitment to at least a semblance of genuine dialogue, which in radio terms translates into exchanges lasting some twenty to thirty minutes on average, the potential interest of a particular personal story for the wider public and the caller's ability to sustain a lengthy, on-air dialogue must be carefully weighed. The more usual pattern of topical selection favors thematic diversity among conversational segments. On rare occasions, the program assumes a thematic focus in response to callers' desire to deal with a topic in particular depth. A case in point was a program aired in the summer of 2000 which dealt with parents' responses to the "outing" of their gay children.

Thus, even though the host is the final arbiter with regards to the inclusion of calls for on-the-air attention, and it is his voice and personality that dominate the program's talk, the program is clearly and explicitly a team production. Production team members routinely emerge from their "backstage" presence through the host's repeated mention of their names and his occasional on-air references to them in broadcast-related matters or in brief, personalizing exchanges such as the mention of personal life events—birthdays, the arrival of a newborn, vacation plans. These exchanges reinforce the program's club-like atmosphere and model companionship as part of its overall message. When listeners actively join the radio exchange between the caller and host, and the program moves beyond the dyadic format, it acquires an even more palpable club-like flavor. The listeners' interventions are expected to fit into the program's overall discursive frame—that is, be cast in the form of personal experience stories that in some way address the original caller's predicament.

The *Third Night Club* program privileges personal experience narratives as emblems of authentic life situations. Like other self-help programs on the media, it is a primary contemporary site for the cultural performance of personal experience stories in the public domain.[49] Personal experience stories constitute a dominant feature of the program's discourse, and departures from this genre, especially attempts to engage in abstract discussions of general issues, are not well taken. The expression of opinions is not welcome even as part of the multiparty discussions that follow the host's appeal to listeners to join in the radio conversation. On a few occasions, I heard listeners intervene by trying to lead the conversation about a caller's problem into a discussion of principled positions. Persisting in their attempt, they were cut short by the host, who urged them to "stop lecturing" and share the personal experience on which their opinion rested, using the first-person singular.

Notably, however, even though the host participates in the callers' narrative construction through question-answer-comment exchanges, the personal narratives told on this program belong to the callers, not the host. Indeed, Yovav Katz makes a special point of keeping his own personal life out of the radio show. So while the program foregrounds—indeed, celebrates—the personal voices of anonymous callers, the host, who is not protected by anonymity, guardedly protects the privacy of his personal life by avoiding any but the most cursory references to it. In one of my interviews with him, he claimed that this was in line with the call-in program's goal of giving callers the floor and putting them at the center of attention without eclipsing their stories with his own personal accounts, stressing that "the program is about them, not about me." He also said that maintaining a separation between home and work is essential for his own well-being, noting that just as his personal life is kept out of the broadcast, he also tries to avoid people's attempts to generalize his media role and to draw him into "consulting" exchanges in everyday life.

He was aware, however, that despite these self-distancing measures, he remained at the center of what he himself called the "drama" of the exchange. Yet his presence was not accomplished through self-disclosures but rather through his performance of the supporter role. Yovav Katz supported my speculation that listeners are drawn to the program not only because of their interest in the problems presented by callers, but also because of their curiosity regarding his way of handling the calls. As he put it, "A great part of the program has to do with the drama of 'how he is going to handle this one, how he will handle whatever is happening there,' the risk of it all on live broadcast."[50]

The personal experience stories heard on the program can be described as "distress narratives" of one kind or another. Since they often involve delicate, personal issues that are usually not openly discussed in public, they tend to include interpersonal as well as intrapersonal conflicts or "life dilemmas," as they are referred to in the program's formulaic opening. Broadly speaking, these narratives cover the range of conflicts, mishaps, life strains, and deliberations that are typical of confessional and quasi-therapeutic programs of this type and of contemporary life more generally. Callers are given the opportunity to share their personal stories of distress and have others attend to them in the public medium of radio broadcasting. This is intended to help them and others cope with pressing dilemmas and with what may turn out to be the nontrivial task of "getting through the night." What is a self-empowering move for the callers themselves also has a wider communal resonance. In narrating and discussing their own life dilemmas, callers are also believed to benefit others, those many "absent listeners" who tune into the program, identify with many of the problems raised in it, relish its introspective idiom or are intrigued by the way the host navigates the program's exchanges. At times, though much more rarely, callers share more lighthearted personal anecdotes, which the host clearly considers a welcome change of tone, a respite from the program's more usual scene of human suffering.

The particular broadcasting format and tenor of the *Third Night Club* program, as Yovav Katz testified, are the result of long years of experience and very serious and laborious crafting on his part. The scheduling of the program as part of late-night broadcasting was an outcome of the discovery of this post-midnight temporal niche during the Gulf War, when the radio served as an important communication channel for people enclosed in sealed rooms during the night. By then Yovav Katz was a highly experienced, respected, and fairly well-known radio personality. He had, in fact, pioneered the "therapeutic" call-in format on Israeli radio in the late 1960s, broadcasting his programs in the late evening hours. He is a family man in his early sixties, a kibbutz-born Ashkenazi Jew, who as a young man opted for life in the city. He has a broad-ranging academic background in theater, philosophy, and the behavioral sciences, an area in which he earned his Master's degree. He has worked as a journalist and at one time wrote a regular column in the daily *Ma'ariv*. He has had an ongoing involvement with community theater productions of all sorts both as writer and director, including the staging of kibbutz festivals. He is also the author of many popular lyrics, some of which have become a staple of Israeli popular song culture. In addition, he has gained considerable experience as a family counselor.

Katz's professional experience covers a variety of radio production formats for more than thirty years, including current affairs and entertainment programs, but he has made a name for himself mainly through his hosting of early and late-night therapeutically oriented call-in programs. He describes his contribution to Israeli radio culture as an effort to create an alternative brand of radio broadcasting, which he refers to as "making humanistic radio," locating it within a broader frame of societal concerns. In the aforementioned interview he said: "This may sound overblown, but I consider this work a kind of mission. It is creating the model of a humanistic radio, tolerance, a sense of humanity, the love of mankind. That's what guides me, I'm servant to this idea."[51]

These programs won him two prestigious awards in the 1980s, a journalistic award in 1986, and in 1989 a Tolerance Prize awarded by the chairman of the Israeli Parliament. In 1990 Yovav Katz placed second in the competition for the coveted Golden Apple Award of the Israeli Broadcasting Authority, which is awarded on the basis of a special listenership survey. His program trailed only slightly behind the all-time favorite of Israeli radio audiences, the Saturday afternoon broadcast from the soccer field, *Shirim Ushe'arim* (Songs and goals).[52]

The first therapeutically oriented call-in program introduced by Yovav Katz in 1969 was devoted to parenting dilemmas. He then developed a program dealing with marital relations, and other programs in which he introduced a variety of psychological themes. At the time the material for this study was gathered, Katz regularly hosted two call-in late-night programs. In addition to the *Third Night Club*, he hosted another program broadcast on Thursday nights between midnight and 2 a.m., again following the midnight news bulletin. In that program, *Together and Apart (shneynu beyahad vekol ehad lehud)*, he is joined in the studio by professional psychologists, who are actually the ones who engage callers in extended conversations, while Katz serves as a nonexpert host and as occasional commentator. In contrast to the caller-initiated, free-floating topics that populate the *Third Night Club* program, many of the programs that include professional psychologists are constructed around preadvertised special themes, which are often objectifications of named emotional states, such as "envy," "sibling ri-valry," or "loneliness." Others are devoted to dream interpretation, and only a small part are open-ended, with the psychologists responding to callers' immediate concerns. The exchanges on this expert-driven program, which is much shorter than the *Third Night Club*, are not separated by musical interludes and listeners are not invited to respond to the callers' stories.

Even though the *Third Night Club* program does not have the stamp of expertise on it, as do programs involving professional psy-chologists, its overall tone and the forms of discourse typically found in it suggest its great affinity with a Western-style quasi-therapeutic ethos. Callers to this program obviously choose not to call the Thurs-day night program, which might allow them to engage in conversations with experts. Yet they nevertheless affiliate themselves with Yovav Katz's middle-class, quasi-therapeutic conversational idiom, which invites the mode of self-examination. Callers often share a sense of personal inad-equacy, which in this context replaces the sense of sin associated with religious confession. The intrusion into callers' personal sphere is taken as testimony of their willingness to embark on a therapeutic path of introspection and inner change.

Reflecting back on the history of the program, Katz told me he had initially sought to include more anecdotal and less problem-oriented personal stories in it, but callers' preferences gave the program its cur-rent emphasis on stories of distress and personal hardship. Not in all matters was he as accommodating to audience desire, however. He told me that he had made an effort to prevent the program from turn-ing into an arena for the solicitation of practical help—financial and otherwise. In his view—which is obviously not shared by Yossi Saias—helping the needy through such a program is a highly problematic and questionable affair as it opens the door to all kinds of manipulations on the part of callers. Such requests, he claimed, also tend to dominate the program at the expense of all other program contents, diverting it from its focus on the discursive management of life problems.

The a priori framing of the problems discussed on the program as life dilemmas suggests that proper candidates for this program are problems that call for verbal treatment and clarification rather than weighty and unsolvable problems such as terminal illness or the death of a loved one. The latter may become proper material for this pro-gram when what is at stake is the caller's perspective on his or her predicament, which can possibly be renegotiated and reconfigured, not when all the program can do is give voice to the caller's despair at the finality and irreversibility of the situation. The meaningfulness of the program's discourse lies in the prospect it holds for effecting a change in the caller's perspective through its quasi-therapeutic, exploratory style, or, in Katz's parlance, through its "psychological work."

Thus, in the program's implicit, quasi-therapeutic interpersonal ideology, both the roots of and the solutions to life's problems are to be sought in individuals' attitudes, actions, and decisions, not in external, sometimes overwhelming, life circumstances. It is believed that individuals can and should be empowered by talk to take responsibility for their actions and gain control over their lives. In this scheme of things, the radio exchange is seen as a contribution to this process of inner self-development, not as a vehicle for providing immediate solutions to the callers' problems. Usually, callers comply with the program's definition of its discursive agenda and bring up difficult situations, moments of indecision, wavering, and inner struggles. These then become the topic of discussion, which may lead to a new appreciation of one's own possibilities, or a glimpse into the perspective of others enmeshed in similar situations.

Callers' dilemmas are ideally presented in a straightforward manner. When they are, the problem-talk can proceed smoothly. An example of such an exchange was a call from an eighteen-year-old girl, the daughter of well-educated and well-to-do parents, whose childhood was marred by parental abuse. She said that her father's brutal treatment, backed by her mother's silence, left her deeply scarred and insecure. At the time of the call, she had not spoken to her father for five years, but since she was about to leave home and go to the army, she had decided to try and mend the rift between them. To that end she enlisted the help of a relative whom both she and her father trusted, and who could therefore act as a liaison between them. The father's uncompromising response to her initiative was a demand that she apologize for all the aggravation she had brought him. She felt she had done nothing she should apologize for, and was debating whether to do so anyway, pro forma, so as to bring an end to the family dispute. This was the dilemma she presented to the host, seeking his help in making her decision.

The girl sounded quite agitated, and the host, as usual, helped her unpack her story and clarify the contours of her dilemma and the possible implications of following the courses of action that lay open to her. At a certain point, he also solicited the responses of other listeners who narrated relevant life experiences of their own, providing additional perspectives. The caller's problem presentation in this case was ideally suited for this program's particular agenda—she presented her predicament in dilemmatic terms. This presentation could readily support a deliberative, reflective discussion of motivations, lines of conduct, and expected outcomes. The caller, while distressed, was able to formulate the dilemma she was immersed in. She also sounded both willing and able to take charge of her life. All she needed was some assistance in doing so. She expected to get such help from the host, and he joined her in exploring her dilemma and weighing the options she had in choosing a line of action.

One important feature of this exploratory, problem-solving talk involves the presentation of alternative points of view that can help to expand and perhaps reshape the caller's view of his or her problem. Obviously, given the highly personal nature of the callers' stories, callers themselves are profoundly enmeshed in their own version of the situations they describe. The opportunity to hear additional points of view is believed to provide an antidote to the one-sidedness that tends to accompany people's narratives of their deeply felt personal concerns and conflicts. It is a self-distancing gesture, which turns participants into partial observers of their own lives.

The host, as sympathetic outsider, is felt to be in a position to propose just such an expansion of the caller's perspective, offering a point of view that is untouched by personal interest or deep emotion. When he invites the listeners to contribute to the radio conversation and turn it into a multiparty exchange, additional viewpoints are brought into play, further problematizing the meanings and trajectories of the caller's dilemmatic situation. This play of perspectives is an essential underlying feature of the program's quasi-therapeutic ethos, which is marked by an exploratory search for authenticity as an act of self-creation.

In accordance with the overall exploratory and introspective nature of the talk, it is also fraught with disfluencies, self-interruptions, and reformulations. This halting quality of the talk can be attributed to the caller's emotional enmeshment as well as to the unfamiliarity of the radio situation. The disfluency is simultaneously spontaneous and performed—and it is completely appropriate to the situation at hand. It is the performance of a person who feels distressed enough to appeal for support, yet collected enough to seek empowerment through a process of reasoned discourse. Overly emotional displays subvert the possibility of a reflective approach to the caller's problem. At the same time, an overly fluent and smooth telling of one's personal distress narrative risks the appearance of being unduly rehearsed, as lacking in immediacy and credibility. It is, indeed, a balancing discursive act.

Quite a number of the calls, however, are initially not presented in anything approaching a dilemmatic format, so that their opening does not facilitate the kind of deliberative, reflective exchange to which the program is geared. In such cases, the host has to help callers to reformulate their stories in terms that would enable him or her to redirect the talk so as to better suit the program's quasi-therapeutic agenda. An example of this can be found in a call placed by a young soldier, in which he told about the difficulties he was having with his girlfriend's mother's obvious inhospitality toward him. The caller opened with some preliminary comments expressing his distress at the way he was being treated by his girlfriend's mother and his excitement at being given air-time to share his story. All this came in a plaintive outpouring that did not point to any specific dilemma that the host could address.

The host's attempt to get the caller to clarify the dilemma that lay behind his story was unproductive—in fact, it turned out that the mother was acting in similar ways toward many other people as well, and that the girlfriend was wholly supportive of him so that the mother's attitude did not threaten their relationship. At a certain point, therefore, the host interrupted the caller's litany and posed the direct question: "So, actually, is there something you're asking?" The caller was clearly unprepared for it and asked: "What do you mean?" So the host repeated his question: "Is there any question you're asking me?" At this juncture, the caller's misunderstanding of the genre was revealed as he said in response: "I just wanted to tell you about the topic of the mother." The requirement that a call to the program should have a "point" inviting further discussion and deliberation had not sunk in. The young man did not realize that "just stories" that do not facilitate the kind of reflective, problem-solving exchange typical of this program's discourse are inappropriate contributions. The litany of complaints about the girlfriend's mother through which the caller vented his feelings of frustration and sense of confusion was not taken by the host to justify the time on air.

Another such example of mismatching orientations to the program's discourse was the case of a woman who called in and said she wanted to share the sense of loneliness she felt as a result of her divorce six months earlier. She expressed her own surprise at finding herself enmeshed in feelings of agony over her loneliness, particularly given her strong desire to get divorced in the first place. Similarly to the previous case, she did not formulate her concern in dilemmatic terms either; rather, she dramatized her sense of isolation and anxiety through repetition and amplification of the emotional condition she was in. This led the host to ask: "What's your story?" His question jerked her out of her emotion talk and elicited a skeletal tale. It was a story full of gaps, yet one that then served as a basis for elaboration and formulation in dilemmatic terms following the host's probings.

The strategy of initially using a "kernel" or "minimal" narrative,[53] which is then gradually fleshed out in a nonchronological fashion, gives the caller's account a spurt-like quality as he or she brings in more information as the exchange proceeds. In performing his or her communicative role, the caller sets out the theme and the general tone of the exchange, foregrounding his or her current emotional state (usually despair, anguish, panic, and the like). It is this subjectively experienced state and the events leading to it that form the main topic of what follows. The caller's life story, as it is brought forth in narrative spurts, provides the discursive material for further reflection and for a more introspective look.

In the case of the woman who professed her profound loneliness, the host's questions invited her to provide more and more details concerning her recently disrupted marriage. The additional information she volunteered gave substance and meaning to her skeletal tale and to her expressions of anguish. Asked by the host whether her young sons were living with her, she answered in the negative, and her explanation brought out a much longer history of marital strife than her account had initially suggested. She revealed that in the past she had run away from home with the children on several occasions and that this finally led her to give up everything, including custody over the boys, and get out of the house. Disclosing this bit of information, which she obviously found difficult to do, appeared to be a turning point in terms of her ability to tell her story. In response to the host's probings, she then reconstructed more and more aspects of her painful marital experience, and readdressed her present emotional stress with greater insight into her situation, exploring possible things she might want to do in trying to alleviate her emotional distress.

In this as in other cases, the caller and host overcame the initial haltingness and misunderstandings that accompanied their exchange, falling into a shared conversational rhythm. In such cases, the growing ease with which the radio conversation then flows comes to stand for the possibility of the caller's move out of the emotional and, perhaps, cognitive impasse that has underwritten the call to begin with. Such a move is considered necessary for reaching a deliberative exchange that may lead to some kind of resolution. The host's reassuring comments to hesitant callers at the outset of the conversational exchange, and at various points in its unfolding, highlight his role as facilitator of both talk and introspection. Thus, while the caller clearly has a story to tell, and a desire to do so, his or her story must be contextually interpretable by the host as having a "point" or purpose in terms of the caller's current life agenda and with reference to the program's discursive format. The callers' tentativeness and hesitancy in presenting their stories reinforce the role of the host as a partner in a collaborative construction of their own personal tales, warranting his interjection of new materials and overall control of the conversational flow.

The host's questions and comments serve to elicit new information, redirect the unfolding narrative, and renegotiate some of its meanings. This collaborative process is the heart and soul of this call-in program, which gains both its flavor and its poignancy from this particular dynamic of spurt-like narration and gradual, retrospective, reconstruction.

Navigating the Program's Discourse

The distress narratives heard on this program are jointly constructed by the caller and host. The phenomenon of collaborative storytelling has attracted the interest of scholars working on narrative as an interactional accomplishment. On Yovav Katz's program, the host's and caller's joint narrative construction serves to "thicken" the minimal story initially provided by the caller. The exchange is designed to create a coherent and complete enough story line that will illuminate the caller's motivations and his or her handling of the current dilemma. In moving the caller's story along, the host's questions may reshape the caller's narrative in significant ways.

In line with the program's quasi-therapeutic goals, these redirecting and reframing moves purport to offer the caller new insights into his or her problem, possibly a new way of viewing the situation at hand. The alternative perspective the caller is presented with may result in an actual derailment of his or her original story line and the introduction of alternative ways of thinking. Within this context, such an intervention is taken to be a well-intentioned, potentially empowering, outcome rather than an attempt to discredit the caller's narrative authority and point of view.

The following example is a case in point. It involves the story of an angry young man whose wife had betrayed him with his best friend. At the point in the call at which we enter (early in the conversation), the caller had indicated that he had already filed for divorce. The dilemmas he was facing stemmed from his realization that a divorce was just what his wife was looking for, and that by following through with his divorce plans he would be actually rewarding her for her betrayal of him. The host (H) proceeded by attempting to help the caller (C) clarify his feelings and motivations. Thus,

Excerpt 1

1 H: That is, what she wants is to live with the boyfriend, and because

2 you're angry with her you don't want to make it possible.

3 C: In the meantime, there's a lot of anger, and I wouldn't like to reach

4 a divorce agreement, and give her a divorce, so she can live with the

5 so-called boyfriend.

6 H: If it weren't for this reason, if you knew the relationship with the

7 friend would not continue, would you be worrying about whether to get

8 a divorce or not?

9 C: Perhaps I would, but it doesn't seem logical. It looks like she really

10 wants to be with him. And he refuses to talk to me, I wanted to meet

11 with him and talk, but he's not prepared to, perhaps rightly so. But she

12 doesn't say this, she doesn't say she'll go live with him, marry him.[54]

In this segment, the host made a first reframing move by introducing a hypothetical situation (lines 6–8), using the subjunctive mood ("if clause"). He thus invites the caller to step out of the reality of his situation and imagine an alternative, unreal, but possible state of affairs. This kind of shift from the realm of actuality to that of speculation in radio talk has been identified by Frank Gaik as a feature of therapeutic discourse, marked by an exploratory turn toward "irrealis."[55] In making this move, the host collaborated in the storytelling, inviting the caller to disengage from his anger and desire for revenge and to consider his perspective about the possibility of divorce apart from his current state of turmoil.[56] The caller rejected this distancing move and the reframing suggested by the host, and insisted on sticking with the facts of the case, supplying some more aggravating bits of information about the wife's and boyfriend's treatment of him (lines 10–11).

Following some further discussion of the caller's misgivings and anger, the host, cued by the caller's comment that he had been too much in love to notice the wife's betrayal, initiated a new line of discussion. He questioned the caller's self-presentation and tried to probe more deeply into the nature of the caller's relationship with his wife before the crisis occurred:

Excerpt 2

1 H: What did you love about her? What attracted you?

2 C: At first what I loved about her, today it sounds funny perhaps, was

3 the mutual trust we had.

4 H: Really? You felt you could trust her?

5 C: At the beginning it was the trust we had for each other that

6 attracted me to her. We spent a lot of time together before we got

7 married, and that's it, and all this time together makes love grow.

8 H: You, when you look back on your relationship over the past five

9 years, did you take an interest in her? Did you pay attention to her?

10 Did you show her you cared? Did you know what was going on with

11 her? Did you show interest in her, talk to her, try to find out?

12 C: Maybe during the more recent period, the last two fatal years I did

13 not show interest in her like I did at the beginning. I didn't try to find

14 out and go into things in terms of caring. You become less interested,

15 or there are pressures at work and things like that.

16 H: You got into a routine?

17 C: We got into a routine life, and it's not, obviously it can't be like it

18 was at the beginning, like a fresh love, the romance and everything.

19 H: You stopped investing in the relationship, and you felt this.

20 C: No, look, on the one hand, when I think about it, I feel things

21 deteriorated. I felt this, but when you live from day to day, you don't

22 say "wait a minute, things are going down, today I didn't say a good

23 word," or anything like that.

24 H: What was it, do you think, she loved in you when she did?

25 C: Again, the mutual trust between us, we told each other everything.

26 H: And when did you stop telling each other everything?

27 C: When, well. . . . Look, it's hard to know, I can't tell when we stopped,

28 because if we didn't, it was probably because there was nothing to

29 tell, we stopped having open conversations, or what you call more

30 interesting conversations.

31 H: And you think it's your responsibility or hers?

32 C: It's both our responsibilities.

33 H: Both your responsibilities.

34 C: Because if I didn't press her and ask what happened, and what

35 and how, she should have done the same.[57]

As we can see here, the host once again attempted to reframe the caller's story. Shifting attention away from the wife's betrayal, he first took the husband back to the initial stages of the relationship (line 1). Then he led him to question his own marital conduct in the years preceding the crisis (lines 8–11). In the host's formulation, investing in the marriage was a matter of "work" that needs to be done toward the improvement of marital communication. This communicative labor is seen mainly as the work of talk in clarifying, elaborating upon, and coping with emotions.[58] The emphasis on communication goes hand in hand with the host's humanistic, quasi-therapeutic approach to radio counseling. Indeed, it echoes nondirective approaches to counseling, which orient clients toward their "potential self" through tentative statements of possibility and potentiality.

The host used a variety of discursive devices typical of therapeutic discourse as studied by Adriene Chambon and Daniel Simeoni. They have identified a category of "open modalizations" that encompasses a wide range of linguistic and discursive devices whose function is to foreground possible alternate realities. As these authors point out, therapists' uses of open modalization are designed to "soften the clients' rigid modes of interpersonal exchange through language. Therapists avoid expressions of definitive certainty and discursive closure. Instead, they consistently use "tentative expressions" of irresoluteness with an open-ended quality—to encourage the exploration of stances and new ways of relating."[59] Other than the use of conditionals ("if-clauses"), as illustrated earlier, the strategic (though not necessarily conscious) use of "open modalizations" by this host included open questions designed to leave the formulation of issues in the callers' hands, information-eliciting tellings, mitigators and euphemisms, hedges functioning as downtoners that diffuse the emotional intensity of statements, and so on.

In this case, the host led the husband to think about his own active part in shaping the relationship, not allowing him to become entrenched in his victim-role. The caller readily admitted that after the first years of romance he did not invest as much in the marital relationship (lines 12–15), describing what had happened in terms of a natural process of routinization (lines 17–18, 20–22, 27–30). He seemed to both buy into the interpersonal ideology constructed around the creed of "communication" and to readily excuse himself from the expectations it entails.

Directing attention to what the husband and wife did and did not do for each other in emotional terms during their years together, the host suggested that marriage is an accomplishment of marital partners, not a natural process they have no control over. The caller went along by supplying the bits of information the host demanded. At that point, having foregrounded the notion of agency, the host explicitly raised the issue of responsibility for what had happened to the marriage (line 31). The caller admitted that the responsibility for the deterioration of the relationship had to be shared by both him and his wife (line 30). He insisted, however, on an egalitarian view of relationships, noting that his wife, too, should be held responsible for not having nurtured their marriage (lines 34–35).

The negotiation of perspectives in this case took the form of a free-flowing conversational exchange to which the host contributed significantly by offering topical shifts, such as the aforementioned shift from a discussion of the wife's conduct to a consideration of the husband's role. At the same time, the host also verbally signaled his alliance with the caller by helping him with the formulation of his account. Thus, the host assisted in the caller's search for suitable words (for example, in line 16 he suggested the term "routine" to help the caller restate his account in summary form), or indicated his affirmation by echoing the caller's formulation through repetition (lines 32–33). His interactional contribution took the form of a blend of discursive initiatives that enabled him to control and redirect parts of the conversation even while signaling his overall responsiveness to the caller's agenda.

Through a gradual process of reinterpretation and reformulation, then, the host gently offered an alternative point of view to the one initially presented by the caller. The caller ultimately accepted it and the end result was a new story, one the caller would probably have rebuffed if it had not grown out of his own discursive co-construction. The exchange that followed the "problem presentation" phase was both tentative and exploratory, allowing for unexpected turns in the conversation to emerge.

In this interactional context of openness and flexibility, the reframing of issues is both expected and acceptable. Consequently, a radical change in point of view can be induced without an accompanying sense of imposition on the caller's part. In fact, although the host refrained from openly passing judgment or moralizing, he spoke from an ideology which assumes and values the possibility of personal change through the active search for new insights. The host's attempts at reframing and redirecting the talk were the discursive moves through which such insights could be attained. The sense of anticipation that accompanies the active participation of the callers who take part in the construction of the radio exchange has to do with its emergent quality and its projection of an open world where all manner of things can—and do—happen.

Given the host's subtle position of authority as media personality with expertise, this collaborative work can be thought of as an act of persuasion. Its effectiveness is predicated on the caller's acceptance of two relevant cultural premises that are central to the therapeutic ethos and to middle-class contemporary interpersonal ideologies modeled on it: 1. that the purpose of therapeutic talk is to transform the client's life narrative, and 2. that communication through verbal, emotionally oriented exchanges is the main road to nurturing marital relations. A rejection of any one of these premises would probably have prevented such a smooth-flowing, cooperative exchange. It may even have resulted in open misunderstanding or confrontation. The example discussed in the following section was an occasion in which these premises were not fully shared.

Meaning Negotiations and Interactional Alignments

Surprising moments and unanticipated responses are most noticeable on those occasions when host and caller have very different views of either the topic at hand, or the program's interactional agenda, or both. In such cases, as is to be expected, the interactional alignment between them is not as smoothly accomplished as in the foregoing account. Rather, the exchange is marked by open resistance and negotiations of meanings. The exchange considered below exemplifies typical ways in which such disagreement is negotiated within the framework of this program. Its consideration will help me to further probe underlying dimensions of the interactional ethos in which it is embedded.

In this instance, it was obvious from the very start that the host and caller were talking at cross-purposes. The call opened with an account of the caller's abject state of mind and a detailed narration of the abuse she had suffered in her marriage. Since in this case the call was made after the divorce had gone through rather than during the time of the crisis itself, when the caller was weighing the option of divorce and fretting about it, her extensive recounting of the marital abuse she had suffered seemed out of place and was left dangling. She then testified that at the time of the call her relationship with her ex-husband had improved considerably, and that she was in the process of forming a new relationship with a man she had recently met. Thus, it was not clear from the opening phase what the "point" of the call was, what life dilemma was to be wrestled with. As the conversation unfolded, the host indicated his growing sense of unease by asking her to try and articulate what it was that she wanted out of the conversation, and why she thought her story was a special one, which might justify the air-time and attention it was getting.

The central task of the ensuing conversation became the attempt to give a name to the caller's problem. This process of clarification revealed how deeply entrenched the caller was in a passive, unassertive, even self-effacing, attitude in all of her relationships. This attitude was utterly unacceptable for the host, for whom a solid sense of self and active agency are preconditions for quality interpersonal relationships. The exchange that followed turned into an infelicitous attempt to negotiate these crucial assumptions that underlie the therapeutic ethos and the discourse of the program itself.

The following excerpt demonstrates some of the discursive negotiations and reframings that emerged. It is taken from the middle of the conversation, following the woman's description of the marital abuse she had endured and her self-description as an extremely passive and dependent person, whose main concern had been to maintain the marital framework and protect it against all odds. Even though she testified that she had ended the marriage by her own choice, she felt that its dissolution was a failure on her part and this feeling seemed to haunt her at the time of the call. The host tried to lead her along an introspective path of inner exploration that would help to clarify her underlying motives and her reactions to the hardships she experienced. Thus:

Excerpt 3

1 H: You were passive in your own terms.

2 C: Because there was a lot of hurt. I received the blows in a passive

3 manner, swallowed them without fighting back.

4 H: You didn't exist at all.

5 C: Right, I didn't exist, right.

6 H: How do you explain the fact that you made such a concession on

7 your own self, your existence, your honor, your place? How do you

8 explain it?

9 C: I explain it as my focus on the marital framework. From my point of

10 view, the marriage stood above all else, and everything else was

11 dwarfed in comparison.

12 H: I'm interested, what image did you have of marriage when you say

13 "marriage above all else"? What, what was the picture that you saw in

14 marriage when you thought how it should be?

15 C: Nothing, I saw the ring on the finger and the rabbinate's stamp, and

16 nothing else, I saw nothing more.

17 H: Tell me a bit about your childhood.[60]

From the host's point of view, the caller's main problem lay in her stance of extreme passivity and in her narrowly institutional, nonrelational view of marriage as a matter of "a ring on the finger and the rabbinate's stamp." For her, marriage was not an arena that invites mutual nurturance and personal growth. The caller accepted the host's diagnosis of her attitude (given in line 1), and even went along with his intensifying description of her situation as involving some kind of existential void (lines 4, 6–8). This intensification move was uncharacteristic of this host.

Yovav Katz's more usual stance involved a rhetoric of control, employing "downtoners" that are designed to diffuse the emotional situation rather than "intensifiers" that can serve to heighten its impact. In fact, in one of our interviews he told me that when a caller gets too emotional, as in becoming audibly tearful in mid-conversation, he asks him or her to take time out in order to calm down. He then puts some soothing music on the air and contacts the caller again a few minutes later. The out-of-character use of intensifiers in this case was obviously designed to push the caller toward a clearer view of her situation and conduct. Its thinly disguised judgmental tone was a rare occurrence on this program. The significance of this point will become evident when compared to Yossi Saias's extensive employment of intensification strategies in the next subsection.

While the host tried to lead the caller in the path of introspection, asking her to clarify her view of marriage (lines 10–12), all she could offer in response was a reiteration of the importance she placed on the conventional signs of this institution (lines 13–14), with no reference to any of the emotional values that fuel a good deal of the discussion of marriage on late-night programming. The host did not debate her perspective but rather initiated another step of self-exploration, inviting her to go back to her childhood, apparently in order to come up with an explanation for the roots of what on this program sounded like a rather bizarre, barely comprehensible, approach (lines 15–16).

She went along with this quasi-therapeutic move, drawing a line between her present state of extreme passivity to her childhood trauma over her parents' divorce. Using the wording earlier proposed by the host, she said she had at the time responded with the same level of self-effacement she later displayed in her marital relations, saying: "I was simply nonexistent from their point of view." She then moved on to explain her lack of assertiveness as related to her sense of inferiority toward her siblings, who were better educated and more accomplished professionally than she was (although she herself had a university degree). This response, again, could be taken as either an uncomprehending or an evasive move. She either did not understand the host's invitation to an inner-directed dialogue concerned with psychological motives and feelings or else she refused to follow it. Whatever the case, she did not present her story in dilemmatic terms, so that the host was eventually forced to push the point and put the question directly:

Excerpt 4

1 H: I want to jump a moment, some distance ahead, what, what do you

2 want out of this conversation?

3 C: My wish in this conversation is like this. I, before I got divorced, and

4 because the wedding ring is so important to me, the stamp of the

5 rabbinate, my condition was, my theoretical condition was, my wishful

6 condition was, that I would not have to pass much time without a

7 wedding ring and the rabbinate's stamp, that it would be as short a

8 time as possible, or zero time—[I fancied] that I would meet

9 someone on the stairs leading down from the rabbinate [where the

10 divorce proceedings are concluded]. It was a wish. Look, it sounds

11 like a dream, or some fantastic thing, but I don't want to go into my

12 personal case, but this condition felt realistic, not fantastic.

13 H: I want to ask you, in your new relationship.

14 C: Yes.

15 H: Did you continue to be the same person or did you look for some

16 change or correction of the place you occupy in a relationship?

17 C: No, no, I didn't look for any change, I sought to be in a relationship

18 like I was in the marriage and almost not to exist as myself, but

19 simply to be the wife of husband-number-two, that's simply what I

20 wanted. He simply, he simply doesn't understand it to this day.

21 H: It's true for today, too, then.

22 C: Yes.

23 H: Now, do you want to hear listeners' responses to what you told us?

24 C: Yes, gladly.[61]

As we see, she interpreted the host's question about what she wanted
out of the conversation (lines 1–2) in substantive rather than interactional terms, as an invitation to self-disclose. She did not see the
program as providing an occasion for clarification but as an invitation
to make an appeal. She did so profusely (lines 3–11). The problem she
faced, as she saw it, lay in the fact that she did not enjoy the social
legitimation and status that in her view seemed to come with the role
of married women. Following her divorce, she harbored a deeply felt
desire to become "the wife of husband-number-two," as she put it,
as soon as possible. From the host's point of view, as his interventions
suggested, the problem lay not in the fact that her wish was not fulfilled
but in the nature of her desire, and in the mutilated sense of self that
her statements revealed to him. He asked her not only to explain her
passivity, but to justify it. He clearly rejected her externalized, socio-
centric perspective, repeatedly redirecting the conversation toward her
internal responses and feelings.

Toward the end of the exchange, however, it became quite clear
that the caller did not really subscribe to the program's quasi-therapeutic ethos after all. Specifically, she rejected a major tenet underlying this ideational system—the belief in the possibility and desirability
of self-transformation through introspective talk. She proposed self-
acceptance, a reconciliation with "who you are" as an alternative to
self-transformation. In response to the host's question about the way
she positioned herself in the new relationship she had recently formed,
whether anything had changed for her (lines 15–16), she declared in
no uncertain terms that she was not interested in self-change and refused to pursue it as a personal goal (lines 17–20). Given her resistance
to the imperative for self-transformation that underlies the program's
discursive agenda, the host's gentle proddings could take the exchange
only so far.

For a passive and self-effacing person, she was surprisingly adamant in resisting the psychological parlance of inner change and the implicit demand the host made on her to retell her life story in a different key. She insisted on her view of marriage as a social arrangement whose main point is to confer security and status. She refused to view the condition of marital dissolution as an issue to be discussed and clarified in terms of partners' motivations and conduct but saw it as an inexplicable falling-out-of-grace. She resisted the host's marital narrative that was grounded in respect for human agency, in relational expectations of mutuality and sharing, and in a recognition of the value of expressive communication.

Toward the close of the conversation (not reproduced here), when the host exhorted her to seek therapy so she could become more self-aware and be empowered in new ways, she complained: "Look, you're using terms that are not quite clear to me. Despite the fact that I'm supposed to be educated and understand exactly every word you said, I didn't quite understand you and I'm not ashamed to admit it." They seemed to be back to square one, and the host broke out of the communicative impasse they had reached by suggesting that they turn the floor over to the program's "absent listeners," inviting them to join the radio conversation and engage in a session of "group dynamics on the air." The radio program thus turned into a virtual forum, apparently in the hope that listeners give voice to opinions and judgments that the host could not openly express given the program's avowedly nonjudgmental ethic.

Listeners' comments seemed to fulfill the host's expectations. In this instance, the three listeners who went on the air (all men) were clearly judgmental of the woman's self-effacing and submissive stance, offering explicit advice about how she should and should not act. This advice followed various directions. The first listener exhorted the caller to be more in touch with her feelings, to be less inhibited and withdrawn, and to think more about herself and not only about others. He then suggested that she should seek professional help, which he himself had found fruitful in the past.

The second respondent offered a different, rather surprising, point of view. He argued for a relational view of marriage, claiming that reciprocity—interpreted both positively and negatively—was the heart and soul of the marital bond. Given this assumption, he radically reframed the caller's narrative, reinterpreting her self-effacement in light of her husband's infidelity as a violation of the rule of reciprocity.

He saw it as a sign of indifference and lack of interest on her part rather than as selflessness designed to save the marital framework. He recommended that in the future she should try and seek reciprocity in any new relationship she was to form.

The third commentator questioned the effectiveness of her coping strategies, including the appeal to the radio program, and urged her to pull herself together and to throw herself into her new life, putting her trust in the healing power of sheer living. He offered specific advice, too, mainly to get into a new relationship and to "flow with it." Flowing with it, in his view, meant replacing talk with action—going out to the beach, going to the movies, attending dances—"without any stories, without any psychologists."

Taken as a whole, this exchange reflected different fundamental stances toward the meaning and conduct of marital life on the one hand and the nature and potential value of therapeutic dialogue on the other. What emerged out of this exchange was a rather discordant multivocal text. The caller's presentation and interpretation of her life story was challenged in a number of ways, but she did not budge. In rejecting the changes of perspective proposed by the host and other listeners, she finally linked her view of marriage as an ultimate seal of social approval to the authority of the family network in which she was embedded, concluding her part of the discussion by saying: "Look, I don't want to change, that's how I am, and it's the people I am close to who made me think this way. . . . It's not just me here, it's my family that stands behind the position I presented."

The host, however, as regulator and not just facilitator of the talk, retained the right to the last word. He, too, stuck to his guns, though he did so in a highly empathetic and conciliatory tone. In the universalizing language of psychotherapy, the very language of whose basic tenets she had rejected, he reassured the caller of the rich possibilities of her hidden self, asserting that she had many undetected and unexplored strengths and virtues within her. Ignoring her explicitly stated self-acceptance ("I don't want to change, that's how I am"), a psychological state whose attainment is often considered a major goal of the therapeutic process, he concluded by urging her to recognize her worth as a human being and look ahead to a better future.

Notably, despite the overall goodwill that animated this program, there was no meeting of minds at the end of this exchange. Each of the participants, the caller and the host first and foremost, was deeply entrenched in his or her own perspective. As the listeners' comments and the caller's and host's final statements most clearly revealed, their respective views were grounded in differences of opinion on fundamental issues such as conceptions of human agency, the role of self-knowledge, the demand for personal accountability, the possibility of change, and the ideal of relational reciprocity. The program provided an arena in which these differences could be explored, but not necessarily agreed upon. After reading a previous version of this account, Yovav Katz confirmed to me that in this and in other cases, he solicited listeners' responses when he felt the conversation was going nowhere. He said he was aware at the time that he was not getting to this woman and was very frustrated about it, but stressed that he insisted on making his point since he felt he was not only speaking to her but to a much wider audience and that it was for the sake of this wider circle that he wanted his views to be made clear.

This is an intriguing example of what Paddy Scannell has called the "double articulation" of the call-in radio format: the host explicitly testifies to the program's broader pedagogical agenda vis-à-vis "absent listeners" over and above its social support function. In discussing this point, Yovav Katz stressed that the fact that he was addressing a much broader listenership while talking to a particular person was very much on his mind as he was running his program. As a public performance, this exchange involved an attempt to promote an interpersonal ideology and discursive regime modeled upon the therapeutic process that is familiar to members of the Israeli middle class, but is by no means equally embraced by all audience members.

This was evident on another occasion, when a caller to one of the *Third Night Club* programs clearly shared none of the assumptions or discursive strategies associated with the quasi-therapeutic ethos. The call was so out of tune with the program's style that Yovav Katz seemed quite taken aback by it. The caller was a man in his mid-sixties, who spoke in a heavily Yemenite accent that marked him ethnically from the very start. He complained that his ex-wife and six children were constantly making financial demands on him, yet none of them was offering any help or companionship. Speaking bitterly of his feelings of hurt and loneliness, he asked the host to help him find a new mate through the program, a woman who would take care of him and make no demands on his resources.

The host's attempts to lead him to reflect on his relational expectations and his assumptions about his parental role were utterly unsuccessful. Finally, stressing that mate-seeking was not a service usually performed on his program, he nevertheless let him repeat his telephone number several times so that interested listeners might call him. Even though this was quite out of line with his own program's code of providing social support, Yovav Katz generously offered the caller the kind of practical help that is the staple of Yossi Saias's program. Indeed, this man's mode of appeal, as well as that of the passive woman's plea in the previous segment, came closer to the style of supplication employed by callers to Saias's program. In both cases, Yovav Katz's assumptions about the values of introspection and inner change were not upheld within the framework of the program's communicative practice and needed to be explicitly reaffirmed. Thus, even while violating his own program's rules, Katz could not resist the temptation to reiterate a central tenet of the quasi-therapeutic ethos. In closing the exchange he reasserted the primacy of the program's quasi-therapeutic agenda. Thus, he urged the caller to probe into his own heart, to try and consider what might have brought him to a place where his interpersonal life was in such a disarray, and to take responsibility for his situation.

Clearly, such direct tutoring in ways of feeling, acting, and speaking arises on those rare occasions when callers' expectations clash with those of the host. Such occasions highlight the pedagogical role of these radio programs in exposing listeners to the therapeutic ethos and its underlying ideological premises. Such media exposure is part of the promotion of the expert system of therapeutic knowledge and its social authority. This obviously ideological dimension of the broadcasting of quasi-therapeutic talk fits in well with the hegemony of modern-liberal ideologies in contemporary capitalist societies. The host defines the parameters of the talk and, as we have seen, subtly regulates the dialogue in both form and substance. Most callers are familiar enough with the quasi-therapeutic code to slide more or less comfortably into its cadence. In this case, however, the gap seems to have been insurmountable. The host and the caller were similarly entrenched in their respective positions, unwilling and probably unable to accept the viability of each other's point of view, or to reflect upon the differences of opinion between them with any measure of reflexivity.

Thus, the dynamics of the exchange of the first divorce narrative presented in this subsection (excerpts 1 and 2) reveal the possibility of shifting perspectives and reaching a point of convergence and a sense of resolution between host and caller on this radio program. The exchanges constituting the second divorce narrative (excerpts 3 and 4) and the story of the Yemenite caller (which I do not have on tape) suggest the kind of communicative difficulties that may arise when participants' perspectives are and remain so fundamentally at odds. The sense of emergence, openness, and movement that was so strongly felt with respect to the divorce narrative in the first example was absent from the second. Apparently, the host's decision to appeal to the listeners for their comments was an unconscious attempt to compensate for the lack of movement he sensed in the internal dynamics of his exchange with the caller in the second example.

In the club-like radiophonic forum thus established, the personal is narratively constructed as a communal resource and community is enacted through discursive collaboration and interactional negotiations centered on notions of personhood and relational life. This is the case whether the exchange follows a consensus-building line, as in the first divorce narrative, or it is discordant in tone, as in the second one. On the occasions discussed here, the call-in radio encounter, through its discursive organization and definition of performative roles, became a context in which a precarious dialogic exchange could emerge for a few fleeting moments in the one case, and its impossibility became apparent in the other.

Indeed, this program's quest for authentic dialogue can be productively engaged in only if participants share in the tenets of a modernist psychotherapeutic ethos. The major components of this ethos have been summarized by McLeod as involving a legitimacy based on science; as drawing on the cultural resonance of medicine; as reinforcing cultural trends in the direction of individualism; as becoming a specialized, marketable product; and as marking a retreat from engagement in public, moral debate.[62] In its sociolinguistic manifestations, according to Cameron's account, this ethos involves the development and cultivation of a language "for being self-reflexive: for understanding one's feelings and behavior through introspection, disclosing feelings verbally to others and responding appropriately to others' disclosure of what they feel."[63]

Within this radio framework, an individually oriented, self-reflexive discourse is constructed and promoted. Potential listeners are lured into its nocturnal circle by its intimate tones. By participating in these exchanges, either actively or passively, individuals who are separated by distance and anonymity become linked through a shared focus of attention and emotional force. Unlike viewers of confessional television talk shows, in which personal experience stories become blatantly manipulated and commodified for public consumption, listeners to these radio programs are not just voyeurs of emotional displays and human suffering. Rather, they are also attentive students of the uncertain, vulnerable scene of interpersonal communication, where our contemporary everyday dramas play themselves out. Listeners to these conversations become vicarious participants in a widely accessible form of the quest for authentic dialogue that marks our time and age.

My foregoing discussion has dwelt on the ways in which these call-in radio exchanges were discursively organized so as to enable participants to play out a culturally coded version of their quest for dialogic authenticity, one modeled on a Western therapeutic ethos. The cultural coding of the social support function enacted on Yovav Katz's program becomes all the more evident when it is considered within a comparative framework. In the next section I therefore turn to the second Israeli call-in radio program I have chosen to focus on, the one hosted by Yossi Saias, which enacts a different code of social support, as I will try to show. The comparative account of languages of social support offered in these pages brings out fundamental cultural differences which may be relevant to other contexts of Israeli social discourse as well.

WEAVING THE WEBS OF COMMUNITY

It's already five years that I am coming here every Monday night, and every time the studio is differently colored—last week there was a war climate here,[64] and this week there's an after-war climate. We want to go back to some sort of daily routine, to a measure of restraint, a word that has become much discussed. . . . The world changes all the time, and we remain here, trying again to utter the words and to translate the feelings through this little microphone, and there's a woman on the line, hello. . . . [65]

The opening words of the second program I want to focus on, *Night-Time Conversations with Yossi Saias,* clearly anchor it in a different discursive world from the one constructed in and through the *Third Night Club* program. On this program, issues related to current affairs, which are self-consciously kept out of the programs hosted by Yovav Katz, are allowed to seep in. In his opening remarks, and throughout the program, Yossi Saias shares his thoughts and feelings about events in the public sphere as well as many intimate details of his personal life. He projects a highly engaged and emotional radio persona, one very different from the empathetic, well-focused, yet somewhat distant persona projected by Yovav Katz.

Yossi Saias is a well-known radio personality in Israel. At the time of research he was in his late thirties, but could already boast a substantial radio career, which began after he completed a special course run by the Israeli Broadcasting Authority in 1985. He has also contributed a personal column to the evening paper *Ma'ariv* focusing largely on his experiences of fatherhood, and in recent years he has become even better known as the host of television programs dealing with stories of love and romance. These programs involve personal interviews about the joys of love, enduring marriages, and family life. His first television program was aired daily for four seasons (totaling some 700 love stories) on a marginal Israeli television channel (Channel 3), and enjoyed many reruns, reinforcing Yossi Saias's image as the Israeli "Mr. Love." Subsequently, the show was moved to a much more prominent position on the Israeli TV broadcasting scene and aired daily on the popular Channel 2 during the early afternoon hours.

Yossi Saias's family immigrated from Morocco in the 1950s as part of the mass immigration of North African and Middle Eastern Jews following the establishment of the State of Israel in 1948. Like many Middle Eastern and North African immigrants to the new Israeli state, he grew up on Israel's social margins. In his case, it was the poverty-stricken neighborhood of Wadi Salib in Haifa in the 1960s. His childhood was marked by deprivation and parental neglect, and he still carries with him the wound of his parents' divorce and his father's subsequent absence from his life. These early traumatic experiences continue to give special urgency to his oft-expressed desire for love and family.

The themes of blissful love and parental devotion ground Yossi Saias's responses to the tales of personal distress and loneliness that constitute the bulk of his program. In fact, he voices a unique blend of anti-macho, feminized masculinity and a highly traditional, conservative view of family life, filled with romance and parental love. He promotes the values of simplicity, compassion, and charity, and expresses distaste for life on the fast track. He draws attention to the high price of modernity—the heartlessness of an alienated world, the evils of conspicuous consumption, and the tyranny of calculating rationality in matters that, in his mind, properly belong to the heart (such as marital commitment, childbearing, and child rearing). Many of his responses sound openly moralizing and judgmental, particularly when contrasted with the carefully nonjudgmental approach practiced by Yovav Katz, and his belief in the power of love and commitment endows his program with a relentless optimism despite the painful and negative emotions that are often voiced in it.

At the time this study was underway, Yossi Saias was happily married and the father of five young children whom he adored and frequently mentioned on his program. With no more than a high-school education, he could not boast any training in counseling or any of the helping professions. Initially, this had caused some concern among radio staff and therapists alike, who felt that the program brushed too closely against the therapeutic-type programs of the kind hosted by Yovav Katz (which had also triggered the objection of professionals when first introduced). Like Yovav Katz, who views his mission as "humanizing radio broadcasting," Yossi Saias considers his broadcasting style as an alternative to mainstream radio. Rather than talking about "humanizing" radio, however, he talks about democratizing it in the sense of foregrounding ordinary people's experiences and inviting them to articulate issues of concern in their own authentic voices. He considers his program explicitly "anti-elitist," and prides himself on making it accessible to people from all walks of life. His frame of reference is more social than personal, but his main concern is with the implications of dire social conditions, such as poverty, institutional failure, and neglect, on people's personal lives.

At my prompting, he compared his program to the one hosted by Yovav Katz. He said that Katz's program appeared to him more "academic" and "orderly" in style than his own. Using a metaphor to clarify his point, he said that these two radio shows compare to each other like a training-suit might compare to an evening gown. Through this appeal to the world of dress codes, he thus contrasted the informality of his own program with what he perceived to be the formality, or even stuffiness, of the program hosted by Yovav Katz. When I asked him to compare the audiences, he replied "in their gut they are totally different" (*yesh lahem mitzei keiva aherim legamrei*). His own program's audience, he felt, was in touch with the raw and harsh realities of life and was seeking both human warmth and actual relief, both of which he was trying to provide.

Yossi Saias's career trajectory was marked by a two-pronged struggle—both to gain legitimacy for a highly emotional and personal style of broadcasting and to gain public acceptance for Middle Eastern and North African music, natively known as *muzika mizrahit*

(Oriental/Middle Eastern, or Mizrahi, music) that is part of the heritage of Jews from Muslim lands. Acting as his own musical producer, he consistently played music whose sounds were barely heard in mainstream radio broadcasting at the time. At one point, Yossi Saias's activism involved a vociferous campaign against the radio authorities—which included his threat to resign and a demonstration in front of the studio in Jerusalem. He demanded to be allowed to broadcast more traditional Moroccan music than the more familiar Middle Eastern and Mediterranean musical style that had already become part of the mainstream popular music scene as a result of the moderately successful struggle of ethnic musicians over musical taste and its social place.

For many years, Israeli radio broadcasts privileged the Westernized popular Israeli music associated with the European heritage of Israeli Jews. Contemporary popular Western music was also prevalent on Israeli radio. However, Middle Eastern (Mizrahi) music—whose soundscapes were apparently too closely associated with the surrounding Arab world Israeli mainstream culture was trying to distance itself from—was not welcome. The exclusion of Mizrahi music from mainstream broadcasting channels, or its containment in the ghettoized soundscapes of officially defined "ethnic" music, became a symbol for the social marginalization of Middle Eastern and North African Jews more generally. Mainstream radio music broadcasting turned into a major battleground on which the Israeli ethnic war was waged. Yossi Saias mobilized his program to this struggle. In recent years, when Middle Eastern music had become a more standard feature of Israeli state-controlled public radio broadcasts, Yossi Saias decided that the battle over the public legitimacy of this music had been won, and that he could indulge his personal preferences and play a broader selection of ethnically colored World Music (muzikat olam).

He told me that it was not at all easy to get either his musical tastes or his interactional style accepted within the radio establishment. In the first years of his broadcasting career he got into repeated confrontations with his superiors over his personalized and sentimental style of performance on air. The fact that he involved audiences in the intimacies of his own life was particularly objectionable to his superiors. For example, as he smilingly recounted, he was rebuked for bursting into tears of joy right on the air the day that his son was born. What kept the program going despite this kind of criticism, he said, was the resounding support he received from the audience. Ultimately, it outweighed the institutional and professional objections voiced by some radio and mental health professionals. As time went by, his style gained wider acceptance, and listeners to his program looked forward to hearing about his everyday concerns and pleasures and his ruminations about the world around him.

In his own self-reflexive construction of his program, Yossi Saias relegated his verbal broadcasting style to the domain of individual personality while his musical selections were held to signal ethnic affiliation. His self-description as a spontaneous conversationalist was an implicit polemic against the norms of controlled, calculated, interactional patterns that he associated with middle-class, European-oriented (Ashkenazi) style—in other words, with the style heard on the program hosted by Katz. When I told him I knew quite a number of people in my social surroundings of middle-class, Ashkenazi, well-educated Jews who liked to listen to his program, he readily countered by saying that the program attracted them because of its unusual warmth. He said they were drawn to it because it gave them a "heat-shock" *(makat hom)*, implying that it was a warmth they were lacking in their own lives and social milieu. He also explained his refusal to read a draft version of this chapter, saying that he feared that exposure to my analysis would have a detrimental effect on the spontaneity and warmth of his style.

Despite its confessional tone, then, Yossi Saias's program does not give voice to the Western therapeutic ethos that legitimates asymmetrical relations of one-sided self-disclosure. Rather, it establishes a relationship with the audience that is based on mutual self-disclosure, promoting an idiom of emotional reciprocity and authenticity. He believes this mutuality enhances his ability to have a genuine impact on his callers' lives through a variety of direct interventions that often take the form of practical help. This practical help may take concrete material expression, but often it involves various forms of interpersonal mediation. Yossi Saias frequently initiates the active involvement of significant others in the caller's situation—either the people the caller is in conflict with or people who can help him or her in some tangible way. In this sense, the radio exchange is just the beginning of a much longer process and may well continue beyond the confines of the program itself. Yossi Saias's program is not an enclosed discursive enclave, a matter of group dynamics on the air, but is intimately implicated in callers' everyday worlds.

Moving between words and deeds, Saias transcends the boundaries of the radio studio. He attempts to alleviate his callers' suffering in tangible and direct ways. He counts on his listeners to join his efforts in verbally generating positive feelings as well as in undertaking good deeds. Whether he solicits companionship, gives advice, or offers solace, or whether he initiates the redistribution of secondhand appliances, children's clothes, food, or medicine, he always engages the radio audience in his endeavors and they are invited to share in his successes.

In attempting to transcend the limitations of the mass-mediated encounter, Yossi Saias used to allow people to visit the studio during broadcasting hours, seeking companionship or soliciting urgent help. Sometimes visitors would bring gifts of food and drink, turning the program into an on-air party. Soon the number of visitors grew and Yossi Saias had to apologetically discourage listeners from in-person appearances at the studio. At the time of the research, studio visits were not allowed unless initiated by Saias himself, if he felt the occasion demanded it. One such case involved a teenage runaway girl who called Saias's program from a public telephone after many hours of roaming the streets. He invited her to the studio and even enlisted a cab driver who was listening to the program to volunteer to bring her there.

Such urgent, crisis situations are rare, however. Increasingly, it seems to me, Yossi Saias seeks to establish clear limits to what his program can and cannot do, focusing it on forms of supportive discourse and practical help that are more or less kept within the confines of the radiophonic exchange. The decision to give a caller air-time has to do with whether Saias feels he or she can be effectively helped. At times such a decision involves balancing out conflicting pulls, such as the urge to respond to a call for help on the one hand and the caution advised by Saias's limited possibility to offer help on the other.

Thus, when a young woman called in on the night I visited the studio, saying that her boyfriend was threatening to kill her, I was alarmed by her panic and thought that this call would be attended to immediately. The production assistant, who took the call while Saias was playing some music, told him about it as soon as the song ended and he proceeded to select the next caller. I felt she shared my response. Yossi Saias, however, more cautious and perhaps more prudent, did not select this call. He told the assistant to tell the woman that she should turn to the police for help. Aware of the limitations of his program, he felt it would be irresponsible for him to intervene in such a potentially violent situation, subordinating the woman's sense of urgency and his sense of drama to what he felt would be socially responsible conduct on his part.

Yossi Saias's program seems to be grounded in traditional forms of communal support, which is extended within the framework of ordinary life events in an ongoing, spontaneous way. As the boundaries between the host's and callers' lives dissolve, the distance between the radio studio and the life outside its walls diminishes. In this respect, Yossi Saias's program differs significantly from the *Third Night Club* program, which is modeled on the spatially and temporally bounded psychotherapeutic encounter. For Saias, the radio is not a self-enclosed sphere separated both from his personal life and from current events. Rather, it is an arena in which the hardships of ordinary people's lives can be shared and sometimes eased.[66]

Rejecting the culture of expertise, Yossi Saias emphasized that he refuses to invite professional psychologists into his studio because he believes this would work against the intimate and spontaneous nature of his program. Where he came from, he said, people didn't go to psychologists; they tried to solve their problems within the family context or with the help of friends.

Thus, while unabashedly putting himself at center stage, Saias capitalizes on his position as an authentic spokesperson of "the simple folk." By penetrating his listeners' hearts with his warm, caressing voice, he speaks for and to people who have no public voice and encourages them to speak for themselves. Even though he gets calls from a wide range of people—Arabs and Jews, religious and secular—he agreed with my suggestion that many of the callers to his program come from Middle Eastern and North African backgrounds, saying that "people from the Oriental world find it easier to relate to me." Many of these callers seem to belong to a socioeconomically weak segment of the population—the poor and lower-working-class of Oriental heritage. An expression that crops up repeatedly in conversations and press accounts of Yossi Saias's programs is that he deals with "the poor and destitute" *(helka'im venidka'im)*. Saias readily confirmed this description, impatiently waving aside the disrespectful tone that attaches to it.

It is apparent from the kinds of stories of hardship callers narrate that many of them belong to the most disadvantaged sections of the Israeli population. These stories testify to extremely precarious life conditions associated with economic deprivation and social marginality. These difficult life circumstances color the relational problems callers share so that even when they tell distress narratives that are similar in substance to the stories heard on the program hosted by Yovav Katz (conflicts related to divorce, parent-child relations, drug addictions, and so on), the troubles they share are of a different order. Callers' difficulties are clearly shaped by socioeconomic hardship and a general sense of helplessness vis-à-vis prevailing social and institutional arrangements. Yossi Saias spoke angrily of society's inability or unwillingness to handle the profound distress and acute need of so many of its weaker members. He said that he often felt listeners expected him to do more for them than he possibly could. Criticizing those who are officially entrusted with the well-being of the poor and needy, he said: "I wonder if the government or anybody up there ever listens to my program and what they think about what they hear." That so many of these callers are of Oriental (Mizrahi) heritage confirms the well-known overlap between class and ethnicity in Israeli society.

Yossi Saias recognizes the far-reaching implications of his callers' social positions and its relation to ethnicity, but he also highlights the pleasures of ethnic affiliation. On occasion, he foregrounds his Moroccan roots by recounting personal anecdotes associated with his family and childhood. At times, he exchanges intimate notes of recognition with callers from North African extraction concerning ethnic customs and foods, or distinctive elements of traditional Jewish-Moroccan ritual practice, such as the veneration of Saints' Tombs. He also underscores his personal affiliation with the well-known Rabbi Kaduri, an elderly rabbi who is highly venerated among Moroccan Jews as a spiritual leader, and who has been an honorary guest at the circumcision parties of his newborn sons. This connection has elevated Yossi Saias's status in the eyes of many of his Oriental listeners, and at times he uses it to promote his philanthropic activities. Thus, Yossi Saias organized a mass Bar-Mitzvah celebration at Rabbi Kaduri's Yeshiva for eighty boys from socioeconomically deprived homes. This event, which included a blessing by the Rabbi, was broadcast live on radio and selected segments of it were broadcast again as part of Saias's late-night program.

Yossi Saias's visibility on the Israeli popular culture scene has been buttressed by many journalistic portraits that have appeared in the daily press and in a variety of weekly magazines over the years. These articles are often accompanied by vivid, full-page pictures of Yossi Saias in dramatic postures and colorful apparel that help to bring out his handsome looks and soulful appearance. On February 22, 1994, Channel 1 of Israel's Public Broadcasting Service aired a documentary about Yossi Saias, which focused on his late-night radio broadcasting. This show created a flurry of cynical commentary about his style and do-gooder mentality, but—more significantly—many appreciative calls from viewers requesting that he be given a chance as a television host, which, as noted, he eventually became. His television appearances thus provide a visual image for his listeners, making him less of a disembodied voice than Yovav Katz.

The various journalistic portraits of Yossi Saias tend to foreground, even celebrate, his simplicity, authenticity, and romanticism as well as his enterprising spirit and ability to mobilize individuals and institutions on behalf of the needy and destitute. Many of the articles echo Saias's on-air self-presentations, revealing details of his past and present private life. Others are more focused on his public activities as an informal social-radiophonic institution of compassion and help. Whatever their focus, they never fail to give expression to Saias's familial and communal ethic of love and care.[67]

Not all responses to Yossi Saias's media persona are equally enthusiastic, however. In fact, my study began with the observation that there was something about the program's style that irritated many middle-class Ashkenazi listeners. The negative responses I encountered ranged from outright disdain for the program's plaintive talk to a cynical attitude about Saias's do-gooder naivete and his outspoken sentimentalism. This latter attitude is evident in some press coverage of the program. Thus, an article that appeared in an issue of the local Tel Aviv newspaper *Ha'ir*, which was devoted to the themes of "good and evil," was titled "I Cry When I See All the Evil around Me." It was topped by a picture of Yossi Saias with angel's wings appended to his back. The subtitle read: "Yossi Saias, a private contractor for good deeds and a standard dish for cynics, can't understand the popularity of evil. A friend from another planet." And the article's opening lines ran as follows:

> Baba Yossi [an appellation reserved for Moroccan Saints] is alive and well, and continues to perform good deeds on live broadcast, to feed the hungry, dress the naked, look for shoes for the barefoot and homes for the homeless, to find love for whoever needs it, to listen to people who have a phone but nobody to talk to, and caress them with his dreamy, sad voice and with his optimistic, if not always coherent, reflections about human existence, about hope and mainly about love, as he understands it. There are people for whom Saias is a little God in a box, or at least the Messiah. There are people who have nothing but this voice of his to hang on to. Where do they come from, all these lonely people, the Saias broken-heart club? What is it about this young man, a non-affluent employee of the public broadcasting authority, that attracts them like a magnet? And how come there will always

be those who treat him as a curiosity, an easy prey for vicious journalists, who will make a ball out of his part-naive, part-outrageous statements, out of his sometimes strange and pointless stories that have no trace of humor or irony about them.[68]

The ambivalent portrayal of Yossi Saias in the Israeli press seems to echo the mixture of admiration and suspicion that is associated with the popular appeal ascribed to televangelists in American culture. The cultural role played by Yossi Saias has become increasingly clear since he moved into the television scene. Thus, in May 2000, when the second television program hosted by Saias was launched on Channel 2, this became one more occasion for a Saias-centered publicity campaign. A short review of the new program in *Ha'aretz*, the Israeli high-brow daily, underscored the sentimentality of Yossi Saias's romanticism and the religious overtones it carried. It compared the tenor of Yossi Saias's program to that of some popular American TV talk shows, saying:

> A bit like Oprah Winfrey, Saias is a missionary, he has a task in life, a mission, a message to disseminate, and he is in fact the only ideological host on Israeli television, a local version of the American Christian television preachers. In the shows they host—one of which, "700 Club," is aired here nightly on the Middle East Channel—new believers tell how they saved their souls (and were healed of cancer and alcoholism) when they discovered Jesus. Saias' Messiah is true conjugal love that is anchored in familialism, and he uses his guests in order to demonstrate that it is a life philosophy that can bring happiness and redemption to one's soul, the model to which one should aspire, and his program, like "700 Club," begins and ends in a short sermon designed to uplift the spirit of those who sought to give up, to strengthen the faith. Saias is the image of niceness. All flows pleasantly. He both sermonizes about the power of love and lives up to his preachings in the way he lives and speaks: he is content and calm because he has attained true love. In America he would have had a church and millions in the bank, and a following that calls "Amen, brother" after every heart-warming story.[69]

Yossi Saias himself seems ambivalent about the missionary intentions attributed to him. While he finds satisfaction in the companionship and help he is able to extend to his listeners, he rejects the image of *zaddik* (Jewish saint) that has been attached to him by some of them. He insists he is just an ordinary person who happens to have been given the opportunity to talk on radio and to share his life and feelings with others. While he is aware of the voyeuristic motivations and sensationalist overtones sometimes attached to his program and its listenership, he insists on the authenticity of his radio persona in giving voice to his feelings and stating his opinions. He is also authentic in his desire to help, providing mediation and practical assistance whenever he can. The discursive strategies Saias employs in attaining the programs' goals deserve further consideration.

Practical Solutions and Emotional Responsiveness

Yossi Saias accomplishes his program's practical and expressive goals by activating a nationwide, ephemeral network of anonymous listeners, who are prepared to act toward one another both as a community of practical action and as a resource for emotional replenishment. The dexterity with which he mobilizes the material and social resources of his individual listeners on behalf of his callers is often remarked upon with great admiration, and, in a popular idiom that blends the practical and the spiritual, he is sometimes referred to as a "miracle-worker."

Yossi Saias's efficacy lies in his ability to provide a proper combination of practical help and verbal support. He values talk primarily as an instrument of emotional expression. As noted, his programs sound as a saga of human plight and adversity, foregrounding issues such as disabling disease, extreme poverty, homelessness, acute helplessness in handling abusive family relations, bereavement, loneliness, substance abuse, sexual disorientation, and so forth. Many of the callers speak in a mode of appeal, seeking help in situations that range from the very difficult to the insoluble. Callers' appeals are evocative, seeking to mobilize emotional support or solicit practical help.

Indeed, callers to this program often express inconsolable feelings of distress and hopelessness, telling heartrending stories of their extremely difficult personal life situations. Callers' problems on this program are rarely formulated as dilemmatic situations inviting deliberative discourse, and the host makes no effort to reformulate them in such terms. In fact, when no practical intervention seems possible, the host does not try to lead the caller through an introspective process of questioning and discussion. Rather, he dramatizes his empathy through displays of emotional support. These displays of support are responses to callers' self-disclosive personal stories and serve to reaffirm the callers' sense of self rather than to recreate it.

The two hosts thus have different conceptions of what counts as offering social support. These are intimately associated with the hosts' understanding of the communicative agenda that animates their exchanges with the callers, and it is this understanding that affects the discursive shape each program takes. As we have seen, Yovav Katz's invitation to callers to tell stories that include a dilemmatic component fits in with his quasi-therapeutic conception of the program as providing callers with an occasion in which to engage in an open, introspective exploration of their problems and view them from a different, more detached perspective. For Yossi Saias the main psychological value of the exchanges on his program lies in the opportunities they provide callers to iterate their sense of personal agony and to address their difficulties to sympathetic ears. He and his callers are not heard fumbling around in an attempt to discover what the caller's problem actually is, or what he or she really wants out of the radio conversation. The callers' words are taken at face-value, and find confirmation as literal accounts of their current emotional state and as heartfelt expressions of their pressing needs.

The discursive frame dominating the program is one of appeal-and-response, not psychologically oriented problem-solving talk. Thus, for example, when a twenty-five-year-old woman called to share her sense of loneliness and sadness, tracing these feelings to the harsh and neglectful parental home she had come from, Yossi Saias did not invite her to elaborate on her childhood situation, or to reflect upon the reason for the particular intensity of her feelings of deprivation at the time of the call, nor did he ask her why she chose to call the program at that particular time. Instead, he turned to the listeners and asked if there was anyone "out there" who might be willing to offer a warm home to a young woman with a history of unmet emotional needs.

Saias rarely solicits listeners' responses to callers' problems. The sense of community that envelopes the program is generated by actual and potential acts of generosity that help to acknowledge and alleviate individuals' pain and need. Listeners are not invited to provide each other with tutoring over coping strategies. In that sense, Saias's communal idiom confirms the particularity of individual cases, the wholeness of individual selves, and the singularity of emotions. Each story is taken on its own terms, not as a token of a type, and it is in its human particularity that it becomes a resource for triggering communal mechanisms of sharing and mutual support. Each of the calls, at the same time, dramatizes the general themes underlying the program—that life is hard and full of pain, and that its harshness can be redeemed through acts of love and caring. Yossi Saias acknowledges the depths of this pain both by providing an arena for heightened emotional displays and by offering help and solace through communicative strategies that build up to what I call a "rhetoric of presence." As in the case of the early pioneers' soul talks, here, too, it is the all-inclusive sense of community that allows individual feelings to be properly articulated and attended to.

This stands out in particular when compared to the idiom of individuality and subjectivity employed by Yovav Katz. Focusing on personal dilemmas, Katz explores conflicting emotions and fragmented selves. His discourse on emotions explores individual motivations and feelings in a self-distanced manner. The talk on Katz's program is designed to help callers regain emotional control through self-reflection and reasoned discourse. The symbolic force of this discourse can be described, in Weberian terms, as the "charisma of reason."[70] It is enacted in a restrained, measured style that is miles apart from Yossi Saias's "rhetoric of presence."

In responding to accounts of emotional distress, Yossi Saias seems to be particularly sensitive to anguished stories that give voice to feelings of loneliness. Such accounts confirm his general view of the centrality of marriage, family, and close relationships in human life, and buttress his insistence on the role of human companionship as the key to overcoming hardships. He both preaches his relational view of the world, with a premium on romantic relationships, and does what he can to promote it by bringing people together in any way he can. He plays the role of mediator, harmonizer, and, at times, matchmaker. Even though he stops short of turning the program into a matchmaking operation, he willingly opens it up to calls from people who are interested in finding a mate.

The program's caller-initiated crisis line activity described so far is complemented by a range of ongoing projects initiated and regulated by the host. Yossi Saias's program became an outlet for individuals and small businesses for donations that are transferred to needy families and individuals. Holidays are particularly common occasions of such giving (Purim costumes for children, Hanukka trips to sacred or historical sites, and so on). For a while, Saias also ran a secondhand clothing store in Jerusalem that served the needs of many families in the area (including his own), using his program both to solicit and advertize donations.

The program's agenda also includes well-publicized calendrical events initiated and orchestrated by Yossi Saias. A well-known occasion is the annual Passover night celebration *(seder)* for about a hundred impoverished or lonely participants. This annual celebration is made possible by listeners' donations, mainly in the form of food products, facilities, and transportation arrangements. The preparations for this *seder* color Yossi Saias's program with a sense of anticipation for several weeks before the occasion itself. A good part of the mobilization of resources required for its success is done on air, turning the event into an extended communal undertaking that is later shared—on air, of course—with all the program's listeners. Another form of practical help typically offered by Saias's program involves the search for persons whose whereabouts are unknown—a runaway son, a wife who has vanished with all the family savings, a parent or sibling from whom the caller was inadvertently separated many years before, and so forth. Yossi Saias's success with such searches builds on the special qualities of radio transmission and depends crucially on the wide dissemination of his program. In this case, his popularity has a great deal to do with his efficacy, and vice versa.

Even among those who do not employ the folk-religious idiom that casts Yossi Saias as "miracle-worker," or "zaddik," Saias has earned the status of a one-person social institution. This position was officially recognized by the Parliament's Education and Culture Committee in 1994. Yossi Saias was invited to a festive meeting of this parliamentary body and received a commendation for his unmatched role in promoting a positive interchange between the media and the public. Saias was gratified and commented: "After all the cynics made a great joke of me and of my program, they suddenly understand that it is a serious one."[71]

Action and presence are the heart of the matter in Yossi Saias's radio program, not a reasoned understanding of one's possibilities and constraints in dealing with life problems. His response to his callers' predicaments follows a "let's try this" and "let's try that" approach rather than an invitation to reconstruct the callers' self-narrative. A clear example of such an action-oriented exchange was his response to a woman who was looking for the father of her twenty-five-year-old son. The father had disappeared when she was five months pregnant and then she accidentally discovered that he was about to become engaged to her sister. The host asked her a few questions that led to further details—the man found out about her pregnancy when she arrived at her parents' home for her sister's engagement party (to which she had not been invited). She had never married and had received little support from her family since her sister and mother held her responsible for the breakup of the sister's engagement plans.

Yossi Saias did not ask about her relationship with the man, or why she had not been invited to her sister's engagement party. He did not even ask why she had decided to look for the man at that point in her life rather than earlier, when she might have solicited financial help in raising her son. Yossi Saias's main concern was whether the son wanted to meet his father. When he discovered that the woman didn't know, he decided to call the son, who was woken up in the middle of the night and his desire to meet his father was confirmed. The line of action that might eventually lead to the son meeting his father was thus triggered.

This case exemplifies Yossi Saias's preferred strategy of involving all relevant parties in the solution to the caller's problem. This is true especially in cases dealing with interpersonal conflict. In such cases, the partner to the conflict mentioned by the caller is contacted and asked to articulate his or her feelings about the conflictual situation and to share thoughts about possible ways of resolving the conflict. Recipients of such rather intrusive calls have included a romantic partner who had decided to break up with the caller; a live-in romantic partner who hesitated to commit himself to a marital relationship; a parent who had difficulty in accepting a child's homosexuality; and a grown son who shunned an elderly parent's company. All these were asked to explain their positions and motives on air in response to Yossi Saias's surprise call. Through these gestures of mediation, Saias felt he invited both parties to "open a new page" and resume communication.

Opening a new page may take more surprising forms, too. Thus, on one memorable occasion, a middle-aged woman called in to share her pain over the many bitter marital conflicts she and her husband were experiencing. She said that they had not had a proper conversation for months and that he had been spending his nights on the living-room couch (an ultimate symbol of marital estrangement in Yossi Saias's discourse of love-in-marriage). The host responded to the caller's story by asking her to put down the telephone receiver. He said he was going to play some romantic music and instructed her to invite her husband, who was asleep in the living room, to dance with her. He promised to call back after a while and try to help them end the conflict.

Yossi Saias's late-night calls to unsuspecting individuals, who happen to be party to some interpersonal conflict that comes his way, often jolt that person out of his or her sleep. This is obviously a blatant intrusion into people's private space. When this is done on air, the surprised party becomes involved in a public enactment of a private conflict without prior notice, let alone consent. Often people comply with the intrusive call and join the conversation, even though they may offer only evasive or disgruntled responses and refuse to disclose themselves on air. It was, in fact, surprising to me how rarely people refused to participate in such unsolicited exchanges by cutting off communication altogether. The opening line, "It is Yossi Saias from the radio here," spoken in his warm, assured voice and casual tone, appears to carry a good deal of weight for listeners even in cases in which their discomfort is evident for all to hear. His self-appointed role as arch-mediator, and his cultural position as media-friend, seem to override the awkwardness of these moments in most cases.

On some occasions, however, this rather blatant interventionist strategy does not work and Yossi Saias's efforts are rejected or even rebuffed. In one such case, he attempted to assist a caller who was not able to tell her long-time boyfriend that she wanted to break up with him and called Saias's program, asking him to do it for her. His phone call to the rejected boyfriend, which woke the fellow in the middle of the night, resulted in a fiasco that led to public rebuke. The boyfriend, shocked to be awakened by this piece of news, was in no condition to engage in an on-air dialogue with either Yossi Saias or his girlfriend. He angrily declared that he was severing all ties with her. A scandalized radio critic responded to this incident by calling Saias "Yossi Springer," pointing to the crude sensationalism associated with the American television talk show hosted by Jerry Springer, which is broadcast in Israel on cable television. The subtitle to that critique ran: "A caller told Yossi Saias that she is finding it difficult to tell her partner that she no longer loved him. Saias was happy to break the guy's heart."[72] The critic attributed this increasingly sensationalist broadcasting approach on Yossi Saias's part to the growing competition of similar programs on the regional radio stations that were established in Israel in recent years. A number of them established programs modeled on that of Yossi Saias. The critic concluded: "Yossi Saias built an impressive career on his extroverted good heart. You can either buy it or not. What is sure, he never tried to make it through sheer cruelty. Today, so it seems, the market is much more competitive."[73]

In my interview with Yossi Saias, I explicitly asked him about this highly interventionist strategy and found that he was aware of the criticism raised against him. He said it was a matter of balancing options, indicating that things did not always work out as projected. Alluding to the mini-scandal of the rejected-boyfriend case, he said that the girl was afraid of the man's potential aggressive response if she broke the news to him on her own. He argued that if he had refrained from intervening in that case, and the boyfriend had become violent, he would have been accused of insensitivity to the girl's plight. With reference to another case, in which his call was an unpleasant surprise to a father who had been out of touch with his son for some eight years, he said he did not regret his intervention, although the father was less than enthusiastic about it. In his view, the embarrassment it caused was a mild punishment for such neglectful conduct. The man, he said, deserved to be reminded that he had a child out there, and that he had a responsibility to him.

Even when he does not use such strategies and confines himself to more standard on-air discussions, Yossi Saias's talk signals a high level of emotional responsiveness. This emotional display is accomplished through the employment of a variety of discursive strategies of emotional intensification. These strategies are typical of this program's idiom of social support and of the "rhetoric of presence" that so clearly distinguishes it from the quasi-therapeutic discourse of the program hosted by Yovav Katz. They are exemplified in the following discussion.

Emotional Intensification Strategies

Calls dealing with such insoluble issues as death and other forms of irreparable loss cannot be addressed within a practical, action-oriented frame of reference; they can only be met with displays of emotional support. Saias signals his emotional identification with the callers' plights in a number of ways. One of them involves the posing of unanswerable questions in responding to callers' agonizing stories. The following call is a case in point. It was aired on a day in which a nationwide campaign for road safety was held as a response to the growing number of fatal road accidents in the months preceding it.

In this exchange, Yossi Saias spoke to a father who had lost a twenty-year-old son in a dreadful car accident. The young man's sister had initially made contact with Saias and told him about the terrible loss her family had endured and about her father's attempt to give expression to this loss by composing songs. This expressive venture was a new turn for this middle-aged man, who worked in a technological field and had shown no artistic inclinations before this tragedy. This backstage preparation, though not frequent, is another example of the ways in which Yossi Saias's program crosses boundaries between the world and the on-air dialogue.

The call itself consisted of a highly emotional exchange between Yossi Saias and the father of the young man, in which the bereaved father expressed his inconsolable pain as well as his anger at the prevalence of careless driving and the authorities' leniency toward it. The host's display of empathy took the form of a series of "unanswerable questions" that repeatedly acknowledged the sense of loss expressed by the caller. He thus reassured him that he was not alone in his grief, and that it was acceptable for him to express it in public.

Unanswerable questions—like rhetorical ones—do not fulfill the preconditions of the speech act of questioning. In this case, however, their posing is "irregular" not because the person asking the question knows the answer, as in the case of rhetorical questions, but because he knows that the only possible answer involves undermining the validity of the question itself. Thus, a question such as "How can you bear it?" is properly answered only by a reiteration of "I can't." The posing of the question, therefore, invites such reiteration or implicitly signals its appropriateness within the context of the dialogue. Yet, by being asked the unanswerable question, the caller is also told that he or she may be the source of an answer the host and his listeners have all been seeking. As someone who knows the pain of living, he or she may be able to impart such knowledge to others. Again, a pattern of reciprocity is established, one that departs from the patterns of empowerment found in the quasi-therapeutic discourse of the kind found in the program hosted by Yovav Katz. Empowerment in Yossi Saias's program is not a one-way road—giving is receiving, as he reiterates again and again, often stressing that he stands at the receiving end, getting from his listeners more than he can give.

Examples of the use of such unanswerable questions are foregrounded in the following excerpt from the exchange in which the bereaved father expressed his grief:

Excerpt 5

1 H: Tell me, *how can one go on living?*

2 C: This is a difficult question. I was asked today in the middle of the day how one

3 goes on living, and I said it is almost impossible.

4 H: *Where does one cull out the strength to get up [in the morning], the strength*

5   *to . . .*

6   C: You simply don't sleep. Your question is out of place. You stop getting up in

7   the morning because you don't sleep at night. You don't go to bed happily. It's

8   over, all this. You stop rolling out of your blanket in the morning, no more of that.

9   You're only left with the pain.

10 H: As you speak, I look at this picture all the time [of the son, sent by the sister].

11 C: I'm in his room now and I have pictures around me. He's looking at me from all

12 sides.

13 H: You fall asleep in his room?

14 C: Yes.

15 H: How does the family try to lessen the pain?

16 C: The family is broken up.

17 H: Yes, it's something you cannot get over.

18 C: You can't get over it.

19 H: There's no way one can.

20 C: No way. Whoever tells you [there is a way] is simply lying and ashamed to tell

21 the truth.[74] (emphasis added)

The host can do little in this exchange beyond encouraging the caller's expressivity, confirming his pain and giving him the feeling that he is not alone. He does this by echoing the caller's sense of helplessness through the standard use of paraphrase and repetition (lines 18 and 20), but more intensely by asking questions that clearly have no answers (lines 1 and 4). These are the very same questions the caller has presumably been asking himself out of the depth of his trauma: How can one go on? Where does one find the strength? What does one do? By asking these questions, the host seems to signal his deep empathy for the caller's situation—he is there with him. He doesn't imply that he knows what one can do in such a situation. The only solace he can offer is the acknowledgment of the immobilizing effect of such pain, the recognition that they have come to a point where speaking is reduced to its phatic function—to a verbal caress. It is a place where the questions one asks can have no answers. They remain dangling, feebly evocative signs of mutual presence. The exchange is "therapeutic" in the way that holding a friend's hand would be, touching it and feeling the pain on one's skin. The caller's subsequent echoing responses, where he repeats some of the host's wording (lines 17–18 and 19–20), seem to confirm that the host's response was well received, that it was indeed interpreted as intended—as signaling emotional presence.

This capitalizing on emotional displays gains special meaning within the context of Israeli society, where Middle Eastern and North African Jews are stereotyped as overly emotional, perhaps engagingly "warm," in a way reminiscent of colonialist representations of Middle Eastern "natives." Rather than trying to rehabilitate this image, Yossi Saias underwrites it by flagrantly embracing it in uninhibited displays of sentimentality. He unabashedly plays up the devalued (and feminized) image of the emotional Jew of Middle Eastern heritage, thereby making this image ironic and taking the sting out of it. In so doing, he dismisses the negative valence attached to this stereotype by Israeli Jews of European heritage whose interactional preferences and social sensibilities have set the expressive standards for mainstream Israeli culture since pioneering days. Yossi Saias uses the radio program as an occasion to celebrate the warmth of simple folks' genuine feelings, exploring the limits of their emotional displays, and reworking them within the contours of a commodified, mass-mediated structure of feeling. The lure of the program lies partly in the indexical dimension of Yossi Saias's style, which is heard as pointing to an ethnically anchored sensibility. Some of the program's allure, however, is to be found in its flamboyant moments of unreserved emotionality that become magnified in and through the publicness of the radio exchange.

Even though most of the problems presented by callers are very difficult and pressing, they do not always involve irreversible, intractable situations such as death and loss. Rather, many of the calls involve problems that can be solved through some form of interpersonal negotiations. These calls invoke Yossi Saias's powers of mediation and, indeed, form a substantial part of the problems he chooses to put on air. Marital problems and family conflicts are prominent among them, looming as large on Yossi Saias's program as on the program hosted by Yovav Katz. His ways of dealing with such problems are particularly revealing since they bring out the specific flavor of his discursive style and the premises underlying his life-world.

Given Yossi Saias's standing as a champion of love and marriage, the stories of marital failure recounted by some of the program's callers seem to hold his particular attention, violating his vision of what romance and family life could and should be. Such stories drive him to engage in musings about the insufferable gap between the promise of love and the realities of love gone sour. Like Yovav Katz, he repeatedly asks callers to recall the first stages of the romantic relationship of which they complain, to recapture its moments of joy. He does not, however, usually use these personal recollections to bring forth accounts of how and why things went wrong. Rather, he chastises callers, pointing out the inexplicable gap between past and present, rhetorically asking how relationships can sour to the degree that they apparently have. This is clearly another version of the "unanswerable question" strategy discussed earlier, and, of course, it is a question that nobody expects to answer. Yossi Saias in fact joins his callers in asking how a marriage that began under the sign of love and passion could have turned into a battlefield overflowing with vengeance and hate. Calls about marital conflict leave him with the vexing sense of one more inexplicable missed opportunity for human happiness.

Whenever he can, he tries to mend relationships by creating direct contact between the parties involved. In a somewhat attenuated version of the interventionist strategy described earlier, he makes great efforts to get people to talk to each other on and off the air. When the whereabouts of one of the parties to the conflict is not known and no direct contact can be made, he uses the radio outlet to give voice to, and amplify, the caller's search for the missing party. The following case is an example of such a call. The caller's story deals with an acute marital crisis that led to a complete breakdown in communication between husband and wife, a typical example of the kind of "falling out of love" that never ceases to perplex and sadden Yossi Saias. The caller appealed to Saias for practical help in finding her husband. They had an argument and he disappeared and left her stranded a few days before she was due to give birth to their first child. She called Yossi Saias's program on the assumption that her husband, or someone who knew where he was, would be listening to it and would help her find him.

The woman sounded desperate, again and again repeating her request in a tone of supplication, as if prostrating herself on a Saint's tomb.[75] Yossi Saias's response indicated that this accentuated mode of supplication was not out of line on his program. Indeed, he did not press her, either by requesting that she supply more information about the details of her situation (beyond reiterating the fact that she was all alone and hated it), or by probing the circumstances that could clarify the marital conflict that had triggered the husband's disappearance.

The exchange showed no trace of the inner exploration and search for self-understanding that such a situation might have triggered within the quasi-therapeutic framework of the *Third Night Club*. Rather than being encouraged to reflect on her situation, the woman became more and more emotionally enmeshed in it as she repeated her appeals: "Yossi, I am begging you," "Yossi, Yossi, find him." The exchange was thus basically an occasion for emotional display, providing the caller with a platform for the dramatization of her distress without any sense of invading her private space. Her distress was heard as a lived reality, not as an embarrassing personal fact that invites clarification. The program's heightened emotionality served as a cathartic measure, carrying the woman's appeal as far as it could go.

Listeners were invited to participate vicariously in the search for the truant husband. After first putting the woman on the air, Yossi Saias followed up by checking back with her through the night to find out if she had heard anything from the missing husband. As he did so, he repeatedly employed a strategy of "intensification," which is clearly exemplified in the following excerpt. The section cited here followed some preliminary remarks in which the caller described her distraught emotional state and the host expressed his sympathy while encouraging her to give more details.

Excerpt 6

1   C: I am about to give birth, any day now I'll be giving birth. Yesterday I had an

2   argument with my husband, he left the house. I want him to come back very

3   much, I have nobody, he's the only one I had. I have no parents and I want him

4   back at home, just now when I am nine months pregnant. Yossi, Yossi. . . .

5   H: When are you due?

6   C: I am into the ninth month, I have to give birth any day now.

7   H: And why did he leave? What was the argument about? What was the topic?

8   C: We had an argument, he left for Tel Aviv yesterday, it has happened to

9   him three times before.

10 H: Three times, yes [correcting her gender inflection].

11 C: Three times this last week.

12 H: What do you mean, three times a week? He, like, he goes out and

13 *comes in and pulls a sulky face or doesn't talk to you?*

14 C: No, no, he didn't pull a sulky face, but yesterday I was very angry because he

15 came back late at night, at one thirty, and every minute that he's away from home

16 feels like eternity to me.[76]

In this excerpt, the caller laid out her predicament in general terms, appealing for help (lines 1–4); she did not respond to the host's question concerning the nature of the argument she and her husband had been having before his disappearance, but elaborated on her case by indicating that it was his third departure in the past week. The host didn't reiterate his question, but rather expressed his astonishment at the frequency of the husband's neglectful conduct (ignoring what could have been the soothing fact that he had already come back twice). He intensified her account by vividly describing the husband's purportedly sulky behavior around the house (lines 12–13). Notably, the caller rejected the factual accuracy of the host's account, but she nevertheless supported the host's assessment of the severity of the husband's conduct by providing other details of his ongoing neglect of her needs at this special time in her life (lines 14–16). Thus, a basic alignment of tone was established between caller and host.

The next few lines of the exchange are also oriented toward emotional intensification. The host shifted his line of questioning and invited the caller to recapture the past, reimagining the love she and her husband must have felt for each other when they got married. She claimed she still loved her husband, an assertion that obviously ran counter to the story of marital strife she had just told, perhaps rendering it even more poignant. This did not lead the host to solicit more details or a richer account of the caller's personal and marital history. Rather, he countered with reiterative uses of the "intensification" strategy, directly or indirectly condemning the husband's conduct. In the following excerpt, I have emphasized the host's use of the intensification strategy:

Excerpt 7

1 H: *So how come, what brings a man to leave a woman in such a way?*

2 C: Eh . . .

3 H: . . . *in such an unfeeling and ugly way? You're pregnant, too, and you're the*

4   *woman he has chosen to marry, a fresh bride, right?*

5   C: No.

6   H: Freshly married, how long have you been married?

7   C: We've been married ten years.

8   H: And it's the first pregnancy. . . .

9   C: It's the first pregnancy.

10   H: *Wow, this should be a source of very great excitement. . . .*

11   C: Yes.

12   H: *So, where's this excitement, why did he go just when it all gets so*

13   *exciting around him?*[77]

Yossi Saias invoked the first stages of the caller's love relationship with her recalcitrant husband only to brush aside her statement that they still loved each other, expressing his exasperation at the fact that such a love relationship could have gone awry. He began by posing a generalized version of an "unanswerable question" that neither he nor his caller, nor any of the "absent listeners," could answer—what makes a man leave a woman whom he has once loved enough to marry and father a child with (line 1)? He then proceeded to paint her situation in aggravated terms. With the knowledge that it was her first pregnancy, Saias marveled that the husband had behaved so harshly toward the woman he had just married (line 4). Even after she had clarified that they had been married for ten years, he did not redirect his condemnation. Rather, he maintained his judgmental tone, suggesting that a pregnancy for which the couple had been waiting for ten years should have been a source of even greater joy. He claimed that the husband was missing out on the best part of his life (lines 12–13).

The husband's conduct was incomprehensible to Yossi Saias; he could not reconcile it with the emotions he so decisively attributed to expectant fathers. He did not interpret the flight response as arising from conflicting emotions. It seems that no such emotional conflict was conceivable within his ideological frame with regards to parenting, let alone acting on such emotions. He also rejected the caller's attempt to explain the husband's flight as a response to the tension they had both experienced during her pregnancy. Instead, he suggested tension-reducing techniques one could engage in during moments of stress—such as yoga or walks in the park—so as to highlight the futility of the husband's flight response. Although their conversation did not seem to be going anywhere, the host continued to employ versions of the intensification strategy, at times in the form of "unanswerable questions," at times with a directly accusative note, as in the italicized material in the excerpt below:

Excerpt 8

1 H: *And he didn't leave a note, didn't write, didn't say anything, didn't leave any*

2 *message explaining the reason [for his disappearance]?*

3 C: He didn't write anything, he left when we were both very upset.

4 H: So, *with you things are upside down, a child draws you apart, usually it*

5 *draws couples together, especially couples after ten years of waiting and*

6 *anticipation and desire [for a child]. How do you explain what happened to*

7 *two people who loved each other and decided [to have a child], and just as it is*

8 *about to arrive, everything suddenly comes to an end, at least as far as he [the*

9 *husband] is concerned?*

10 C: It's hard for me to explain this, we've been through an especially difficult time,

11 these past few months.[78]

At this point the host seems to have reached the end of his resources. His earlier offer to have the caller send her husband a song on the radio, one that would melt his heart if he was listening, was rejected by the woman, and he went back to recirculating his accusatory comments and unanswerable questions in a slightly different guise—he condemned the husband for having left no note even though this was hardly to be expected given that he had quit the house in the heat of argument. He then directly accused both husband and wife of mishandling their relationship, which he claimed to be the opposite of everybody else's (lines 4–6), posing an "unanswerable question" concerning the inconstancy of human feelings (lines 6–9). The final excerpt from this radio exchange illustrates an even more accentuated use of aggravating strategies on the part of the host.

Excerpt 9

1 H: Yes, and can you feel the movements [of the baby]?

2 C: Yes.

3 H: *But isn't it fun when the guy can feel them, too, when he puts his hand on the*

4 *belly. . . .*

5 C: *I am sure my husband loves me and I love him, too.*

6 H: *So why do you get into such stupid arguments when the essence of life is so*

7 *great? Soon you'll have a child, soon there'll be a new person in the world who*

8 *comes from both of you, why this separation at the wrong time?*

   C: Yossi, I'm begging you, help me get my husband back home.[79]

As we see, the host further aggravated the picture of the caller's situation by invoking an imaginary scene of marital intimacy in which husband and wife share the joy of feeling the unborn child's stirrings. He suggested that the husband should have been with her, able to put his hand on her belly and feel the child's movements (lines 3–4). At this point, the use of the aggravation strategy seems to have exceeded its emotional efficacy. Rather than feeling supported, the woman was pushed into a self-defensive posture, recycling her belief in her marital relationship (line 5). This open rift led Yossi Saias to reiterate his annoyance at what he now blatantly called the couple's "stupid argument." He was annoyed at their lack of appreciation for the preciousness of that time in their lives (lines 6–8). The conversation ended where it started—with the caller's explicit, desperate plea for help. The host responded to the caller's final plea by formulating a direct appeal to the husband—who might be listening—coaxing him to go home to his loving wife. The exchange closed with the caller's final words of thanks.

Throughout this exchange, the host increasingly intensified the emotional coloring of his comments. While feeling for the woman, he was obviously outraged by the husband's conduct and did not hesitate to say so. He started out by asking an essentially neutral question: why did your husband leave? This question was never really answered, and with each reiteration Saias sounded more disgusted with the man's conduct. He accused the husband of selfishness and lack of feeling, and both the husband and the wife of mishandling their relationship. They represented his worst fear—the disintegration of what he assumed began as a loving marital bond—and he had no qualms about making his position known to the caller and his other listeners. At times he sounded as exasperated as the caller herself, rather awkwardly balancing support and censure.

Indeed, Yossi Saias's judgmental attitude, as exemplified in this excerpt, provides a notable contrast to the strictly nonjudgmental orientation promoted within the quasi-therapeutic idiom employed by Yovav Katz. Some of the remarks Yossi Saias made in the foregoing exchange (and on other occasions) sounded to me rather insensitive, at times even abrasive. I wondered how they could possibly soothe or empower distressed callers. Had it not been for the enveloping warmth of Yossi Saias's voice, his intensification and dramatization of the woman's plight might have been heard as a put-down. However, I believe this was neither the host's intention nor the effect of his style, even though at one point he seemed to have pushed too hard, calling forth the woman's defensiveness.

The program indeed dangled between Yossi Saias's desire to provide emotional support and his irrepressible urge to express his opinion and offer moral guidance. Indeed, in his scheme of things, the two went hand in hand. Thus, rather than taking the caller out of her predicament by inviting her to explore the issue in a somewhat detached way, Yossi Saias intensified her sense of helplessness. He "thickened" her story with additional, imaginary details (such as the baby's movements in her womb); he compared her responses unfavorably with those of others (stating that usually a first child brings couples together); he compounded her doubts about her husband's whereabouts, repeatedly asking why he had gone away and how he could have done so. Furthermore, he amplified the severity of her situation by declaring it as not only difficult but also incomprehensible. The woman voiced only very mild objections to the host's judgmental outpourings, correcting some of his factual comments. She accepted the liberty he took to speak for her, presenting her story as a narrative of relational failure.

She offered rather flimsy explanations for her and her husband's conduct. These were grounded in a folk psychology that associates emotional tension with loss of control and a subsequent flight-response. Yossi Saias's commentary on her story was implicitly anchored in normative definitions of marital roles and commitments as well as in an ethic of romance and care. Thus, when later that night he found out that the husband had not yet made contact, he resumed his verbal hand-wringing, dramatizing the sense of crisis once again. At that point he became even more directly reproachful, impatiently repeating questions he had already asked without waiting for her reply, and finally accusing her of holding something back from him, which she denied.

Although at this point he sounded suspicious of her story, he did not try to fill in the gaps with further questioning. He was obviously frustrated by his inability to help her, and seemed somewhat rebuffed that the husband was either not tuned in to the program or was dismissive of its appeals. As his frustration grew, his judgmental attitude increasingly overshadowed his personal warmth. His responses conveyed an irritation with the caller's story. This was not the only time I had heard this happen. Once he asked, in a tone that sounded almost accusatory, a middle-aged woman caller, who shared her feelings of loneliness, why she was living alone. On another occasion, a young woman called in to share her anxiety about an unwanted pregnancy. He apparently found it so hard to construct the arrival of a new baby in negative terms that it took a while for him to shift from a congratulatory to a commiserating tone.

Clearly, a less emotional and more practical response to the abandoned wife's problem might have been more helpful in this case (as in others). For example, such a response was supplied by a clear-headed listener who called and suggested that the woman get a printout from the telephone company of all the calls made from her home in the days preceding her husband's disappearance. This could perhaps give her some clue as to who the husband was in contact with and eventually lead to his whereabouts. This commonsensical idea had not occurred to Yossi Saias, who seems to favor grand gestures of appeal and response over detective-like, logical reasoning.

Yossi Saias did not only express his judgment of the callers' conduct and of the ethics of their interpersonal life, he also felt that people call into his program in order to hear his opinion on issues that concern them and not just to be helped during moments of crisis. Whether they ask for his opinion or not, they invariably get it. Yovav Katz, on the other hand, stressed that he was trying hard to avoid any trace of a judgmental tone in responding to callers' stories. He believed that any attempt on his part to pass judgment would only inhibit their willingness to open up and share their problems.

Yovav Katz's verbal maneuverings are no less value-laden and control-oriented than Yossi Saias's use of explicit censure. In some cases, both hosts reject the caller's position. In the case of the passive divorcee who called Katz, passivity and a refusal to change were not treated as acceptable interpersonal options. Rather paradoxically, it was by insisting on her right to be self-effacing in her relations with significant others that she asserted a position of autonomy vis-à-vis the program's ethos. Yossi Saias, as we have seen, is sometimes explicitly judgmental of his callers' conduct, as he was in the case of the pregnant woman whose husband had run away, and is never worried about blocking his callers' expressivity.

Speaking from within an explicitly articulated moral framework that he assumes is shared by his audience, Yossi Saias does not see it as his role to guide them into new ways of thinking about themselves. Rather, the exchanges on his program act as moral reminders of some of the fundamental values he assumes they must uphold. Therefore, despite the emotionally charged and occasionally contentious spirit of the exchanges on his program, the negotiation of meanings generated by them is considerably less radical than the shifts in perspective that are sometimes heard in the radio dialogues hosted by Yovav Katz. Although Katz is always soft-spoken and sees it as his role to help callers find their own answers to their life dilemmas, his approach is actually more intrusive in its goal of effecting inner change.

Cultural Subversions

Saias's callers rarely challenge his worldview head-on. This can be attributed either to the fact that they share his views or to their reluctance to contradict him. As we saw in the case of the woman who rejected Yovav Katz's therapeutic call for change, there are rare cases of resistance on Yossi Saias's program as well, which become occasions for an open negotiation of the program's assumptive framework. One such example involved a woman caller's open resistance to Yossi Saias's cherished ethic of love-and-marriage. A thirty-five-year-old woman called during the week of Hanuka, the Festival of Lights. In celebration of the festival and of their shared heritage, she offered to give him the recipe of a Moroccan dish she had prepared. After ascertaining her age, he asked if she was married, and when she answered in the negative, he continued:

Excerpt 10

1 H: So you made a big dish and ate it on your own?

2 C: I didn't eat it on my own. I invited about twenty of my friends.

3 H: It sounds sad.

4 C: Why sad? I'm not sad at all. You have no idea how happy I am.

5   H: No, no, it sounds like, like some scene, if they filmed it for a scene, they'd say:

6   "A person lights the Hanuka candles on her own." . . . Ah, it's really hard.

7   C: Yes, no, but look, that is, I'm really not sad. I'm a very happy girl.

8   H: Great.

9   C: I'm happy that I'm not [married]. Does the fact that I'm not married mean I have

10 to be unhappy?

11 H: No, of course not, right.

12 C: There are married women who are very unhappy.

13 H: Yes, no, it's not a matter of sadness and happiness. It's simply an

14 existential state, what a person does for himself.[80]

Here, clearly, the caller challenged Yossi Saias's view that marriage represents the ultimate human good, that one can find emotional fulfillment only in a loving, preferably institutionalized, conjugal relationship. He often equated unhappiness with the perceived emotional deprivations of single life. Since the caller identified herself as a Yossi Saias fan, she was surely aware of his position on the blessings of marital life and the misery of life alone. Her call, however, was a departure from the program's regular pattern of appeal-making. She used the special holiday atmosphere frame to make a light-hearted call, offering a recipe rather than requesting help. Then she resisted the program's customary agenda by rejecting the image of the "poor old spinster" who had nobody with whom to share the wonderful food she had prepared (line 1). He didn't hear her when she insisted that she invited some twenty friends to share her traditional Moroccan dish (line 2), and responded to this tour-de-force of sociability by saying it sounded sad (line 3). She rejected this depiction and demanded that he explain his evaluation of her situation (line 4). Again, he didn't hear her, both justifying and enlivening his unfounded claim concerning the woman's loneliness by fantasizing a scene in which a lonely person is lighting the Hanukka candles (lines 5–6). She did not join his flight into *irrealis* but instead reiterated how happy she actually was (line 7). She further challenged him by explicitly asking if being unmarried necessarily means one is unhappy (lines 9–10). She then pushed her point by stating that there are many married women who are unhappy (line 12). Yossi Saias conceded this point and tried to extricate himself from the argument by changing the terms of discussion from a question of one's happiness to what he vaguely called one's "existential state" (line 14).

As their conversation continued, the caller clarified her views on marriage—views that in fact resonated with those of Saias. They both had very high expectations of this institution. Indeed, she stated that she had remained single because she was not willing to marry someone she did not feel was right for her. She did not see her refusal to compromise as a failing on her part. In fact, her parents' relationship had convinced her that a perfect marriage was possible, even if difficult to attain. Saias, nevertheless, refused to relent, again "rubbing it in" by countering her choice with a final "But tonight you are sleeping alone." In Yossi Saias's terms, "sleeping alone" epitomizes the wretched life. However, undaunted, she responded by saying, "And it's great fun."

Although quite resistant to subversive callers, Yossi Saias's own discourse is in some ways subversive vis-à-vis the larger social field. As a cultural form, it presents an alternative idiom of social support, challenging the hegemony of the mainstream, quasi-therapeutic ethos of psychological expertise. While this challenge usually remains implicit, occasionally it is verbalized explicitly. In one case, a psychologist called the program in order to comment on a previous caller's problem. After she presented herself in her professional role, Yossi Saias cut her short, saying: "We don't need psychologists here. We are our own psychologists here."

The "we" in this case, one may assume, refers to the program's intended audience—those many anonymous listeners whose life problems resonate with those of Saias's callers, many of them of Middle Eastern heritage, who comprise the program's regular patronage. In brushing aside the culture of expertise represented by the Western psychotherapeutic ethos, Yossi Saias reaffirmed the ethic of care and the communal values that animate his world and program. For his listeners, Yossi Saias's seriousness and naivete, his well-wishing sentimentality, romanticism, and moral zeal, as well as his many proven successes in solving people's problems and alleviating their pain—all give him the authority and the charisma they are looking for.

The parasocial relationship listeners seem to have developed toward Yossi Saias is itself culturally inflected—it combines intimate warmth with veneration and, at times, the attribution of a quasi-saintly aura. His charisma appears to lie in the special combination of his caring, his unabashedly sentimental attitude, and his down-to-earth

practical organizational skills. Not surprisingly, perhaps, this intertwining of emotional expressivity and a functionally oriented practical
approach resonates with patterns of social support associated with a
traditional "psychotherapy" in McLeod's account. The major components of this form of "therapy" as a cultural system involve religious
belief, including spiritual direction, the free expression of feelings,
including the detailed confession of sins and doubts, and a sense of
developmental movement toward some ideal personal state, which in
this case has been incarnated in relational terms as marital and parental
bliss. Another dimension of traditional "therapies" is their enactment
as collective ritual.[81] Yossi Saias's program is thus constructed as a
site of communal participation and social mobilization. Listeners are
repeatedly invited to share material resources and extend their goodwill
to those in need. Even in those cases when practical help is not possible,
distressed callers nevertheless find themselves enveloped in the assuring
sounds of a communal conversation that assures them that they are
not alone.

Yossi Saias's invocation of a communal ethos brings to mind the
code of honor discussed by Gerry Philipsen in his study of a blue-collar
American speech code.[82] It privileges group values and norms over the
authenticity of individual, inner experience. Yet Yossi Saias's worldview
is not organized around notions of social place and hierarchy, as in
the case studied by Philipsen, but rather around notions of belonging
and inclusion. It rests on an affiliative vision of human connectedness
tested against human suffering and an ethic of mutual responsibility
and care. Yovav Katz's program reinforces the view that solutions to
life's problems are to be found mainly in individuals' inner worlds,
whereas Saias's program reinforces the view that solutions are to be
found in a community of well-intentioned others. The two programs
chart alternative public spheres that overlap in some ways yet differ in
the ways in which they articulate the quest for human dialogue.

Saias's program is a radiophonic, self-styled, version of a traditionally oriented "psychotherapy." It is, however, colored by such
modern and postmodern themes as romanticism, the authenticity of
feeling, the primacy of pure relational concerns, and an awareness
of the tension between autonomy and human connectedness. Saias's
self-constructed radio persona is that of a spontaneous, self-directed,
idiosyncratic personality, animated by authentic feeling and a caring
spirit. He responds to callers' distress by giving expression to meanings
and values that are part of the texture of traditional communal life.

Both he and his callers interpret human distress in terms of a shared vision of the good life—as life filled with love and caring. This vision informs a practical morality which is frequently articulated by the host and callers. In discussing the callers' concrete problems, all participants in this program join hands in formulating social guidelines for desired interpersonal conduct, negotiating its contours and sanctioning behavior that falls short of their implicit ideals.

Furthermore, although Yossi Saias identifies himself as nonreligious, his program is infused with spiritual overtones. He encourages the celebration of family-oriented, life-cycle rituals and festivals, and cherishes folk-religious pilgrimages and such religious practices as the veneration of Saints' tombs. Yet at the same time he preaches the value of romance, insists on individuals' agency in shaping their own life, is open about sexual matters, and prods his listeners to cultivate moments of passion in order to sustain and revive matrimonial life. At times, he implicitly acknowledges the limits of his communal social-support model and even urges distressed callers to seek professional help.

Thus, Yossi Saias's vision of human connectedness is deployed in a flexible and context-sensitive manner. He is aware of the repressive potential of social norms and constraints. In some cases, indeed, I have heard him urge callers to disengage themselves from webs of connectedness that they find overly constraining and fight for their personal autonomy. On the night I visited his studio, for example, an ultra-Orthodox teenager called to tell about how stifled he felt within his own family and neighborhood, whose faith he no longer shared. Yossi Saias encouraged the boy to protect himself by finding a way out of his current predicament, even if this meant he had to give up his current environment. In this case Yossi Saias clearly rooted for the values of individuality despite the heavy costs this would entail in terms of familial relations and communal affiliation.

Yossi Saias's program is by and large concerned with the personal experience stories of its callers, and dwells mainly on interpersonal relationships and familial affairs. Yet it does not construct the personal in psychologized terms, as separable from the social world surrounding individual selves. It is therefore both thematically and situationally more porous. As we have seen, Yossi Saias constructs his program as an arena where boundaries are systematically blurred— those between host and audience, those between his radio persona and his everyday life, those between the studio and the world outside, between callers and noncallers. His interventionist strategies may turn nonlisteners into participants in radio conversations; until recent years, his open-door policy brought people to the studio in emergency situations. He sometimes follows up on callers whose problems could not be properly attended to within the confines of the radio program and updates his listeners on past calls. No less significantly, the program is porous in that it sometimes allows the public sphere of current events to penetrate its enclosed space of late-night intimacy.

Let me then conclude my discussion of Yossi Saias's program with one memorable example in which the drama of Israeli public life pervaded the program, creating a dialogic moment that blended the program's intimate tones with the stridency of political events. It took place in the spring of 1996, following a series of suicide bus bombings perpetrated by the Palestinian Hamas movement in several Israeli cities. Yossi Saias, whose radio studio was quite close to the sites of the bombings in Jerusalem, found himself inevitably embroiled in this drama as his program was repeatedly interrupted with news updates reporting the names of casualties in one of the bombings. On this occasion the line between politics and communal relations became blurred. Yossi Saias responded to the public anxiety that filled the air through effusive verbal commiseration and dramatic gestures of solidarity both on and off the air.

Thus, in his penchant for the grand gesture, he organized a live broadcast of a festive ride on the eighteen bus line in Jerusalem, which connects a poor neighborhood to the city, and where two bus bombings had occurred a week earlier. This was a much-publicized show of popular support for the terror-stricken neighborhood whose inhabitants had no choice but to continue to use this bus line. He also approached the mayor in order to arrange for a protective roof over the commemorative candles individuals lighted at the site of the bombings, where people gathered to share their grief. And without changing the usual personalized tenor of his program, he helped create a special kind of dialogue, in which political actors and private citizens spoke to each other out of the depths of their emotions in a way that was probably not possible anywhere else on the Middle Eastern scene at the time.

This contribution of the program was acknowledged in an article that appeared in the local Jerusalem weekly *Kol Ha'ir* on the week following the bombings, where Yossi Saias was given much credit for his performance both within and outside the studio walls.[83] This article also gave him a platform from which to reflect on his social mission and its potential political implications. It was titled "Yossi, Yossi, Make Peace," in imitation of the mode of appeal so commonly heard on his program when callers share pressing problems related to their personal lives. Saias was described in terms that frequently appear in both press accounts and conversational exchanges in which he figures—as a "wailing wall," as an "improvisational social welfare service for the poor and destitute," and as a "national psychotherapist." The article described some of the unusual calls Yossi Saias received that week from political figures—from the far Jewish right and, even more surprisingly, from Palestinian listeners from Gaza, some of whom belonged to the *Hamas* movement itself.

The Palestinian callers chose Yossi Saias's program as a platform for expressing their desire for peace, their outrage at the bombings, but also to publicize their annoyance at the travel restrictions that came in their aftermath. In what became a landmark broadcast, Saias stood up to the task of navigating this unusual flood of calls. Despite his highly explicit expression of support for Prime Minister Shimon Peres, Yossi Saias insisted that he was not making a political statement but an emotional one, expressing support for the man who was shouldering the burden of navigating the nation at that difficult time. His response to a Bedouin caller from Beer-Sheva, who expressed his pain at the terrorist attack and wanted to offer his help in some way, was a typical Saias response: "Let's establish a love army. Would you like to be its first soldier?"

Yet despite Yossi Saias's posture, the article about him detected the political statement embedded in the program: "Nevertheless, the program manages to convey a political message. Perhaps unintentionally, but one that underscores mutual openness and tolerance." In this context of apolitical politics, Sheikh Nimer Darwish, the head of the Islamic movement in Israel, who had openly denounced the suicide attacks, denying the claim that they had roots in Islamic teachings, found himself in dialogue not only with Yossi Saias but also with Avi Farhan, a right-wing activist and settler. Sharing his agony at the terrorist attacks, Darwish complimented Yossi Saias on his program, saying:

> I follow your program, Yossi, you have done excellent deeds, but today you performed the best deed of your life by addressing Peres and saying: "We hug you and love you." If there are killers who are listening now, they are saying: Now we've blown it. There's all the military efforts and the espionage, but with love you can destroy not only snakes but all evil. I

commend you on the statement "there's no political atmosphere here." You penetrated right into my heart with this sentence.

Avi Farhan, a leader of the Gaza Strip settlement movement, reciprocated by saying: "I commend Darwish's words. I as a settler and you as an Arab spiritual leader have to call out to those people in Gaza, to encourage them to make their voices heard. Let them take the risk, too, and call Saias' program." Saias seconded by asking Arab listeners to call in, and many, indeed, took up the challenge. In the interview he gave to the paper, Yossi Saias concluded: "This program was an important document. Look how reticent they [the Palestinians] are. Nobody gave them an open line, perhaps because the feeling in the media is that it is our time to talk now. It's our turn, our right. But I believe in dialogue. I know that no political solution will come out of here, but perhaps we can find the common ground between neighbors. Just two [individuals]. Nations are beyond my size."

Thus, personalizing and humanizing a bitter political struggle in this particular moment of shared grief, Yossi Saias offered his own version of nonpolitical politics, which for a moment sounded a note of human sanity in a chaotic, violent world. On this as on other occasions of radiophonic solidarity, Yossi Saias capitalized on the boundary-dissolving character of his program, on its ability to transcend the lines between host and audience, between the studio and the world outside, and this time also dissolve the invisible line that runs between the political and the communal. Even while addressing a national conflict, all callers spoke in an idiom of personal address, keeping in line with the program's regular intimate texture and tone. This way, arch-enemies, too, could openly share similar sentiments in what turned into a hesitant but poignantly real moment of mutual recognition.

This particular program stands out among the programs in my corpus in that it was concerned with a public event that had penetrated people's personal lives in a way that forced a renegotiation of customary boundaries between the personal and the communal. Most of the exchanges on the call-in programs I have studied move in the opposite direction, bringing personal concerns into the public sphere rather than casting communal-political themes in the program's intimate tones. Whether public concerns are collapsed into the private sphere, as in this case, or personal concerns claim public resonance, as in most others, call-in radio programs emerge as a cultural arena which invites an ongoing negotiation of the tensions between the private and public, the individual and the collective, dialogue and transmission. These tensions, as I have argued, are central themes of social life as we have come to know it, and have been addressed as constitutive of the early pioneers' soul talks and of the *dugri* way of speaking as well.

CALL-IN RADIO AS A MULTIVOCAL ARENA

The two radio programs I have attended to in the foregoing account exemplify the role of contemporary broadcasting in shaping the public sphere in idioms that simulate and recreate the immediacy of face-to-face interpersonal encounters. Paddy Scannell has attended to this possibility in noting that radio (and television) hosts "have learned to treat the communicative process not simply as the transmission of content, but as a relational process in which how things are said is as important as what is said. All this has, I think, contributed to new, interactive relationships between public and private life which have helped to normalize the former and to socialize the latter."[84]

The call-in radio format makes this dimension of broadcasting particularly visible. It is first and foremost an invitation to diversify the kinds of voices that can be heard on radio, providing a venue for people who rarely appear on daytime radio. On these programs ordinary people's personal experience narratives are worthy of attention in and of themselves. They are not just colorful illustrations of more important themes, as personal stories tend to be when appearing in current events programming. In this context these stories affirm the role of the personal domain, constructed in relational terms, as a locus of authenticity. The programs thus serve to disseminate a shared vision of authentic dialogue as a moment of human contact. Yet, in learning to treat radio broadcasting in relational terms, the two hosts, whose communicative styles I have considered here, have taught themselves to do different things, signaling different stances toward their broadcast talk.

The many points of difference I have pointed out between the two programs' broadcasting styles can perhaps make better sense when subsumed under the two overarching orientations that have been identified in the study of art and popular culture: the mode of realism and the mode of melodrama. As expressive modes, the two broadcasting styles addressed here diverge in some basic epistemological assumptions which Christine Gledhill has discussed with reference to realism and melodrama.[85] According to her account, the mode of realism is grounded in the assumption that the world can be adequately explained and represented. Melodrama lacks such confidence in the possibilities of rational explanation due to its focus on often inexplicable forces such as the desires and fears that shape human life.

Thus, while realism cultivates a discourse oriented toward understanding, melodrama, in the words of Peter Brooks, is a "language of presence and immediacy."[86] Viewing these programs in these terms, as popular-discursive formations oriented toward realism in the one case (Yovav Katz) and toward melodrama in the other (Yossi Saias), takes us beyond a point-to-point comparative analysis of cultural style and allows us to see these programs as part of larger cultural configurations associated with the construction of social-cultural hierarchies. Given the long history of associating melodrama with the popular and the feminine, the kind of disdain I have sometimes encountered for Yossi Saias's melodramatic style among members of the educated middle class, including Yovav Katz himself, becomes less surprising. The more encompassing context of the differences summarized below is therefore important to keep in mind.

In Yovav Katz's program, the host acts mainly as a guide leading the caller toward self-reflection and inner exploration. He helps callers discover and clarify their motivations, desires, possibilities, and limitations. The radio exchange empowers callers by offering them an opportunity to create a reflective distance from their experience. The interpersonal exchange between host and caller assists the latter in reshaping his or her sense of self through the "cooling function" of narrative (as identified by Bruner and Lucariello[87]). These explorations of alternative points of view also allow listeners to identify with the quasi-therapeutic process that is modeled for them on the program. Yossi Saias's program offers personal empowerment by allowing callers to give voice to their experiences and feelings in a highly immersive mode. Furthermore, callers' personal plight becomes embedded within the larger framework of an ephemeral community of sympathetic listeners who are actively mobilized to extend emotional support and even practical help.

In the quasi-therapeutic discourse of Yovav Katz's program, issues of interpersonal ethics are psychologized and their moral dimensions are thereby attenuated. In this discourse, the social is subordinated to the personal and talk is the vehicle for inner change. Moral issues become a matter of personal choices and preferences, and answers are to be sought in individual motivations and feelings even as they cultivate interpersonal bonds. Essentially, each caller is expected to find his or her own solution to problems after articulating them as personal dilemmas concerned with the vicissitudes of interpersonal life.

Yossi Saias's program enacts a communal conversation in a cultural world where words and deeds are interchangeable, social distance is minimized, and the studio walls are permeable. The self-absorbed yet caring host cultivates his personal charisma through both self-disclosures and emotional displays. Sharing in his callers' difficult moments, he also explicitly instructs them in the basic tenets of what he considers to be the good life. He replaces the abstract notion of individual uniqueness that is so central to Yovav Katz's idiom with a concrete attachment to individuals with whom one feels a shared sense of belonging. In Saias's view, individual problems are interpreted as failures of the communal ethic of love and caring, and he chides callers who he feels have failed to live up to its standards.

Both hosts use particular forms of talk through which their different worldviews and interpersonal ideologies are enacted. They both model ways of speaking for their audiences and regulate callers' participation by incorporating them within the programs' discursive regimes. In the case of Yovav Katz's program, audiences align themselves with a self-reflective, problem-solving mode of talk. In the case of Saias's program, they are invited to express their emotions in an open, melodramatic manner. Unlike cases of explicit linguistic regulation, the guidelines for talk on these call-in radio programs remain largely implicit, and are mainly made visible through the actual unfolding of the radio exchange. A major difference between the stylistic idioms employed in these two programs lies in their underlying attitudes toward emotional display. I have described these difference in terms of contrasting rhetorics—Yovav Katz's rhetoric of emotional control and Saias's rhetoric of emotional presence.

These two rhetorics are embedded within larger cultural configurations of meanings and values. I have attempted to present the main points of my analysis in a schematic form. The picture is obviously more complex than the polarities I have sketched here can possibly capture. Yet the foregoing account, despite its inevitably reductionistic flavor, draws together the main points of comparison that have emerged as significant to the understanding of the cultural idioms animating these two programs.

What can be said about the ways in which these two communicative styles interact on the Israeli cultural scene? And further, what are
the implications of these stylistic observations for our understanding of
the role such radio programs play in the larger social field? As indicated
in the above discussion, some of the presumptions and sensibilities
that inform the programs' idioms of social support are diametrically
opposed while others overlap. The voluntary nature of participation
in these radio exchanges minimizes the misunderstandings and conflicts generated by them. Since callers are self-selected, those who feel
uncomfortable with a program's style usually refrain from calling in;
listeners who find the talk on such a program irritating—as some do—
simply tune out if they happen to hit on it when moving between radio
channels. As my account shows, however, callers may be out of tune
with the particular idiom that governs the exchanges on the program
they have contacted.[88] I have used a number of examples of such stylistic mismatches in my foregoing analysis as a strategy for exploring
the rules and premises underlying the smooth construction of these
programs and which tend to remain invisible when not violated in
some way.

The hosts themselves are aware, each in his own way, of providing
a communicative alternative to the other's program. Yossi Saias, as we
have seen, is rather dispassionate about these differences, attributing
them to differences in sensibility related to ethnic background and
social class. He plays up the image of the emotional Middle Eastern Jew
in a flamboyant and subversive manner. As I found out in discussing
an earlier version of this account with Yovav Katz, he too points to
the ethnic roots of Yossi Saias's style but has a clear aversion to it.
As he phrased it, he was put off by Saias's apparent self-absorption,
his rampant sentimentality, his carelessness in dishing out opinions
and advice, and his encouragement of the callers' self-pity. Although
he conceded that my account gave him new insights into Yossi Saias's
program, he felt I was overly accepting of its style.

Replicating the rejection of Mizrahi heritage, whose "Arabness"
many Israelis of European descent openly disdained, he told me that the
program's discourse resonated with "everything that's now happening
with Shas," the orthodox party of Oriental Jews whose electoral success has led to recharting the Israeli political map. As a social-political
movement, Shas has been instrumental in foregrounding ethnic and
class issues within Israeli politics, thereby contributing to the erosion
of the hegemony of Ashkenazi Jews, who trace their heritage to Europe.

Not surprisingly, Yovav Katz did not view his own program in ethnic terms. The hegemonic standing of the Western-based quasi-therapeutic idiom renders its cultural inflections invisible. Yossi Saias, on the other hand, was more attuned to the social anchoring of this style in middle-class, bourgeois culture. Although he was not interested in commenting on my analysis, his own account of Yovav Katz's program emphasized its orderly and distanced nature (captured, inter alia by the epithet "academic"). In contrasting it with the simple, spontaneous, and impassioned style of his own program, he explicitly drew a class line between the simple folk and the educated classes. Class and ethnicity are largely overlapping categories in discussions of the Israeli-Jewish population. Thus, both Yovav Katz's comments on Yossi Saias's program and Saias's characterization of the two programs reinforced my sense that they should be understood within the larger context of interethnic relations in Israel today.

Admittedly, Yovav Katz's own measured and reasoned style comes closer to my own cultural baggage. Some of the discourse on Yossi Saias's program, especially its melodramatic tone and use of intensification strategies, sometimes sounded grating to my Ashkenazi ears. I have at times found myself cringing at a response casually delivered by the host. Some of these responses sounded as if they could only accentuate the caller's problem, "rubbing it in" as it were, or moralizing where I would have wanted to hear acceptance. But few of the callers' responses indicated that they shared my moments of unease. They were clearly quite better aligned with the program's expressive regime. Despite my occasional inner resistance toward the program's emotional overload, I did not share Yovav Katz's sense of annoyance. Indeed, his authoritative condemnation of Saias's program reminded me of some of the responses I encountered among professional psychologists with whom I discussed my study. To them Yovav Katz's program seemed no less jarring than Yossi Saias's program was to Yovav Katz. They rather vehemently asserted that such short, one-shot radio encounters were meaningless and potentially harmful, similarly invoking the culture of expertise and the language of professional responsibility to criticize any form of "media psychology."

Within my present account, these programs are viewed as alternative venues of social support that emerged in the last two decades of the twentieth century in response to the need to maintain radio's vibrancy as a medium of communication in a television-saturated age. I do not seek to evaluate their effectiveness beyond pointing out the need to consider cultural differences in expressive style, the ways in which they are played out in this media context, and the implications they carry as assertions of social and moral authority.

For me and for other middle-class Western (or Westernized) listeners, understanding and appreciating Yossi Saias's program may involve more of a cognitive leap. It may require an effort to render the strange familiar. Understanding and appreciating Yovav Katz's program, on the other hand, requires an ability to exoticize the therapeutic ethos that permeates so much of Western bourgeois life. Both are movements of mind and heart. Both require attention not just to "what" but also to "how" things are said. I believe that the positive as well as the negative "gut reactions" to these programs I have encountered among informants while working on this research, however expressed, can be traced to their style no less than to their particular focus on personal contents. It is mainly through their performative style that these programs are constituted as distinctive yet mutually defining cultural arenas.[89] As I have tried to show, the expressive idioms they employ are themselves ongoing cultural constructions. The Israeli radio scene is a stylized human environment that gives voice to diverse, ethnically anchored "structures of feeling."[90] These programs' soundscapes are crafted by the hosts, rearticulating the dialectical tension between the personal and the communal in a society that has partially embraced Western individualism.[91]

Most significantly, however, each of these radio programs, while employing its own cultural idiom, is multivocal in the sense that it is the product of what Bakhtin views as processes of hybridization, or "a mixture of two social languages within the limits of a single utterance, an encounter . . . between two different linguistic consciousnesses, separated from one another by an epoch, by social differentiation, or by some other factor." Bakhtin further distinguishes two types of hybridity. One is "organic hybridity," which involves a mixture that "merges and is fused into a new language, world view, or object."[92] The other is "intentional hybridity," which "sets different points of view against each other in a conflictual structure."[93] In the latter case, even when only one language is present in an utterance, "it is rendered in the light of another language."[94]

More than the hybridity of style-mixing, these programs manifest "intentional hybridity"—each implicitly responds to the other's emotional idiom. The language of emotional detachment and control employed in the program hosted by Yovav Katz can be seen as an implicit rejection of the rampant emotionalism typical of Yossi Saias's ethnic style and its social implications. Similarly, Yossi Saias's accentuated emotionalism can be seen as an implicit, playful rejection of the bourgeois ethos of emotional control, which stands in the way of spontaneous expression and immediacy in human relations. The cohabitation of these two alternative voices on the same channel of Israeli public radio (albeit on different nights of the week) has the political effect Bakhtin associates with intentional hybridity—as each voice unmasks the other, the authoritative discourse of both programs is to some extent undone.

The Politics of Counterpolitics

I have argued that the radio programs considered in this study can be viewed as constituting an alternative, nocturnal public sphere (very different from—yet also reminiscent of—the communal sphere charted by the early pioneers' nightly soul talks). As noted, these alternative social spaces thematize personal concerns that have traditionally been relegated to the private sphere, responding to what Peter Berger has referred to as the increasing "unreality" or "weightlessness" of social institutions and the public sphere in the experience of the inhabitants of late modernity. In his words: "As the public sphere continues to slide into unreality, the private sphere emerges as the major plausibility structure for the self and ipso facto for an increasingly sophisticated concern with subjectivity."[95] Both these programs constitute alternative social spaces that combine the thematics of the private sphere with the social resonance provided by articulations of shared cultural codes. Yovav Katz's program is an alternative social space in the sense that it circumscribes a depoliticized domain of self-oriented intimate talk. Yossi Saias's program similarly delineates an alternative social space, but one in which voices and problems that are usually marginalized by mainstream institutions and excluded from daytime broadcasting can be heard.

Focusing on personal problems and problematic interpersonal relations, both programs insert into the public sphere the tormented voices of ordinary people who struggle with the hardships of their troubled selves and interpersonal lives. Their authenticity lies in the disclosure of their sense of vulnerability and failure to sustain meaningful lives as well as satisfying close relations. These programs put forth the image of the deeply distressed individual and his or her confessional discourse as a cultural icon that personifies the search for authentic dialogue. Clearly, this image of the troubled self is considerably removed from the image of the straight-talking Sabra, that is, the personal ideal of the morally driven, socially responsible agent who acts in the service of collective ends by speaking his or her mind in confrontational encounters. Indeed, the troubled self of the 1990s has at least partially replaced the assertive self of the Israeli nation-building era of the 1940s and 1950s as a locus of authenticity. Whereas the idealized image of the Sabra was reaffirmed, as we have seen, through the staging of ritualized performances of straight talk, the confessional telling of distress narratives on the nocturnal radio programs studied here ritually reaffirms the image of the troubled and flawed person who is struggling to hold his or her personal life together in a fragmented and disheveled world of burdensome family and interpersonal relations.

Studies of such alternative radio programs can support feminist and other critiques of Habermas's idealized image of the bourgeois public sphere as a democratic arena of free and equal participation in reasoned debate.[96] Taken together, these critiques have argued that the bourgeois public sphere "has, from its inception, been built upon powerful mechanisms of exclusion."[97] These mechanisms are predicated on the deeply ingrained monolingualism of liberal philosophies and institutions.

The insertion of alternative voices into the public sphere of Israeli radio broadcasting is a democratizing move that carries an oppositional flavor. Like alternative radio broadcasting in other cultural contexts, such as the Basque "free radio" movement discussed by Jacqueline Urla, the Israeli radio programs considered here are examples of popular cultural forms that have proliferated "in the interstices of the bourgeois public."[98] They similarly construct counterpublics that "give lie to the presumed homogeneity of the imaginary public."[99] These counterpublics are comprised of sleepless listeners who reject the overwhelming primacy given to current events and national-political struggles in Israeli politics-driven daytime broadcasting. They use the liminality of late-night programming to carve out a publicly recognized personal sphere. In other words, they enact a politics of counterpolitics. Even though they are dominated by the powerless modes of advice-seeking or supplication, these programs provide arenas where marginalized and vulnerable people—the poor, the miserable, the disoriented, the suffering—can speak for themselves rather than be spoken about. As Kress has pointed out, the new voices and genres that thereby emerge may have far-reaching social implications despite their marginality, or even because of it. In his words: "Genres which have an existence in certain private domains can emerge in the arena of the public, and there perhaps act as new models of social interaction not at the moment available."[100]

Indeed, the programs' hosts generally rely on the potential of this private-idiom-turned-public and do not usually encourage callers to seek institutional help even when this might seem a reasonable move from an outside observer's point of view. In those rare cases in which callers tried to cast their narratives in broader institutional terms, they were unsuccessful. On one such occasion, a woman called Yovav Katz's program and said that she had been physically abused by her husband for many years. The host launched a line of questioning that sought to explore her feelings of vulnerability, but the woman did not appear interested in this exploratory move. Rather, she talked angrily about the policeman's casual attitude when she tried to file an official complaint against her spouse. She sounded much more like a feminist-activist, who was disgusted with paternalistic sociopolitical arrangements than like the heartbroken, disoriented victim of marital abuse who was the more typical caller to these late-night programs.

Her approach was so out of tune with the program's quasi-therapeutic idiom that Yovav Katz repeatedly tried to redirect her talk toward a mode of expression more commensurate with his own vision of the program's agenda. Failing to do so, he said that her problem seemed more in line with the kinds of issues dealt with on daytime radio, and suggested that she call one of these programs the following day. He then gently but firmly terminated the conversation. What this caller and listeners to this particular exchange were implicitly told was that feelings of anger and frustration directed at social institutions or structural arrangements were not among the emotions that Yovav Katz's program was designed to accommodate.

Similarly, yet for different reasons, Yossi Saias's strategy of communal mobilization, with its preference for spontaneous, informal invocation of individuals' goodwill and resources, precludes the activation of social welfare institutions. Thus, for example, when a woman called Saias's program and said that she had lost her husband in a car accident, was disabled, had two small children she could not feed, and was about to be evicted from her apartment with no alternative housing in sight, he did not ask her about institutional interventions she might have sought, nor did he refer her to the welfare authorities for the help they could and should have given her. Rather, he asked for her telephone number and appealed to his listeners to offer whatever help they could give to the woman in a direct, informal gesture of empathy and support.

The sociopolitical sphere, which dominates mainstream, daytime radio programming, becomes momentarily marginalized and loses some of its pressing actuality when listeners of the programs hosted by Yovav Katz and Yossi Saias immerse themselves in callers' personal problems. As noted, in this rather unusual radiophonic environment, personal and interpersonal concerns command center stage. In phenomenological terms this is experienced as a sort of reversal. The social-political sphere of current affairs, which is the paramount reality of radio broadcasting, is kept out of the program's range. Hourly news updates are often experienced as an unwelcome intrusion into the program's conversational flow. These intrusive news breaks take listeners back to the officially ordained "reality" of current affairs coverage, for a moment overshadowing the programs' personal focus and their implicit claim that the private sphere is where the action really is.

The study of late-night call-in radio programs thus points to a cultural arena where different versions of the quest for authentic dialogue are played out. It is a uniquely constructed arena of public dissemination in which the possibility of dialogic communication is reclaimed through the blurring of the customary lines between media producers and consumers, between private and public, between words and deeds. At the same time, as we have seen, each of the programs studied here is an arena of cultural production with qualities of its own, where culturally inflected styles of social support are creatively reproduced and reinterpreted. These styles coexist, and in some implicit ways stand in dialogic relation to each other in what is essentially the shared cultural space of public broadcasting. The characteristics that Paddy Scannell claims are constitutive of public service broadcasting hold in the case of these radio programs: "the provision of a service of mixed programs on national channels available to all."[101]

These call-in radio programs are clearly part of a larger media phenomenon, which Peter Gibian has referred to as the "airwaves dialogue boom." He described the 1980s trend toward media dialogues as such: "Where we were used to static 'talking heads' handing down The Word in monologue—*talking at us*—we are increasingly hearing a wild multiplicity of voices, of tones, of stances in dialogue, fighting for the floor, arguing about that Word—*talking all around us.*"[102]

Indeed, even the most cursory exposure to the contemporary Israeli media scene can only amplify this observation, which was originally formulated nearly two decades ago for a different cultural context. Moreover, a glance at some prime-time television talk shows suggests that the diversity of voices heard on self-help call-in radio programs, such as self-disclosive, therapeutic discourses, or the teary-eyed stories of personal distress and hardship, as well as the charitable gestures of communal mobilization, have all become an increasingly prominent part of mainstream Israeli broadcasting in recent years. Talking all around us, media personalities, studio guests, online chatters, and anonymous callers to radio programs engage in mediated dialogues in which they openly share their personal concerns and opinions with the nation-at-large. The many radio and television programs in which this outpouring of personal information and feelings takes place are often modeled on American formats. Yet they chart Israeli cultural spaces in which new forms of "public intimacy" and communal participation are circulated in daytime and nocturnal dialogues that have become part of Israel's increasingly multivocal and complex mediascape.

By viewing these radio exchanges as a version of the Israeli search for authentic dialogue, I suggest that they echo earlier dialogic quests in Israeli culture, such as the early pioneers' soul talks and the Sabra's *dugri* confrontational mode. This thread of cultural continuity weaves together evanescent "dialogic" moments whose promise has reverberated through Israel's shifting cultural scene. This shifting scene is also the scene of changing communication technologies and the human longings and possibilities that attend them. With the advent of contemporary digital technologies, both the powers of dissemination and the possibilities for dialogue have increased many-fold. How these recent changes will affect the "spokenness" of radio voices is a question that will have to be asked in years to come.

Conclusion
Writing against the Text

This book chronicles the role of the quest for "authentic dialogue" in the Israeli dream of communal solidarity, as well as the souring of such dialogue in the shifting context of Israeli society through the twentieth century. My focus has been on the role played by culturally focal ways of speaking and speech occasions in shaping and reflecting this process. While I tried to recapture some past moments, my account was obviously written from the standpoint of the present—the standpoint of a participant-observer of the culture. My particular position within the field of study has inevitably colored my account with the blend of nostalgia and disillusionment that have shaped so much of the contemporary Israeli cultural scene. Whether it was interpreted as a quest for a transcendent communion of souls, as a direct and confrontational style that facilitates collective action, or as a public, mass-mediated display and elaboration of personal problems and feelings, the search for genuine dialogue has been a central dimension of the production and negotiation of Israeli identity over the years. The utopian promise of a harmony-filled communal solidarity generated by enactments of "authentic dialogue" has been a powerful force in the dynamics of Israeli culture and provides a particularly rich site in which to explore the interplay of culture and speech.

Thus, taking speech to be a profoundly cultural activity, these studies attend to the cultural dynamics of the Israeli scene from the perspective of its verbal-expressive repertoire, offering an extended exploration of the fluctuations of culturally focal speech styles, speech events, and speech ideologies over time. Throughout the book, I have addressed speech-related activities in terms of the meanings and values in which they are grounded. In conclusion, therefore, let me address the larger story suggested by the three "case studies" that make up this book by revisiting the central thematic and conceptual threads that have figured in the foregoing account such as the shifting cultural conceptions of "community" and "authentic dialogue"; the cultural negotiations attending locally shaped binaries such as "words" and "deeds"; the cultural construction of face-to-face as well as mass-mediated social relations; and the tensions entailed by the twin processes of social affinity and solidarity-building as against social differentiation, boundary maintenance, and exclusion.

While all three case studies are centrally concerned with the role played by the quest for authentic dialogue in the production of community, their exploration has revealed subtle shifts in the cultural configurations associated with the notions of "community" and "authentic dialogue" alike. It has also revealed shifting conceptions of the notion of the individual and its position in relation to communal life. All three studies indicate that in Israeli ethno-sociology, which draws on Jewish conceptions of the individual/community dialectic, the underlying relationship is one of mutual actualization of self and society rather than of opposition and struggle (as in the case of modern Western culture). This localized interpretation of personhood and sociality has been affected by Western modernity in a variety of ways, and has given different inflections to the construction of Israeli identity over the years. As I have tried to show, some version of the search for authentic dialogue has been a major discursive tool in this cultural project.

In the case of the early pioneers' soul talks of the 1920s, community building, as a central social goal, was anchored in a vision of the face-to-face context of the small, "intimate group" of like-minded individuals whose shared quest for authenticity involved an interpretation of dialogue as a "communion of souls." Communal life within the "intimate group" was a total, all-encompassing experience, yet it was largely constituted through the interplay of group-oriented individual voices. The notion of authenticity that informed these gatherings combined self-discovery and self-creation in confessional encounters in which individuals probed their innermost hearts and lay them open before the group. Self and community were thus mutually constituted, merging personal feelings and public concerns, giving as much weight to "words" as to "deeds." The high value placed by these groups on speech as a vehicle of personal exploration and communal expression endowed them with a rarified "spiritual" aura in a social climate that privileged productive labor and pragmatically oriented deeds.

Later reenactments of the soul talk format, such as the fighters' talks following the 1967 war, replicated this overall cultural configuration, yet at this point the group discussions were not part of a total communal experience and were largely confined to the emotionally loaded but restricted experience of participation in war. While still conducted in a face-to-face setting, these postwar, highly tormented fighters' talks were expressive enclaves oriented to the larger community of kibbutz members. They became emblems of troubled soldierhood due to their focus on difficult emotions and moral dilemmas associated with war and combat. The fictional reassessments of the soul talk ethos, as found in some Israeli plays, provide further reflections on the basic values of community and authenticity that originally animated the soul talk ethos, not only questioning the present consequences of pursuing them but also undermining the very credibility of such a pursuit.

While I have referred to the soul talk ethos as a road not taken in the Zionist enterprise, the *dugri* ethos has marked a well-recognized path to the construction of the Sabra identity and Israeliness more generally, representing a dominant strand in Israeli culture in the decades immediately preceding and following the establishment of the State of Israel (in 1948). Taking action rather than expression as its main theme, the *dugri* ethos has been associated with a pragmatic orientation that is grounded in a polarity between words and deeds. In this context, "authentic dialogue" is not a matter of a communion of souls but rather a matter of socially meaningful action and personal commitment to collective goals. Talking straight involves authenticity in the sense of being able to represent one's thoughts, attitudes, and feelings faithfully, out of a sense of collective responsibility rather than a yearning for a communion of souls, without the soul-searching of the early pioneers. *Dugri* speech involves authenticity in the sense that it affirms and displays rather than creates the culturally privileged image of the Sabra. The social warrant to be direct in potentially confrontational encounters ideally generates trust between individuals who join in cooperative action, whether in face-to-face communities or in larger communities that diffusely share a distinctive cultural style. The cultural authority of this style has rested on the vitality of speech codes whose effectiveness has been undermined with the growing social segmentation and differentiation of Israeli society.

The hegemonic *dugri* ethos has always been problematic as a vehicle of in-group solidarity in what was, in effect, a society of immigrants. With the renunciation of the melting pot ideology that sought to turn all immigrants into Sabra-like Israelis, its implementation in the self-consciously multicultural society of contemporary Israel has turned it into a major site of cultural contestation. I have traced this dynamic with reference to Jewish ethnicity in Israel, attending specifically to the issue of Ashkenazi-Mizrahi relations through a consideration of a much-publicized social drama, known as the Ori Or Affair, in which the meanings of *dugri* speech came to be renegotiated in the public arena. The growing multivocality of the Israeli cultural scene is accompanied by a growing sense of disorientation vis-à-vis the changing contours of Israeli speech culture. This is reflected in periodic "moral panics" in press accounts that evaluate the Israeli ethos, which frequently focus on styles of speech and social conduct.

The greater diversity of the Israeli social scene is addressed in the study of two late-night call-in radio programs. These programs construct loosely demarcated "media communities" of listeners who remain anonymous yet share fleeting moments of self-disclosure in dialogue within the dependable framework provided by these regular radio broadcasts. These radio dialogues work to foreground a discursive arena where national themes are pushed backstage and attention is drawn to the personal domain. Focusing on personal feelings and problems, on well-being, self-help, and betterment, they attend to the problematic of interpersonal and familial relationships. In response to the collectivism, rationality, and mechanization that have come to dominate the Israeli progressive, nation-building ethos, these radio programs offer a contrapuntal theme grounded in a "therapeutic" and communal culture. They thus become cultural sites for generating mass-mediated versions of "authentic dialogue." While both programs thrive on self-disclosure and emotional display, the expressive strategies employed by the hosts point to the use of very different idioms of social support and to differences in the notion of "authentic dialogue" they articulate.

The program hosted by Yovav Katz gives voice to a Western-based psychotherapeutic ethos that views dialogue as a tentative vehicle for self-probing and self-transformation. Its efficacy lies in the belief that well-chosen words can heal and that this healing is a discursive process. The possibility of creating a "media community" in this case rests with the universality of the human predicament and the consequent similarities between the problems people face. The program hosted by Yossi Saias, on the other hand, is more about self-display than self-exploration. It is about affirming the suffering of individual persons and changing their circumstances, not about changing them, and it is grounded in the view that emotional support and practical action are equally relevant and necessary responses to human distress. The "media community" in this case is continuous with actual communal networks that are activated through the program's talk.

As we have seen, over the years the quest for "authentic dialogue" has been a centerpiece of the cultural project of creating a new Israeli culture, community, and personhood. The shape of the "dialogic moments" encompassed within this quest, the nature of the communal experiences they engendered, and the notion of authenticity cultivated in them were all subject to subtle cultural negotiations and shifts. In particular, these shifts concerned rearticulations of the individual/community dialectic.

The different versions of the interplay of self and community traced in the three studies that make up this book narrate the tale of the production of Israeli identity in and through culturally focal speech styles and speech events. Taken together, they offer a practice-oriented and complex picture of cultural change that complicates the accounts suggested by macro-level sociological sketches that portray a linear movement from collectivism to individualism in Israeli culture. At the same time, we note that the Israeli nation-building project, like others of its kind, has been blind to the implications it held for the groups excluded from or marginalized by it. Cultivating the value of authentic expression, the "dialogic moments" I have studied have at times turned into sites of social regimentation, erecting boundaries and exclusions through their very language of commitment and community. The inwardly directed look associated with the nation-building project and its exclusionary dimensions has generated an increasingly self-feeding lack of regard for the rights and suffering of those not invited into the privileged circle of "Israeliness," or only half-heartedly invited to do so—Palestinians, Middle Eastern Jews, newcomers, and women.

The nature of the nation-building project itself has been renegotiated over time, reinterpreting the "words" versus "deeds" dialectic that has been so central to Israeli speech culture and giving different valence to each of its terms. During early pioneering days, "doing" mainly referred to collectively oriented, productive engagements in construction and agricultural work. As the conflictual nature of relations with the indigenous Arab population became inescapably clear, combat activities became more and more central in the arsenal of the Jewish settlers' "deeds." It is worth noting that from very early on the spirit of group solidarity envisaged among the early pioneers was modeled on the fighting ethos of the close-knit combat unit. Indeed, as Rina Peled points out, even Martin Buber, the philosopher of dialogue, "regarded the community of fighters as an ideal model for the organic community he promoted."[1]

This suggests that the promotion of group solidarity is intimately linked to the potential for group violence. Inclusion and exclusion strategies—verbal and otherwise—feed into each other through an intricate web of half-acknowledged mutual justifications. Within this context, the vision of communication as "authentic dialogue" has played an important role in helping to cement group boundaries— for better and for worse. The utopian visions of true dialogue seem to have generated more yearnings and evasions than livable realities. The "dialogic moments" delineated in this book demarcate domains of discursive activity in which spiritual, emotional, and moral sentiments are thematized and ritualized in ways that divorce them from the reality of power struggles, conflicts of interest, diversity, and political strife. They thus mark highly enticing—but also potentially problematic— social spaces. As valorized models of and for social discourse, they celebrate affinity and like-mindedness, promote a yearning for ritual moments of transcendence, and privilege expressive over deliberative discourse genres in the conduct of communal affairs.

Despite their rather loose formal organization, I suggest that the Israeli dialogic moments I have explored function in a way reminiscent of the South American ceremonial dialogues studied by Greg Urban and others. These South American dialogic forms are ceremonial in the sense that they ritualize aspects of the interchange such as the regulation of turn-taking in a way that enhances the dialogue either through the exchange of turns-at-talk or through the use of backchannel cues. In the South American ethnographic data surveyed and analyzed by Urban within a semiotic framework, these ceremonial dialogues convey a culture-specific message about linguistic and social solidarity "by means of an indexical connection between the ceremonial dialogic form, as a sign vehicle, and the type of linguistic interaction for which it is employed—negotiation, myth-telling, greeting and so forth—as meaning, as well as by a culture-specific iconicity."[2]

Like these ceremonial dialogues, the ritualized communicative events I have focused on convey particular messages about solidarity, about what social integration is and how it can and should be achieved. The instances of ritualized authentic dialogues I have studied can be considered in terms of the cross-cultural category of "ceremonial dialogue" posited by Urban. As instances of coordinated linguistic action, they become sign vehicles that serve as "a model of and for [social] coordination more generally, this coordination in turn representing a fundamental building block of social solidarity."[3] The different kinds of dialogic moments, or ceremonial dialogues, I have considered in this book thus represent different paths to the production of different kinds of social solidarity through coordinated linguistic action that is grounded in the overarching theme of the quest for authentic dialogue in Israeli cultural history.

In tracing this central theme in Israeli speech culture through its different manifestations in the evolving saga of modern Israeli ethos, I have been attentive to the changing ideals and articulations of social solidarity that have informed the Israeli quest for authenticity in dialogue over the past century. I find Urban's analytic distinction between three ideal types of solidarity helpful in contemplating my own case studies. It includes: 1. the shared culture model grounded in common tradition; 2. the exchange model grounded in the complementarity of acknowledged difference; and 3. the balance of power model grounded in mutual respect and a recognition of interactants' mutual capability to coerce one another in the context of social exchanges.

I believe the first two types are most relevant to the emergent models of solidarity that animated the early Zionist settlers' soul talks, the Sabras' style of straight talk, and the supportive exchanges between radio hosts and their callers. The third type of solidarity, which seems to be intrinsic to hierarchical societies, is an important feature of premodern cultural configurations such as those found in traditional Judaism as well as the Arabic ethos of *musayra* (to name only examples directly relevant to my analysis). It has been rejected within the Israeli egalitarian ethos. Consequently, issues of power have been under-thematized and under-ritualized in Israeli speech culture and remain a troubling, yet barely acknowledged and poorly regulated, element in it. The reluctance to recognize the working of power seems to have given rise to unrecognized paternalism toward cultural outsiders on the one hand and to a widespread discontent and sense of decline associated, for example, with such aberrations as the Big Mouth phenomenon, on the other.

As Urban points out, there is a link between contexts of potential conflict and the ritualization of dialogue since ceremonial dialogues provide, so to speak, social bridges in contexts in which solidarity is rendered problematic by social distance. This is certainly true for each of the case studies considered here, which involve different ways in which talk is mobilized for the purpose of creating community and common culture in the public sphere, in response to social alienation and in the face of potential conflict. The various interactional models of solidarity enacted in these contexts serve as blueprints of social conduct more generally, so that "each dialogic performance suggests how that solidarity can be achieved in other social interactions, e.g., in ordinary conversation."[4] How the "dialogic moments" studied here may have affected the emergence of speech patterns and speech ideologies in other domains of Israeli discourse, such as the political domain, is an intriguing question that goes beyond the confines of this study.

In offering a series of interlinked ethnographic accounts of ways of speaking, I see this work as contributing to the overall agenda of the ethnography of communication in a number of ways.

First, by casting a wider net than is usually done in such studies, which tend to be synchronic, I have offered an intertwined set of studies that provide a diachronic view of culturally focal ways of speaking within one national society. My study has thus moved from the culture's formative stages in the days of early settlement, through its nation-building communal idiom in the years preceding and following the establishment of statehood, to its contemporary accommodations of internal diversity and globalized trends. In sketching this temporal trajectory, I have studied ways of speaking as forming an interrelated set of cultural alternatives that anticipate and respond to each other as part of the ongoing dynamics of social life.

Second, I have explicitly attended to the role of ideological struggle and resistance in addressing the cultural shaping of hegemonic ways of speaking. While my work has been centrally concerned with the individual-community dialectic, with questions of individual autonomy and social solidarity, I have moved beyond a focus on the notion of speech codes as cultural resources, which is central to the approach formulated by Dell Hymes and Gerry Philipsen,[5] to a concern with the cultural politics of language use, the role of language ideologies in identity negotiations and their fluctuations over time.

Third, these studies have problematized rather than assumed the existence of "speech communities" and "social identities." Working within a performative perspective informed by the work of Goffman and others,[6] I have discussed both communities and identities as constituted through speech practices. This is a departure from a more traditional sociolinguistic position which views communicative conduct as reflecting preformed identities and groupings. In the view adopted here, communities and identities are seen as ongoing cultural projects constituted through speech. Discursive processes of ritualization, regimentation, and stylization, which operate against a backdrop of resistance and subversion, work to figure and refigure particular identities and group boundaries.

Fourth, in acknowledging the constant flow of forms, meanings, and messages between the interpersonal and public domains in contemporary cultures, this book has combined the study of face-to-face encounters with the study of mass-mediated communication forms and formats. Moving among everyday cultural settings, public rituals, and commodified verbal performances, I have addressed both the constraints and the possibilities of various communication channels and settings. The analysis has thus provided insights into the changing contours and meanings of face-to-face encounters on the one hand, and offered glimpses of the personal and communal possibilities of mass-mediated ones, on the other.

Finally, given the broad-ranging temporal trajectory of these three studies, each of them has called for and enabled different methodological foci, producing an inevitable yet potentially enriching unevenness in the kinds of data collected and presented. Thus, the study of the soul talk ethos has been mainly based on the availability of historical materials and a variety of popular and high culture texts. It has involved an attempt at sociolinguistic reconstruction and a tracing of intertextual relations. The study of the *dugri* ethos and the language ideology associated with it has been grounded in a prolonged exploration of Israeli speech symbolism based on participant observation, interviewing, and text analysis. The study of radio talk has a synchronic focus, and capitalizes on the medium-based possibilities of attending to recorded talk and amplifying its meaning within an interpretive account.

Indeed, the study of ways of speaking and speech events that have become culturally focal in the contexts of modernity and late modernity must take into account both developing communication technologies and the social implications of changing economic and social conditions. In John Peters's terms, as discussed earlier,[7] the ideologies and practices of communication-as-dialogue have to be interpreted against the background of the increasingly important role played by mass-mediated dissemination in people's lives. In Deborah Cameron's framework, as elaborated in the introduction,[8] the quest for dialogue in late modernity must be considered in relation to the existential task of reflexively constructing self-identities and with reference to the growing impact of institutional forces of linguistic regimentation. Both authors have made arguments that blur the traditional disciplinary lines between interpersonal and mass communication while remaining sensitive to the historically situated nature of studies of communication. Such sub-disciplinary intersections suggest that new media forms and changing social conditions may call for new answers to old questions just as they invite us to pose new questions in addressing old themes.

I cannot help but note a confluence of themes relevant to this book, whose roots are historically traceable to the 1920s and whose impact has been felt throughout the twentieth century. Peters has noted the intellectual fervor surrounding communication as a topic of intellectual debate after World War I and World War II, pointing out that "all the intellectual options in communication theory since that time were already visible in the 1920s."[9] During the same period, Martin Buber's philosophy of dialogue was a central strand in this intellectual conversation and had far-reaching ramifications for the Zionist youth groups who tried to weave its spirit into a life of dialogue in the context of their nocturnal soul talks. At about the same time, too, psychoanalytic orientations gave impetus to the development of a therapeutic ethos that became central to generations of middle-class Westerners in later years, giving rise to speech cultures grounded in notions of authentic dialogue, openness, and directness. The cultural specificity of these expressive values was brought out through my discussion of the Arabic ethos of *musayra* and the interactional values associated with the expressive idiom of Middle Eastern (Mizrahi) Jews.

Moreover, the 1920s were also the years in which radio listening and broadcasting became an integral part of people's lives in industrialized nations, serving to reconfigure both collective and individual identities. As Susan Douglas points out in her illuminating history of American radio,[10] its incorporation into people's lives involved many contrary and ambivalent effects. It gave rise to "media communities" that partook of the immediacy of transient moments of shared listening at the national level, but also reinforced subcultural and regional identities. It thus promoted national cohesion on the one hand and social differentiation on the other.

Radio broadcasting has opened up the domestic sphere to a host of external voices that affected listeners' involvements and emotions. Most poignantly, perhaps, from the standpoint of my analysis, the listening experience provided by radio in the 1920s was closely associated with the era's spiritual strivings, which were also encapsulated in quests for dialogue formulated by intellectuals and social activists at the time. Susan Douglas describes the experience of radio listening as one involving "disembodied voices" emanating from "the sky," saying: "Emphasizing radio's connection throughout the twentieth century to a persistent sense of spiritual longing and loss is essential to any understanding of what radio has done to us and for us."[11] She further refers to popular responses to the emergence of radio listening as a "spiritualism craze" in American 1920s culture, explaining:

> The way radio was first written about, as a magical, supernatural phenomenon, suggests that "the ether" and its disembodied voices from around the country somehow bridged the widening gap between machines and spirituality, and helped create an imaginative space where these two were reconciled. Radio burrowed into this unspoken longing for a contact with the heavens, for a more perfect community, for a spiritual transcendence not at odds with, but made possible by, machines.[12]

As we have seen, the quest for a community of dialogue infused with spiritual longings has only partly faded into the mists of the past. Clearly, radio broadcasting and listening have become routinized and have undergone many changes since their inception in the 1920s. Yet the emergence of the call-in format as a central development in radio programming since the late 1970s has reinfused radio listening with a new kind of aura. Thus, despite the increasing commercialization of the medium, radio listening has retained traces of the intimacy and spirituality that were associated with it in its early days.

Let me therefore conclude by admitting that the design of this book seeks to encompass a broader range of phenomena than those usually covered by more localized and synchronic studies of ways of speaking tend to cover. The book is also ambitious in its attempt to capture my increasingly complex authorial attitude toward the cultural themes encompassed in these studies as they have evolved over some twenty years of scholarly engagement with Israeli culture and its speechways. Initially, I was primarily concerned with delineating the processes and products of the emergence of new expressive forms that were part of the larger culture-making enterprise of modern Israel, and exploring their role in the production of group solidarity and identity formation. The basically affirmative flavor of this focus on the constructive dimension of Zionist cultural production has been gradually tempered by a more nuanced understanding of the exclusionary and totalizing strands associated with the culture-making and nation-building project.

This growing understanding has been grounded in a recognition of the two different pulls that Bakhtin has metaphorically referred to as *centrifugal* forces of differentiation in language and culture versus *centripetal* forces of standardization. The struggle between the centrifugal forces of diversity and the centripetal forces of unification and totalization characterizes the social life of language. This view of language as a site of struggle has far-reaching consequences for the ways we engage in the study of ways of speaking. As Bakhtin has remarked: "Such is the fleeting language of a day, of an epoch, a social group, a genre, a school and so forth. It is possible to give a concrete and detailed analysis of any utterance, once having exposed it as a contradiction-ridden, tension-filled unity of two embattled tendencies in the life of language."[13]

Thus, the crystallization of culturally focal ways of speaking inevitably entails the potential for cultural exclusion, and is experienced in very different ways by various participants in the wider social-cultural scene. My account has highlighted the self-making and communal dimensions of the cultural processes that give rise to the emergence of shared ways of speaking. It has sought to encompass the sense of promise, hope, and thrill such processes hold for cultural members without disregarding the blindness, loss, and denials that are an integral part of them as well. Indeed, for anyone familiar with the Israeli scene, my focus on the quest for genuine dialogue as a central cultural theme in the Israeli ethos may appear highly counterintuitive. The pervasiveness of conflict and violence in Israeli life—in the form of war, terrorism, occupation, militarism, and irreconcilable ideological rifts—is widely recognized. So are their manifestations in Israeli speech culture.[14] In this context, therefore, my decision to foreground the quest for dialogue and the cultural configuration associated with it may at first glance seem quite bizarre.

I hope the foregoing account has demonstrated the centrality of this quest in Israeli communicative life through the years, whether it took the form of harmony-building group processes, mass-mediated interpersonal encounters, or culturally sanctioned patterns of confrontation. The dialogic moments explored here have been described as ritualized enclaves, which point to a cultural alternative against a backdrop of potential violence and social strife. Indeed, the public and scholarly conversations concerning contemporary Israeli social and political life highlight issues of social fragmentation and draw attention to the dangers attending the conflict-ridden public sphere. In the 1980s and 1990s the fear of social breakdown and lack of solidarity has led to the emergence of dozens of dialogue groups that attempted to bridge some of the major social rifts considered to be a threat to the body politic. Thus, for example, flourishing cultural "industries" concerned with promoting dialogue between Israelis and Palestinians, or between secular and religious Jews, emerged. They constituted deliberate efforts to establish cultural enclaves in and through which group identities and group relations could be explored and overcome. These efforts can be viewed as institutionalized attempts to create moments of dialogue in a social setting filled with the shrillness of competing voices. Some of these attempts, which have been largely dominated by official versions of cultural conciliation, were the subject of study and critique by scholars from a variety of analytical perspectives.[15]

Notably, I do not argue that the larger social reality, against which the dialogic moments I have studied are set, represents a failed social utopia. In fact, this exploration has led me to believe that the reality of strife and violence is entailed by the vision of dialogue as a communion of souls, which has been so central to the Israeli ethos. The vision of genuine contact among those who share a cultural world, with its primordial and mystical overtones, implies the potential for exclusion and violence toward those whose difference cannot be encompassed within the group's cultural world. Verbal violence and social rifts, in this view, do not mark trouble in utopia; rather, they constitute its dark shadow.[16] In other words, the utopian vision explored in these pages carries its own impossibility. Somewhat paradoxically, therefore, it generates repeated attempts to reinvigorate itself in a variety of sociocultural contexts. The quest for genuine dialogue thus becomes a measure of its absence and colors the cultural conversation with both limitless yearning and unbounded desperation.

The studies presented here sketch only a small part of the cultural landscape to which they pertain. I believe, however, that they touch upon themes that have been central to the making of Israeli culture. Attending to the specificity of the Israeli case, these studies have illuminated the more general themes of identity formation and nation-building as ongoing sites of cultural struggle and negotiation. Through their distinctive focus on communication practices, they have provided a useful lens through which to contemplate both past and present processes of cultural production and change. This sustained exploration of the rise and fall of culturally focal ways of speaking in the Israeli arena has emphasized the role of speech as a constitutive activity in this overall process. It has also stressed the role of ideological shifts in reshaping speaking patterns and speech events.

While each of the preceding case studies could be read in its own right, I hope to have persuaded the reader that both the substantive and methodological significance of this work lies in the intertwining of the three. The nonlinear process of "writing against the text" that I have followed has taken me back and forth from one study to the other, enabling me to trace the strands of meaning that weave these cultural fragments into a larger whole. By foregrounding the migration of communication patterns across contexts and times, I have been able to encompass the cultural yearnings and struggles that have animated, destabilized, and revitalized the quest for "authentic dialogue" in Israeli culture over the past century. I have tried to show how cultural patterns of communication can be problematized and relativized as a necessary step toward recognizing the multivocal scene in which they have gained their legitimacy and privilege. Hopefully, future studies of the changing contours of Israeli ways of speaking will add subtlety and complexity to this account by focusing more fully on the marginalized and suppressed voices that have contributed to the making of Israeli speech cultures over the years, and trace the new cultural formations that inevitably arise in such dynamic scenes of cultural contact and change.

Notes

INTRODUCTION

1. For a discussion of the philosophical treatment of the notion of authenticity in continental philosophy, see Golomb, *In Search of Authenticity*. A critical approach toward this concept has been articulated in Adorno, *The Jargon of Authenticity*.
2. Golomb, *In Search of Authenticity*, 81.
3. Taylor, *The Ethics of Authenticity*, 66.
4. See, for example, Trilling, *Sincerity and Authenticity*. Trilling's treatment of the development of the notions of "sincerity" and "authenticity" is discussed from a sociological perspective in Berger, "'Sincerity' and 'Authenticity' in Modern Society." Trilling posits an oppositional relation between the ideas of sincerity and authenticity. This opposition will be further discussed with reference to the accent of sincerity attributed to *dugri* speech (see chapter 2 of this book). The role of the idea of authenticity in the development of the field of folklore studies as a scholarly pursuit is discussed in Bendix, *In Search of Authenticity*.
5. In her theory of cultural scripts, Anna Wierzbicka has emphasized the cultural inflection of meta-linguistic terms, including the notion of dialogue itself. As my analysis will show, her discussion of Bakhtin's notion of dialogue-as-communion in its Russian inflection echoes at least some versions of the notion of dialogue that informs Israeli speech culture. See Wierzbicka, "Russian Cultural Scripts."
6. Buber, *Between Man and Man*, 19. See also Buber, *I and Thou*.
7. Cf. Taylor, *Sources of the Self*.
8. Communication studies that have drawn heavily on Buber include Stewart, "Foundations of Dialogic Communication"; Arnett, *Communication and Community*; Anderson, Cissna, and Arnett, *The Reach of Dialogue*.
9. Cissna and Anderson, "Theorizing about Dialogic Moments," 65.
10. Ibid., 74.
11. Among social theorists, phenomenologists have made the most distinctive contributions to the study of human communication as a site of intersubjectivity. Cf. Schutz, *On Phenomenology and Social Relations*, and more recently Gurevitch, "The Break of Conversation."
12. Bendix, *In Search of Authenticity*, 8.
13. Ibid., 16.
14. Ibid., 10.
15. Peters, *Speaking into the Air*, 2.
16. Ibid., 59.
17. Ibid., 21.

18. Benedict, *Patterns of Culture;* Bateson, *Naven;* Brown and Levinson, *Politeness.*

19. Brown and Levinson, *Politeness,* 243.

20. Ibid.

21. Cameron, *Good to Talk?* See also Cameron, *Verbal Hygiene.*

22. Giddens, *Modernity and Self-Identity.*

23. Cameron, *Good To Talk?,* 4.

24. Ibid., 4–5.

25. Ibid., 182.

26. Carpanzano, "On Dialogue," 271.

27. Ibid.

28. Ibid., 270.

29. A number of widely read collections of ethnographic studies have greatly contributed to the growing interest in an ethnographic perspective on the study of speech behavior, among them Gumperz and Hymes, *Directions in Sociolinguistics;* Bauman and Sherzer, *Explorations in the Ethnography of Speaking;* Brenneis and Myers, *Dangerous Words;* Hill and Irvine, *Responsibility and Evidence in Oral Discourse.* Books offering panoramic views and integrative statements of the ethnography of communication approach include Hymes, *Foundations in Sociolinguistics;* Saville-Troike, *The Ethnography of Communication.* Some of the monographs I have found particularly useful include Ochs, *Culture and Language Development;* Sherzer, *Kuna Ways of Speaking;* Schieffelin, *The Give and Take of Everyday Life;* Philips, *The Invisible Culture;* Briggs, *Learning How to Ask.*

30. Kenneth Burke's works include *Permanence and Change, The Philosophy of Literary Form, A Grammar of Motives, A Rhetoric of Motives,* and *Counter-statement.*

31. Cf. Bakhtin, *The Dialogic Imagination.* The different senses in which the notion of dialogue has come to be used in the study of language, reflecting Bakhtin's influence, are reviewed in the introduction to Mannheim and Tedlock, *The Dialogic Emergence of Culture.* The formal sense involves the economics of verbal exchange; the functional sense involves the struggle of multiple voices; the ethical/political sense counterposes the multivocality of a text or social interaction to the authoritarianism of closed texts; and the ontological sense involves a view of structure as emerging from social action rather than precipitating it.

32. Hymes, "Ways of Speaking."

33. Carbaugh, "Fifty Terms for Talk: A Cross-Cultural Study." For a further application of this framework, see Carbaugh, " 'Just Listen.' "

34. Hymes, "The Ethnography of Speaking."

35. A performance-oriented approach to the study of everyday discourse is elaborated in Bauman, *Verbal Art as Performance;* Bauman, *Story, Performance, Event;* Briggs, *Competence in Performance.* For further discussion of this perspective, see Bauman and Briggs, "Poetics and Performance."

36. K. Burke, *The Philosophy of Literary Form,* 66.

37. Ibid., 77–78.

38. See Ray, "The Ethnography of Nonverbal Communication in an Ap-

palachian Village"; Carbaugh, *Talking American;* Braithwaite, "Cultural Communication among Vietnam Veterans"; Philipsen, *Speaking Culturally;* Fitch, *Speaking Relationally.*

39. Philipsen, "The Prospect for Cultural Communication," 245. See also Carbaugh, *Cultural Communication and Intercultural Contact.*

40. For theoretical elaborations and methodological implications of this perspective, see Philipsen, "A Theory of Speech Codes." For a review and an assessment of this approach, see Carbaugh, "The Ethnographic Communication Theory of Philipsen and His Associates."

41. Turner, *Dramas, Fields and Metaphors,* 38.

42. Ibid.

43. Ibid., 39.

44. Ibid., 43.

45. See van Gennep, *The Rites of Passage;* Turner, *The Ritual Process.* For a theoretical discussion on liminality and dialogue, see Swearingen, "Dialogue and Dialectic."

46. Turner, *From Ritual to Theater,* 48.

47. Ibid., 49.

48. Philipsen, "The Prospect for Cultural Communication," 245. See also Carbaugh, *Cultural Communication and Intercultural Contact.*

49. Buber, *Meetings,* 32.

50. Goffman, *Interaction Ritual;* Brown and Levinson, *Politeness.*

51. The literature dealing with philosophical and communication perspectives on dialogue is clearly much older and richer than I can even point to here. In addition to Buber's anthropological philosophy and Bakhtin's views on speech, I have been particularly influenced by Gadamer's phenomenological approach to conversation; see Gadamer, *Truth and Method.* For attempts to elaborate on interdisciplinary approaches to the study of dialogue, see Dascal, *Dialogue,* and Maranhao, *The Interpretation of Dialogue.*

52. Bauman, *Let Your Words Be Few.*

53. P. Burke, *The Art of Conversation,* 7.

54. Cf. R. Peled, *"The New Man" of the Zionist Revolution.*

55. These land-related activities fell under the folk-epistemological category of "knowledge of the land" (*yedi'at ha'aretz*). Cf. Katz, "The Israeli Teacher-Guide."

56. R. Peled, *"The New Man" of the Zionist Revolution,* 47.

57. Katriel and Philipsen, " 'What We Need Is Communication.' " See further elaboration in Carbaugh, *Talking American.*

58. Chapter 2 is based on Katriel, *Talking Straight.* The current chapter offers an expansion, update, and reassessment of the earlier study by recontextualizing it in relation to the other two case studies explored in this book.

59. For an early seminal discussion of the cultural-linguistic role played by indexical signs, see Silverstein, "Shifters, Linguistic Categories and Cultural Description."

60. A preliminary formulation of the first part of the study of soul talks appears in Katriel, "The Dialogic Community." It was also delivered as a Van

Zelst Lecture in Communication at the School of Speech, Northwestern University, on May 30, 1996.

61. Avraham Shapira, *Si'ah Lohamim* and *The Seventh Day* (see chapter 1).

62. The plays include Sobol, *Leil Ha'esrim*, Peled, *Hevre*, and Lerner, *Ahavot Bitaniya* (see chapter 1).

63. Beit-Hallahmi, *Despair and Deliverance*.

64. Ibid., 109.

65. Ibid., 115.

66. Ibid., 119.

67. Ibid., 154.

68. A preliminary consideration of call-in radio programs of this genre is found in Katriel, "Mon histoire est comme ca.'"

69. See Elster, *Sour Grapes*. Elster's discussion of states that are essentially byproducts may provide a way to think of the social-ritual production of emotional states such as solidarity.

70. Bakhtin, *The Dialogic Imagination*, 272.

71. Ibid., 276–77.

72. The translations from Hebrew in this book are my own, unless indicated otherwise. In transcribing Hebrew words, I have used "h" for the letter *het*, "kh" for *kaf refuyah*, and "y" for *yod*. Since my analysis is not conducted within a discourse-analytic framework, I have opted for more reader-friendly rather than accurate transcriptions of spoken texts.

CHAPTER 1

1. The extensive research literature on the Israeli kibbutz includes a great deal of discussion with regards to ideological tensions associated with its social organization and the dilemmas attending the implementation of the communal and egalitarian ethos. See, for example, an early treatment in Spiro, *Kibbutz* and later in the collection of essays in Krausz, *The Sociology of the Kibbutz* and Evens, *Two Kinds of Rationality*. The far-reaching changes in the social and economic organization of *kibbutzim* as they adapted to the wider societal transformations in the increasingly "capitalist" and less egalitarian Israeli society has drawn both public and research attention in the 1990s. See, for example, Rosner and Gets, *The Kibbutz in the Era of Changes*.

2. Cf. Zerubavel, *Recovered Roots*. Nahman Ben-Yehuda, *The Masada Myth*. See further discussion of Israeli myths in Nurith Gertz, *Myths in Israeli Culture*, and Weiss, *The Chosen Body*.

3. Cf. Katriel, *Performing the Past*. Some of the activities typically engaged in by settlers preparing the land for settlement in the areas surrounding the Sea of Galilee included the uprooting of native trees. For a related discussion with reference to a later settlement effort, see Bar-Itzhak, "'The Unknown Variable Hidden Underground' and the Zionist Idea."

4. Cf. Katriel and Shenhar, "Tower and Stockade."

5. A. Ufaz, *Document and Fiction*, 20. See also Erez, *The Third Aliyah Book*; E. Margalit, "*Hashomer Hatza'ir*"; Ben-Avram and Near, *Studies in the*

Third Aliyah. For oft-cited literary treatments of the Third Aliyah, see Shaham, *Even Al Pi Habe'er* and *Hahar Vehabait.*

6. The cultural figure of the New Jew as elaborated in Hashomer Hatza'ir movement is extensively discussed in a recently published book by R. Peled, *"The New Man" of the Zionist Revolution.* See also E. Margalit, *"Hashomer Hatza'ir"*; Mintz, *The Bonds of Youth;* Schatzker, *Jewish Youth in Germany between Judaism and Germanism;* Lamm, *The Zionist Youth Movements in Retrospect;* Lamm, *The Educational Method of Hashomer-Hatza'ir Youth Movement.* For precursors in the German youth culture, see Laqueur, *Young Germany* and Stachura, *The German Youth Movement.*

7. Tonnies, *Community and Society.*

8. Buber, *Paths in Utopia,* 164. For later discussions of the idea of the "intimate group" and the kibbutz utopian ideology of communal life, see, for example, Tzur, "The Intimate Group"; Yas'ur, "Buber's Social Thought and the Study of the Kibbutz"; Near, "Post-Utopian Thought in the Kibbutz"; Near, "I-Thou-We"; S. Almog, "Pioneering as an Alternative Culture"; Tal, "Myth and Solidarity."

9. M. Buber, *Paths in Utopia,* 162, Hebrew.

10. Ibid., 164.

11. For a consideration of religious motifs in the Labor movement, see Fishman, "Religion and Communal Life in an Evolutionary-Functional Perspective," and Anita Shapira, "The Religious Motifs of the Labor Movement," in *New Jews, Old Jews,* 248–75.

12. For an excellent treatment of the notion of "camaraderie" in Hashomer Hatza'ir movement, see Weiler, "The Camaraderie of Hashomer Hatza'ir."

13. Tsur, *Kehiliyatenu,* 5–6.

14. The concept of "liminality" has been elaborated within anthropology by Turner, *The Ritual Process.* See discussion in the introduction.

15. Tsur, *Kehiliyatenu.*

16. Liban and Goldman, "Freud Comes to Palestine," 893. On the puritan spirit of the pioneering groups of the early 1920s, as well as the myths of sexual liberation associated with them, see Biale, "Zionism as an Erotic Revolution," in *Eros and the Jews,* 176–203. For other illuminating studies of Zionism and sexuality, see Gluzman, "The Yearning for Heterosexuality," and Boyarin, "The Colonialist Carnival."

17. Shulamit, in Tsur, *Kehiliyatenu,* 229–30.

18. Meir Ya'ari, in Tsur, *Kehiliyatenu,* 277.

19. Cf. Katriel, "Gibush" in *Communal Webs,* 11–34.

20. An insightful study of Yehoshua Sobol's historical plays by literary scholar Yael Feldman similarly interprets the Bitaniya Ilit saga as "the road not taken" of Zionist settlement. Cf. Feldman, "Zionism."

21. David Horowitz, in Tsur, *Kehiliyatenu,* 152–53.

22. A. Ufaz, *Document and Fiction;* Keshet, *Underground Soul;* Govrin, *Keys,* 203–25; Shaked, *Hebrew Narrative Fiction,* 3:70–79; Shenhar-Alroy, "From Oral to Written Myth"; Sadan-Loebenstein, *Israeli Prose in the Twenties,* 119–60; Weiler, "Magic, Comradeship and Reform [*tikkun olam*] as Clusters of a New Identity"; Hess, "Will You Ask about the Stature of a Rug?"

23. A. Ufaz, *Sefer Hakvutza* and *Sefer Ha-hayim*. See A. Ufaz, *Document and Fiction*.
24. Bistritsky, *Days and Nights*.
25. David Horowitz, *My Yesterday*.
26. Sobol, *Leil Ha'esrim*.
27. Buber, *I and Thou*, 230–33.
28. Keshet, *Underground Soul*, 55–56.
29. A. Ufaz, *Document and Fiction*, 38.
30. David Kahana, in Tsur, *Kehiliyatenu*, 53.
31. Bistritsky, *Days and Nights*, 158–59.
32. Elyahu Rapaport, in Tsur, *Kehiliyatenu*, 177–79.
33. David Kahana, in Tsur, *Kehiliyatenu*, 175.
34. Shimon, in Tsur, *Kehiliyatenu*, 42.
35. For an insightful discussion of "re-enchangment" within the pioneering ethos, see Weiler, "The Magic of Hashomer Hatza'ir."
36. A. Ufaz, *Document and Fiction*, 25.
37. Cf. Naveh, *The Confession*.
38. A. Ufaz, *Document and Fiction*, 30–31.
39. Ibid., 31.
40. Buber, *The Knowledge of Man*.
41. Gurevitch, "The Dialogic Connection and the Ethics of Dialogue," emphasis mine. See also Taylor, "The Need for Recognition," in *The Ethics of Authenticity*, 43–53.
42. Moshe, in Tsur, *Kehiliyatenu*, 77.
43. David Horowitz, in Tsur, *Kehiliyatenu*, 81.
44. Dovie, in Tsur, *Kehiliyatenu*, 55.
45. Yehoshua, in Tsur, *Kehiliyatenu*, 90–91.
46. Yehuda, in Tsur, *Kehiliyatenu*, 94.
47. On women in *Kehiliyatenu*, see A. Ufaz, "The Feminist Issue." On images of womanhood in *Kehiliyatenu*, see Hess, "Will You Ask about the Stature of a Rug?" n. 22. My discussion is based on these two studies.
48. A discussion of eroticism in eighteenth-century Hasidism appears in Biale, *Eros and the Jews*, 159–95. On the homoeroticism associated with the Hashomer Hatza'ir pioneering groups, see Mintz, *The Bonds of Youth*, n. 6. For a discussion of the gendered, masculinist nature of the German "cult of friendship" that forms part of the cultural heritage of the Hashomer Hatza'ir youth groups, see Mosse, "Friendship and Nationhood."
49. On eroticism in the age of Jewish enlightenment, see Biale, *Eros and the Jews*, 196–230.
50. Meir Ya'ari, in Tsur, *Kehiliyatenu*, 276.
51. Ibid., 288.
52. Binyamin Dror, in Tsur, *Kehiliyatenu*, 29–30.
53. Ibid., 30.
54. Ibid., 31.
55. Meir Ya'ari, in Tsur, *Kehiliyatenu*, 282.
56. Eliyahu Rapaport, in Tsur, *Kehiliyatenu*, 184.
57. A. Ufaz, "The Feminist Issue" 111.

58. Shenka, in Tsur, *Kehiliyatenu*, 117.
59. Ibid., 117–18.
60. A. Ufaz, "The Feminist Issue," 115.
61. M. Ya'ari, "Rootless Symbols."
62. A. D. Gordon had visited the group and developed warm relations with its members. See Gordon, *Selected Works*, and for a recent study of Gordon's thought in Avraham Shapira, *The Kabbalistic and Hasidic Sources of A. D. Gordon's Thought*. Shapira was the editor of the volume of soldierly conversations published in 1967 under the title of *Si'ah Lohamim*.
63. The article "*Smalim Tlushim*" was reprinted in *Shdemot*, 72 (1980): 9–16; the reference here is to pp. 14–15.
64. Ben-Aharon, "A Conversation with Meir Ya'ari," 21.
65. It was published in the 1988 edition of *Kehiliyatenu* edited by Muky Tsur; see pp. 281–90.
66. David Horowitz, *My Yesterday*, 105–6.
67. Meir Ya'ari, "A Glimpse of a Man's Life (A) (*miktzat mehaiyei adam*)," *Al Hamishmar*, August 28, 1970; "My First Year in the Country (*shnati harishona ba'aretz*)," *Al Hamishmar*, September 4, 1970; "The Long Furrow (*hatelem ha'arokh*)," *Al Hamishmar*, September 11, 1970.
68. Amos Elon, *Ha'aretz*, July 17, 1970.
69. Yitshak Lofben, in *Hapoel Hatza'ir* 13 (1921): 6–7, cited in Tsur, *Kehiliyatenu*, 265.
70. Bistritsky, *The Hidden Myth*.
71. Bistritsky, *Days and Nights*, 63.
72. Ibid., 280.
73. Ibid.
74. This statement is cited on the jacket of the 1978 edition of *Days and Nights*.
75. Avraham Shapira, *Si'ah Lohamim*. The English translation appears in Shapira, *The Seventh Day*. To enhance the smoothness of the reading, I will use the English title in referring to the book, even though for speakers of Hebrew it lacks the resonance attached to the Hebrew original.

    Notably, between *Kehiliyatenu* and *Si'ah Lohamim*, after the 1948 war, there also developed a commemorative genre of books that emerged out of conversational situations in which friends reminisced about a fallen comrade. They are identified as the testimonial genre of "*Haverim mesaprim al . . .*" (Friends tell about). Some were widely disseminated and became part of the public domain, others remained within family and friendship circles. Probably the best known among these texts is the book put together by the artist Menahem Shemi in memory of his son, Jimmy, titled *Haverim Mesaprim al Jimmy*.
76. G. Ufaz, "The Ties of the Kibbutz to Jewish Sources"; G. Ufaz, "The Shdemot Circle Members in Search of Jewish Sources."
77. In addition to Bistritsky's novel, David Horowitz's memoir, and Sobol's play, which have already been mentioned, artistic invocations of the saga of Bitaniya Ilit included Y. Ya'ari's *Ke'or Yahel*, and the more recent TV play by Lerner, *Ahavot Bitaniya*.
78. Yoel Bin-Nun, *Ha'aretz*, June 6, 1997.

79. The book's sales figure was cited in a commemorative radio program broadcast on the thirtieth anniversary of *Si'ah Lohamim* in Galei Zahal, the military radio station, on June 10, 1997, in which some of the original participants in the fighters' talks engaged in a retrospective discussion of the volume. All the citations that follow are taken from the 1971 English version of the book.

80. Amnon Barzilai, "The Messianic Were Taken Out," *Ha'aretz*, June 16, 2002.

81. Muky Tsur in Shapira, Avraham, ed., *The Seventh Day*, 269–70.

82. Haim Bar'am, "The Torments of *Hashomer Hatza'ir*," *Kol Ha'ir*, June 24, 1988.

83. For a link between combat soldiers' positioning along the fighter/non-fighter dimension and their reconstructions of their wartime experiences, see Lumsky-Feder, *As If There Was No War*, and Lumsky-Feder, "The Meaning of War through Veterans' Eyes."

84. Henry Near in introduction to Shapira, Avraham, ed. *The Seventh Day*, 4. Further references to *The Seventh Day* will be cited parenthetically by page numbers in the text.

85. Barnea, *Shooting and Crying*. The expression "shooting and crying" inspired the title of a psychological study of Israeli soldiers' civil disobedience. See Linn, *Not Shooting and Not Crying*. In a later book by the same author, the *Si'ah Lohamim* volume is described in more positive and less critical terms than is usually suggested by the use of the phrase "shooting and crying," and is said to be the "foremost expression of the moral tradition in military life." See Linn, *Conscience at War*, 150. Indeed, as Uri Ben-Eliezer has argued, the "shooting and crying" syndrome has deeper cultural roots than usually suggested by students of Israeli society. This discussion of the emergence of Israeli "civil militarism" since the late 1930s brings out the tension between "words" and "deeds" as culturally central categories in Israeli nation-building ethos. See Ben-Eliezer, *The Making of Israeli Militarism*. The intergenerational context of the emergence of a deeds-oriented militarism in prestate years is also significant in understanding the cultural construction of Sabra "straight" talk, as will be discussed in the section on *dugri* speech.

86. Mosse, "Friendship and Nationhood," 362.

87. Shapira, Avraham, ed., *The Seventh Day*, 253.

88. Ibid., 112.

89. Ibid., 230.

90. Ibid., 109.

91. Tsur, Ben-Aharon, and Grossman, *Among Young People*.

92. An encounter of young kibbutz members held in Ein-Shemer to mark the first anniversary of the Six Day War, which was coordinated by the editor of *Si'ah Lohamim*, Avraham Shapira, was recorded and parts of it appeared in the November 22, 1968, issue of *Ha'aretz*, a nonkibbutz publication, under the headline: "The Hashomer Hatza'ir Youth Question: Is There a Justification for the State of Israel?" It was accompanied by an

editorial statement saying that the issues raised in this encounter, while partly specifically concerned with kibbutz life, gave voice to the thoughts and feelings of Israelis more generally.

93. Tobin, "In the Shadow of Wars."
94. Israel Ring, "The Culture of Dialogue (Tarbut Hasihim)," *Hashavu'a Bakibbutz Ha'artzi,* December 24, 1969.
95. David Sha'ari, "From Confessional Talks to a Clarifying Discussion (*Misihot Vidui—Ledyun Mevarer*)," *Tmurot* 4 (1970): 12–16.
96. Luz, "Between Necessity and Volition," 60.
97. Amnon Barzilai, "The Messianic Were Taken Out," *Ha'aretz,* June 16, 2002.
98. Rubik Rosenthal, "Uri Izhar and Yoni Rokhel in a Debate Concerning *Siah Tzeirim,*" *Hashavua Bakibbutz Haartzi,* February 6, 1970, p. 3.
99. Ibid., p. 5.
100. Aharon Bakhar, "*Si'ah Lohamim*—Ten Years After," *Shiv'a Yamim, Yediot Ahronot* Weekend Supplement, June 3, 1977, p. 7.
101. Ibid., p. 8.
102. Amiram Cohen and Rubik Rosenthal, "*Si'ah Lohamim,* Chapter B," *Al Hamishmar,* April 13, 1987.
103. Ibid.
104. Shlomit Tene, "'*Si'ah Lohamim:* Where Are They Today?" *Yediot Ahronot,* June 5, 1992.
105. Cf. "Conversation in Harav Kook Yeshiva," *Shdemot* 29 (1968): 15–27.
106. Barzilai, "The Messianic Were Taken Out," *Haaretz,* June 16, 2002.
107. Oz, *In the Land of Israel,* 132–33.
108. For example, transcribed conversations that appeared in a kibbutz publication under the heading "From Fighters' Mouth," *Mibefnim* 24 (1982): 234–45.
109. For example, Mazal Mualem, "*Si'ah Lohamim '68, Si'ah Mefakdim* [commanders talk] 89," *Ma'ariv,* May 8, 1989; Yerah Tal, "'The Dilemmas Facing Fighters Today Are More Difficult Than in the Past,'" *Ha'aretz,* April 19, 1989 [a short interview with Muky Tsur]; Yosi Amir, "*Si'ah Lohamim '89,*" *Davar,* April 27, 1989; Avner Avrahami, "*Si'ah Lohamim '94,*" *Ma'ariv,* April 13, 1994; Gideon Levy, "The Professionals," *Ha'aretz,* May 20, 1994.
110. Gertz, *Myths in Israeli Culture,* 96.
111. Ibid.
112. Ibid., 97.
113. Mazal Mualem, "*Si'ah Lohamim '68, Si'ah Mefakdim* [commanders] 89," *Ma'ariv,* May 8, 1989.
114. Alex Fishman, "Siiah Lohamim," *Hadashot,* May 17, 1991.
115. "Following the *Shofar* in the *Kotel,*" a selection from a radio program commemorating the thirtieth anniversary of the Six Day War, *Ha'aretz,* June 6, 1997.
116. Lili Galili, "Today There Are Those Who Shoot and Those Who Cry," *Ha'aretz,* May 27, 2001.
117. Ibid.

118. An interesting discussion of conscientious objection in the Israeli context as a site for ideological struggle and the social negotiation of citizenship has been proposed by Sara Helman in her dissertation and in a series of articles: "Conscientious Objection to Military Service"; "Redefining Obligations, Creating Rights"; "War and Resistance"; and for an article specifically devoted to the veteran organization Yesh Gvul, see "*Yesh Gvul.*"

119. Interviewed in an article in *Ha'aretz* upon his receiving the Oscar Romero award in Texas, Yisahi Menuhin, the spokesperson of the veteran *Yesh Gvul* movement, expressed his pride in the fact that the notion of "selective refusal" was "born in Israel." The whole article is devoted to the gap between the marginalization of peace activists in Israel and the recognition they receive abroad in the form of prestigious, international awards. See Aviv Lavie, "Stars Outside," *Ha'aretz Supplement,* April 4, 2003.

120. The full text of the letter can be found in the Hebrew and English versions of the refusers' Web site: http://seruv.org.ie.

121. Lili Galili, "*Si'ah Lohamim* 2002 Has Gone Underground," *Ha'aretz,* September 18, 2002.

122. Aviv Lavie, "We Have Sobered Up," *Ha'aretz,* December 27, 2002.

123. The personal statements appear in the Courage to Refuse Web site: http://www.seruv.org.il. *Yesh Gvul* has its own Web site: http://www.yesh-gvul.org. The Web site of a women's organization devoted to the demilitarization of Israeli society, called New Profile, which began its activities in the late 1990s, is http://www.newprofile.org. All three organizations have been active separately and in coordination since the outbreak of the Palestinian uprising in the fall of 2000.

124. Haim Bar'am, "The Torments of Hashomer Hatza'ir," *Kol Ha'ir,* June 24, 1988.

125. The village of Ein Hod, previously Ein Hud, has a special place in the history of Israeli settlement and Palestinian displacement. It is now an artists' colony. Cf. Slyomovics, *The Object of Memory.*

126. Dov Bar-Nir, "The Night of the Twentieth in *Tzavta,*" *Al Hamishmar,* February 4, 1976.

127. Sobol, *Leil Ha'esrim,* program of the 1976 production of the play at Haifa Municipal Theater.

128. Yedidyah Shoham, "From a Different Angle," *Hedim* 105 (1976): 63.

129. Sobol, *Leil Ha'esrim,* 12–13.

130. Ibid., 50.

131. Ibid., 19.

132. Ibid., 67.

133. Interview with Sobol conducted before the 1976 production of the play, reproduced in the program for the 1990 production.

134. Yotam Reuveni, "Sobol. Committed for Life," *Yediot Ahronot,* July 26, 1985.

135. Rachel Shklovsky, "A Search for Roots," *Ha'aretz,* September 9, 1977.

136. Giora Manor, "The Elite of Bitaniya Ilit," *Hotam,* January 23, 1976.

137. Dov Bar-Nir, "Leil Haesrim in *Tzavta,*" *Al Hamishmar,* February 4, 1976.

138. Shauli Beskind, "Undressing Again," *Kolbo,* August 24, 1990.

139. Sarit Fuchs, "Leil Ha'esrim. The End Is the Beginning," *Ma'ariv,* September 7, 1990.

140. Elyakim Yaron, "Doubts That Are Part of All of Us," *Ma'ariv,* September 28, 1990.

141. Aryeh Palgi, "*Leil Ha'esrim* and the Nineties," *Al Hamishmar,* September 28, 1990.

142. Yehoshua Sobol, "Greetings to Materialistic Israel [Israel *Haboazit*]," *Hotam,* February 8, 1974.

143. Cf. Urian, *The Arab in Israeli Theater.* See also Ofrat, *Earth, Man, Blood.* For a discussion of the image of the Palestinian in Israeli film, see Shohat, *Israeli Cinema.*

144. On "*gibush*" as a cultural metaphor, see reference in note 19, chapter 1. Given the centrality of the notion of *gibush,* it is probably not surprising that the demise of the Zionist ethos has been described in terms of "falling apart" or "deconstruction." A discussion of plays exploring this process in the 1990s, which includes reference to Hevre, can be found in Urian, "Between Zionism and Post-Zionism in Israeli Theater."

145. Michael Handelaltz, "*Hevre, Hevre, Rega, Rega*" [Buddies, just a moment; based on the lyrics of a popular song], *Ha'aretz,* August 21, 1989.

146. Shosh Avigal, "Group Dynamics on a Mountain in the Galilee," *Hadashot,* August 11, 1989.

147. Miri Paz, "With the White Hairs and the Dust (*Im Haseiva Veha'avak*)," *Davar,* August 20, 1989.

148. H. Peled, *Hevre,* unpublished play script, February 1989, p. 13.

149. Shimeon Levy, "Hevre, From the *Tanakh* to the *Palmah* (From the Bible to the Pre-State Underground)," *Kol Ha'ir,* September 22, 1989.

150. The theme of group bonding mobilized for criminal intent has been compellingly addressed in the film produced by the brothers Uri and Benny Barabash titled *Ehad Mishelanu* (One of Us).

151. Boaz Evron, "Entrapped Friends," *Yediot Ahronot,* August 20, 1989.

152. H. Peled, *Hevre,* 81.

153. Heda Boshes, "Destroying the Myth out of Sobriety," *Ha'aretz,* April 22, 1994.

154. Susie Rosk-Osherov, "I Am Not Pleased with What's Happening," *Tzomet Hasharon,* July 23, 1993.

155. Aryeh Palgi, "Confession unto Death (*Vidui ad Tzet Hanshama*)," *Al Hamishmar,* September 14, 1993.

156. Lerner, *Ahavot Bitaniya,* 7. I am grateful to Professor Dan Urian for making this manuscript available to me before the TV play actually aired. It was then tentatively titled "The Spirits of Bitaniya."

157. Cf. Katriel, *Performing the Past.*

158. Lerner, *Ahavot Bitaniya,* 12.

159. Ibid., 14.

160. Ibid., 24.

161. Ibid., 27.

162. Ora Armoni, "In Bitaniya, Under Ya'ari's Watchful Eye," *Kibbutz,* April 20, 1994.

163. In 1988, the brothers Uri and Benny Barbash produced an English-speaking film titled *Haholmim* (The dreamers; the English-language title was *Unsettled Land*), which is based on the Bitaniya Ilit story and includes readings of excerpts from *Kehiliyatenu*. This filmed version of the story is congruent with the spirit of Sobol's play, but it was not nearly as successful in Israel of the late 1980s. This film was described as a Zionist Western by Gertz in *Motion Picture*, 209–17. Some further discussion of this film as part of the genre of "group films" appears in Talmon, *Israeli Graffiti*, 99–110.
164. Cf. Ofrat, *Earth, Man, Blood*, 13.

Chapter 2

1. See Dan Horowitz, *The Heavens and the Earth*; O. Almog, *The Sabra*; Anita Shapira, "Dor Ba'aretz," in *New Jews, Old Jews*, 122–54. For an anthropological deconstruction of the Sabra ethos, see Hazan, *Simulated Dreams*. On the decline of Israeliness, see Ohana, *The Last Israelis*.
2. Kimmerling, *The Invention and Decline of Israeliness*, 89.
3. Ibid., 89–111.
4. See Gilman, *The Jew's Body*.
5. For empirical studies that discuss Jewish confrontational style in the American setting, cf. Schiffrin, "Jewish Argument as Sociability"; Tannen, "Ethnicity as Conversational Style"; Myerhoff, *Number Our Days*.
6. Netiva Ben-Yehuda, *1948—Between Calendars*.
7. Ibid., 76.
8. Elon, *The Israelis*; Rubinstein, *To Be a Free People*; Segev, *1949: The First Israelis*; O. Almog, *The Sabra*.
9. Oring, *Israeli Humor*, 24.
10. Schoenbrun, *The New Israelis*, 231.
11. Yair Kotler, *Ma'ariv*, January 8, 1982.
12. *International Herald Tribune*, October 18–19, 1981.
13. Yair Kotler, *Ma'ariv*, June 12, 1981.
14. Orly Azulai-Katz, *Yediot Ahronot*, December 6, 1985.
15. Tamar Avidar, *Ma'ariv*, December 12, 1980.
16. Akiva Eldar, *Ha'aretz*, September 9, 1999.
17. Doron Rosenblum, *Ha'aretz*, December 1, 1995.
18. Sagi Green, *Ha'aretz*, November 4, 1995.
19. Sagi Green, *Ha'aretz*, November 7, 1995.
20. Ran Kislev, *Ha'aretz*, November 2, 1998.
21. Turner, *Dramas, Fields and Metaphors*, 14.
22. Ortner, "On Key Symbols."
23. Geertz, "From the Native's Point of View."
24. K. Burke, *Permanence and Change*, 50.
25. Liebman and Don-Yehia, *Civil Religion in Israel*; Handelman, *Models and Mirrors*; Zerubavel, *Recovered Roots*; Gertz, *Myths in Israeli Culture*; Katriel, *Performing the Past*; O. Almog, *The Sabra*.
26. Goffman, *Interaction Ritual*.

27. Schieffelin, Woolard, and Kroskrity, *Language Ideologies.*
28. Sappan, *The Ways of Slang.*
29. Oring, *Israeli Humor.*
30. Sornig, *Lexical Innovation;* Sappan, *The Ways of Slang.*
31. The second comment from 1. is quoted from an article by S. Keshet, *Ha'aretz,* Dec. 26, 1969. Number 2. is from Ben-Amotz and Ben-Yehuda, *The World Dictionary of Hebrew Slang.*
32. Winch, *Ethics and Action.*
33. Brown and Levinson, *Politeness.*
34. Cf. Ezrahi, *Rubber Bullets.*
35. Netiva Ben-Yehuda, *1948—Between Calendars,* 13.
36. Ibid., 12.
37. Ibid., 49.
38. Bloch, *Political Language and Oratory in Traditional Society.*
39. See Lanham, *Style.*
40. Cameron, "Restrictive Practices: The Politics of Style," in *Verbal Hygiene,* 67.
41. Ibid., 75.
42. Lionel Trilling describes a historical shift from a culture of sincerity, grounded in a symmetrical relation between individuals and social roles, to a culture of authenticity, grounded in a fundamental opposition between them. This, however, is not necessarily a linear process. As Peter Berger points out, the crisis of modernity and the alienation from social institutions that has given rise to the culture of authenticity also produces "powerful countervailing forces" expressed as a hunger for stability and integration. See Berger, " 'Sincerity' and 'Authenticity' in Modern Society," 88. The reinvocation of an ethos of sincerity gives expression to such countervailing forces. The utopian quest for genuine dialogue in this context, while marking a state of alienation from traditional and bourgeois Jewish diaspora cultures, posits the possibility of overcoming social alienation by cultivating a particular form of social discourse, not by bypassing it.
43. See Trilling, *Sincerity and Authenticity,* 25.
44. Kurzweil, *Our Modern Literature—A Continuation Or a Revolution?*
45. Stachura, *The German Youth Movement.*
46. Berlin, *Russian Thinkers.*
47. Gordon, *Selected Works,* 254.
48. Rousseau, *The Essential Rousseau.*
49. M. Douglas, *Natural Symbols;* M. Douglas, *Implicit Meanings.*
50. Turner, *The Ritual Process;* Turner, *From Ritual to Theater.* See introduction for an explication of the concepts of "liminality" and "communitas" in Turner's analytic framework.
51. Turner, *The Ritual Process,* 106–7; Oring, *Israeli Humor,* 123.
52. See the account of American "tough talk" that appears in Gibson, *Tough, Sweet and Stuffy.* Also, the account of the notion of "honest speech" as manifested in the Phil Donahue talk show, as elaborated by Carbaugh, *Talking American.*
53. Peters, *Speaking into the Air,* 18.

54. Goffman, *Interaction Ritual,* 56.
55. Brown and Levinson, *Politeness.*
56. Ibid., 244.
57. Ibid., 94–101.
58. Katriel and Dascal, "What Do Indicating Devices Indicate?"
59. Atelesk, "An Anatomy of Opinions."
60. Silverstein, "Shifters, Linguistic Categories and Cultural Description," 34.
61. Simmel, *Conflict and the Web of Group Affiliations.* See also Myerhoff, *Number Our Days.*
62. Hymes, "Models of the Interaction of Language and Social Life."
63. Press correspondents, *Ma'ariv,* July 23, 1982.
64. Bitzer, "The Rhetorical Situation."
65. Ibid., 10.
66. Katriel, *Communal Webs,* 35–49.
67. Cf. Robinson, *Corporate Personality in Ancient Israel.*
68. Prell-Foldes, "The Reinvention of Reflexivity in Jewish Prayer."
69. An intriguing conceptual link between action and conflict is pointed out by Victor Turner, who notes that the words *act* and *agon* (from which stem many conflict-related words such as *antagonism*) are etymologically related.
70. In the terminology developed by Laban, *The Language of Movement,* the elements of movement are described in terms of the Effort/Shape factor and temporality. Thus, the movements accompanying a sustained stretch of *dugri* speech manifest the quality of strength (rather than lightness) on the weight dimension, and the quality of directness in spatial orientation (focusing on each other). They are also characterized by quickness or abruptness on the time factor.
71. Netiva Ben-Yehuda, *1948—Between Calendars,* 71.
72. Turner, *Dramas, Fields and Metaphors,* 36.
73. Cf. Feldman, *No Room of Their Own,* 177–91, where this novel and its sequel are discussed within the framework of a feminist analysis of Is-raeli women authors' writings. For a feminist historical account of the experience of Palmah women, see Efron, "Sisters, Fighters and Mothers."
74. Tamar Avidar, *Ma'ariv,* March 20, 1981.
75. Kenneth Burke, in *The Philosophy of Literary Form,* proposes that the examination of "critical moments" in a work of art can offer a key to its overall meaning (as discussed in the introduction to this book).
76. Netiva Ben-Yehuda, *1948—Between Calendars,* 162.
77. Ibid.
78. Ibid., 170.
79. Ibid., 171.
80. Ibid.
81. Naomi Gal, *Kol Yerushalaim,* June 5, 1981.
82. Dan Omer, *Ha'olam Haze,* March 25, 1981.
83. Netiva Ben-Yehuda, *1948—Between Calendars,* 5.
84. Dan Meron, *Hado'ar,* summer 1981.
85. Dalia Shhori, *Al Hamishmar,* March 30, 1981.

86. Tamar Avidar, *Ma'ariv,* March 20, 1981.
87. Miriam Oren, *Mozna'im,* December 1, 1981.
88. Oring, *Israeli Humor.*
89. Hulda Gur-Raz, *Ma'ariv,* May 26, 1981.
90. Daniel Ben Simon, *Ha'aretz,* July 29, 1998.
91. The issue of nomenclature as related to Jews from Muslim lands has been helpfully addressed in an article by Pnina Lahav titled "A 'Jewish State . . . to Be Known as the State of Israel': Notes on Israeli Legal Historiography," where she says:

    > The history of Mizrahi Jews in Israel is captured by the various terms used to define them. Just as African Americans have changed from colored people to Negroes to Black to African-Americans, so have the Mizrahi Jews changed their preferred appellation. In the beginning they were called Sephardim (those from Spain) to denote their origin in Spain before the expulsion in 1492. They were then dubbed "members of the Eastern sects" to designate the fact that they had arrived from various countries of the Orient (in English, Orientals) as distinct from the West. In the 1990s, as Israeli society became more sensitive to issues of equality and prejudice, the term was changed to Mizrahim (those from the East). (413)

    I will use the terms "Oriental Jews" and the more recent "Mizrahim," which, as Lahav further points out, unlike earlier references to Jews from Muslim lands as "sects" (*edot*) offers a terminological equalization with Ashkenazim, Jews of European descent, rather than using the latter as a baseline for the former.
92. Said, *Orientalism.*
93. A critical approach to representations of "Oriental Jews" is discussed in Shohat, "Sephardim in Israel" and "The Invention of Mizrahim."
94. Herb Keinon, *Jerusalem Post,* October 1, 1997.
95. Cf. Weingrod, "Ehud Barak's Apology"; A. Margalit, "Ehud Barak and the Penance of the Labor Party," in *Views in Review,* 31–51.
96. Daniel Ben Simon, *Ha'aretz,* July 29, 1998.
97. Or's "pardon" by the party was widely covered in the press, too. A typical press item was, for example, the article by journalist Ron Levin, which appeared in *Ma'ariv,* November 15, 1998, under the title "The Labor Puts Or Back in Key Positions in the Party," and the article by Nehama Duek and Haim Shivi of the same day in *Yediot Ahronot,* which was titled "Labor Will Cancel Ori Or's Suspension Tomorrow."
98. Yosi Dahan, *Yediot Ahronot,* July 30, 1998.
99. Nehama Duek, *Yediot Ahronot,* August 2, 1998.
100. Gideon Levi, *Ha'aretz,* August 2, 1998.
101. Nathan Zach, *Ma'ariv,* August 2, 1998.
102. Tami Shemesh-Kritz, *Ma'ariv,* August 5, 1998.
103. Sever Plotzker, "Kol ha'am popolitika," *Yediot Ahronot,* May 9, 2000. In this survey, conducted by *Dahaf* Institute, 24 percent of the respondents listed *hutzpa* and 20 percent listed "directness devoid of politeness" as Israeli characteristics, yet only 20 percent considered themselves as typical Israelis (compared to 30 percent a decade earlier).

104. Sered and Tabory, " 'You Are a Number, Not a Human Being.' "
105. Katriel, "*Lefargen.*"
106. The hedges *kaze* and *ke'ilu* have been analyzed by linguists. See Henkin, "*Ma bein 'hashama'im khulim kaele.*' " Yael Maschler has used an earlier version of this chapter in her recent analysis of the hedges *kaze* and *ke'ilu* in spoken Hebrew; see "*Veke'ilu haraglayim sh'xa nitka'ot bifnim kaze.*" Cultural reflections about the younger generation of Israelis, which are described as "the generation of kaze-keilu" appear in a special issue of the now extinct magazine *Politika* 34 (1990).
107. Kimmerling, *The Invention and Decline of Israeliness,* 208–28.
108. Gideon Samet, *Ha'aretz,* October 11, 1985.
109. Ben-Amotz and Ben-Yehuda, *The World Dictionary of Hebrew Slang.*
110. *Koteret Rashit,* March 9, 1983.
111. S. Cohen, *Folk Devils and Moral Panics.*
112. Cameron, "Dr. Syntax and Mrs. Grundy: The Great Grammar Crusade," in *Verbal Hygiene,* 82.
113. A forthcoming paper has studied readers' responses to a section in a popular evening paper (*Ma'ariv*) in which they were asked to respond to the question, "What makes one an Israeli?" The author, Rakefet Sela-Sheffy, has found that the most prominent image depicted by respondents who fall under the category of middle-class Ashkenazi Jews was that of the "Ugly Israeli," whose traits contained features of style similar to the ones depicted in articles such as the "Big Mouth" piece discussed here. Working-class Mizrahi respondents tended to depict a patriotic image of the Israeli that came closer to that of the mythological Sabra. The author accounts for this difference in terms of center-periphery relations, arguing that those respondents who come from more established layers of society can afford to express detachment from hegemonic values, signaling sophistication and refinement. This mechanism may explain why the elite weekend magazine of *Ha'aretz* published most of the style-related moral panics I have noted in the past few years. See Sela-Sheffy, " 'What Makes One an Israeli?' "
114. The illustration by Bary Goodbar may be familiar to some readers: it was taken from the jacket of band King Crimson.
115. *Ha'aretz,* September 24, 1999. Further references to this article will be cited parenthetically by page numbers in the text.
116. Yehiam Weitz, "A Myth That Collapsed," *Ma'ariv,* May 30, 2000.
117. "Medinat Vulgaria," *Ha'aretz,* September 14, 2001, p. 34.
118. Ibid., 36.
119. For an interesting recent discussion of Israel between East and West within a postcolonialist perspective, see Eitan Bar-Yosef, "Printer or Hunter?"
120. For a detailed discussion of the initial contact phase between Arabs and Jews in Palestine of the turn of the twentieth century, as depicted in literary texts, see Yaffah Berlovitz, " 'The Other People,' The Arab Question," in *Inventing a Land, Inventing a People,* 113–66.
121. Further elaboration appears in Griefat and Katriel, "Life Demands *Musayra.*" Cf. also Bourdieu, "The Sentiment of Honor in Kabyle Society."

122. The notion of "honor" has figured in a variety of analyses of Islamic cultures—for example, Antoun, "On the Significance of Names in an Arab Village"; Assadi, "Deference"; Beeman, *Language, Status and Power in Iran;* Gilsenan, "Lying, Honor and Contradiction"; Koch, "Presentation as Proof"; Khuri, "The Etiquette of Bargaining in the Middle East"; Shipler, *Arab and Jew.*
123. Keddie, "Symbol and Sincerity in Islam."
124. Caplan, *Arab and Jew in Jerusalem.*
125. Rosen, *Bargaining for Reality.*
126. Ferguson, "Myths about Arabic."
127. Patai, *The Arab Mind.*
128. Uzi Benziman, *Ha'aretz,* October 19, 1997.
129. Doron Rosenblum, *Ha'aretz,* November 5, 2000.
130. Gideon Samet, *Ha'aretz,* December 28, 2001.
131. Katriel and Philipsen, " 'What We Need Is Communication.' "

CHAPTER 3

1. Spitulnik, "Media," 144.
2. Ibid., 144–45.
3. Tacchi, "Radio Texture," 242.
4. See Anderson, *Imagined Communities.* In recent years, there has been a great deal of interest in "media communities" of various kinds. Examples of studies of radio-based "media communities" can be found in Cowlan, "A Revolution in Personal Communications"; and Powell and Ary, "Communication without Commitment." The notion of "media community" has great currency in writings about the Internet. For one of the first statements related to electronic communication, cf. Rheingold, *The Virtual Community.* See also Danet, *Cyberplay.*
5. S. Douglas, *Listening In,* 5.
6. Gibian, "Newspeak Meets Newstalk," 138.
7. Peters, *Speaking into the Air.*
8. Ibid., 214.
9. Ibid.
10. Habermas, *The Structural Transformation of the Public Sphere.*
11. Brecht, *Brecht on Theater,* 52.
12. This said, some interesting work has been done on talk radio as an interpersonal phenomenon and on the discourse of call-in radio from a variety of analytic perspectives. In addition to the work already cited, it includes, for example, Turow, "Talk Show Radio as Interpersonal Communication"; Mendelsohn, "Listening to Radio"; Avery and Ellis, "Talk Radio as an Interpersonal Phenomenon"; Schwebel, "Radio Psychologists"; Crisell, *Understanding Radio;* Armstrong and Rubin, "Talk Radio as Interpersonal Communication"; Avery, "Talk Radio"; Gaik, "Radio Talk-Show Therapy and the Pragmatics of Possible Worlds"; DeCapua and Dunham, "Strategies in the Discourse of Advice"; Kuo, "Agreement and Disagreement Strategies in a Radio Conversation"; Herbst, "On Electronic Public

Space"; Hutchby, "Aspects of Recipient Design in Expert Advice-Giving on Call-In Radio"; Hutchby, *Confrontation Talk;* Panese, "Calling In"; Franco, "Hello, You're on the Air"; Kupferberg and Green, "Metaphors Enhance Radio Problems Discussions."

13. There is a rather extensive literature on TV talk shows, which includes studies that consider them as a form of "self-help talk": Crow, "Conversational Pragmatics in Television Talk"; Carbaugh, *Talking American;* White, *Tele-Advising;* Munson, *All Talk;* Livingston and Lunt, *Talk on Television;* Peck, "TV Talk Shows as Therapeutic Discourse"; Priest, *Public Intimacies;* Mehl, *La television de l'intimite;* Shattuc, *The Talking Cure;* Abt and Mustazza, *Coming after Oprah;* Gamson, *Freaks Talk Back;* Lowney, *Baring Our Souls;* Illouz, "That Shadowy Realm of the Interior."

14. Kress, "Language in the Media," 400.

15. Jenkins, *Textual Poachers.*

16. Scannell, *Radio, Television and Everyday Life,* 19.

17. Scannell, "Introduction: The Relevance of Talk," in *Broadcast Talk,* 1.

18. Analyses of TV talk shows range from critical approaches to the study of this media form as epitomizing "trash TV" and cultural approaches that attempt to "read" them as meaningful texts of contemporary popular culture. Both approaches are represented in the studies mentioned in note 13 above.

19. Spitulnik, "The Social Circulation of Media Discourse and the Mediation of Communities," 176.

20. Gibian, "Newspeak Meets Newstalk," 139.

21. Cameron, *Good to Talk?* 21.

22. Gibian, "Newspeak Meets Newstalk," 144.

23. Studies of "radio psychology" include: Bouhoutsos, "The Mental Health Professions and the Media"; Balter, "Giving Away Child Psychology Over to the Airwaves"; Barzel, "Advice on the Air"; Raviv, Raviv, and Yunivitz, "Radio Psychology and Psychotherapy"; Raviv, Raviv, and Arnon, "Psychological Counseling over the Radio"; Raviv, "Radio Psychology."

24. Cf. Horton and Wohl, "Mass Communication and Para-Social Interaction."

25. Horton and Strauss, "Interaction in Audience-Participation Shows," 587.

26. Studies of social support tend to view it as a universal function of social interaction, although cultural differences in patterns of seeking and offering support are also acknowledged. Communication-centered approaches to the study of social support are found in Albrecht and Adelman, *Communicating Social Support.* The study of social support is closely linked to the study of help-seeking behavior. An Israeli study, which attempted to develop a measure for "the willingness to seek help," has concluded that the relationship of ethnic origin to help-seeking should be further pursued. See B. Cohen, "Measuring the Willingness to Seek Help." As I will argue, these unexplored cultural inflections have implications for delimiting the audiences of self-help radio programs.

27. Gibian, "Newspeak Meets Newstalk," 140.

28. Pratt, "So She Really Loves Eggs," 165.

29. Geertz, *The Interpretation of Cultures.*
30. The notion of liminality as a state of between-and-betwixt is discussed in Turner, *The Ritual Process.* It is further explicated in the introduction. For a discussion of the night as a liminal zone, see Melbin, *The Night as Frontier.* An informative discussion of all-night radio in the United States can be found in Keith, *Sounds in the Dark.* Keith argues that all-night radio is becoming more and more pervasive in American life due to changes in work patterns and lifestyles that are moving society toward a "24/7" (hours/days) activity pattern.
31. The notion of "talking cure" is traced to psychoanalytic parlance. See also Shattuc, *The Talking Cure.*
32. Buber, *Meetings,* 32.
33. Lutz and Abu-Lughud, "Introduction: Emotion, Discourse, and the Politics of Everyday Life," 11.
34. Ibid., 13 (my emphasis).
35. Lutz, "Engendered Emotions."
36. Lutz and Abu-Lughud, "Introduction: Emotion, Discourse, and the Politics of Everyday Life," 6.
37. Bourdieu, *Distinction.*
38. For a discussion of the category of "Mizrahim," see note 91 in chapter 2.
39. Cf. E. Cohen, *The Moroccans.*
40. Katriel and Philipsen, " 'What We Need Is Communication.' "
41. Cameron, *Good to Talk?* 154.
42. Bellah et al., *Habits of the Heart.*
43. Cameron, *Good to Talk?* 158.
44. Giddens, *Modernity and Self Identity,* 6.
45. Cameron, *Good to Talk?* 29–30.
46. Cf. McLeod, *Narrative and Psychotherapy,* for another discussion of pre-modern, modern, and postmodern therapeutic codes.
47. Pratt, "So She Really Loves Eggs," 177.
48. Yovav Katz, February 6, 1996. The corpus of transcribed programs I have worked with encompasses twenty programs recorded in 1995 and 1996. They lasted about four hours each and usually contained seven to ten exchanges with callers. I cannot report any gender or age-related patterns on the basis of this corpus.
49. Cf. Thornborrow, "Having Their Say."
50. I held two lengthy interviews with Yovav Katz, one in November 1998 and one on August 11, 2000. I also spent a night in the radio studio in Tel Aviv on July 11, 2000, which gave me an opportunity to observe the "backstage" of the program's production and talk to the hosts and producers on their own professional turf. My visit to Yossi Saias's studio on July 15, 2000, was followed by a long telephone interview on August 20, 2000.
51. Second interview with Yovav Katz, August 11, 2000.
52. As Yovav Katz told me, Yossi Saias's program was third, at a wide margin from the first two. This attests to the fact that both the hosts whose programs are dealt with here have been recognized favorites of Israeli radio listeners for quite a while.

53. The notion of "kernel narrative" has been proposed in Susan Kalcik's early article on personal experience narratives. See Kalcik, "'Like Ann's Gynecologist.'" A similar use is made of the term "minimal narrative" in Linde, *Life Stories.*

54. Yovav Katz, November 28, 1996. The line segmentation in these excerpts was introduced for ease of reference only. It carries no significance from the standpoint of linguistic analysis.

55. Cf. Gaik, "Radio Talk-Show Therapy and the Pragmatics of Possible Worlds."

56. For work that illuminates various aspects of collaborative storytelling, including recipient redirecting of the teller's talk, which stresses the interpersonal work they do, see Mandelbaum, "Interpersonal Activities in Conversational Storytelling" and "Assigning Responsibility in Conversational Storytelling."

57. Yovav Katz, November 28, 1996.

58. The creed of "communication" and its relation to the therapeutic ethos were discussed in the introduction. See Katriel and Philipsen, "'What We Need Is Communication'"; Bellah et al., *Habits of the Heart;* Carbaugh, *Talking American;* Cameron, *Good to Talk?* A more therapeutically centered version of this creed appears in the discussion of therapy as a cultural form in Woolfolk, *The Cure of Souls.*

59. Cf. Chambon and Simeoni, "Modality in the Therapeutic Dialogue," 253. There is a considerable literature on psychotherapeutic discourse in nonmediated settings. Although my approach is interpretive rather than discourse-analytic, I found some of this work quite helpful in terms of sensitizing me to this genre. Among the works I consulted are: Labov and Fashnel, *Therapeutic Discourse;* Gale, *Conversation Analysis of Therapeutic Discourse;* Bergmann, "Veiled Morality"; Ferrara, *Therapeutic Ways with Words;* Gerhardt and Stinson, "The Nature of Therapeutic Discourse"; Capps and Ochs, "Out of Place"; Buttny, "Clients' and Therapists' Joint Construction of the Clients' Problems."

60. Yovav Katz, February 6, 1996.

61. Ibid.

62. McLeod, *Narrative and Psychotherapy,* 19–20.

63. Cameron, *Good to Talk?* 139.

64. Shortly before this program was aired, on two separate occasions, there were bus explosions in Jerusalem that caused many casualties. The explosions occurred quite close to the location of the radio studio.

65. Yossi Saias, March 12, 1996. The corpus of transcribed programs I have worked with encompasses fifteen programs recorded in 1995 and 1996. They lasted about five hours each and usually contained seven to ten exchanges with callers. I cannot report any gender- or age-related patterns on the basis of this corpus.

66. Yossi Saias's program has also become a template for other forms of broadcasting. Thus, a well-known "pirate" network of late-night conversations on field radio was created by front-line IDF soldiers on the lookout for entertainment and company and has been dubbed *Reshet Saias* (the Saias network).

67. A few examples of full-fledged journalistic portraits devoted to Yossi Saias over the past decade, most of them accompanied by one or more color-ful, even cover-page, photographs, appeared at various junctures in his life. On October 29, 1993, the Haifa local weekly *Kolbo* carried a colorful full-page picture of Saias on the occasion of the fortieth anniversary of a community club he had frequented as a child in a poor area, making him a local icon; on February 18, 1994, an article in the weekend supplement of *Ma'ariv* appeared on the occasion of the airing of the documentary about Saias. A colorful front-page picture was titled "Saias Ltd."; on March 8, 1996, there was extensive coverage in the Jerusalem weekly *Kol Ha'ir* of Saias's efforts following local bus explosions; on July 12, 1996, he was prominently featured in the weekly supplement of *Yedi'ot Ahronot,* and the story of his professional battles within the Broadcasting Authority was laid out in detail; on August 28, 1998, another extended portrait appeared in the weekly supplement of *Yedi'ot Ahronot,* covering new developments in his life (a fifth son) and career (a new television program); on April 5, 1999, the women's weekly *La'isha* published an interview with Yossi Saias, getting his personal view of the organizational politics of the Broadcasting Authority and reconfirming his commitment not to sell himself to com-mercial interests; finally, *Yedi'ot Ahronot* also carried another sprawling interview with Saias, complete with full-page, color portrait, in its festive Independence Day supplement of May 9, 2000, under the heading of "The National Psychologist." Yovav Katz, on the other hand, indicated that his program attracted media attention in the first few years in which it was aired, but has become a taken-for-granted part of the Israeli broadcasting scene since. He doesn't want media attention and the "public relations" dimension associated with it, which Saias seems to relish and which he uses to serve his personal as well as ethnic-political agenda. A similar function was served by a book he published in which he included seventy-seven letters sent by audience members to a program he hosted on Channel 3 of Kol Israel, *Reshet Gimel,* under the name of *Ahava Yomyomit* (Daily love). See Saias, *Love Day by Day.*
68. Yaron Fried, *Ha'ir,* September 2, 1994.
69. Rogel Alper, *Ha'aretz,* June 2, 2000.
70. I have adopted the term "charisma of reason" from a discussion of Weber by Roth, "Charisma and the Counterculture."
71. Dalia Shhori, *Ha'aretz,* June 28, 1994.
72. Yaacov Levitam, *Yediot Ahronot,* November 26, 1999.
73. Ibid.
74. Yossi Saias, January 1, 1996; my emphasis.
75. On pilgrimages to Saints' Tombs in contemporary Israel, see Bilu and Ben-Ari, "The Making of Modern Saints." For a discussion of saint worship as a cultural practice among Moroccan Jews, see Ben-Ami, *Saint Veneration among the Jews in Morocco.*
76. Yossi Saias, March 12, 1996; my emphasis.
77. Ibid, my emphasis.
78. Ibid, my emphasis.
79. Ibid, my emphasis.

80. Yossi Saias, December 18, 1995.
81. McLeod, *Narrative and Psychotherapy,* 7.
82. Philipsen, *Speaking Culturally.*
83. Ronit Tzach, *Kol Ha'ir,* March 8, 1996. All subsequent references are taken from the same article.
84. Scannell, "Public Service Broadcasting and Modern Public Life," 343.
85. Gledhill, "The Melodramatic Field."
86. Brooks, *The Melodramatic Imagination,* 67.
87. Cf. Bruner and Lucariello, "Monologue as Narrative Recreation of the World," 76.
88. A well-known example of such a clash of codes within the context of the anthropology of Jewish life is Myerhoff's discussion of the clash between the communicative code of the elderly residents of the Jewish Old People Home she studied in Los Angeles and the Western-educated, middle-aged psychologist who was invited to help work out the conflicts among group members in a chapter tellingly titled "We Fight To Keep Warm." See Myerhoff, *Number Our Days.*
89. See Scannell, "Public Service Broadcasting and Modern Public Life."
90. See Williams, *Marxism and Literature,* for a discussion of the notion of "structures of feeling."
91. Cf. Roniger, "Cultural Prisms, Western Individualism and the Israeli Case."
92. Bakhtin, *The Dialogic Imagination,* 361.
93. Ibid.
94. Ibid., 362.
95. Berger, "'Sincerity' and 'Authenticity' in Modern Society," 87.
96. Cf. Habermas, *The Structural Transformation of the Public Sphere.* Various critiques of Habermas's position can be found, for example, in Fraser, "Rethinking the Public Sphere." The interest that the distinction between the private and public domains holds for communication scholarship is evidenced in a special journal issue devoted to it. Cf. Rawlins, *Communication Theory.*
97. Urla, "Outlaw Language," 245.
98. Ibid., 247.
99. Ibid., 246.
100. Kress, "Language in the Media:," 417.
101. Scannell, "Public Service Broadcasting and Modern Public Life," 320.
102. Gibian, "Newspeak Meets Newstalk," 138.

CONCLUSION

1. R. Peled, *"The New Man" of the Zionist Revolution,* 61.
2. Urban, "Ceremonial Dialogues in South America," 371.
3. Ibid., 376.
4. Ibid., 384.
5. See the extensive discussion of this approach in Philipsen, "A Theory of Speech Codes."
6. Goffman, *The Presentation of Self in Everyday Life.*

7. Peters, *Speaking into the Air.*
8. Cameron, *Good to Talk?*
9. Peters, *Speaking into the Air,* 10.
10. S. Douglas, *Listening In.*
11. Ibid., 40.
12. Ibid., 41.
13. Bakhtin, *The Dialogic Imagination,* 272.
14. For examples of different kinds of studies dealing with the pervasiveness of verbal violence in Israeli public discourse, see Peleg, "The Peace Process"; Cromer, *The State and Violence.*
15. Studies exploring the dynamics of Israeli-Palestinian dialogue groups include: Gurevitch, "The Power of Not Understanding"; Halabi, *Identities in Dialogue;* Helman, "Monologic Results of Dialogue"; Maoz, "Power Relations in Intergroup Encounters"; Rabinowitz, "Natives with Jackets and Degrees"; Suleiman, "Planned Encounters between Jews and Palestinian Citizens."
16. A somewhat similar argument has been proposed in a recent study of encounter groups promoting dialogue between secular and religious Jews in Israel. Cf. Yanay, "Mandatory Reconciliation."

References

Abt, Vicki, and Leonard Mustazza. 1997. *Coming after Oprah: Cultural Fallout in the Age of the TV Talk Show.* Bowling Green, OH: Bowling Green State University.

Adorno, Theodor W. 1974. *The Jargon of Authenticity.* London: Routledge.

Albrecht, Terrance L., and Mara B. Adelman, eds. 1987. *Communicating Social Support.* Newbury Park, CA: Sage.

Almog, Oz. 2000. *The Sabra: The Creation of the New Jew.* Berkeley: University of California Press.

Almog, Shmuel. 1993. "Pioneering as an Alternative Culture." *Zion* 58 (3):329–46 (in Hebrew).

Anderson, Benedict. 1991 [1983]. *Imagined Communities: Reflections on the Origin and Spread of Nationalism.* London: Verso.

Anderson, Rob, Kenneth Cissna, and Ronald Arnett, eds. 1994. *The Reach of Dialogue: Confirmation, Voice and Community.* Cresskill, NJ: Hampton Press.

Antoun, Roger. 1968. "On the Significance of Names in an Arab Village." *Ethnology* 7:158–70.

Armstrong, Cameron, and Alan Rubin. 1989. "Talk Radio as Interpersonal Communication." *Journal of Communication* 39:84–94.

Arnett, Ronald. 1986. *Communication and Community: Implications of Martin Buber's Dialogue.* Carbondale: Southern Illinois University Press.

Assadi, Rezza. 1980. "Deference: Persian Style." *Anthropological Linguistics* 22:221–24.

Atelesk, Jean. 1981. "An Anatomy of Opinions." *Language in Society* 10 (1):217–25.

Avery, Robert. 1990. "Talk Radio: The Private-Public Catharsis." In *Talking to Strangers: Mediated Therapeutic Communication,* ed. G. Gumpert and S. L. Fish, 87–97. Norwood, NJ: Ablex.

Avery, Robert K., and Donald G. Ellis. 1979. "Talk Radio as an Interpersonal Phenomenon." In *Inter/Media: Interpersonal Communication in a Media World,* ed. G. Gumpert and R. Cathcart, 108–15. New York: Oxford University Press.

Bakhtin, Mikhail. 1981. *The Dialogic Imagination: Four Essays.* Austin: University of Texas Press.

Balter, Lawrence. 1983. "Giving Away Child Psychology Over to the Airwaves." *The Clinical Psychologist* 36 (2):37–40.

Bar-Itzhak, Haya. 1999. "'The Unknown Variable Hidden Underground' and the Zionist Idea: Rhetoric of Place in an Israeli Kibbutz and Cultural Interpretation." *Journal of American Folklore* 112 (446):497–513.

Barnea, Nachum. 1981. *Shooting and Crying.* Tel Aviv: Zmora, Bitan, Modan (in Hebrew).

Bar-yosef, Eitan. 2002. "Printer or Hunter? Nahum Gutman, *Lobengulu King of Zulu* and the South African Book." *Theory and Criticism* 20:113–36 (in Hebrew).

Barzel, Esther. 1986. "Advice on the Air: The Use of Radio as a Guidance Medium." Ph.D. diss., Hebrew University.

Bateson, Gregory. 1958. *Naven*. Stanford: Stanford University Press.

Bauman, Richard. 1983. *Let Your Words Be Few: Symbolism of Speaking and Silence among Seventeenth-Century Quakers*. Cambridge: Cambridge University Press.

———. 1984 [1977]. *Verbal Art as Performance*. Prospect Heights, IL: Waveland Press.

———. 1986. *Story, Performance, Event*. Cambridge: Cambridge University Press.

Bauman, Richard, and Charles Briggs. 1990. "Poetics and Performance as Critical Perspectives on Language and Social Life." *Annual Review of Anthropology* 19:59–88.

Bauman, Richard, and Joel Sherzer, eds. 1989 [1974]. *Explorations in the Ethnography of Speaking*. Cambridge: Cambridge University Press.

Beeman, William. 1986. *Language, Status and Power in Iran*. Bloomington: Indiana University Press.

Beit-Hallahmi, Benjamin. 1992. *Despair and Deliverance: Private Salvation in Contemporary Israel*. Albany: State University of New York Press.

Bellah, Robert, Richard Madsen, William M. Sullivan, Ann Swidler, and Steven M. Tipton. 1985. *Habits of the Heart: Individualism and Commitment in American Life*. Berkeley: University of California Press.

Ben-Aharon, Yariv. 1980. "A Conversation with Meir Yaari on His Article 'Smalim Tlushim.' " *Shdemot* 72:20–30 (in Hebrew).

Ben-Ami, Issachar. 1998. *Saint Veneration among the Jews in Morocco*. Detroit: Wayne State University Press.

Ben-Amotz, Dan, and Netiva Ben-Yehuda. 1972. *The World Dictionary of Hebrew Slang*. Tel Aviv: Levin Epstein (in Hebrew).

Ben-Avram, Baruch, and Henry Near. 1995. *Studies in the Third Aliyah: Image and Reality*. Jerusalem: Yad Yitshak Ben-Zvi (in Hebrew).

Ben-Eliezer, Uri. 1998. *The Making of Israeli Militarism*. Bloomington: Indiana University Press.

Ben-Yehuda, Nahman. 1995. *The Masada Myth*. Madison: University of Wisconsin Press.

Ben-Yehuda, Netiva. 1981. *1948—Between Calendars*. Jerusalem: Keter (in Hebrew).

Bendix, Regina. 1997. *In Search of Authenticity: The Formation of Folklore Studies*. Madison: University of Wisconsin Press.

Benedict, Ruth. 1946. *Patterns of Culture*. New York: Mentor.

Berger, Peter. 1973. " 'Sincerity' and 'Authenticity' in Modern Society." *Public Interest* 31:81–90.

Bergmann, Jorg R. 1992. "Veiled Morality: Notes on Discretion in Psychiatry." In *Talk at Work: Interaction in Institutional Settings*, ed. P. Drew and J. Heritage, 137–62. Cambridge: Cambridge University Press.

Berlin, Isaiah. 1978. *Russian Thinkers*. London: Hogarth Press.

Berlovitz, Yaffah. 1996. *Inventing a Land, Inventing a People.* Tel Aviv: Hakibbutz Hameuchad (in Hebrew).

Biale, David. 1992. *Eros and the Jews: From Biblical Israel to Contemporary America.* New York: Basic Books.

Bilu, Yoram, and Eyal Ben-Ari. 1992. "The Making of Modern Saints: Manufactured Charisma and the Abu-Hatseiras of Israel." *American Ethnologist* 19 (4):672–87.

Bistritsky, Nathan. 1978 [1926]. *Days and Nights.* Tel Aviv: Sifriyat Hapoalim (in Hebrew).

————. 1980. *The Hidden Myth.* Tel Aviv: Yahdav.

Bitzer, Lloyd. 1968. "The Rhetorical Situation." *Philosophy & Rhetoric* 1:1–14.

Bloch, Maurice, ed. 1975. *Political Language and Oratory in Traditional Society.* London: Academic Press.

Bouhoutsos, Jacqueline. 1983. "The Mental Health Professions and the Media." In *Innovations in Clinical Practice: A Source Book,* ed. P. A. Keller and L. G. Ritt. Vol. 2:361–70. Sarasota, FL: Resource Exchange Incorporated.

Bourdieu, Pierre. 1966. "The Sentiment of Honor in Kabyle Society." In *Honor and Shame: The Values of Mediterranean Society,* ed. J. Peristiany, 191–241. Chicago: University of Chicago Press.

————. 1979. *Distinction: A Social Critique of the Judgment of Taste.* Cambridge, MA: Harvard University Press.

Boyarin, Daniel. 1997. "The Colonialist Carnival: Zionism, Gender, Mimesis." *Theory and Criticism* 11:123–144 (in Hebrew).

Braithwaite, Charles. 1990. "Cultural Communication among Vietnam Veterans: Ritual, Myth and Social Drama." In *The Cultural Legacy of Vietnam,* ed. R. Morris and P. Erenhaus, 145–70. Norwood, NJ: Ablex.

Brecht, Berthold. 1974. *Brecht on Theater: The Development of an Aesthetic.* Ed. and trans. John Willett. London: Eyre Methuen.

Brenneis, Don, and Fred Myers, eds. 1984. *Dangerous Words: Language and Politics in the Pacific.* New York: New York University Press.

Briggs, Charles. 1986. *Learning How to Ask.* Cambridge: Cambridge University Press.

————. 1988. *Competence in Performance: The Creativity of Tradition in Mexicano Verbal Art.* Philadelphia: University of Pennsylvania Press.

Brooks, Peter. 1976. *The Melodramatic Imagination.* New Haven: Yale University Press.

Brown, Penelope, and Stephen Levinson. 1987. *Politeness: Some Universals in Language Usage.* Cambridge: Cambridge University Press.

Bruner, Jerome, and Joan Lucariello. 1989. "Monologue as Narrative Recreation of the World." In *Narratives from the Crib,* ed. K. Nelson, 73–97. Cambridge, MA: Harvard University Press.

Buber, Martin. 1958. *I and Thou.* New York: Charles Scribner's Sons.

————. 1965. *The Knowledge of Man.* New York: Harper and Row.

————. 1972. *Between Man and Man.* New York: Macmillan.

————. 1973. *Meetings.* La Salle, IL: Open Court Publishing.

————. 1983. *Paths in Utopia.* Tel-Aviv: Am Oved (in Hebrew).

Burke, Kenneth. 1935. *Permanence and Change.* Indianapolis: Bobbs-Merrill.

————. 1941. *The Philosophy of Literary Form*. New York: Random House.

————. 1945. *A Grammar of Motives*. Los Angeles: University of California Press.

————. 1950. *A Rhetoric of Motives*. New York: Prentice-Hall.

————. 1957. *Counter-statement*. Chicago: University of Chicago Press.

Burke, Peter. 1993. *The Art of Conversation*. Ithaca: Cornell University Press.

Buttny, Richard. 1996. "Clients' and Therapists' Joint Construction of the Clients' Problems." *Research on Language and Social Interaction* 29 (2):125–53.

Cameron, Deborah. 1995. *Verbal Hygiene*. London: Routledge.

————. 2000. *Good to Talk? Living and Working in a Communication Culture*. London: Sage.

Caplan, Gerald. 1980. *Arab and Jew in Jerusalem: Explorations in Community Mental Health*. Cambridge, MA: Harvard University Press.

Capps, Lisa, and Ohs, Elinor. 1995. "Out of Place: Narrative Insights into Agoraphobia." *Discourse Processes* 19:407–39.

Carbaugh, Donal. 1988. *Talking American: Cultural Discourses on Donahue*. Norwood, NJ: Ablex.

————. 1989. "Fifty Terms for Talk: A Cross-Cultural Study." *International and Intercultural Communication Annual* 13:93–120.

————, ed. 1990. *Cultural Communication and Intercultural Contact*. Hillsdale, NJ: Lawrence Erlbaum.

————. 1995. "The Ethnographic Communication Theory of Philipsen and His Associates." In *Watershed Research Traditions in Human Communication Theory*, ed. D. P. Cushman and B. Kovacic, 269–91. Albany: State University of New York Press.

————. 1999. " 'Just Listen': 'Listening' and Landscape among the Blackfeet." *Western Journal of Communication* 63 (3):250–70.

Carpanzano, Vincent. 1990. "On Dialogue." In *The Interpretation of Dialogue*, ed. T. Maranhao, 269–91. Chicago: University of Chicago Press.

Chambon, Adriene, and Daniel Simeoni. 1998. "Modality in the Therapeutic Dialogue." In *Linguistic Choice across Genres: Variations in Spoken and Written English*, ed. A. Sanchez-Macarro and R. Carter, 239–63. Amsterdam: John Benjamins.

Cissna, Kenneth N., and Rob Anderson. 1998. "Theorizing about Dialogic Moments: The Buber-Rogers Position and Postmodern Themes." *Communication Theory* 8 (1):63–104.

Cohen, Ben-Zion. 1999. "Measuring the Willingness to Seek Help." *Journal of Social Service Research* 26 (1):67–82.

Cohen, Eitan. *The Moroccans: The Negative of the Ashkenazim*. Tel Aviv: Resling, 2002 (in Hebrew).

Cohen, Stanley. 1987. *Folk Devils and Moral Panics: The Creation of the Mids and Rockers*. Oxford: Basil Blackwell.

Cowlan, Bert. 1979. "A Revolution in Personal Communications: The Explosive Growth of Citizens' Band Radio." In *Inter/Media: Interpersonal Communication in a Media World*, ed. G. Gumpert and R. Cathcart, 116–21. New York: Oxford University Press.

Crisell, Andrew. 1986. *Understanding Radio*. London: Methuen.

Cromer, Gerald. 2004. *The State and Violence: Public Debates about Political Violence in Israel*. London: Frank Cass.

Crow, Bryan K. 1986. "Conversational Pragmatics in Television Talk: The Discourse of *Good Sex.*" *Media, Culture and Society* 8:457–84.

Danet, Brenda. 2001. *Cyberplay: Communicating Online.* Oxford: Berg.

Dascal, Marcelo, ed. 1985. *Dialogue: An Interdisciplinary Approach.* Amsterdam: John Benjamins.

DeCapua, Andrea, and Joan Findlay Dunham. 1993. "Strategies in the Discourse of Advice." *Journal of Pragmatics* 20:519–31.

Douglas, Mary. 1973. *Natural Symbols.* New York: Vintage Books.

———. 1975. *Implicit Meanings.* London: Routledge and Kegan Paul.

Douglas, Susan. 1999. *Listening In: Radio and the American Imagination.* New York: Random House.

Efron, Yonit. 2000. "Sisters, Fighters and Mothers: The Ethos and Reality of the 1948 Generation." *Iyunim Bitkumat Israel: Studies in Zionism, the Yishuv, and the State of Israel* 10:353–80 (in Hebrew).

Elon, Amos. 1971. *The Israelis: Founders and Sons.* New York: Holt, Rinehart, and Winston.

Elster, Jon. 1983. *Sour Grapes: Studies in the Subversion of Rationality.* Cambridge: Cambridge University Press.

Erez, Yehuda. 1964. *The Third Aliyah Book.* Tel Aviv: Am Oved (in Hebrew).

Evens, T. M. S. 1995. *Two Kinds of Rationality: Kibbutz Democracy and Generational Conflict.* Minneapolis: University of Minnesota Press.

Ezrahi, Yaron. 1997. *Rubber Bullets: Power and Conscience in Modern Israel.* New York: Farrar, Straus, Giroux.

Feldman, Yael. 1987. "Zionism: Neurosis or Cure? The 'Historical' Drama of Yehoshua Sobol." *Prooftexts* 7:145–62.

———. 1999. *No Room of Their Own.* New York: Columbia University Press.

Ferguson, Charles. 1969. "Myths about Arabic." In *Readings in the Sociology of Language,* ed. Joshua Fishman, 375–81. The Hague: Mouton.

Ferrara, Kathleen. 1994. *Therapeutic Ways with Words.* Oxford: Oxford University Press.

Fishman, Aryei. 1987. "Religion and Communal Life in an Evolutionary-Functional Perspective: The Orthodox *Kibbutzim.*" *Comparative Studies in Society and History* 29 (4):763–96.

Fitch, Kristine. 1998. *Speaking Relationally: Culture, Communication and Interpersonal Connection.* New York: Guilford Press.

Franco, Jean. 1997. "Hello, You're on the Air." In *Mass Culture and Everyday Life,* ed. P. Gibian, 153–63. London: Routledge.

Fraser, Nancy. 1993. "Rethinking the Public Sphere: A Contribution to the Critique of Actually Existing Democracy." In *The Phantom Public Sphere,* ed. B. Robbins, 1–32. Minneapolis: University of Minnesota Press.

Gadamer, Hans-Georg. 1975. *Truth and Method.* New York: Continuum.

Gaik, Frank. 1992. "Radio Talk-Show Therapy and the Pragmatics of Possible Worlds." In *Rethinking Context,* ed. A. Duranti and C. Goodwin, 271–89. Cambridge: Cambridge University Press.

Gale, Jerry E., ed. 1991. *Conversation Analysis of Therapeutic Discourse: The Pursuit of a Therapeutic Agenda.* Norwood, NJ: Ablex.

Gamson, Joshua. 1998. *Freaks Talk Back: Tabloid Talk Shows and Sexual Nonconformity.* Chicago: University of Chicago Press.

Geertz, Clifford. 1973. *The Interpretation of Cultures.* New York: Basic Books.

―――. 1976. "From the Native's Point of View: On the Nature of Anthropological Understanding." In *Meaning in Anthropology,* ed. K. Basso and H. Selby, 221–37. Albuquerque: University of Mexico Press.

Gerhardt, Julie, and Charles Stinson. 1994. "The Nature of Therapeutic Discourse: Accounts of the Self." *Journal of Narrative and Life History* 4.3:151–91.

Gertz, Nurith. 1993. *Motion Picture: Israeli Fiction in Film.* Tel Aviv: The Open University (in Hebrew).

―――. 2000. *Myths in Israeli Culture: Captives of a Dream.* London: Vallentine Mitchell.

Gibian, Peter. 1997. "Newspeak Meets Newstalk." In *Mass Culture and Everyday Life,* ed. P. Gibian, 137–52. London: Routledge.

Gibson, William. 1966. *Tough, Sweet and Stuffy: An Essay on Modern American Prose Styles.* Bloomington: Indiana University Press.

Giddens, Anthony. 1991. *Modernity and Self-Identity: Self and Society in the Late Modern Age.* Cambridge: Polity.

Gilman, Sander. 1991. *The Jew's Body.* New York: Routledge.

Gilsenan, Michael. 1967. "Lying, Honor and Contradiction." In *Transaction and Meaning: Directions in the Anthropology of Exchange and Symbolic Behavior,* ed. B. Kapferer, 191–219. Philadelphia: Institute for the Study of Human Issues.

Gledhill, Christine. 1987. "The Melodramatic Field: An Investigation." In *Home Is Where the Heart Is,* 5–39. London: British Film Institute.

Gluzman, Michael. 1997. "The Yearning for Heterosexuality: Zionism and Sexuality in Alteneuland." *Theory and Criticism* 11:145–60 (in Hebrew).

Goffman, Erving. 1959. *The Presentation of Self in Everyday Life.* New York: Doubleday.

―――. 1967. *Interaction Ritual: Essays on Face-to-Face Behavior.* New York: Doubleday.

Golomb, Jacob. 1995. *In Search of Authenticity: From Kierkegaard to Camus.* London: Routledge.

Gordon, Avraham David. 1943. *Selected Works.* Ed. N. Taradyon. Tel Aviv: Stiebel (in Hebrew).

Govrin, Nurith. 1978. *Keys.* Tel-Aviv: Hakibbutz Hameuchad (in Hebrew).

Griefat, Yusuf, and Tamar Katriel. 1989. "Life Demands *Musayra:* Communication and Culture among Arabs in Israel." In *Language, Communication and Culture: Current Directions,* ed. Stella Ting-Toomey and Felipe Korzenny, 121–38. London: Sage.

Gumperz, John, and Dell Hymes, eds. 1972. *Directions in Sociolinguistics: The Ethnography of Speaking.* New York: Holt, Rinehart and Winston.

Gurevitch, Zali. "The Power of Not Understanding: The Meeting of Conflicting Identities." *Journal of Applied Behavioral Science* 25 (2):161–73.

―――. 1990. "The Dialogic Connection and the Ethics of Dialogue." *British Journal of Sociology* 41 (2):181–96.

―――. 1998. "The Break of Conversation." *Journal for the Theory of Social Behavior* 28 (1):25–40.

Habermas, Jurgen. 1989. *The Structural Transformation of the Public Sphere.* Cambridge: Polity.

Halabi, Rabbah. 2000. *Identities in Dialogue.* Tel Aviv: Hakibbutz Hameuchad (in Hebrew).

Handelman, Don. 1990. *Models and Mirrors: Toward an Anthropology of Public Events.* Cambridge: Cambridge University Press.

Hazan, Haim. 2001. *Simulated Dreams: Israeli Youth and Virtual Zionism.* New York: Berghan Books.

Helman, Sara. 1993. "Conscientious Objection to Military Service as an Attempt to Redefine the Contents of Citizenship." Ph.D. diss., Hebrew University (in Hebrew).

————. 1999a. "Redefining Obligations, Creating Rights: Conscientious Objectors and the Redefinition of Citizenship in Israel." *Citizenship Studies* 3.1:45–70.

————. 1999b. "War and Resistance: Israeli Civil Militarism and Its Emergent Crisis." *Constellations* 6.3:391–410.

————. 1999c. "*Yesh Gvul.*" In *Fifty to Forty-Eight: Critical Moments in the History of the State of Israel,* ed. A. Ophir, 313–19. Tel Aviv: The Van Leer Jerusalem Institute/Hakibbutz Hameuchad (in Hebrew).

————. 2002. "Monologic Results of Dialogue: Jewish-Palestinian Encounter Groups as Sites of Essentialization." *Identities: Global Studies in Culture and Power* 9:327–54.

Henkin, Roni. 1999. "*Ma bein 'hashama'im khulim kaele,' 'hashama'im khulim kaze,' ve'hashama'im khulim ke'ilu'?*" In *Ha'Ivrit Safa Haya II* [Hebrew as a living language], ed. Rina Ben-Shachar and Gideon Toury, 2:102–22. Tel Aviv: Hakibbutz Hameuchad (in Hebrew).

Herbst, Susan. 1995. "On Electronic Public Space: Talk Shows in Theoretical Perspective." *Political Communication* 12:263–74.

Hess, Tamar. 1995. "Will You Ask about the Stature of a Rug? Images of Femininity in 'Kehiliyatenu' and in the Novel 'Days and Nights.'" Master's thesis, Hebrew University, Jerusalem (in Hebrew).

Hill, Jane, and Judith Irvine, eds. 1993. *Responsibility and Evidence in Oral Discourse.* Cambridge: Cambridge University Press.

Horowirz, Dan. 1993. *The Heavens and the Earth: A Self-Portrait of the 1948 Generation.* Jerusalem: Keter (in Hebrew).

Horowitz, David. 1970. *My Yesterday.* Jerusalem: Schocken (in Hebrew).

Horton, Donald, and Anselm Strauss. 1957. "Interaction in Audience-Participation Shows." *American Journal of Sociology* 62:579–87.

Horton, Donald, and Richard R. Wohl. 1956. "Mass Communication and Para-Social Interaction." *Psychiatry* 19:215–29.

Hutchby, Ian. 1995. "Aspects of Recipient Design in Expert Advice-Giving on Call-In Radio." *Discourse Processes* 19:219–38.

————. 1996. *Confrontation Talk: Arguments, Asymmetries, and Power on Talk Radio.* Mahwah, NJ: Lawrence Erlbaum.

Hymes, Dell. 1962. "The Ethnography of Speaking." In *Anthropology and Human Behavior,* ed. T. Galdwin and W. C. Sturtevant, 13–53. Washington, DC: Anthropological Society of Washington.

————. 1972. "Models of the Interaction of Language and Social Life." In *Directions in Sociolinguistics,* ed. J. Gumperz and D. Hymes, 35–71. New York: Holt, Rinehart and Winston.

————. 1974. *Foundations in Sociolinguistics*. Philadelphia: University of Pennsylvania Press.

————. 1989 [1974]. "Ways of Speaking." In *Explorations in the Ethnography of Speaking*, ed. R. Bauman and J. Sherzer, 433–51. Cambridge: Cambridge University Press.

Illouz, Eva. 1999. "That Shadowy Realm of the Interior: Oprah Winfrey and Hamlet's Glass." *International Journal of Cultural Studies* 2 (1):109–31.

Jenkins, Henry. 1992. *Textual Poachers: Television Fans and Participatory Culture*. London: Routledge.

Kalcik, Susan. 1975. " 'Like Ann's Gynecologist or the Time I Was Almost Raped.' " *Journal of American Folklore* 88:3–11.

Katriel, Tamar. 1986. *Talking Straight: 'Dugri' Speech in Israeli Sabra Culture*. Cambridge: Cambridge University Press.

————. 1991. *Communal Webs: Communication and Culture in Contemporary Israel*. Albany: State University of New York Press.

————. 1993. "Lefargen: A Study in Israeli Semantics of Social Relations." *Research on Language and Social Interaction* 26 (1):31–53.

————. 1997. *Performing the Past: A Study of Israeli Settlement Museums*. Mahwah, NJ: Lawrence Erlbaum.

————. 1998a. "The Dialogic Community." In *Media, Culture, Ritual*, ed. T. Liebes and J. Curran, 114–35. London: Routledge.

————. 1998b. " 'Mon histoire est comme ca. . . .' Recits d'experiences personelles a la radio Israeillienne." *Cahiers de Litterature Orale* 44:207–28.

Katriel, Tamar, and Marcelo Dascal. 1984. "What Do Indicating Devices Indicate?" *Philosophy and Rhetoric* 17 (1):1–15.

Katriel, Tamar, and Gerry Philipsen. 1981. " 'What We Need Is Communication': Communication as a Cultural Category in Some American Speech." *Communication Monographs* 48:301–17.

Katriel, Tamar, and Aliza Shenhar. 1990. "Tower and Stockade: Dialogic Narration in Israeli Settlement Ethos." *Quarterly Journal of Speech* 76 (4):359–80.

Katz, Shaul. 1985. "The Israeli Teacher-Guide: The Emergence and Perpetuation of a Role." *Annals of Tourism Research* 12:49–72.

Keddie, Nikki. 1963. "Symbol and Sincerity in Islam." *Studia Islamica* 19:27–63.

Keith, Michael K. 2001. *Sounds in the Dark: All-Night Radio in American Life*. Ames: Iowa State University Press.

Keshet, Shula. 1995. *Underground Soul*. Tel Aviv: Tel Aviv University-Hakibbutz Hameuchad (in Hebrew).

Khuri, Fuad. 1968. "The Etiquette of Bargaining in the Middle East." *American Anthropologist* 70:698–706.

Kimmerling, Baruch. 2001. *The Invention and Decline of Israeliness: State, Society, and the Military*. Berkeley: University of California Press.

Koch, Barbara. 1983. "Presentation as Proof: The Language of Arabic Rhetoric." *Anthropological Linguistics* 25:47–70.

Krausz, Ernest, ed. 1983. *The Sociology of the Kibbutz*. New Brunswick, NJ: Transaction Books.

Kress, Gunther. 1986. "Language in the Media: The Construction of the Domains of Public and Private." *Media, Culture and Society* 8:395–419.

Kuo, Sai-hua. 1994. "Agreement and Disagreement Strategies in a Radio Conversation." *Research on Language and Social Interaction* 27 (2):95–121.

Kupferberg, Irit, and David Green. 1998. "Metaphors Enhance Radio Problems Discussions." *Metaphor and Symbol* 13 (2):103–23.

Kurzweil, Baruch. 1959. *Our Modern Literature—A Continuation or a Revolution?* Jerusalem: Schocken (in Hebrew).

Laban, Rudolf. 1966. *The Language of Movement*. Boston: Plays.

Labov, William, and David Fashnel. 1977. *Therapeutic Discourse: Psychotherapy as Conversation*. New York: Academic Press.

Lahav, Pnina. 2001. "A 'Jewish State . . . To Be Known as the State of Israel': Notes on Israeli Legal Historiography." *Law and History Review* 19 (2):387–433.

Lamm, Zvi. 1991. *The Zionist Youth Movements in Retrospect*. Tel Aviv: Sifriyat Hapoalim (in Hebrew).

———. 1998. *The Educational Method of Hashomer-Hatza'ir Youth Movement: The Story of Its Formation*. Jerusalem: Magnes Press (in Hebrew).

Lanham, Richard. 1974. *Style: An Anti-Textbook*. New Haven: Yale University Press.

Laqueur, Walter. 1962. *Young Germany: A History of the German Youth Movement*. London: Routledge and Kegan Paul.

Lerner, Moti. 1994. *Ahavot Bitanyia* [The loves of Bitanyi]. Unpublished television play (in Hebrew).

Liban, Alex, and Dodi Goldman. 2000. "Freud Comes to Palestine: A Study of Psychoanalysis in a Cultural Context." *International Journal of Psychoanalysis* 81:893–906.

Liebman, Charles, and Eliezer Don-Yehia. 1983. *Civil Religion in Israel: Traditional Judaism and Political Culture in the Jewish State*. Berkeley: University of California Press.

Linde, Charlotte. 1993. *Life Stories: The Creation of Coherence*. Oxford: Oxford University Press.

Linn, Ruth. 1989. *Not Shooting and Not Crying: Psychological Inquiry of Moral Disobedience*. Westport, CT: Greenwood Press.

———. 1996. *Conscience at War: The Israeli Soldier as a Moral Critic*. Albany: State University of New York Press.

Livingston, Sonia, and Peter Lunt. 1994. *Talk on Television: Audience Participation and Public Debate*. London: Routledge.

Lowney, Kathleen. 1999. *Baring Our Souls: TV Talk Shows and the Religion of Recovery*. New York: Aldine de Gruyter.

Lumsky-Feder, Edna. 1995. "The Meaning of War through Veterans' Eyes: A Phenomenological Analysis of Life-Stories." *International Sociology* 10.4:463–82.

———. 1998. *As If There Was No War: Life Stories of Israeli Men*. Jerusalem: Magnes Press (in Hebrew).

Lutz, Catherine. 1990. "Engendered Emotions: Gender, Power, and the Rhetoric of Emotional Control in American Discourse." In *Language and the Politics of Emotion*, ed. C. Lutz and L. Abu-Lughud, 69–91. Cambridge: Cambridge University Press.

Lutz, Catherine, and Lila Abu-Lughud. 1990. "Introduction: Emotion, Discourse, and the Politics of Everyday Life." In *Language and the Politics of Emotion*, ed. C. Lutz and L. Abu-Lughud, 1–23. Cambridge: Cambridge University Press.

Luz, Ehud. 1971. "Between Necessity and Volition." *Shdemot* 40:60–65 (in Hebrew).

Mandelbaum, Jenny. 1989. "Interpersonal Activities in Conversational Storytelling." *Western Journal of Speech Communication* 53:114–26.

———. 1993. "Assigning Responsibility in Conversational Storytelling: The Interactional Construction of Reality." *Text* 13 (2):247–66.

Mannheim, Bruce, and Dennis Tedlock, eds. 1995. Introduction to *The Dialogic Emergence of Culture.* Urbana: University of Illinois Press.

Maoz, Ifat. 2000. "Power Relations in Intergroup Encounters: A Case Study of Jewish-Arab Encounters in Israel." *International Journal of Intercultural Relaions* 24:259–77.

Maranhao, Tullio, ed. 1990. *The Interpretation of Dialogue.* Chicago: University of Chicago Press.

Margalit, Avishai. 1998. *Views in Review.* New York: Farrar, Straus, Giroux.

Margalit, Elkana. 1971. *"Hashomer Hatza'ir"—From Youth Community to Revolutionary Marxism.* Tel Aviv: Hakibbutz Hameuchad (in Hebrew).

Maschler, Yael. 2001. *"Veke'ilu haraglayim sh'xa nitka'ot bifnim kaze:* Hebrew *kaze* (like), *ke'ilu* (like) and the Decline of Israeli *dugri* (direct) Speech." *Discourse Studies* 3 (3):295–326.

McLeod, John. 1997. *Narrative and Psychotherapy.* London: Sage.

Mehl, Dominique. 1996. *La television de l'intimite.* Paris: Editions du Seuil.

Melbin, Murray. 1987. *The Night as Frontier: Colonizing the World after Dark.* New York: Free Press.

Mendelsohn, Harold. 1979. "Listening to Radio." In *Inter/Media: Interpersonal Communication in a Media World,* ed. G. Gumpert and R. Cathcart, 89–98. New York: Oxford University Press.

Mintz, Matityahu. 1995. *The Bonds of Youth: Hashomer Hatza'ir 1911–21.* Jerusalem: Zionist Library (in Hebrew).

Mosse, George. 1982. "Friendship and Nationhood: About the Promise and Failure of German Nationalism." *Journal of Contemporary History* 17:351–67.

Munson, Wayne. 1993. *All Talk: The Talk Show in Media Culture.* Philadelphia: Temple University Press.

Myerhoff, Barbara. 1978. *Number Our Days.* New York: Dutton.

Naveh, Hanna. 1988. *The Confession: A Study of Genre.* Tel Aviv: Papyrus (in Hebrew).

Near, Henry. 1982. "Post-Utopian Thought in the *Kibbutz.*" *Hakibbutz* 8:213–31 (in Hebrew).

———. 1988. "I-Thou-We: Buber's Theory of Community and the *Kibbutz.*" *Hakibbutz* 12:195–212 (in Hebrew).

Ochs, Elinor. 1988. *Culture and Language Development: Language Acquisition and Language Socialization.* Cambridge: Cambridge University Press.

Ofrat, Gideon. 1980. *Earth, Man, Blood: The Myth of the Pioneer and the Ritual of Earth in Eretz-Israel Settlement Drama.* Tel Aviv: Tscherikover (in Hebrew).

Ohana, David. 1998. *The Last Israelis.* Tel Aviv: Hakibbutz Haneuchad (in Hebrew).

Oring, Elliot. 1981. *Israeli Humor: The Content and Structure of the "Chizbat" of the Palmach.* Albany: State University of New York Press.

Ortner, Sherry. 1973. "On Key Symbols." *American Anthropologist* 75:1338–46.

Oz, Amos. 1983. *In the Land of Israel.* New York: Harcourt Brace Jovanovich.

Panese, Marcello. 1996. "Calling In: Prosody and Conversation in Radio Talk." *Pragmatics* 6 (1):19–87.

Patai, Raphael. 1983. *The Arab Mind.* New York: Charles Scribner.

Peck, Janice. 1995. "TV Talk Shows as Therapeutic Discourse: The Ideological Labor of the Televised Talking Cure." *Communication Theory* 5 (1):58–81.

Peled, Hanan. 1989. *Hevre* [Buddies]. Unpublished play (in Hebrew).

Peled, Rina. 2002. *"The New Man" of the Zionist Revolution.* Tel Aviv: Am Oved (in Hebrew).

Peleg, Muli. 2002. "The Peace Process and the Failure of Public-Political Discussion in Israel." *State and Society* 2 (3):421–43.

Peters, John Durham. 1999. *Speaking into the Air.* Chicago: University of Chicago Press.

Philips, Susan. 1982. *The Invisible Culture: Communication in Classroom and Community on the Warm Springs Indian Reservation.* New York: Longman.

Philipsen, Gerry. 1987. "The Prospect for Cultural Communication." In *Communication Theory: Eastern and Western Perspectives,* ed. L. Kincaid, 245–54. Orlando: Academic Press.

———. 1992. *Speaking Culturally.* Albany: State University of New York Press.

———. 1997. "A Theory of Speech Codes." In *Developing Communication Theories,* ed. G. Philipsen and T. L. Albrecht, 119–56. Albany: State University of New York Press.

Powell, Jon, and Ary Donald. 1979. "Communication without Commitment." In *Inter/Media: Interpersonal Communication in a Media World,* ed. G. Gumpert and R. Cathcart, 122–25. New York: Oxford University Press.

Pratt, Mary Louise. 1997. "So She Really Loves Eggs: Fighting It out on Call-in Radio." In *Mass Culture and Everyday Life,* ed. P. Gibian, 164–77. London: Routledge.

Prell-Foldes, Riv-Ellen. 1980. "The Reinvention of Reflexivity in Jewish Prayer: The Self and Community in Modernity." *Semiotica* 30 (1/2):73–96.

Priest, Patricia. 1995. *Public Intimacies: Talk Show Participants and Tell-All TV.* Cresskill, NJ: Hampton Press.

Rabinowitz, Dan. 2001. "Natives with Jackets and Degrees: Othering, Objectification, and the Role of Palestinians in the Co-Existence Field in Israel." *Social Anthropology* 9 (1):65–80.

Raviv, Amiram. 1993. "Radio Psychology: A Comparison of Listeners and Non-Listeners." *Journal of Community & Applied Social Psychology* 3:197–211.

Raviv, Amiram, Alona Raviv, and Gilad Arnon. 1991. "Psychological Counseling over the Radio: Listening Motivations and the Threat to Self-Esteem." *Journal of Applied Social Psychology* 21 (4):253–70.

Raviv, Amiram, Alona Raviv, and Ronith Yunivitz. 1989. "Radio Psychology and Psychotherapy: Comparison of Client Attitudes and Expectations." *Professional Psychology: Research and Practice* 20.2:67–72.

Rawlins, William K., ed. 1998. *Communication Theory* 8, no. 4.

Ray, George. 1987. "The Ethnography of Nonverbal Communication in an Appalacian Village." *Research on Language and Social Interaction* 21:171–88.

Rheingold, Howard. 1993. *The Virtual Community: Homesteading on the Electronic Frontier.* Reading, MA: Addison Wesley.

Robinson, Henry. 1964. *Corporate Personality in Ancient Israel.* Philadelphia: Fortress.

Roniger, Luis. 1994. "Cultural Prisms, Western Individualism and the Israeli Case." *Ethnos* 59 (1/2):37–55.

Rosen, Larry. 1984. *Bargaining for Reality: The Construction of Social Relations in a Muslim Community.* Chicago: University of Chicago Press.

Rosner, Menahem, and Shelomoh Getz. 1996. *The Kibbutz in the Era of Changes.* Tel Aviv: Hakibbutz Hameuchad Publishing House (in Hebrew).

Roth, Gunther. 1979. "Charisma and the Counterculture." In *Max Weber's Vision of History: Ethics and Method,* ed. G. Roth and W. Schluchter, 119–43. Berkeley: University of California Press.

Rousseau, Jean Jacques. 1974. *The Essential Rousseau.* New York: New American Library.

Rubinstein, Amnon. 1970. *To Be a Free People.* Tel Aviv: Schocken (in Hebrew).

Sadan-Loebenstein, Nili. 1991. *Israeli Prose in the Twenties.* Tel Aviv: Sifriyat Hapoalim (in Hebrew).

Saias, Yossi. 1988. *Love Day by Day.* Haifa: Gestelit (in Hebrew).

Said, Edward. 1979. *Orientalism.* New York: Vintage Books.

Sappan, Raphael. 1963. *The Ways of Slang.* Jerusalem: Kiryat Sefer (in Hebrew).

Saville-Troike, Muriel. 1982. *The Ethnography of Communication: An Introduction.* Baltimore: University Park Press.

Scannell, Paddy. 1989. "Public Service Broadcasting and Modern Public Life." *Media, Culture and Society* 11:317–48.

———, ed. 1991. *Broadcast Talk.* London: Sage.

———. 1996. *Radio, Television and Everyday Life: A Phenomenological Approach.* Oxford: Blackwell.

Schatzker, Haim. 1998. *Jewish Youth in Germany between Judaism and Germanism.* Jerusalem: Zalman Shazar Center for Jewish History (in Hebrew).

Schieffelin, Bambi. 1990. *The Give and Take of Everyday Life.* Cambridge: Cambridge University Press.

Schieffelin, Bambi, Katherine Woolard, and P. Kroskrity, eds. 1998. *Language Ideologies: Practice & Theory.* New York: Oxford University Press.

Schiffrin, Deborah. 1984. "Jewish Argument as Sociability." *Language in Society* 13:311–35.

Schoenbrun, David. 1973. *The New Israelis.* New York: Atheneum.

Schutz, Alfred. 1970. *On Phenomenology and Social Relations.* Chicago: University of Chicago Press.

Schwebel, Andrew. 1982. "Radio Psychologists: A Community Psychology/Psycho-Educational Model." *Journal of Community Psychology* 10:181–84.

Segev, Tom. 1986. *1949: The First Israelis.* New York: Free Press.

Sela-Sheffy, Rakefet. In press. " 'What Makes One an Israeli?': Negotiating Identities in Everyday Representations of 'Israeliness,' " *Nations and Nationalism.*

Sered, Susan, and Ephraim Tabory. 1999. " 'You Are a Number, Not a Human

Being': Israeli Breast Cancer Patients' Experiences with the Medical Establishment." *Medical Anthropology Quarterly* 13 (2):223–52.

Shaham, Nathan. 1956. *Even Al Pi Habe'er* [A stone on the well's mouth]. Tel Aviv: Sifriyat Hapoalim (in Hebrew).

———. 1984. *Hahar Vehabait* [The mountain and the home]. Tel Aviv: Sifriyat Hapoalim (in Hebrew).

Shaked, Gershon. 1988. *Hebrew Narrative Fiction 1880–1980.* Vol. 3. Tel Aviv: Hakibbutz Hameuchad (in Hebrew).

Shapira, Anita. 1997. *New Jews, Old Jews.* Tel Aviv: Am Oved (in Hebrew).

Shapira, Avraham, ed. 1967. *Si'ah Lohamim.* Tel Aviv: Publication of Young Members of the Kibbutz Movement (in Hebrew).

———. 1971. *The Seventh Day: Soldiers' Talk about the Six-Day War.* Trans. H. Near. London: Penguin.

———. 1996. *The Kabbalistic and Hasidic Sources of A. D. Gordon's Thought.* Tel Aviv: Am Oved (in Hebrew).

Shattuc, Jane. 1997. *The Talking Cure: TV Talk Shows and Women.* New York: Routledge.

Shemi, Menahem, ed. 1952. *Haverim Mesaprim al Jimmy.* Tel Aviv: Hakibbutz Hameuchad (in Hebrew).

Shenhar-Alroy, Aliza. 1990. "From Oral to Written Myth: On Nathan Bistritsky's *Days and Nights*." In *Kibbutz and Literature: Research and Criticism,* ed. S. Shur and L. Hadomi, 66–90. Tel Aviv: Sifriyat Hapoalim (in Hebrew).

Sherzer, Joel. 1993. *Kuna Ways of Speaking: An Ethnographic Perspective.* Austin: University of Texas Press.

Shipler, David. 1986. *Arab and Jew: Wounded Spirits in a Promised Land.* New York: Times Books.

Shohat, Ella. 1988. "Sephardim in Israel: Zionism from the Standpoint of Its Jewish Victims." *Social Text* 19/20:1–35.

———. 1989. *Israeli Cinema: East/West and the Politics of Representation.* Austin: University of Texas Press.

———. 1999. "The Invention of Mizrahim." *Journal of Palestine Studies* 29 (1):5–20.

Silverstein, Michael. 1976. "Shifters, Linguistic Categories and Cultural Description." In *Meaning in Anthropology,* ed. K. Basso and H. Selby, 11–55. Albuquerque: University of New Mexico Press.

Simmel, Georg. 1955. *Conflict and the Web of Group Affiliations.* New York: New Press.

Slyomovics, Susan. 1998. *The Object of Memory: Arab and Jew Narrate the Palestinian Village.* Philadelphia: University of Pennsylvania Press.

Sobol, Yehoshua. 1990 [1976]. *Leil Ha'esrim* [*The Night of the Twentieth*]. Tel Aviv: Or-Am (in Hebrew).

Sornig, Karl. 1981. *Lexical Innovation: A Study of Slang, Colloquialisms and Casual Speech.* Amsterdam: John Benjamins.

Spiro, Melfrod E. 1956. *Kibbutz: A Venture in Utopia.* New York: Schocken Books.

Spitulnik, Deborah. 1996. "The Social Circulation of Media Discourse and the Mediation of Communities." *Journal of Linguistic Anthropology* 6 (2):161–87.

————. 2001. "Media." In *Key Terms in Anthropology*, ed. A. Duranti, 143–46. Oxford: Blackwell.

Stachura, Peter. 1981. *The German Youth Movement, 1900–1945*. New York: St. Martin's Press.

Stewart, John. 1978. "Foundations of Dialogic Communication." *Quarterly Journal of Speech* 64:183–201.

Swearingen, C. J. 1990. "Dialogue and Dialectic: The Logic of Conversation and The Interpretation of Logic." In *The Interpretation of Dialogue*, ed. T. Maranhao, 47–71. Chicago: University of Chicago Press.

Suleiman, Ramzi. 1996. "Planned Encounters between Jews and Palestinian Citizens of Israel as a Microcosmos: Social Psychological Aspects." *Studies in Education* 1 (2):71–85.

Tacchi, J. 2002. "Radio Texture: Between Self and Others." In *The Anthropology of Media: A Reader*, ed. K. Askew and R. Wilk, 241–57. Oxford: Blackwell.

Tal, Uriel. 1981. "Myth and Solidarity in the Zionist Thought and Activity of Martin Buber." *Hatziyonut* [Zionism] 7:18–35 (in Hebrew).

Talmon, Miri. 2001. *Israeli Graffiti: Nostalgia, Groups, and Collective Identity in Israeli Cinema*. Tel Aviv: Open University and University of Haifa Press (in Hebrew).

Tannen, Deborah. 1981. "Ethnicity as Conversational Style." *International Journal in the Sociology of Language* 30:133–49.

Taylor, Charles. 1989. *Sources of the Self: The Making of Modern Identity*. Cambridge, MA: Harvard University Press.

————. 1991. *The Ethics of Authenticity*. Cambridge, MA: Harvard University Press.

Thornborrow, Joanna. 1997. "Having Their Say: The Function of Stories in Talk-Show Discourse." *Text* 17 (2):241–62.

Tobin, Yehuda. 1969. "In the Shadow of Wars." *Hedim* 34.90:3–11 (in Hebrew).

Tonnies, Ferdinand. 1957. *Community and Society*. East Lansing: Michigan State University Press.

Trilling, Lionel. 1971. *Sincerity and Authenticity*. Cambridge, MA: Harvard University Press.

Tsur, Muky. 1971. "The Intimate Group." *Shdemot* 39:62–68 (in Hebrew).

————, ed. 1988 [1922]. *Kehiliyatenu* [Our commune]. Jerusalem: Yad Yitshak Ben-Zvi (in Hebrew).

Tsur, Muky, Yariv Ben-Aharon, and Avishai Grossman, eds. 1969. *Among Young People [Bein Tzeirim]: Talks in the Kibbutz*. Tel Aviv: Am Oved (in Hebrew).

Turner, Victor. 1969. *The Ritual Process*. Ithaca: Cornell University Press.

————. 1974. *Dramas, Fields and Metaphors*. Ithaca: Cornell University Press.

————. 1982. *From Ritual to Theater*. New York: Performing Arts Journal Publications.

Turow, Joseph. 1974. "Talk Show Radio as Interpersonal Communication." *Journal of Broadcasting* 18:171–79.

Ufaz, Aviva. 1996. *Document and Fiction*. Tel Aviv: Hakibbutz Hameuchad (in Hebrew).

————, ed. 1996. *Sefer Hakvutza*. Jerusalem: Yad Yitshak Ben-Zvi (in Hebrew).

————. 2000. "The 'Feminist Issue' and Feminine Self-Expression in a Pioneering Society: A Rereading of *Kehiliyatenu*." *Cathedra* 95:101–18 (in Hebrew).

———. 2001. *Sefer Ha-hayim: Yomanah shel Kevutzat Kiryat Anavim.* Jerusalem: Yad Yitshak Ben-Zvi (in Hebrew).

Ufaz, Gad. 1986. "The Ties of the Kibbutz to Jewish Sources as Expressed in the Thought of Shdemot Circle." Ph.D. diss., University of Tel Aviv (in Hebrew).

———. 1999. "The Shdemot Circle Members in Search of Jewish Sources." In *In Search of Identity: Jewish Aspects in Israeli Culture,* ed. Dan Urian and Efraim Karsh, 132–45. London: Frank Cass.

Urban, Greg. 1986. "Ceremonial Dialogues in South America." *American Anthropologist* 88:371–86.

Urian, Dan. 1996. *The Arab in Israeli Theater.* Tel Aviv: Or-Am (in Hebrew).

———. 2002. "Between Zionism and Post-Zionism in Israeli Theater." *Kesher* 31:37–46.

Urla, Jacqueline. 1995. "Outlaw Language: Creating Alternative Public Spheres in Basque Free Radio." *Pragmatics* 5 (2):245–61.

van Gennep, Alfred. 1960. *The Rites of Passage.* London: Routledge and Kegan Paul.

Weiler, Yael. 1996. "Magic, Comradeship and Reform [*tikkun olam*] as Clusters of a New Identity." Master's thesis, Hebrew University, Jerusalem (in Hebrew).

———. 1998. "The Magic of *Hashomer Hatza'ir.*" *Cathedra* 88:73–94 (in Hebrew).

———. 2001. "The Camaraderie of *Hashomer Hatza'ir.*" *Cathedra* 102:63–96 (in Hebrew).

Weingrod, Alex. 1998. "Ehud Barak's Apology: Letters from the Israeli Press." *Israel Studies* 3 (2):238–52.

Weiss, Meira. 2002. *The Chosen Body: The Politics of the Body in Israeli Society.* Stanford: Stanford University Press.

White, Mimi. 1992. *Tele-Advising: Therapeutic Discourse in American Television.* Chapel Hill: University of North Carolina Press.

Wierzbicka, Anna. 2002. "Russian Cultural Scripts: The Theory of Cultural Scripts and Its Applications." *Ethos.*

Williams, Raymond. 1977. *Marxism and Literature.* Oxford: Oxford University Press.

Winch, Peter. 1972. *Ethics and Action.* London: Routledge and Kegan Paul.

Woolfolk, Robert L. 1998. *The Cure of Souls: Science, Values and Psychotherapy.* San Francisco: Jossey-Bass.

Ya'ari, Meir. 1923. "Rootless Symbols (*Smalim Tlushim*)." *Hedim* 2:93–106. Reprinted in *Shdemot* 72 (1980): 9–16 (in Hebrew).

Ya'ari, Yehuda. 1981 [1937]. *Ke'or Yahel* [Like the dawn of light]. Tel Aviv: Sifriyat Hapoalim (in Hebrew).

Yanay, Niza. 2003. "Mandatory Reconciliation [*tzav piyus*]: The Violent Discourse of Moderation." *Israeli Sociology,* 5 (1):161–91.

Yas'ur, Avraham. 1982. "Buber's Social Thought and the Study of the *Kibbutz.*" *Hakibbutz* 8:183–209 (in Hebrew).

Zerubavel, Yael. 1995. *Recovered Roots: Collective Memory and the Making of Israeli National Tradition.* Chicago: University of Chicago Press.

Index